MW01617153

Risk Work

Risk Work

Making Art and Guerrilla Tactics in Punitive America, 1967–1987

Faye Raquel Gleisser

The University of Chicago Press

Chicago and London

The University of Chicago Press, Chicago 60637
The University of Chicago Press, Ltd., London

Published 2023
Printed in China

32 31 30 29 28 27 26 25 24 23 1 2 3 4 5

ISBN-13: 978-0-226-82646-2 (cloth)
ISBN-13: 978-0-226-82647-9 (e-book)
DOI: https://doi.org/10.7208/chicago/9780226826479.001.0001

Publication is made possible in part by a gift from Elizabeth Warnock to the Department of Art History at Northwestern University.

Library of Congress Cataloging-in-Publication Data

Names: Gleisser, Faye Raquel, author.
Title: Risk work : making art and guerrilla tactics in punitive America, 1967–1987 / Faye Raquel Gleisser.
Description: Chicago : The University of Chicago Press, 2023. | Includes bibliographical references and index.
Identifiers: LCCN 2023000226 | ISBN 9780226826462 (cloth) | ISBN 9780226826479 (ebook)
Subjects: LCSH: Art and revolutions. | Guerrillas in art. | Performance art—United States.
Classification: LCC N8236.P5 G59 2023 | DDC 702.81—dc23/eng/20230113
LC record available at https://lccn.loc.gov/2023000226

♾ This paper meets the requirements of ANSI/NISO Z39.48-1992 (Permanence of Paper).

For Brian and Pamela Gleisser

In memory of Marcus and Helga Gleisser,

and Ted and Idarose Luntz

Contents

Introduction. Punitive Literacy and Risk Work 1

[1] Hit-and-Run Aesthetics: Asco, Chris Burden, and Relational Geographies of Risk, 1971–1976 33

[2] Deputized Discernment: Adrian Piper, Jean Toche, and the Politics of Antiloitering Laws, 1974–1978 69

[3] Rethinking Endurance: Pope.L, Tehching Hsieh, and Surviving Safety, 1978–1983 108

[4] "¿Why *Won't* You See Us?": The Guerrilla Girls, PESTS, and the Limits of Anonymity, 1985–1987 148

Epilogue. At the Edges of Guerrilla 181

Acknowledgments 197

Notes 203

Bibliography 241

Index 259

Dear Lil: October 30, 1969.

Jon Hendricks and I are doing today another guerilla at 2.30pm. at MOMA. If you decide to join us, don't stay to close to us, because my lawyer thinks this time you may be arrested (charges would be penal, i.e., several years of jail. Ha-Ha-Ha) We are going to take off the wall a painting at Moma, and replace it with our included statement. If for some reason we cannot do this (painting screwed to the wall or possible damage to the painting) we will drape in black the work and pin our statement to the draperie. We decided not to damage any work, because Jon pointed out very correctly that it would be in itself a form of repression or fascism, and therefore would defeat our purpose. Love Toche

[I.1] Jean Toche, handwritten letter to Lil Picard, October 30, 1969. Lil Picard papers, 1955–1972, Archives of American Art, Smithsonian Institution. Courtesy of Jon Hendricks.

Introduction

Punitive Literacy and Risk Work

Don't stay too close to us, warns the artist Jean Toche in a letter scrawled in cursive on a piece of notebook paper. Written in haste, the note, dated October 30, 1969, tells his friend, the white art critic and artist Lil Picard, "Jon Hendricks and I are doing today another guerrilla at 2.30 pm. at MoMA. If you decide to join us, don't stay to [*sic*] close to us, because my lawyer thinks this time you may be arrested (charges would be penal, i.e., several years of jail. Ha Ha Ha)" (figure I.1).[1] Toche, a white Belgian-born artist, and his collaborator, Jon Hendricks, a white American artist and art gallery director at Judson Church, had recently begun staging unannounced actions during Art Worker Coalition (AWC) protests in New York City.[2] "We are going to take off the wall a painting at Moma, and replace it with our included statement," Toche continues. "If for some reason we cannot do this (painting screwed to the wall or possible damage to the painting) we will drape in black the work and pin our statement to the draperie. We decided not to damage any work because Jon pointed out very correctly that it would be in itself a form of repression or faschism [*sic*], and therefore would defeat our purpose. Love, Toche."

As planned, at 2:30 that afternoon, Toche and Hendricks initiated their "guerrilla" at the Museum of Modern Art. Picard decided to join but, heeding Toche's caution, kept her distance from the artists. Janice (Jan) Van Raay, a white, New York–based artist and friend of Toche and Hendricks, was also present, photographing the event. Like Picard, Van Raay had likely received an invitation warning that the cost of participation might be jail. Van Raay's images show Hendricks and Toche standing beside the painting they've just removed and leaned against the wall: Kazimir Malevich's iconic *Suprematist Composition: White-on-White* (1918; fig. I.2). In the foreground, two unidentified women sit on

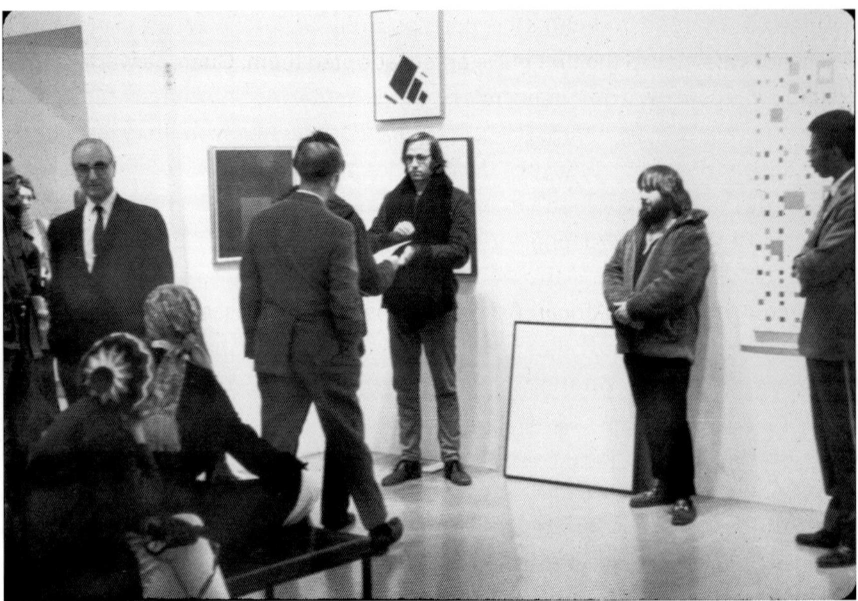

[I.2] "Removal of Malevich's *White on White* Action by Guerrilla Art Action Group," October 30, 1969. Black-and-white photograph. Photo © Jan Van Raay.

[I.3, facing page] Alberto Korda, *Guerillero Heroico*, 1960. Black-and-white photograph. bpk Bildagentur/Alberto Korda/Art Resource, NY. © 2021 Estate of Alberto Korda/Artists Rights Society (ARS), New York.

a museum bench with their backs to the camera; on the right, a Black security guard watches with his arms crossed.

When white museum staff arrive, including the director of public relations, Elizabeth Shaw, and the director of painting, Wilder Green, Hendricks hands them a statement listing three demands: that MoMA deaccession one million dollars' worth of art and give the funds to poor communities to use as they wish; decentralize its white power structure, including devoting a wing to Black artists; and close its doors until the war ends in Vietnam. The list was modeled on the communiques of the Black Panther Party for Self-Defense, Black Emergency Cultural Coalition, and Puerto Rican Young Lords. Toche and Hendricks signed their names as the founding members of their newly established art collective: Guerrilla Art Action Group (GAAG).

By identifying as "guerrilla" artists, Toche and Hendricks sought to harness the cultural currency of guerrilla warfare. This form of low-tech physical and psychological irregular tactics had become synonymous with anticolonial battles in Algeria, Cuba, and Vietnam. Of course, guerrilla tactics did not originate in the 1960s, nor was the US the first place artists adopted them. Guerrilla warfare has existed for hundreds if not thousands of years, as long as there have been states and dissenters to resist them. The term *guerrilla* appeared in military discourse in the early nineteenth century to describe the "small wars" fought by Spanish insurgents against Napoleon's invading forces during the Peninsular War.[3] The United States has its own long and enduring history of guerrilla warfare. It was used by Indigenous nations to combat settler-colonial violence and genocide; by enslaved Africans and African Americans resisting and escaping slavery; and by Black, Indigenous, and other people of color seeking to survive ongoing state-sanctioned violence.[4] Yet the concept of the guerrilla tactic has been defined by US military historians as invariably *external* and *imported*: something that comes from somewhere else; something inherently foreign.

Contrary to the long-standing history of tactical interventions in America, US security experts working for the government in the 1960s promoted the idea that guerrilla tactics first entered this country by way of Soviet-backed training in Spain during the 1930s and its influence on American communists. When the concept of the "guerrilla" gained unprecedented widespread attention in the 1960s, it arrived via the rising profile of anticolonial revolutionaries fighting in third world liberation wars. Ernesto "Che" Guevara, for one, became famous throughout the world for opposing US domination in Latin America and leading guerrillas in the Sierra Maestra during the Cuban revolution. His 1961 training manual, *Guerrilla Warfare*, which called for guerrillas to be both fighters and social reformers, also gained global traction following his execution in 1967 by US-backed soldiers in Bolivia. Cuban prime minister Fidel Castro memorialized Che as an "artist of guerrilla struggle," and Cuban leaders declared 1968 "the year of the heroic guerrilla" in his honor.[5] Simultaneously, a photograph capturing Che's steady gaze, leather jacket, and beret with its emblematic star (fig. I.3)—taken by fashion photographer Alberto Korda in 1960 in Havana—became an

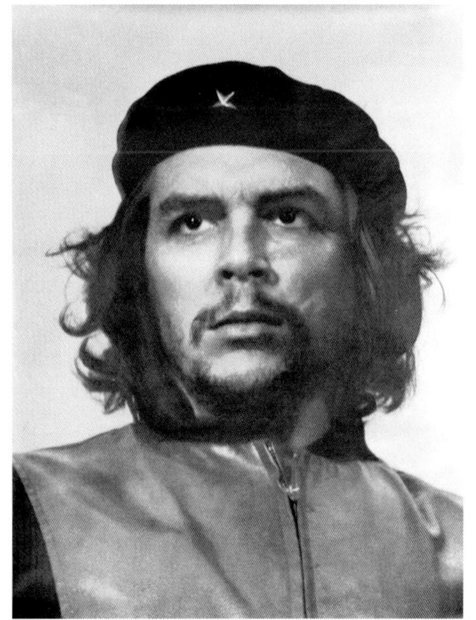

international symbol of revolutionary spirit, appearing on Manhattan subway billboards and in protest posters and graffiti-tagged walls in Paris, Mexico City, Havana, and beyond. Urban guerrilla actions enacted by Palestinian, Uruguayan, and West German groups, among others, also added to the building momentum and visuality of an emergent global "guerrilla generation."[6]

The idea that such intervention was imminent in the US had been popularized in Robert Taber's 1965 bestseller *The War of the Flea*, which dubbed guerrilla warfare "the political phenomenon of the mid-twentieth century," one that "threatens or *almost* threatens to break out in the United States itself."[7] The circulation of Che's manual and Taber's book, alongside writings by the Martinique clinical psychologist Frantz Fanon, inspired by his experience in the Algerian war for independence, and mini-manuals by Chinese communist revolutionary Mao Zedong, Afro-Brazilian militant Carlos Marighella, and French theorist Regis Debray, cultivated a shared vocabulary of action. These texts helped reveal and forge links among Algerian fighters combating French colonizers, the North Vietnamese fighting American imperialist forces, and the chapters of the Black Panther Party for Self-Defense emerging across the US and facing off with predominantly white police patrols. Framing a particular artistic practice as a kind of guerrilla activity carried a political edge. Artists who used the word "guerrilla" staged solidarities with anticolonial movements, while bridging the glamorization of the guerrilla fighter and exploiting officials' fear of a third world–style guerrilla war in the US. A few days after the "Malevich action," Picard wrote in an op-ed in the *East Village Other* that GAAG's intervention at MoMA should be seen not just as a "political action" but as "a *new art form*," a "happening with meaning in the museum."[8]

I begin this book with GAAG's "Malevich action" at MoMA because, on the one hand, it is an iconic instance of early guerrilla art practice in the late 1960s, when artists in the United States and around the world—from Argentina, Uruguay, and Brazil to Italy, Germany, France, and the Netherlands to Japan—began adapting and experimenting with guerrilla tactics in their practices.[9] On the other hand, Toche and Hendricks's documented action offers more than an art-historical record of guerrilla art. It provides a glimpse of the often unremarked but critically important labor central to the deployment of such tactics in artwork. Namely, how artists anticipate and negotiate the prospect of punitive encounters and consequences.

GAAG's experimental art suffused with advocacy, Hendricks explains, emerged in part from the recognition that he and Toche wanted to protest but "had no preparation for being arrested" and needed to preemptively "clarify how we wanted to approach things."[10] As Toche put it:

> We made *planned* appearances and disappearances. *That* was "guerrilla." I want to reiterate that the actions with Jon were carefully planned, and not hysterical reactions. They were pre-discussed. We made sure to have witnesses each time to watch, in order to have people that could attest to our actions in court. We recorded the plan before hand, with communiques and documents, also for legal protection.[11]

Indeed, Toche's letter forewarning Picard was just one part of this preemptive planning. He and Hendricks invited her to be a witness who could testify in court, if need be. In fact, while the crowd seen in Van Raay's image may seem like an impromptu gathering of museumgoers, at least four of those present were friends of the artists. In addition to Picard and Van Raay, Tom Lloyd, an artist and Black leader of the AWC's calls for museum decentralization, and Howard Wise, a white gallery director, in dark-rimmed glasses and suit and tie, appear at the photo's left edge.

The artists also met with a lawyer, learned about the possibility of arrest and ensuing charges (property damage, trespass, or "inciting a riot," the latter carrying a higher sentence following the 1968 passage of the federal Anti-Riot Act), and shared that information with a number of potential witnesses. In advance of their action, Hendricks also sent an affidavit to *Newsweek* declaring GAAG's intent not to damage any property.[12] In Van Raay's photographs, solicited by the artists as evidence to be used in court (as opposed to merely documenting an art action for future museum acquisition or art criticism), the space between Toche and Hendricks and their friends demonstrates how a simple warning—to stay at a safe distance to avoid arrest—choreographs a scene otherwise perceived as spontaneous and haphazard.

The ability to move freely in the United States—as abolitionists, grassroots activists, artists, and scholars of social movements, critical disability theory, critical race theory, and human geography have long shown—is rooted in a conception of personal freedom based on an idealized heterosexual, white, male, able-bodied citizen.[13] The artists' calculations are based on what queer of color cultural theorist Sara Ahmed calls "social norms legitimized by governing forces that promise the elimination of fear in civil society." These norms, Ahmed explains, produce "the politics of mobility, whereby mobility of some bodies involves and even requires the restriction of the mobility of others."[14] In this system, race—interpellated via its entanglement with gender, sexuality, class, and an array of identifying factors—is a spatializing and temporalizing tool. It is used to uphold normalized hegemonic modes of governance and control that sustain and protect whiteness and the antiblack and colonial configurations of space and resources upon which it depends.[15] Following critical ethnic studies and racial formation, "race" in this book is understood as an epistemic form central to the making of modernity and state formation.[16] Relatedly, racism within American governance, as abolitionist geographer Ruth Wilson Gilmore explains, is the *planned* and normalized "state-sanctioned or extralegal production and exploitation of group-differentiated vulnerability to premature death."[17] Art interventions labeled "guerrilla" are commonly understood as spontaneous, ephemeral actions that disrupt spatial and social order. While these actions have become a key site for studying how artists deploy agency and resist power, the racial politics of mobility, vulnerability to premature death, and policing central to each work has yet to be conceptualized as an integral part of the work's form, reception, and legacy.

Risk Work: Making Art and Guerrilla Tactics in Punitive America, 1967–1987 analyzes the complex relationship between guerrilla tactics in art, state power, risk management, and policing in the United States. While guerrilla war has a long and ongoing history, I start this story at a time when artists adapted guerrilla tactics to artistic production with unprecedented intensity, as emergent surveillance technologies and criminal code reforms expanded the police's punitive discretion. My exploration of art begins in 1967, a period marked by anticolonial movements and President Lyndon B. Johnson's "War on Crime," informed by the perception of a coming guerrilla war, and culminates in 1987, as Ronald Reagan's conservative "law and order" approach to regulation gutted welfare, enhanced police technology, and rebranded guerrilla tactics used in US counterinsurgency as "low-intensity conflict." I argue that the documented expansion of policing and governmentality between the late 1960s and late 1980s—and its impact on what artists did and didn't make—is one of the most significant components linking the artists in this book, as well as a lens through which to examine their use of increasingly securitized spaces and strategies of cultural resistance to state violence and regulation.

At the heart of this book is a racially diverse, multiethnic, cross-class constellation of artists—Jean Toche of Guerrilla Art Action Group, Adrian Piper, Chris Burden, Pope.L, Tehching Hsieh, and the members of the art groups Asco, PESTS, and the Guerrilla Girls—who, between the mid-1960s and the mid-1980s, produced work beyond art-sanctioned spaces and simultaneously explored what guerrilla tactics in art might look like in the United States. They inserted themselves into a range of spaces, from TV studios, parks, and museums to police departments, billboards, and the mail; they experimented with media hijacking, misinformation, perceptual sabotage, and the temporary occupation of space in conceptual and performance-based works. Over the years, the work of each has been retrospectively labeled "guerrilla," a curatorial shorthand that has come to imply little more than an element of surprise and spontaneity.[18] Some, like the members of GAAG and the Guerrilla Girls, explicitly claim the moniker "guerrilla" to link their art actions to a wider visual culture of revolution. PESTS, by contrast, opted for the metaphor of invasion and infestation, while Piper, Pope.L, Hsieh, and Asco envisioned tactics that called into question categories of making, work, and social order itself. In each work, however, these artists expanded the contours of artmaking and reframed relations between punishable subjects, as their varying vulnerabilities to state-sanctioned violence differently informed the decisions and tactical forms each made.

Returning to the illustrative example of GAAG, Toche and Hendricks not only anticipated possible legal consequences but also strategically considered how museum leaders would wield their legal authority. When planning for their "Malevich action," Hendricks recalls that they anticipated that arrest was unlikely:

> Do you arrest the artists, the people doing this? You could. We were trespassing, they said. But that was part of our calculus, too. [Picture the headline:] "Museum Arrests Artists." "Why are they arresting artists?" "Because the artists are angry. Because they feel the museum isn't doing its job, isn't telling the truth." That's an interesting story. So, they realized, "Maybe we better not arrest them. Maybe there's another approach: neutralize them, buy them off."[19]

The artists' correct prediction that they would not be arrested that day relies on their careful evaluation but also, implicitly, on the expectation that two white men could remove a painting from the wall and, if arrested, receive due process and a fair trial. Toche and Hendricks's fastidious planning, court-oriented documentation, protective choreographing of potential collaborators and witnesses, and speculation about the museum's strategic pacification, animates what I call their *punitive literacy*.

Punitive literacy is cumulative knowledge that allows for self-protective mobility in a penal society. It is a calculus of risk based on the body, spaces, and networks one inhabits. Black feminist intersectional and queer of color critiques of patriarchal white supremacist power make possible the framing of the work of calculating risk-taking as relational, embodied, and situated knowledge.[20] The concept of punitive literacy, developed across this book, emerged from a need to name the work of risk-taking in a spatialized racial order that is prevalent but not yet adequately articulated in discussions of artists' deployment of low-tech modes of intervention in conceptual and performance-based practice in the US. When I began this research, I found an art-historical vocabulary insufficient to animate the relational social politics of risk-taking that links artists' seemingly discrete actions. Punitive literacy, as a concept, builds upon the "politics of mobility" and is in debt to a range of crucial work established in the interdisciplinary fields of performance studies, Black studies, and prison studies, which provide a way of speaking about actions shaped by the will for social justice and living, alongside one's awareness of the securitization of space, police presence, and the need for self-protection.

Scholars in early childhood education have written of "punitive literacy practices," addressing the literal punitiveness of standardized literacy testing in schools.[21] I develop "punitive literacy" instead to address a *literacy in punitiveness*, including structures of punishment as well as modes of risk-taking that subvert, delay, or contest those responses. "Punitiveness" is a societal relation of punishment foundational within an ever-expanding disciplinary network—what Michel Foucault famously called "the carceral archipelago"—that extends techniques of punishment within prison to the entire "social body."[22] In sociological terms, punitiveness is "a phenomenological complex operating at a personal, symbolic, political and structural level," a set of relations that ordains "dynamics between punitive and punishable subjects."[23] Broadly speaking, punitive literacy is the ability to assess how one's body will, or will not be, subjected to state violence. It is the knowledge an individual uses (whether consciously or subconsciously) to determine what creative acts they can carry out in a particular place at a particular time and what might be the consequences of those actions.

Punitive literacy, however, is more than anticipating encounters with law enforcement and the consequences of written law. In artists' hands, the work of survival and risk-taking relies on an understanding of the *mutations* of law as well as the range of unsafety it regulates among people with differently complex relations to the state. Punitive literacy, then, involves both an attunement to the possibility of containment and a calculation of its likelihood based on one's exposure to state violence, as well as how the actions of collaborators and intermediaries will potentially unfold. In a society profoundly shaped by racial, gendered, sexualized, and classed hierarchies of power, everyone calculates their risks. But some people do it consciously and under lethal threat, while others rely more comfortably on the law and police to protect them and their rights. The magnitude of this difference has yet to be considered as a central component of tactics in art labeled "guerrilla." This oversight is especially troubling given that riskiness and physical danger-seeking in art discourse formalizes in an unprecedented way in the 1970s and 1980s, as the masochistic art practices of cis-gendered white men (and a few white women) are canonized.[24]

To be clear, there never was a coherent "guerrilla" movement in the US. Instead, a loose constellation of artists, groups, or collectives engaged with differing causes, audiences, and sites. In 1972, for example, Chris Burden, a white male artist, held a TV talk show host hostage on the air in his performance *TV Hijack*. In 1974, members of the Chicano art group Asco staged and photographed a fictional scene of gang war aftermath in East Los Angeles; seeking to upend the white-dominated media's perpetuation of Chicano gang rivalries, they effected conceptual art media hoax, circulating the image, undetected, via local news channels as a real event.

Also in 1974, Piper (who retired from being Black in 2012),[25] donned an Afro wig, reflective sunglasses, and hypermasculine strut and "loitered" on Harvard's campus as part of her conceptual art series *The Mythic Being*. That same year, Toche wrote open letters to the US attorney general and the mayor of Boston, calling for Boston's police chief to resign due to his force's inadequate protection of Black Bostonians from assaults by white antibusing protesters. In 1978 in New York City, Pope.L, a Black man, sought to draw attention to the normalized presence of the unhoused, crawling on his hands and knees in a suit through Times Square in an action that attracted the attention of a law enforcement officer. And Hsieh, an undocumented Taiwanese man, created his own *Wanted by U.S. Immigration Service* poster, also in 1978; he did not publicly display it, however, until 1982, in the midst of his *Outdoor Piece*, twelve months spent living on the streets of Manhattan. The Guerrilla Girls, founded in 1985 by seven white women, wheat-pasted acerbic critiques of art-world sexism near high-end New York art galleries. And PESTS, a collective of women of color that emerged in part in response to the myopic vision of the art world's white feminists, mailed anonymous "PEST strips" decrying "tokenism" and the "racial apartheid" of the New York art world.

These artworks will illuminate how cross-pollinating transnational and spatial ideas of guerrilla tactics shaped mechanisms of social control in the 1970s and 1980s. Of course, the risks calculated by artists in the United States are distinct from those faced by artists living under even more repressive conditions.[26]

The consequences incurred by artists using guerrilla tactics while living under dictatorship and apartheid—arrest, censorship, exile, and worse—have been examined in studies of the Rosario Group in Argentina, the AI-5 ban in Brazil, the Tupamaros in Uruguay, and the tactical maneuvers of anti-apartheid artists in South Africa.[27]

To be sure, the US government has not enacted sweeping restrictions on freedom of expression or threatened artists with death or exile. Nonetheless, the anticipated *threat* of violence—the central function of police power as an arm of the state—and its disproportionate and asymmetrical presence within the lives of minoritized individuals remains a significantly overlooked aspect of US-based artists' decisions to use or avoid certain types of tactical intervention.[28] Thus, while guerrilla tactics were explored through artistic practice transnationally, this book argues that it is important to focus on their formation in the US, to be able to confront the nation's leading and imperial role in developing practices of militarized civil regulation; as well as how framing guerrilla practices as external justified the development of these very practices both at home and abroad. This book and these artists' works show that these practices were always already inherent to US-based political resistance because of the state's unique position in developing and exporting punitive policies and practices globally. Drawing on art history, performance studies, Black feminist and queer of color critique, legal studies, carceral studies, and Black studies, the four chapters of this book track how artists in the US not only negotiated the language and performance of tactics then being glamorized by activists and revolutionary fighters; they also helped bring expressions of confrontation, resourcefulness, and aggression into domestic culture while negotiating, and often altering, a burgeoning security apparatus.

Subsequently, this introduction addresses two key oversights and their implications: first, that interpretations of guerrilla tactics in American art have not yet adequately confronted the rapidly changing landscape of policing and criminal code reform endemic to the 1960s and 1970s within definitions of guerrilla. Second, that the social politics of risk-taking that unfolds contingently across and within the artwork and its interpretation has been underexamined, despite the industrialization of risk in this period.[29]

Unlearning "Guerrilla"

To date, a scholarly consensus on the use of low-tech tactics in the 1960s and 1970s emphasizes conceptualizations of the guerrilla as synonymous with leftist radical change. This consensus is born of the idea of the guerrilla that is linked to anticolonial, heroic, progressive social change—actions intended to intervene, momentarily, in asymmetrical power dynamics. Among the most famously glamorized and lethally surveilled instances in the US, the Black Panther Party for Self-Defense formed in October 1966 in Oakland, California, under the leadership of Bobby Seale and Huey Newton, to provide a Black patrol unit to counter the white police force. While the group's scope expanded far beyond this initial purpose, becoming a national organization focused on community aid, mental health support, education, and nutritional health in the Black community, the inclusion of *Self-Defense* in the original group name connotes a need for protection from violence threatened by a state mired in lethal racialized punitive relations. Those on patrol initially carried not weapons but, as historian Leigh Raiford explains, notepads, tape recorders, and cameras to monitor police activity.[30] It was only after sharing information with the police proved ineffective that the Black Panthers turned to protecting themselves with guns.

Inspired in large part by the Black Panther Party, a number of militant reform groups emerged. The Chicano Brown Berets mobilized in LA in 1967 to draw attention to farm workers' rights, antiwar demands, and the overpolicing of the barrios of Los Angeles County. The Chinese Red Guard Party, paying homage to the Panthers and to the student-led Red Guards, part of the Cultural Revolution in China, formed in 1969 to fight for better living and working conditions in San Francisco's Chinatown. The Native American Indian Movement, initially established in 1968 in Minneapolis, fought for treaty rights and the preservation of Indigenous cultures in the face of congressional relocation acts displacing tribal communities. The Young Lords (initially the Young Lords Organization, or Young Lords Party) emerged in Chicago in 1968 and extended to New York City, where group members staged demonstrations and hosted community programs in support of their thirteen-point program demanding the right of self-determination for Puerto Ricans and Latino nations and an end to capitalist oppression.

Despite differing vested interests, these activist reformers shared a sense of the connection between the anticolonial wars of occupation being fought overseas in Vietnam and Latin America, and the domestic war fronts within American ghettos and barrios. As they wielded guerrilla tactics associated with the third world, but also uniquely bound up within grounded struggles specific to the American terrain and histories of genocide, slavery, and displacement, it was widely understood that the physical was also a symbolic gesture, a way of connecting battlegrounds. As historian Christoph Kalter and others have explained, the third world is not a place but "the concept that allowed for a radical critique of existing systems of power and representations while permitting them at the same time to elaborate equally radical alternatives."[31]

The late 1960s also saw a growing urgency among artists, curators, and art critics to offer a vision of the guerrilla applicable to art, theater, and symbolic cultural warfare that rippled across the 1970s and 1980s. In October 1967, the Italian cultural critic Umberto Eco gave a speech in New York City, urging artists in this country to become "cultural guerrillas."[32] The same year, Italian art critic Germano Celant published his "Notes on a Guerrilla War" in the international publication *Flash Art*, telling art audiences across the world that the "guerrilla war" in art—artists waging war on the art system—had already begun.[33] In Paris, the Situationists, a collective of writers and visual artists, promoted the use of "guerrilla warfare in the mass media."[34] In the US, street theater groups adapted the guerrilla concept; Bread and Puppet Theater, the Living Theater, and the San Francisco Mime Troupe, as well as the Diggers and El Teatro Campesino, radically altered the face of theater, spectatorship, and models of activist-oriented practice in public space.[35]

The range of adaptations of "guerrilla" across the arts was vast. Artist-organized exhibitions in unexpected locations were referred to as "guerrilla gallerizing," while Melvin Van Peebles deemed his method of filmmaking, which looked beyond Hollywood for funding, as "guerrilla film."[36] In 1971, *Guerrilla Television*, a how-to guide authored by Michael Shamberg and designed by Ant Farm, laid out a transhistorical potential for "the use of the word 'guerrilla' [as] a sort of bridge between an old and a new consciousness," while Paul Ryan's essay "Cybernetic Guerrilla Warfare" called for the cultivation of an information ecology and disruptive tactical intervention.[37] As Warren Hinckle, editor of the leftist Bay Area underground paper *Scanlan's Monthly*, wrote, also in 1971, in his preface to an issue on guerrilla warfare in the US, "Guerrilla warfare will become a catchword of the 1970s along with women's liberation and the mini skirt."[38]

Scholars looking back on this period have provided useful reconceptualizations of "guerrilla" that attend to its ethnic and global relations of change-making. Historian Jeremy Varon, in his study of two white groups, the Red Army Faction in Germany and the Weather Underground in the US, succinctly describes the guerrilla as "an anti-authoritarian icon who embodied the mystique of the outlaw."[39] Historian Rychetta Watkins's discussion of guerrilla aesthetics—anchored in discussions of Emory Douglas's *Black Panther* drawings and the imagery printed in *Gidra*, an underground newspaper dubbed the "Voice of the Asian American Movement"—asserts that guerrilla principles became a "type of transitional ethnic consciousness designed to usher people of color from rhetorical change to substantive change."[40]

These ideas are echoed in Kodwo Eshun and Ros Gray's conception of a cinematic "guerrilla imaginary" that draws on the relationship in the late 1960s and early 1970s between the revolutionary struggle of third-world nations against the American military-industrial empire and the struggle of Black urban guerrillas within the "metropole of the principal enemy."[41] When, for example, Gillo Pontecorvo's film *The Battle of Algiers*, featuring guerrilla rebels during the Algerian war, was nominated for Best Foreign Film at the 1967 Academy Awards, movie critics, government officials, and artists alike dubbed it a "primer in guerrilla warfare."[42] In a world increasingly connected by televised news and mass-produced print media, images depicting guerrilla fighters that circulated with exceptional speed made a significant impact on political resistance and cultural production.[43]

These instantiations and descriptions of guerrilla tactics are incisive and capacious but incomplete. They focus on the use of tactics in a countercultural context but do not account for either the figure of the guerrilla as it was simultaneously imagined by the US government or how this process of figuration served the maintenance of state power, not just the making of radical praxis. One reason for this oversimplification might be a result of Michel de Certeau's oft-cited formulation, which aligns *tactics* with the powerless and temporary actions "determined by the absence of space," and *strategy* with established power and the ability to maintain control through the production of space.[44] But as feminist theorist María Lugones has shown in her critique of Certeau's limiting dichotomy, a far more complex "tactical-strategic" intentionality arises from the tactician "having a deep spatio-temporal insight into the social" born of the "double inhabitation of the space that fragments and of the space constituted in relational movement."[45] Conversely, those working within the government, or law enforcement, do not inhabit such rigid relations. In short, guerrilla tactics are not merely temporary redirections of power but a record of situated knowledge that calls forth horizons of tactical possibility for refusing, as well as being co-opted and rebranded by and for the state.

As discussed in the following section, activists and revolutionaries weren't the only ones profiling and defining "guerrilla." Elected officials, law enforcement, urban reformers, and citizens studied the concept of the guerrilla, too, and expanded its discursive meaning. At home and abroad, US police officers were involved in a massive international training mission in which the US military claimed guerrilla tactics as what was later rebranded "low-intensity" counterinsurgency.[46] "Guerrilla," thus, is more accurately a metaphor for a set of relations projected onto particular bodies, places, and temporalities of policing. For this reason, "guerrilla" in this book is not used as a descriptive term but, rather, is positioned as a complex field of negotiation wherein boundaries of "here" and "there," "militant" and "orderly," "risky" and "safe," come into being. It is in this paradox—the guerrilla was both a catalyst for change and an excuse for social control and risk management—that we gain a deepened understanding of the stakes of artists' experimentation with tactics in conceptual and performance-based works through a closer look at the intensified expansion of policing that occurs in the 1960s onward.

Punitive Relations

Remarkably, the story of the "punitive turn" remains the most understudied aspect of artists' use of guerrilla tactics in the US. The phrase is used widely across sociology, geography, history, and criminal law to name the historical impact of harsh sentencing legislation, prison-building, increased police hiring and budgets, and implementation of video and computerized surveillance technology.[47] In short, it underscores the expansion of all aspects of the criminal punishment system, which we see maintained and expanded in the present.

In its common usage, the punitive turn in the US refers to the period of the 1960s and after, when a federal "War on Crime" inaugurated by President Lyndon B. Johnson, elevated the issue of crime from a local concern to one of national urgency.[48] Under the Omnibus Crime Control and Safe Streets Act passed by Congress in 1968, Johnson established the Law Enforcement Assistance Act (LEAA), the first federalized funding stream for local police departments; it would remain active until 1982 (though it continued to function thereafter in less legible ways).[49] Between the 1960s and the 1980s, police budgets skyrocketed, while prisons and prison populations expanded simultaneously, trends that continue to this day: the number of incarcerated people in the US has grown exponentially since the late 1960s, from a hundred thousand to more than 2.4 million people.[50] Since 1973, incarceration rates have risen by a factor of six, even as crime statistics have fallen, while expenditures on the criminal justice system have quadrupled over the past four decades.[51] As historian Khalil Gibran Muhammad puts it bluntly, "The United State is the most punitive country in the world."[52]

Muhammad's observation is tied to the reality that there has been not one but many punitive *turns* at the core of US nation-building and its social governance. He, and a number of scholars of carceral history have challenged the notion of a singular punitive turn in the 1960s by locating racialized punitive turns in the postwar period, the post-emancipation era, and earlier, within the colonialist establishment of the nation, the genocide of Indigenous peoples and the enslavement of African and Black Americans.[53] In this way, the project of the "War on Crime" did not create but expanded upon a penal infrastructure already in place.[54] The policing of guerrilla tactics during the 1960s through the 1980s fits into this larger story and is just part of one chapter in punitive America. However, it is an especially important context for the history of art because it is inextricably bound up with artists' unprecedented use of tactics in art.

Between the late 1960s and late 1980s, as artists began experimenting with guerrilla tactics in art, a number of events coalesced to increase contact with police power and an expanding punitive landscape: the 1968 Anti-Riot Act was used to remove civil rights and antiwar activists from public spaces; new antiloitering laws in the early 1970s regulated gay cruising sites and queer spaces as well as survival economies; antihomelessness laws criminalized poverty throughout the economic recession of the 1970s and the rise of unhoused populations in the 1980s; and a racialized and classist "War on Drugs," begun by Nixon and formalized by Reagan, brought even more youth of color into the cycle of carceral debt. In the 1980s, the undoing of welfare support, and the implementation of nuisance and urban renewal policies normalized the forced, often violent removal of people in the name of protecting property relations and domestic security. Nationally, capital spending on corrections, such as prison construction, reached a high of 16 percent between 1986 and 1988.[55] At the same time, a proliferation of closed-circuit video surveillance, police helicopters, computerized crime databases, and predictive policing algorithms expanded the reach of police discretion in public and private spaces. Within the longer arc of punitiveness foundational to the US, it is a period of intensive police expansion and, as Micol Seigel articulates, a *relegitimization* of policing domestically and globally that has structured our contemporary moment.[56]

This expansive, networked system of punishment—extensive enough to justify the term *punitive America*—is deeply informed by gendered, racialized, and sexualized notions of threat and order that bridge historical and contemporary regimes of surveillance.[57] The years 1967 to 1987, then, demarcate a time of, on the one hand, unprecedented artistic experimentation with regard to tactics and, on the other, an emergent, codified critical vocabulary for risk management and policing, and its consolidation within coercive security paradigms. Changing policing paradigms also engendered strategies of expression, survival, and collective aid, often among the minoritized subjects most vulnerable to state violence, which gave way to transformative forms of tenacity, care, and world-making, including many that remain purposefully fugitive, furtive, and undefined.[58] Thus, artists using guerrilla tactics, while attuned to risk-taking, also negotiated punitive relations and structures born of the entanglement of domestic cultural expression and international relations; as this relationship evolved, the forms through which their artwork manifests offer a unique archive of the making of risk as a social and political phenomenon specific to these Cold War decades. Importantly, "guerrilla" was a device not just animated by activists but instrumentalized by politicians, law enforcement, and national security authorities.

In the late 1960s and early 1970s, the phrase "guerrilla warfare" was used publicly to describe racialized urban police-citizen conflict and in internal government documents to justify expanded police spending. As a 1967 FBI report on "racial disturbances" observed, "We are in a guerrilla war for which our National Guard has not been adequately trained as it should be."[59] During a "safety hearing" held in November 1967 by the new National Advisory Commission on Civil Disorders (also known as the Kerner Commission), organized to research the causes of riots, Los Angeles police chief Thomas Reddin declared, "If we [police and politicians] don't take advantage of what exists in the United States in 1967, we are crazy because we are never going to have it so good again."[60]

Reddin was referring to the rebellions that summer, most explosively those in Detroit and Newark, and to his sense that liberals and conservatives momentarily agreed than aggressive policing was needed to combat urban conflict framed as guerrilla war. As one reporter, writing about the clashes between Black citizens and white police in Detroit in July 1967, asserted, "The big story Tuesday was 'guerrilla warfare,'" the governor having called in National Guard "shock troops to put down the guerrilla warfare."[61] Watching news of the Detroit rebellion from Havana during the first conference of the Organization of Latin American Solidarity, Black power activist Kwame Ture (then Stokely Carmichael) announced that "guerrilla warfare was being organized in the ghettos for a fight to the death."[62]

This fight for survival, apparent in the uprisings—with the 1965 rebellion in Watts as a significant turning point—had been a long time in the making: the US government's systematic state-sanctioned social, economic, and political disenfranchisement of Black people, intensified with mass-urbanization, linked the afterlives of slavery and Jim Crow–era segregation to the ongoing underfunding and policing of Black and brown communities and city neighborhoods.[63]

As Charles W. McKinney Jr. explains, "riots" are "violent revelations that lay bare the systemic inequities that dogged marginalized people," a manifestation of long-standing, day-to-day subordination of Black communities through residential segregation, economic displacement, workplace discrimination and unemployment, and increased tensions due to urbanization and policing, which meant more contact with the state.[64] For this reason, scholars and activists have taken to using the language of "rebellion" or "uprising" to emphasize how these actions contest white supremacist structures that protect and normalize white ascendency.

Law enforcement officers did not acknowledge these causes but instead offered a binary: they narrated Black people's use of guerrilla tactics in urban spaces, such as Watts, Detroit, and Newark, as a senseless, excessive showing of extralegal force, whereas police power was presented as sanctioned and necessary, the officers themselves victims of a battle for social order. Reducing this complex, transhistorical conflict to moralizing, racist stereotypes, Los Angeles police chief Edward Davis asked his superiors in 1967 to choose a side: "Would it be the law of the jungle, or the law of organized society?"[65] The xenophobic and imperialist dichotomies of disorder and order, extralegal and legal force, jungle and civilization—as false as they were persuasive—had gained credibility. American military historians presented the guerrilla as an "agent of *foreign* aggression."[66] Police chief Reddin called for more militarized manpower to combat the coming surge of militants; 1968, he asserted, should be "the year of the cop."[67] Reddin's declaration echoed the Cuban government's announcement, made only a few weeks earlier, that 1968 should be the "year of the heroic guerrilla." Taken together, these statements emphasize how the profiles of guerrilla and police officer were inextricably bound within a global imaginary of force and action.

In response to calls from law enforcement for weapons and training appropriate to a guerrilla war, the LEAA expanded police budgets. In its initial year, it provided police departments with an additional forty million dollars in block grants for riot gear, chemical weaponry, and training programs that bolstered future-oriented risk management.[68] These programs drew on the experience of counterinsurgency units confronting guerrilla fighters in Vietnam and, when authoring riot control manuals for US law enforcement, adapted guerrilla actions based on Viet Cong tactics.[69]

This anti-riot buildup would have implications for artists adapting tactics for cultural production in the following decades. When US government agencies, including the CIA, compiled watch lists to track instances of guerrilla warfare, agents did not differentiate armed militants from cultural producers. Both appeared on rosters of those under surveillance. For example, "Guerrilla Warfare Advocates in the United States," a report commissioned by Johnson and supervised by Edwin Willis, the chair of the House Committee on Un-American Activities, tracked citizens who had voiced communist sympathies, visited Cuba or China (ostensibly to study guerrilla warfare), and promoted various forms of armed liberation. The list, published in 1968, included artists, such as Frank Gillette and Ken Marsh, the white men leading Peoples' Video Theatre, which was using newly available portapak video technology to produce "guerrilla television" in collaboration with the Black Panther Party, alongside Robert Williams, a Black Marxist and outspoken supporter of armed resistance who authored the influential text "USA: The Potential of a Minority Revolution," and Max Stanford, a leader of the Revolutionary Action Movement, a Black group of which Bobby Seale was a member.[70] Willis's report set the groundwork for the state to determine when and at what point an individual *becomes a guerrilla*, and how that determination could lead to designating a dissenting citizen as a foreign enemy who could be stripped of constitutional rights "as in wartime." The report served, in the eyes of the government, to validate FBI director J. Edgar Hoover's expansion of COINTELPRO, a Cold War counterintelligence program initiated in 1956 to track communists. In the late 1960s, the FBI director incentivized local law enforcement to watch and "aggressively penetrate" the Black Panther Party and activist organizations sympathetic to its cause.[71]

Another significant development in 1967 was that Hoover established the National Crime Information Center (NCIC). The NCIC was funded in the wake of the 1967 uprising in Detroit—an event, along with Watts, that prison studies scholar Jordan T. Camp identifies as central to "today's explosive carceral crisis" and the making of "neoliberal racial and security regimes."[72] Behind the scenes, the NCIC worked to standardize metrics for collecting and analyzing crime-related data: by 1976 national regulations had been issued for crime data management, and by 1980 all state governments had access to the centralized, computerized NCIC database, forming an unprecedented network dedicated to tracking and reporting incidents nationwide.[73]

The power to visualize criminality as well as define self-defense through "data-driven approaches" is instrumental in normalizing state-sanctioned violence while outlawing forms of resistance to it. For this reason, the media's (re)presentation of the Black Panthers' armed self-defense provides a deeply relevant lesson for assessing the risk-taking of the artists who populate this book. Chroniclers of the Black Panther Party have discussed the visuality of the Panthers and the myriad responses to, and implications of, the group's rupture of state narratives of control.[74] In response to the Panthers' armed counterpatrols, state senator Don Mulford proposed a bill to prohibit the open carry of loaded firearms in California. Members of the Black Panthers countered with a protest, appearing at the capitol building in Sacramento on May 2, 1967. As reporters took photos, they entered the building, wearing leather jackets and berets and carrying guns, emulating the visual iconography of anticolonial movements emblematized by the look of Che Guevara. The next day, these images ran in national publications, such as *U.S. News and World Report*, *Life*, and *Time*, and in local papers, such the *Sacramento Bee*. The *Bee*'s provocative headline, "CAPITOL IS INVADED," framed the Black Panthers' action not as one by citizens defending their Second Amendment rights but as a foreign infiltration.

On the *Bee*'s front page and elsewhere in the press, the story told through the images codified a cinematic message—what Kara Keeling refers to as "blacks with guns"—that eclipsed the list of demands that had been the purpose of their protest.[75] Meanwhile photographs taken by reporters that countered the insinuation of invasion gained no traction in the news: these lesser-known images show Black Panthers with weapons lowered, pointing to the floor, speaking with white police officers who, having read their printed demands, concluded that the protesters were responsibly exercising their constitutional rights (fig. I.4). While COINTELPRO is often cited as the key example of state efforts to defeat the Panthers, the Mulford Act, signed into law by California governor Ronald Reagan two months later—a harbinger of things to come under his law-and-order federal administration in the 1980s—demonstrates how race-neutral governance legalized antiblack modes of containment vis-à-vis a discourse of perceived risk and public safety. As Erica Edwards explains, pointedly, "COINTELPRO was no exception to *normal surveillance*" of Black radicalism and Black life.[76] This kind of everyday surveillance, traced back to the Black Atlantic slave trade and implemented through policing measures in the US on plantations and after, necessitates furtive negotiations that Black diaspora and surveillance studies scholar Simone Browne calls "dark sousveillance." Drawing upon the Black radical tradition, Browne defines dark sousveillance as imaginative "tactics employed to render one's self out of sight" through methods of "antisurveillance, countersurveillance, and other freedom practices," and a "site of critique" for contesting the antiblack surveillance central to the making of whiteness.[77]

To be clear, the artists studied in this book are *not* armed militants. And yet, the ways they navigate the term "guerrilla" in their art practice—whether claiming or evading the label—manifest as punitive literacy inculcated within the historically specific articulations of *guerrilla* then used by activists and law

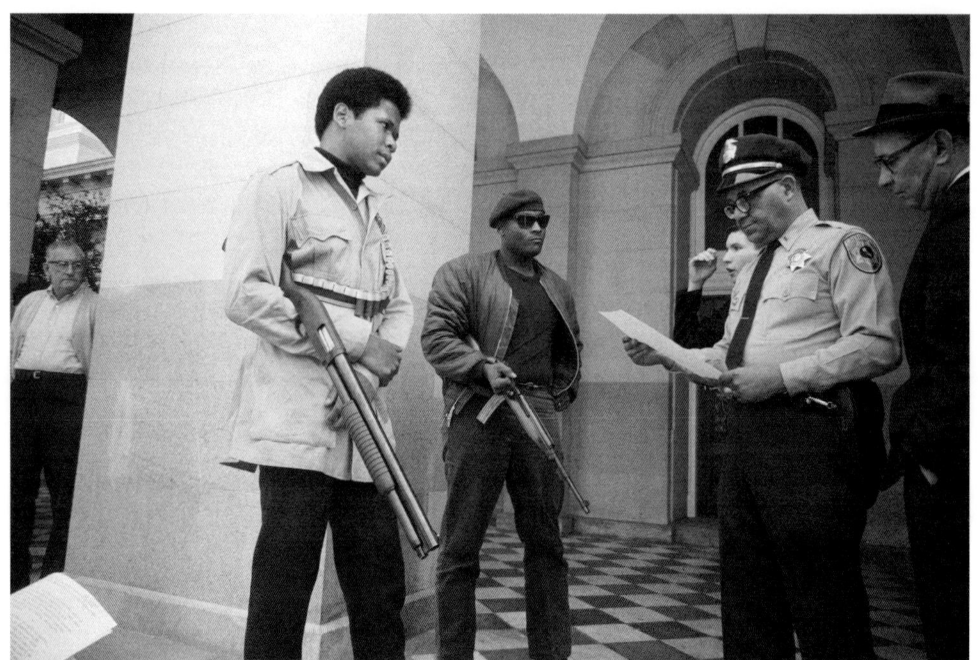

[I.4] *Black Panthers at California State Capitol*, May 2, 1967. Archive caption: "Two members of the Black Panther Party are met on the steps of the State Capitol in Sacramento, May 2, 1967, by Police Lt. Ernest Holloway, who informs them they will be allowed to keep their weapons as long as they cause no trouble and do not disturb the peace. Earlier several members had invaded the Assembly chambers and had their guns taken away." Black-and-white photograph. Bettmann Collection. © Getty Images.

enforcement. As Toche and Hendricks specified in the statement they shared the day they removed Malevich's painting from MoMA's wall, "We are a pacifist group," whose "protest actions are executed on an *art level*, not on a level of political militancy or real violence."[78] Nevertheless, through those symbolic gestures they invited association with the work of the Black Panthers, Weather Underground, and other groups. Depending on who uses it and when, the label *guerrilla* can give rise to what Varon calls "the politics of proving."[79] The Weathermen, a white group, he explains, "fell prey to the seductive optimism of global voices like Che Guevara and Mao Tse-tung." They also "plainly idealized blacks, imputing to them capacities they could not possibly possess."[80] By mobilizing the mythic invincibility of the urban guerrilla, shaped by entangled imaginaries of third-world militancy and policing, white activists seeking to put their bodies on the line and build solidarity at times gained notoriety in ways that inadvertently leveraged the racist fantasies of inhuman strength evoked by police as justification for the surveillance and violent removal of Black and brown people.

By contrast, Asco's conceptual work with media hoax was attuned to the danger of attracting police attention, an awareness that informed their experimental performance and conceptual art practice. As Harry Gamboa Jr., one of Asco's founding members, noted, "We needed strategies to avoid the police," leading to tactics of satirical, humorous play with props and costumes, and actions that intentionally thwarted classification and affiliation.[81] The members of Asco imagined modes of cultural production that confronted inequity yet were nimbly evasive of punitive consequences. As these two examples suggest, "guerrilla" functioned differently but in interrelated ways for artists: for Toche and Hendricks, it provided a visual strategy that connected their critique of the artworld to other solidarities, whereas for other artists, like the members of Asco, it was a necessary survival strategy that was later named as an aesthetic quality within the work.

The artists featured in this book envisioned guerrilla actions just as the militant fighter and his tactics were becoming a global and cultural phenomenon—a figure to be envisioned and celebrated, or forcibly contained and removed. The story of "guerrilla" in art, and its narration, then, is about not merely an individual's momentary gesture or privileges but a structural carceral archipelagic *context*, a collectively managed terrain of possibility and containment through which the terms and legacies of risk-taking come to be. At its most basic level, the book asks that we pay close attention not just to what the concept *guerrilla* means but to what it *does*, and for whom, in the name of articulating risk, resistance, and change.[82]

The Work of Risk—and the Risk of Work

Punitive contexts within the US, and artists' anticipation of them, have not yet been prioritized within art-historical studies of guerrilla tactics in conceptual and performance-based art. Instead, foundational art exhibitions and scholarly texts have taken up the difficult task of anthologizing the pluralism of experimental art between the late 1960s and late 1980s by discussing artists' actions, typically through hyperlocal case studies situated as "interventionist art," "institutional critique," "body art," "agitprop," "protest art," "social practice," "direct action," and "participatory art."[83] While these labels provide useful genealogical frameworks, they tend to prioritize individual agency within a specific time and place, and utilize comparative rather than relational analysis, eliding the ways artists' tactics are not just connected but dialectically linked through mechanisms of social control that generate relations to power in art history and society.

In these anthologies, monographs, and exhibitions, for example, the involvement of police, guards, and lawyers in the making of the art is typically mentioned anecdotally, usually to indicate an end to an art action. Routinely, police presence signals that the artists have come up against a predicted barrier. *Risk Work* proposes that we instead take these moments of potential or realized state violence not as an endpoint or as mere symptoms of artistic transgression, but as a structural field that shapes artists' decisions to act and to make art. When art discourse accepts police presence and security architectures as givens, it reinforces the myth that security is indispensable and obscures the fact that policing is a constantly evolving, mutating form that artists anticipate and *shape* in their tactical work.

Subsequently, one way this book differs from most studies of tactics in art is that each chapter cross-analyzes artists' decision-making processes as a form of situated knowledge that is about not individual agency but *structural* and *relational* fields of manufactured vulnerability. Rather than center the moment of confrontation, so often fetishized in discussions of practice known as guerrilla, I look to the "before" and "after"—artists' anticipation of punitive relations and audiences' assessment of their encounters—to challenge the common narrative that these artworks are merely ephemeral, momentary disruptions or diversions of institutional power or social order. I consider how effects of policing fall disproportionately—and in deeply incommensurate ways—upon Black, Indigenous, brown, and Asian people in the United States, and also dialectically and inversely become the basis of white artists' mobilities and their sense of safety when taking risks with guerrilla tactics in art. Because art emerges through the social and psychological labor of risk, the specific risks of doing artwork labeled "guerrilla" are inextricably bound up in the nonspectacular practices of surviving in a society that maintains antiblack "structural unlivability" within its definitions of safety and security—relations of ontological violence explored in the work of Saidiya Hartman, Orlando Patterson, Hortense Spillers, Jared Sexton, and Frank B. Wilderson.[84]

Developing alongside this wealth of scholarly critique, an unprecedented volume of art and exhibitions making explicit the relations of racism, antiblackness, policing, and incarceration in the twenty-first century has also paved the way for this book's engagement with the racial politics of guerrilla tactics in art. In 2020, Nicole Fleetwood's groundbreaking exhibition *Marking Time: Art in the Age of Mass Incarceration* at MoMA PS.1, introduced the concept of "carceral aesthetics," which she defined as "ways of envisioning and crafting art and culture that reflect the conditions of imprisonment."[85] Looking to the management of penal temporality and materiality both within and beyond the prison, Fleetwood offers carceral aesthetics as a framework than can deepen understanding of the expansive genre of art made by people while imprisoned or in response to relations of incarceration. *Marking Time* joins a number of shows in the last decade that have confronted shared concerns, such as *Walls Turned Sideways*, curated by Risa Puleo; *Necessary Force: Art in the Police State*, organized by Kym Pinder; *Envisioning Justice*, curated by Alexandria Eregbu; and *Promise, Witness, Remembrance*, curated by Allison Glenn in partnership with an advisory board to commemorate the life of Breonna Taylor and condemn antiblack police violence and systemic racism. I hope readers will think of this book as a companion study to these exhibitions that begins from a related but different point of departure: *Risk Work* offers one method for analyzing the role of art and art discourse that does *not* seek to confront police power as a subject but instead indexes the white raciality and antiblack politics of *under*policing that is central to punitiveness in the US.

Accordingly, this book seeks to come to know with the artists the realities that challenge and motivate them to differentially anticipate punitiveness while navigating legalized and socialized notions of punishment and care.[86] To draw out artists' different but intermeshed vulnerabilities and proximities to policing, I employ *risk work*, a framework that centers the relationship between their tactical choices and literacy in punitiveness. The conjunction of "risk" and "work" aims to bring forward (1) *the work of risk-taking*, specifically the labor, time, experience, and skill of becoming literate in its potential consequences (material, legal, social, carceral, and lethal) in a penal society, and (2) *the socially coded value system that determines whether an artist's risks are praised or invalidated as work* (the social risk of the artwork). Risk work as an art-historical interpretative analytic allows us to better see power at work in and across the stories told about resistance, subversion, and deviance.

The meaning of risk work builds from the discourses of "work" and "risk" that have remained siloed. My conceptualization of *work* finds inspiration in Ann Stoler's "concept-work," Micol Seigel's "violence work," and the "wake work" theorized by Christina Sharp, as well as the activists and scholars arguing for the terms "sex work" and "care work."[87] While each neologism mobilizes distinctive aims, these thinkers collectively demonstrate the profound utility of rethinking how *work* can provide an analytic for addressing the ways that seemingly private and mundane acts—from classification and mourning, to desire and violence—are in fact sites for transformative, as well as taxing and costly, modes of being and becoming.

In art history, ideas of "work" became a central point of contention in the 1960s and 1970s among experimental artists pushing the edges of avant-garde practice—whether in Minimalism manufactured using assembly lines and construction yards, or in dematerialized, market-resistant Fluxus, performance art, conceptualism, installation art, and Happenings. As art historians Julia Bryan-Wilson and Helen Molesworth have articulated, the definition and status of "work" in the post–World War II period changed in significant and influential ways.[88] The Art Workers Coalition formed to galvanize artists as workers with worker's rights. (Toche was directly involved with the AWC, Piper attended a few meetings, and other artists in this book knew it well.) Many artists brought forward a feminist Marxist critique of work, rendering visible the tedium and undervalued work of childcare, cleaning, and maintenance in their art. As the feminist movement gained momentum, and "care work" as labor became a fixture of political demonstrations and art of the 1960s and 1970s, Black queer and postcolonial feminist theorists such as Audre Lorde and Trinh T. Minh-ha critiqued white feminists' romanticizing of multicultural notions of togetherness that normalized the exploitation and erasure of women of color's intellectual and domestic labor.[89]

While much has been written on the discourse of "work" in American art, the widely held sociological finding that risk-taking is socially constructed has yet to be made a primary concern in art-historical studies, despite art historian Joan Kee's insightful assertion that "risk" emerged as a new topic of consideration in American art of the 1960s and 1970s. It was during this period, Kee notes, that "risk became as central to the definition of artist as conceptions of labor or intention had been previously."[90] And yet, the discourse of spectacular "riskiness" that emerged through confrontational tactics in art has largely upheld white, heterosexual masculinity—and to a less extent, femininity—as the untroubled baseline of risk-taking. In a representative 1978 essay titled "Risk as the Practice of Thought," part of a *Flash Art* special issue on "Danger in Art," French critic François Pluchart tracked art practices of the 1970s that put pressure on the ethical limits of art through self-harm, reviewing only the work of white male artists such as Burden, Vito Acconci, Joseph Beuys, Dennis Oppenheim, and Ben Vautier.[91] When "riskiness" in performance and conceptual-based art produced by white-presenting artists is considered, the "body" is almost always discussed in universalizing terms. And yet, for white artists, punitive literacy is informed by patterns of public safety, resource distribution, and land ownership historically tailored to protect them.

This tendency to leave gendered and sexualized whiteness unnamed when discussing risk continues into the present. Contemporary reconsiderations of risk in art, such as art historian Jane Blocker's discussion of confrontational art practice in the 1970s, present risk as "a game of one-upmanship that yields to intense, often masculinist struggles for the position of most daring."[92] Though Blocker provides a useful critique of the gender politics at work within the expediency of a "self-congratulatory rhetoric of risk" in art, and questions "who exactly is experiencing risk," her framing suggests that risk-taking is by definition dangerous, competitive, or deviant behavior that is needless or voluntary. She concludes with a query: "I find myself wondering what an artistic boycott of risk might look like."[93] This kind of assessment forecloses discussion of risk-taking that is not danger-seeking or masculinist but fugitive, illegible, quiet, transformative, and unavoidable. Furthermore, this understanding overlooks the *work* of taking *nonspectacular* risks in one's resistive, tactical artwork, risks that are not about one-upmanship but about evading and surviving the harm of state-sanctioned violence, carceral welfare, deportation, or discrimination, as in the work of Hsieh, Pope.L, PESTS, Asco, and Piper. The artists' methods and questions aren't separate—though they have been in art history—but relational, dialectical, and cross-generational. Risk work is an attempt to denaturalize these entanglements and the implications of their ongoing erasure.

When the gendered and sexualized racial politics of risk-taking remains underacknowledged, art-historical analyses of action-taking reproduce the limits of a comparative method and uphold the "juridical privileges of whiteness," defined by Robyn Wiegman as an implicit bias of the law that protects property—values foundational to the establishment of the United States and its justification of the genocide of Indigenous people and the forced migration and enslavement of Africans and African Americans.[94] Furthermore, as white and white-presenting (and, typically, heteronormative) artists' relational protection by the law remains largely invisible, art-historical scholarship overlooks such calculation and reinforces what Black studies scholar George Lipsitz has termed the "white spatial imaginary"—a formulation of mobility and power that "does not simply disadvantage nonwhites by excluding them from the fruits and benefits of mainstream society . . . but also disadvantages whites by preventing them from seeing how we are actually governed in this society, and how new oppositional ideas, actions, and associations might be developed."[95]

Recognizing that there are many facets to risk, of which anticipating arrest is just one, it is important to note that many of our contemporary ideas of riskiness can be traced to significant changes in the management of crime as a national concern in the 1960s through the 1980s. For example, the crime-related data-collecting efforts initiated in the late 1960s would inform the standardized nationwide development of "risk assessment" for decades. Policing increasingly focused on "recidivism risk," a race-neutral, "scientific" term for the likelihood of repeat criminal offenses that ends up disproportionately punishing Black, brown, and working people (all the more so in the age of electronic monitoring).[96] During the 1970s, Congress standardized sentencing outcomes based on a "salient factor score." This score, the product of an eleven-point actuarial calculation, organized prisoners into four risk categories, from low- to high-risk, based on credit scores, education, employment, health, geographic location, and other factors.[97]

These logics were applied not only to prisoners but to individuals deemed "at-risk" based on factors directly related to assumptions police and policy makers made about certain areas of cities being prone to uprising and guerrilla warfare. The pathologizing of certain actions as "irrational" and "self-destructive," as opposed to "strategic," would carry even larger implications, coinciding with the advent of clinical risk assessment in the 1970s and psychiatry's emphasis on anticipating the threat of a "risky person."[98] The perceived objectivity of recidivism risk scores, criminal law scholar Jessica Eaglin explains, justified and accelerated the expansion of risk technologies that would come to define the 1970s and 1980s, a period of increased police funding, police beats based on biased computer analyses, an upsurge in arrests for comparatively minor crimes, and increased contact between law enforcement and Black communities and people of color in segregated, lower-income areas.[99] As Eaglin astutely asserts, "The produced disorder of criminal administration becomes the natural order of things when translated into technical assessments of risk."[100] Meanwhile, the welfare state was dismantled, and poverty—along with the means of surviving poverty—was criminalized through the integration of the government's "wars" on poverty, crime, and drugs.[101] In this light, risk scores don't merely predict exposure to harm; they create future orientations to spaces, people, and behaviors that come to be associated with risk. The profound racism of the criminal injustice system and the "color-blind racism" of laws and metrics of safe-keeping means that the *risk* of risk-taking is exponentially less for gender-conforming white people, and incrementally more lethal for nonnormative whites and queer, nonbinary, and straight people of color in a society that differently polices gendered and sexualized Blackness, Indigeneity, Asianness, and brownness.[102]

By taking up risk work, this book strives to denaturalize the gendered colorblindness of the legal and cultural discourses of risk-taking that underwrite narratives of guerrilla tactics in American art of the late twentieth century. The artists at the focus of these chapters hardly exhaust the subject of guerrilla tactics in art and risk-taking. Rather, their work productively draws out the ways that "guerrilla" encodes gendered, racialized, and sexualized constructions of criminality, innocence, and threat, and how these ideas shaped these artists' maneuvers, as well as the reactions they received.[103] My interdisciplinary approach bridges transtemporal analyses of the afterlives of slavery in contemporary art, developed by art historians such as Huey Copeland, Krista Thompson, and Cheryl Finley and a growing body of scholarship forged by scholars tracking the relations of artmaking, lawmaking, identity formation, and governance.[104] As one of the forerunners of this latter methodology, performance studies scholar Joshua Chambers-Letson, insightfully suggests, the urgent task is to "complicate the distinction between performance and law, demonstrating the aesthetic nature of the law and the legal function of aesthetics."[105]

To think of risk and work together in art discourse exposes how risk calculation (often invisible) and risk-taking (often spectacularly visible) are both forms of work and both require literacy in punitiveness. This approach also offers an opportunity to better understand how artists' arrests and trials (or lack thereof) have given rise to new juridical interpretations of First Amendment rights. Burden and Toche, for example, become central to the emergent art law field established in the late 1970s, when their arrests for *Deadman* (1972) and "Open Letter for Tony Shafrazi" (1974), respectively, become the focus of texts studied by generations of artists and lawyers.[106] While Burden's and Toche's cases become legal precedent and the basis of regulatory protection, Pope.L crawls in a suit, enacting a method of mobility that skirts the terms of loitering policed by New York City statutes. In so doing, he mobilizes his literacy in punitive structures to evade arrest, motivated in large part by the relatively heightened consequences he would face as a Black man in the carceral system. At the same time, his circumvention of arrest means that his work does not become a case study for lawyers seeking to understand (read: standardize) art and liability law, a discourse that continues to shape metrics of concern and consequence today. Risk work is about not just the riskiness of one's artwork, but the limited perception of artists' punitive literacy that informs both art history and American legal history by normalizing white-centering patriarchal structures of governance in stories of resistance and action.

With these efforts in mind, the chapters of this book are organized around pairs of artists differently oriented to guerrilla tactics: Asco and Burden (chapter 1), Piper and Toche (chapter 2), Hsieh and Pope.L (chapter 3), and the Guerrilla Girls and PESTS (chapter 4). The chapters focus on adjacent urban areas that are differently policed—for example, East Los Angeles and West Los Angeles, Cambridge and Boston, and Soho and Chinatown in New York City—to tell a story about the long arc of policing and liberal police reform in the US and its imprint within tactical genealogies of artmaking in the 1960s through the 1980s. The policing of cities is of particular concern: following the Safe Streets Act, Congress allocated increasing amounts each year in discretionary funds to large cities for the unsupervised purpose of "targeting high crime areas and high crime problems," while simultaneously rolling back welfare funding.[107] Through the book's chapters, I aim to show how preparation for and evasion of arrest is an essential element of art often classified as spontaneous and surprising, and one that links artists not casually but intimately, through their learned knowledge of the penal order, its mutations, and its ongoing expansion. Collectively, the chapters chart a series of punitive contexts that unfold beginning with the ascent of the militant guerrilla in the late 1960s, and continue through the expansion of policing, surveillance technology, and idioms of risk. By the late 1980s, resistance—and punitiveness—had come to mean something else.

The year 1987 is offered as a generative, if imperfect, temporal culmination marked by a trifecta of changes occurring in and across risk, art, and policing discourses. The formalizing of a risk industry picks up momentum at this time, following German sociologist Ulrich Beck's 1986 projection that a global "risk society" had emerged, "moving from a world of enemies to one of dangers and risks . . . [wherein] risk, not war, is the determining factor of power, identity, and the future."[108] In the art world, the Guerrilla Girls garnered national attention by 1987, as discussed in chapter 4. Their rise to fame indelibly changed the discourse of "guerrilla" in American art—their stylization of guerrilla becoming a touchstone that unintentionally overshadows other uses of the term in art while also invariably shaping them. Finally, 1987 demarcates a significant shift toward "community and problem-oriented policing" nationwide, in which police became ever more present in schools, parks, and neighborhoods through community partnerships and "quality of life" policing. As police historian Herman Goldstein writes of the cementing of community policing as *the* paradigmatic practice in 1987, "The direction of change in policing has turned an important corner."[109] Taking all of these changes together, then, I mobilize 1987 as marking the threshold of one era of punitive literacy as another begins. The twenty-year period I consider, 1967 to 1987, is one during which contemporary understandings of guerrilla were forged within a crucible of cultural expression, punitive relations, and police reform that produce and justify paradigms of risk which continue to prevail today.

Interlacement as Method

The book is structured such that chapters can be read as stand-alone studies. My goal, however, across the book as a whole, is to bring into view a particular "knot of relations," or durational "event" in Paul Veyne's formulation: namely, the making of risk through the mythologizing of guerrilla tactics.[110] I've gathered stories of artists and their encounters (and collaborations) with lawyers, guards, police, and passersby as if making a weaving: winding together the many seemingly unrelated threads, drawn from various disciplines and many archives, the better to understand the stakes of riskiness in relation to historically specific notions of risk, crime, threat, and militancy. In keeping with my interdisciplinary method, the cross-analysis within each chapter aspires toward a method of *interlacement*: uniting closely or intricately the many threads, while amplifying the tangles of the artists' risk work.

To engage critically with the political history of guerrilla tactics in American art requires moving back and forth across many archives: from government-commissioned studies of guerrilla warfare that intermingle artists and activists, to police records tracking artists' arrests, to underground stories mapping strategies for resistance, to the mythologizing of the guerrilla in art, protest culture, fashion, and film. These relations and archives help reveal how the meaning of "guerrilla" constantly expands, and paradoxically shrinks, as its capaciousness makes for a superficial or generalized catchall status. How artists negotiated a shifting policing and surveillance landscape, how they envisioned rebellious modes of sociality and contact, as well as how interpretations of their work have shaped subsequent generations, constitutes the history of guerrilla tactics in art that exists relationally across the works but has yet to be told.

This story turns first to the sociopolitical, racial geographies of Los Angeles, where a militarized policing structure emerges that will serve as a model for police departments across the country. Los Angeles is significant: it's where computerized predictive policing algorithms were created and implemented in the early 1970s, and where the first SWAT teams were deployed. This, precisely at the time that Chris Burden and Asco created work that indexes the different modalities of police presence shaping West and East Los Angeles. In chapter 1, "Hit-and-Run Aesthetics," I explore how Burden and Asco's work records the temporal and spatial shifts authorized by police in anticipation of urban uprisings in East and South Central Los Angeles. Following the 1968 Anti-Riot Act, which federalized law enforcement's ability to preemptively interrogate individuals deemed potential agitators, computerized risk algorithms and the media's portrayals of racialized criminality also factored into beat patrols' increasing surveillance in predominantly Chicano and Black neighborhoods, while maintaining white, Anglo areas with much less force. This first chapter elucidates the divergent calculations and consequences of the artists' use of "hit-and-run" tactics, providing insight into the ways that artists' perception of the state's wielding of emergency power becomes a kind of temporalized aesthetic response to the racial asymmetries of policing and the white-centering logics of art discourse.

In chapter 2, "Deputized Discernment," I move to the East Coast to consider Adrian Piper's and Jean Toche's interventions in Cambridge and Boston, Massachusetts, where the relative calm of Harvard's campus offsets the explosive antibusing protests in adjacent Boston. This chapter delves into the politics of inscrutability and the policing of inchoate crimes such as loitering in public spaces. As in chapter 1, the analysis centers the role and attendant mythology of the police—both state and federal—and turns to early idioms of liberal police reform and its role in shaping conceptual art practice beyond art-sanctioned spaces to rethink the ways practices of slowness and persistence have been integral to guerrilla tactics in art.

Whereas the first two chapters focus on groupings of artworks that complicate misconceptions of spontaneity, latency, and speed in art made during the first half of the 1970s, the next two chapters look to the period of intensified policing in the late 1970s to mid-1980s and to related changes in artists' punitive literacy. Chapters 3 and 4, each set in New York City, consider the impact of the earlier history's legal precedent while analyzing ways that notions of guerrilla tactics continue to mutate within the framing of resourcefulness, endurance, and anonymity in art. In chapter 3, "Rethinking Endurance," I cross-examine how the then-undocumented Taiwanese artist Tehching Hsieh (now a US citizen) and the Black American artist Pope.L negotiate the irreducible intersections of whiteness, antiblackness, and anti-Asianness within the criminalizing of the unhoused and immigrants, and how this knot shapes policing, art law, exhibitions (such as *Illegal America*), and urban renewal programs in New York City. In the process, they produce distinctive iterations of "endurance." Their art actions in and around Times Square and Chinatown between 1978 and 1983 reveal what it means to endure safety discourse. This chapter brings forward the multiethnic, gendered, multiclass contours of guerrilla tactics, risk, and its myriad distortions as they crystallize within art law.

Chapter 4, "¿Why *Won't* You See Us?" follows the historical arc of guerrilla tactics in art to a time when guerrilla marketing was popularized and the Reagan Administration strategically rebranded counterguerrilla warfare as "low-intensity conflict." It focuses on the graphic art interventions of two anonymous feminist collectives: the Guerrilla Girls, a predominantly white group established in 1985, and PESTS, a largely overlooked group established by women of color artists and curators, active 1987–1989. Pushing beyond the typical contextualization of the groups' practices within histories of agitprop and activism, the chapter situates their tactics instead vis-à-vis the formalization of "freedom fighters," the relationship of "guerrilla" to "terrorist" within the American imaginary, and emergent legislation of racial bias. In so doing, it reframes the Guerrilla Girls' fame, and PESTS' relative obscurity, as revealing of the social politics of anonymity that continues to shape misconceptions about clandestine practice.

The book concludes with an epilogue, "At the Edges of Guerrilla," that looks at the ways contemporary artists—Art v War, Amina Cruz, and Sonic Insurgency Research Group—mobilize expanded punitive literacies in the making of their risk work amid algorithmic predictive policing, the "War on Terror," and an ever-expanding apparatus of surveillance and punishment. I began writing this book in 2014 as the Black Lives Matter movement gained momentum, and completed it in 2022, amid a pandemic, pervasive surveillance, and a prison-abolition movement building in size in the aftermath of the state-sanctioned murders of George Floyd, Breonna Taylor, Ahmaud Arbery, and many other Black Americans. The epilogue considers these contemporary contexts, and the ever-urgent need for critical vocabularies that illuminate the precise skills born of the struggle to survive policing and its many manifestations today. Punitive literacies in the twenty-first century continue to develop through exposure, explicit and insidious, to the patterned racialized criminalization of poverty, repression of social movements, and monitoring of survival economies, as well as in relation to one's sense of privilege and protections. Artists attuned to these contexts and histories are uniquely positioned to provide salient insights into the *work* of becoming literate in, and resistant to, such conditions.

One of the inequities in this book's narratives is that cis-gendered heterosexual men and women are prominent. Without a doubt, the heteronormative structuring of space that informs the American canon of conceptual and performance art is indicative of a larger story about controlling queer mobility. As American studies scholar Christina Hanhardt has shown, for example, the notions of safety and risk espoused in the monitoring and expansion of urbanized space in the 1960s and 1970s are inextricably bound up in the making of lesbian, gay, bisexual, and transgender identity formation and activism.[111] My concern here, though, is to demonstrate how and why the seeming consensus in art history surrounding tactics labeled guerrilla—and commonly associated with the work of cis-gendered heterosexual artists—deserves further scrutiny.

Risk Work seeks to confront how celebrations of resistance and agency can shore up patriarchal white supremacist metrics of order and value when the standardization of risk upon which they rely is left untroubled. This is not a story about the artists' originality or individual modes of resistance, but about how they differently anticipated the possibilities and structural consequences of punitive encounters. This is a story about *how* and *why* some achieved great recognition for their risk-taking, while others were ridiculed or censored—and why this history of tactics carries political implications, then and now. This journey begins, in the following pages, with a decoy gang-war victim in East Los Angeles and the emergencies this diversion reveals at the heart of a new strain of spectacularly confrontational art in America.

[1]

Hit-and-Run Aesthetics

Asco, Chris Burden, and Relational Geographies of Risk, 1971–1976

During a local news broadcast on Mexican American gang violence that aired on KHJ-TV in Los Angeles in the mid-1970s, a photograph of a slain man appeared briefly on screen (plate 1). In the photograph, the unidentified man lies on his back in the middle of a darkened street in the Li'l Valley of East Los Angeles.[1] Around his motionless form, the pink glow of safety flares set to deter traffic offsets a cerulean expanse of pavement. Within the open space that takes up the bottom half of the image, one might perceive the photographer's hesitation to get closer to the body, or a desire to step back and document as much of the scene as possible. Above the image's horizon line, amid another set of flares, out-of-focus headlights silhouette several onlookers standing at the far end of the block. The image was a fiction: a conceptual, performance-based artwork, *Decoy Gang War Victim*, created by the artists Glugio "Gronk" Nicandro and Harry Gamboa Jr., two cofounders of Asco, a collaborative group of independent Chicano artists working in East Los Angeles in the 1970s and 1980s.[2]

The group was active, with some fluctuation, between 1972 and 1987.[3] Its four founding members—Gronk, Gamboa, Willie Herrón III, and Patssi Valdez—became friends as teens at Garfield High School in the late 1960s and established a collaborative practice in the early 1970s comprising myriad forms, from unannounced performances on city streets to conceptual photography to mail art and short films. Each brought a distinct set of skills and interests: Valdez trained in theater makeup and cosmetics and worked as a hairdresser at her mother's salon while studying painting at East LA College part-time.[4] Gronk sketched, painted, and cultivated gender-bending, protopunk self-expression. Herrón incorporated contemporary news events and graffiti into urban murals to process his own run-ins with gang violence and the devastation it wrought within his family through his brother's involvement in urban cholo culture.[5] Gamboa, drawn to the power of text and image, turned to editorial work at *Regeneración*, an avant-garde leftist Spanish-language newspaper. In 1971, he invited Valdez, Gronk, and Herrón to join the paper, an experience that spurred their formation as a collaborative group the following year. Together, they chose the name "Asco," meaning "disgust" or "nausea" in Spanish, a response to the aggressively discriminatory treatment of Chicanos in the US and, more specifically, in East Los Angeles, the predominantly Mexican American, Spanish-speaking barrio where they lived.

Decoy exemplifies the sense of disgust that mobilized the artists' collaborations, and their goal of soliciting critical reflection on the sources of such animosity while expanding the aesthetic language of conceptualism and performance-based art. Gamboa and Gronk staged the photo swiftly, knowing that the police patrols were relentless in the barrio.[6] Gronk covered himself in ketchup and lay down in the middle of a relatively empty residential street, while Gamboa lit the flares and shot color images of the scene. Both then quickly abandoned the scene to avoid arrest.[7]

They created *Decoy*, Gamboa explains, "to throw a monkey wrench into . . . [a] chain of retribution" promoted by derogatory reporting in local newspapers. The *Los Angeles Times* and the *Herald Examiner*, they felt, degraded and denounced Chicano culture at every opportunity. The papers had "latched onto the notion of gang warfare and focused specifically on East L.A. gangs," says Gamboa, "provid[ing] the names of the murder victims, their home addresses, the locations and addresses of where the families worked, so of course in the next issue, they were the ones that had been murdered." In doing so, Gamboa asserts, "the newspapers would basically lay out the murder plan and really they were complicit in the ongoing warfare."[8] He went around to news stations and publications with the staged image, leading to its appearance on KHJ-TV, Channel 9, soon after. *Decoy* used "hit-and-run tactics," Gamboa says, "to provoke the viewer to commit acts of perceptual sabotage,"[9] to set up "decoys so they would think someone had already been killed."[10] The production of *asco* in the viewer was also a potential outcome.

The "hit-and-run" tactics that Asco deploys across a number of performance-based conceptual pieces resonated with actions carried out by artists nationwide. Some used the airwaves and the media, while others experimented with the responses of passersby on the street in their performance and conceptual-based practice. On the East Coast, for example, Abbie Hoffman and John Giorno's 1971 pirate radio station, WPAX Inc., sent rock and jazz, as well as women's programs and speeches by the Black Panther and Young Lords, to soldiers in

Vietnam, a project later exhibited as a work of conceptual art (and investigated by the FBI as an "attempt to subvert the United States Armed Services").[11] In Iowa in 1973, sisters Ana and Raquelín Mendieta created *Moffitt Building Piece*, recording the reactions of passersby to pig blood splattered on the sidewalk. As one secretly filmed the scene from a parked car, the other took photographs through a window, behaving as undercover FBI agents might during a stakeout.[12]

On the West Coast, Terry Fox destroyed a bed of rare Chinese jasmine flowers in front of a San Francisco art museum in *Defoliation Piece* (thinking of Agent Orange and immolation).[13] And in Los Angeles, Chris Burden, a contemporary of the artists of Asco, staged *Deadman* in November 1972 (plate 2). For this work, Burden, like Gronk in *Decoy*, lay prostrate in the street surrounded by lit flares. By contrast to Gamboa and Gronk, who quickly evacuated the scene they'd constructed, Burden pretended to be a hit-and-run automobile casualty, wedging his tarp-covered body against a car tire in the West Los Angeles art district for the duration of the flares' ignition. When an unknowing passerby, walking by the crowd that had gathered to watch, reported the "accident" to police, Burden was arrested for a traffic violation and for causing a false emergency to be reported.

In the early 1970s, these performance and conceptual art works occurring beyond art-sanctioned spaces were just coming to be recognized in art-world discourse. Ursula Meyer's 1973 essay "The Eruption of Anti-Art" was among the first in the US to identify "guerrilla-art-action performers" within the then-burgeoning genre of "anti-art" and conceptualism.[14] Soon after, writers such as *Village Voice* contributor Carman Moore would give a name to this development; in 1974, for example, Moore cited a "guerrilla art movement," evolving since 1965 and made up of "a growing band of artist revolutionaries."[15]

Of the artists named above, Burden, dubbed the "Evel Knievel of art" and "the Art-Martyr" by writers in the early 1970s, gained unprecedented and unparalleled fame for aggressive, confrontational works that challenged ethical boundaries.[16] In November 1971, for example, Burden traveled to Kansas City, Missouri, where for three days he wore a ski mask in public, taking on the "look" of a masked militant or bank robber for a piece he later called *Interiorization: You'll Never See My Face in Kansas City* (fig. 1.1).

A few weeks later, on November 21, Burden enacted one of his most infamous pieces, *Shoot* (fig. 1.2). He invited friends to F Space, a warehouse turned art space in Santa Ana, California, that he and several friends had recently established, to watch as Bruce Dunlap, a fellow artist, aimed a gun at him and pulled the trigger. Dunlap, who'd intended only to graze Burden's skin, reportedly misfired his .22 caliber rifle, causing the bullet to fully enter and exit the artist's arm.

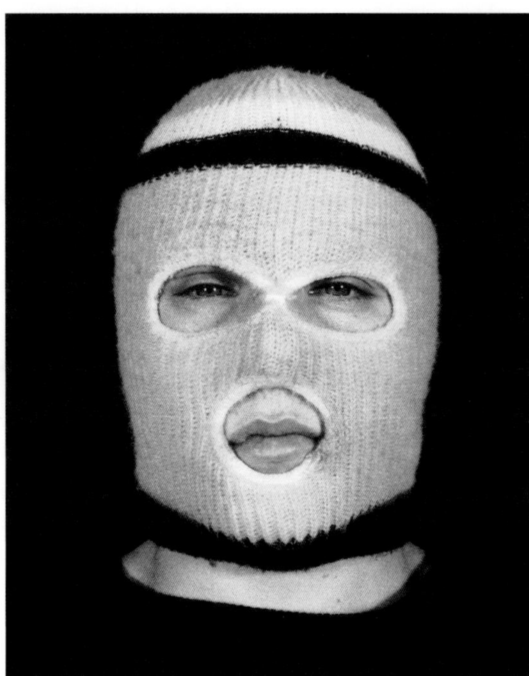

[1.1] Chris Burden, *Interiorization: You'll Never See My Face in Kansas City*, 1971. Black-and-white photograph. © 2021 Chris Burden. Licensed by the Chris Burden Estate/Artists Rights Society (ARS), New York.

Burden explained his motivation for *Shoot* as a desire to respond to daily media images of death in Vietnam and desensitizing gun violence in soap operas and crime dramas: "You see people getting shot on T.V. everyday, so I wanted to find out how it would be to receive a bullet in my body. But it wasn't really the violence or the pain I was interested in, but the mental experience."[17] In the year between *Shoot* and *Deadman*, he held a knife to the throat of Phyllis Lutjeans, a friend and curator, while she interviewed him about his art practice in *TV Hijack*.

These early-1970s artworks formed part of a repertoire of aggressive, short-lived acts in which art-goers came to recognize Burden's signature aesthetic. His arrest and trial for *Deadman* gained wider local and national coverage, his image appearing, for example, on the front page of the *New York Times* art section in 1973. As art critic Douglas Davis put it coyly in *Newsweek*, "Burden is obviously prepared to risk anything, even death. . . . Watch out. Chris Burden may get you next."[18] Art critic Robert Horvitz similarly positioned Burden in 1976 as a man who "knows his limits" and "limits his risks accordingly" to give his work unrivaled "visceral intensity and bite."[19] His national and international reputation continues to this day; art critic Peter Schjeldahl's 2015 essay commem-

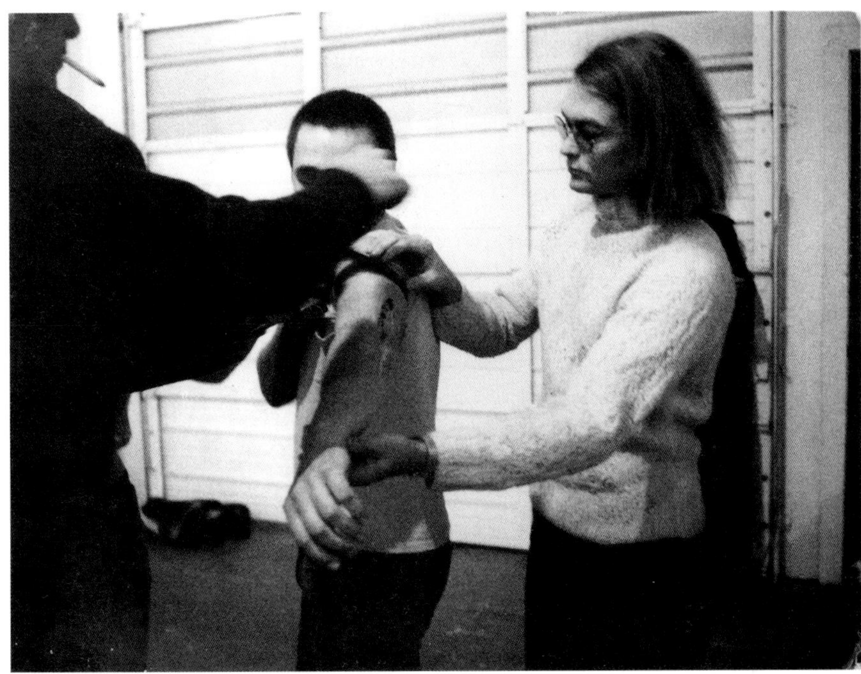

[1.2] Chris Burden, *Shoot #11*, November 19, 1971. Black-and-white photograph. © 2021 Chris Burden. Licensed by the Chris Burden Estate/Artists Rights Society (ARS), New York.

orating his death remarked on how the artist "went to extremes, but he wasn't nuts." The title of the essay posthumously anointed him, "The Danger Artist."[20]

In many ways, Burden and Asco's works exemplify the characteristics commonly associated with guerrilla tactics in art.[21] Each adapts and inverts visual metaphors of violence on a symbolic level to capture attention and directs audiences to reflect on social behaviors and routines by disrupting them. They enact their works beyond art-sanctioned spaces, on street corners or in television studios, garages, and warehouses, or stage surprising, unannounced actions in and around museum and gallery spaces. As the curator Dana Friis-Hansen put it in 1988, in his contribution to the exhibition catalogue for *LA, Hot and Cool, the Eighties*, both Burden and Asco used "aggressive, visible, and provocative actions [to] test the limits of art."[22]

Horvitz's reading of Burden, and Friis-Hansen's reflection on Burden and Asco, are representative insofar as mentions of "limits" are common in scholarship on tactics. But to speak of "limits" without accounting for the construction of risk within perceived bounds of societal norms elides the fact that these bounds, and their effects on artmaking, are asymmetrical, inextricably bound to institutions that uphold patriarchal whiteness (television, film, art museums, policing, law) and punitive relations that manage and maintain these power formations. It is not a coincidence, then, that Burden's spectacular deployment of risk and potential harm—wearing a ski mask, staging a faux-automobile accident, holding a woman hostage on the air, soliciting a gunshot wound—boosted his profile, earning him a great deal of attention, whereas Asco's careful, comparatively quiet, and often satirical negotiation of *asco*-inducing manifestations of imperialist power—police brutality, the horror of the Vietnam war, widespread discrimination against Chicanos in the US—generated a vastly smaller following and art-world status.

In this chapter, I turn to Asco's and Burden's distinctive uses of "hit-and-run" tactics, and their reception in the 1970s, by interlacing a half-dozen nearly contemporaneous artworks carried out in specific geographical areas within Los Angeles. I do so to cross-analyze the ways in which Asco and Burden differently negotiated relations of racialized and gendered punitiveness then directly shaping not only the LA art world but widespread notions of risk, emergence management, and innovation; and how the artists' use of surprise and spatial sabotage reveals distinct but interconnected conditions of enablement and threat that shaped narratives of guerrilla tactics in American art and society. As such, this chapter argues that "the right to the city" and "the right to be" in art history are shaped by policing, emergency management, and anti-riot laws in deeply interconnected ways.[23]

A note about place: Los Angeles is not only a key site for this chapter but a significant part of the larger story of the making of risk and artists' negotiation of punitive literacy. While LA has been discussed as a shared terrain for avant-garde practice, it's significance as a policing hub has not yet been adequately considered in art discourse as an important component of artistic experimentation in the 1960s and 1970s. Los Angeles is a laboratory of police communication and risk management, the first city to implement SWAT teams and among the first to develop proto-predictive policing procedures attuned to anti-riot policies emerging in the late 1960s and early 1970s.[24]

My cross-examination of Asco's and Burden's use of guerrilla tactics in East and West Los Angeles, and the differing policing protocols applied to these areas, draws upon the idea of "geographic relevancy" developed by Black studies scholar Katherine McKittrick. McKittrick theorizes the ways that "social space is inextricably tied up with the differential placement of racial bodies."[25] In her work on Black women's fugitive cartographies, she provides an instructive, expansive definition of geography as a set of relations. "Geography," she writes, "materially and discursively extends to cover three-dimensional spaces and places, the physical landscape and infrastructures, geographic imaginations, the practice of mapping, exploring, and seeing, and social relations in and across space."[26] Building upon this notion, this chapter aims to show how Asco's and Burden's works share much more than a common urban setting; their works and reception histories record and manifest the consolidation of police knowledge central to the relational geographies of LA and art discourse.

The revisionist focus in this chapter also seeks to expand upon the revelatory observations made by several scholars regarding the racial politics inscribed within Burden's work. In the catalogue accompanying the landmark 2013 exhibition *Radical Presence: Black Performance in Contemporary Art*, curator Valerie Cassel Oliver notes in two succinct sentences the differing risks entailed in Burden's and radical Black performance artists' navigation of public space:

> For Burden, who is white, these actions were apparently aimed at testing his own physical limits as well as the limits of what might constitute artistic expression. For black artists, however, the social and political aspects of endurance-based performance are inescapable, specifically because the black body has particular meanings and a particular history in the Americas.[27]

Thinking about the manufacture of Burden's international profile and what it implies for the interpretation of Asco, art historian C. Ondine Chavoya also queries, "How do we work within, and yet against, such genealogies?" observing that the language and lenses of conceptualism do "not account for the ways in which Asco actualized or extrapolated these concepts in order to make social statements."[28] Adding to this conversation in 2018, art historian Huey Copeland reflected on the specific relationship of Asco's *Decoy* and Burden's *Deadman*, asserting in an insightful paragraph that Burden's concerns in *Deadman* and the ensuing trial were "a world apart from those of the average black man, or Hispanics, both demographics more likely than whites to be the victims of murder."[29]

Cassel Oliver, Chavoya, and Copeland each make incisive observations that call for further probing of the neutralizing of whiteness within the canonized narratives of risk-taking in 1970s art. As Black studies scholar George Lipsitz explains, "As the unmarked category against which difference is constructed, whiteness never has to speak its name, never had to acknowledge its role as an organizing principle in social and cultural relations."[30] Given Burden's large international profile and the extent to which ideas of risk-taking in art continue to be informed by his work's prominence in the canon of performance and conceptual art globally, tackling the racialized and gendered conditioning of his "danger artist" mantle is long overdue.

But this examination is about more than simply reckoning with the white-centering societal privileges afforded by Burden's male whiteness or the racial inequity experienced by the Chicanx artists affiliated with Asco. In avoiding Burden's gendered whiteness, and consequent position in relation to state-sanctioned violence, art-historical scholarship has not only obscured his work's racialized spatial politics, but has reinforced the protection of whiteness and, more specifically, white masculinity within narratives of risk-taking in art, his risk-taking normalized as a standard-bearing form. Additionally, Burden's arrest and trial, examined in this chapter, will inform the formation of "art law" discussed in chapter 3, his legal precedent serving as the basis of racialized "colorblind" juridical interpretations of guerrilla tactics for subsequent artists.

As this chapter demonstrates, the normalizing of gendered and sexualized whiteness in art discourse has dialectically informed Asco's work and the artists' own punitive literacy, then and now. The very idea of the "guerrilla tactic" in art, informed by both Burden's fame and Asco's marginalization within art-historical discourses on the "hit and run," perpetuates a predictive policing framework that enables the ongoing standardization of risk vis-à-vis whiteness—and simultaneously obscures the risk work of artists inhabiting more complex relations of vulnerability to state-sanctioned violence, cultural appropriation, and misrepresentation. By scrutinizing the artists' differing but interconnected risk work and its spatialization within Los Angeles, this chapter hopes to continue the work of charting how articulations of risk in art history normalize the racist structures negotiated by historically marginalized artists that have inversely validated white artists' spectacularized encounters with the state.

Beat Patrols and Aftercrimes: Asco's Urban Interventions and No Movies

In 1972, when Gamboa asked a curator at the Los Angeles County Museum (LACMA) about the underrepresentation of Chicano artists in the museum, he was told, dismissively, that Mexicans were not serious "fine artists" but instead made "folk art" or "were in gangs."[31] In the curator's reply, one can discern how pervasive stereotypes of Mexican criminality shaped decision-making in the art world. These ideas, fabricated from crime stories, were substantiated by Hollywood, whose skewed representations in films like *The Magnificent Seven* portrayed Chicanos as aggressive, prone to criminality, and incapable of governing themselves.[32] Meanwhile, the advent of police dramas on primetime TV fashioned an imaginary that privileged the perspective of police officers, who were often hired as consultants.[33] Simultaneously, as art historian and media scholar Chon Noriega points out, ads for the Frito-Lay Corporation featured the Frito Bandito, a Mexican outlaw who stole Anglos' corn chips at gunpoint.[34]

Members of Asco responded to the curator's racist remarks with one of their earliest collaborative art pieces. Under cover of night, Gronk, Herrón, and Gamboa returned to the museum with spray paint and tagged the entrances and exits. A documentary image taken by Gamboa the next morning, *Spray Paint LACMA* (plate 3), shows three signatures—"Gronkie" in red, "Herrón" and "Gamboa" in black—arrayed on a walkway wall. Valdez, in a bright red top, leans on the rail above the wall and looks away from Harry behind the camera. "We didn't do an icon of Che," Gronk explains, and "we didn't do an icon of Zapata—we designed it with our own emphasis."[35] The photo preserves the artists' act, which transmuted the institution, and their exclusion from it, into a temporary conceptual work of art—the "first conceptual work of Chicano art to be exhibited" there, as Gamboa quipped, and one that was almost immediately whitewashed.[36] Asco did not face legal ramifications for *Spray Paint LACMA*, but the social and material risks for Chicano and Chicana artists staging guerrilla conceptual art at this time were high.

Asco also sought to call out stereotypical roles assigned to Chicanos in film and in the media—the gang member, the militant, the Mexican bandit—and to disrupt them through humor and satire. To that end, the artists devised a genre they called "No Movie." These collaboratively produced counterimages—*Decoy Gang War Victim* is an example—used cinematic tropes and the glamor of nearby Hollywood to flirt with, confuse, and challenge stereotypes, while exposing the pervasiveness of white racism and xenophobia shaping their own experience as marginalized minority subjects.[37]

Conceptually, No Movies operate like film stills: images of action cut from movie narratives, at once familiar and untethered, made strange and uncanny through ambiguous messages. Chavoya has described No Movies as "false documents" that deploy "factuality," pointing to a source without an original as a way to critique a history of absence and invisibility.[38] Amelia Jones notes their complicated negative critiques that articulate a conflicted "desire and hatred" for Hollywood.[39] Gronk was the first to articulate the filmic qualities of No Movies, grounded in a desire to create "an image that looked as if there was a preceding image and an image that went after it." Yet he also offers another explanation of the genre, one mired in the *anticipation* of police power:

> We didn't use art terms to describe No Movies at the time they were made . . . it was an activity that we did or an action that we did by going out into the street and acting . . . it was using a hit-and-run kind of tactic. It was to do things in a spontaneous way. But also it was done to do it very quickly, because a lot of things we were doing were against the law on the streets. So it had those tactics of still doing it very, very quickly and then getting away from there because we would probably get stopped by the police or things would happen to us if we did something.[40]

Valdez offers much the same reason for the swiftness of Asco's urban interventions:

> Given the heavy police surveillance in our community at the time, as in many of our performances, we used what we called hit-and-run tactics, meaning we had to do things quickly so we wouldn't get busted or harassed by the cops. We had everything ready—what we were going to wear, how we were going to look—then we would jump in the car, find the location, do our performance and, just as quickly, get back in the car and drive away. I remember being horrified at the thought of ever going to jail![41]

"Because of the way we looked," she recalls, "I must have gotten stopped by the cops twenty-five times in one year alone in my neighborhood."[42] This, then, was the context for Asco's actions: "I had to express myself with what was happening in the community. . . . You know, we were really harassed by the cops. Humiliated. Pulled over constantly. And then I encountered racism a lot."[43]

The harassment of Chicanos by police in East Los Angeles long predates the 1970s and is entangled with urbanization and social control. Between 1900 and 1930, 1.5 million Mexicans migrated to the US, where they were restricted to the lowest-paying menial jobs and to segregated housing and schools that deepened class disparities.[44] Real estate lobbying and government policies throughout the twentieth century had cemented racially discriminatory land grant deeds that excluded Black and Chicano individuals from owning property in much of

West Los Angeles. These barriers pushed minoritized groups into smaller, segregated areas in South Central and East Los Angeles that were then aggressively policed. Historian George Sánchez describes the process as "urban apartheid . . . sustained via a private-public partnership between government officials and private industry, particularly the real estate lobby," wherein "American-born Anglo newcomers" were funneled to the Westside, while "foreign-born and nonwhite residents found themselves largely confined to the Eastside and Southside."[45] In the 1940s, he explains, the Federal Housing Lending Program deemed the predominantly Black residential areas of South Central and predominantly Chicano residential areas of East Los Angeles to be "high risk," thereby disqualifying whole communities from mortgages and loans.[46]

During this period, white gangs such as the "Spook Hunters," protected by the police, beat up Chicano and Black youth.[47] Their attacks reached a peak with a historic assault on Latino men wearing zoot suits, a style born of Harlem dance lounges. In Navy Yard, East LA, and Watts, in June 1943, whites beat and stripped these men of their clothing. The media called the riots "Zoot Suit Warfare," a name that strategically effaces the instigators of the violence and suggests its victims as the culprits.[48] Long before Asco formed, Herrón had heard his uncles' accounts of the attacks they suffered during the riots—and noticed this history's omission from lessons at school.[49]

Asco's No Movies carry both the formal logic of a film sequence and the artists' anticipation of law enforcement's response, conditioned by neighborhood circumstances during the 1960s and early 1970s, when policing and arrest rates intensified.[50] As Noriega insightfully observes, "Gamboa applied text to these images in the same way the LAPD had done to secure a narrative to its visual evidence."[51] The No Movies genre emerged while legal and activist organizations in LA were laboring to materialize such realities. For example, a 1969 report on police malpractice, "Law Enforcement: A Matter of Redress," analyzed two years of data collected from ACLU-run complaint centers in Los Angeles. As police historian Max Felker-Kantor describes in his incisive book documenting the LAPD, the report documented a "dual standard of law enforcement in Los Angeles—one for Negroes and Mexican Americans, and one for whites": of the complainants of malpractice deemed credible by the ACLU, 314 were from Black Americans, 174 from Mexican Americans, 118 from Anglos, and 34 from others. The study, Felker-Kantor emphasizes, also found alarming rates of abuse: one of every ten law enforcement officers in Los Angeles County was engaged in "some form of police malpractice."[52] In a 1970 study on police-community relations in

East Los Angeles (included in Gamboa's personal archives), Frank Sifuentes put these realities into context: "the so-called crime rates are more indicative of *over-enforcement*. There is three more times police coverage in East Los Angeles than there is in the Westside, and in other predominantly Anglo communities."[53]

Overenforcement doesn't merely affect individuals; it is a collective experience that is managed, learned, embodied, and internalized. Sara Ahmed labels "stop and search" policing as a "technology of racism" and reminds us:

> The stop and search does not always end at that point: the search itself can be extended by practices of indefinite detention. Stopping is therefore a political economy that is distributed unevenly between others, and it is also an affective economy that leaves its impressions, affecting the bodies that are subject to its address.[54]

"Those who are stopped," she concludes, "are, perhaps, moved in a different way."[55]

Extending Ahmed's observation, we can see, through the lens of punitive literacy, that stop and search begins not with the stop but with the anticipation of being stopped. "Stop-and-frisk" was legalized federally with the Supreme Court case *Terry v. Ohio* (1968). In the decades since, numerous reports have shown, again and again, that it is race, not crime, that motivates these stops, which predominantly contain the movements of young men and women of color. "It is a ritual of dominance and submission played out hundreds of thousands of times each year," Michelle Alexander observes. Moreover, she notes, these routinized stoppages "are the most effective way for [police] to collect fingerprints, photographs, and other information on young people not yet entered into the criminal databases."[56] In Los Angeles in particular, the frequency of these encounters meant that eventually a criminal database, as revealed in 1992, included eight out of every ten people of color in the entire city.[57]

Gamboa was explicitly instructed to "[move] in a different way" when he learned then that his name had appeared in a 1970 FBI report listing a hundred militants, including Black intellectuals and revolutionaries such as Angela Davis and Eldridge Cleaver, who law enforcement perceived as "involved in the violent disruption of the establishment."[58] Gamboa was identified as a threat due to his activism during high school, when he'd taken a leadership role in the 1968 "Chicano walkouts," when ten thousand students across all five East Los Angeles high schools marched out of class to protest substandard educational conditions.[59] The report also cited as a threat Gamboa's support of the California Black Conference Committee and the Brown Berets; for law enforcement officials, affiliation with these groups signaled an *intention* to possibly incite future action.[60] When LAPD sergeant Robert Thoms presented the list in testimony before the US Senate Subcommittee to Investigate the Administration of the Internal Security Act and Other Internal Security Laws, he framed the activities of those listed as "antiestablishment, antiwhite, and militant."[61]

Gamboa learned of his surveillance in late 1970 or early 1971, when, he recounts, an "unidentified Latino man in Boyle Heights" confronted him; it would be in his best interest, the man told him, to pick up a copy of *Extent of Subversion in the New Left* at the Federal Building bookstore, located in the Civic Center on Los Angeles Street. Gamboa purchased the report that day, realizing later that he had been "fortunate to walk away unharmed" from his encounter with the informant, who'd also suggested that "I might want to change my beliefs if I wanted to avoid serious trouble."[62]

Gamboa's experience was part of a larger effort to curtail mobility in East Los Angeles, an area deemed "high risk" by police. Whereas prediction has always been a part of policing, "predictive policing," today a multimillion-dollar international business, refers to the use of computer algorithms based on geospatial data technology. This mapping of space accelerated in the early 1970s, with the expansion of mainframe computing and emergence of applicable algorithms.[63] In Los Angeles, in particular, Phillip S. Mitchell, an expert in mathematical programming and public systems, began to work with law enforcement in what political theorist and human geographer Brian Jordan Jefferson calls "the first attempt to fuse quantitative geography with policing." Mitchell was, Jefferson contends, "foundational in bringing differential policing into programming language."[64] The California Council of Criminal Justice encouraged these partnerships, seeking ways for the state to leverage newly available computer "optimization" algorithms to modernize its police patrol beats.[65] This "beat patrol" algorithm presaged predictive policing by nearly forty years, remapping routes and increasing the number of police sent to "high incident" areas in Los Angeles County, and specifically in Anaheim, Santa Ana, and Los Angeles, where police had already established checkpoints and curfews in anticipation of riots.[66]

Mitchell's attempt to optimize beat patrols quantified a variety of factors: for patrol unit *k*, for example, he calculated *t(k')*, the average driving time required to respond to an incident, and *S(k')*, the average incident load. His algorithm also relied upon *p* representing the *expected number* of incidents of a particular type based on past events. Mitchell's 1973 publication on this topic included a representative computer-generated map (fig. 1.3) focusing on Anaheim to show readers the utility of the new technology. Landmarks such as the Santa Ana Freeway (Interstate 5, cutting diagonally between areas 5, 6, and 9 and 7, 11, and 12) and the blank rectangular space of Disneyland (included in area # 7) help establish bearings. Whereas the original, hand-generated beat map had included fourteen beat territories, Mitchell's computer-generated map reduces that number to just thirteen. Essentially, with the algorithm, fewer police have been delegated to areas 11 and 12, whereas increased surveillance is recommended for downtown Anaheim (area 10).

As the remapping of Anaheim suggests, historic patterns of racialized overpolicing of particular sections in urban areas are re-presented in Mitchell's computer-generated maps as an efficient and unbiased reallocation of resources. "Equations like these," Jefferson explains, "signified the dawn of a new conception of urban space," creating an idea of objective policing and patrolling, which law enforcement embraced as mathematical and therefore free from bias.[67] This kind of remapping cemented the idea of "high incident" zones, in part by effacing racial geographies of abandonment and surveillance that had created higher incident loads in the first place.[68] Studying Mitchell's maps, Jefferson notes that "the preoccupation with the micro also formed a shield against structural analysis. No thought was given to the relations between hot spot microareas and the externally imposed social and punitive policies used to manage them. All sources of illegal activity are seen as intrinsic characteristics of microspaces."[69]

Asco members were attuned to the microspaces of policing, as well as how the media's misrepresentation of Chicanos construed a broader landscape in which criminality was spatialized and increasingly expansive policing justified. *Decoy*, recall, was an intervention in a news cycle that perpetuated a murder cycle, an attempt by Gronk and Gamboa to stop a "chain of retribution" killings. Such strategies weren't just sensitive to local space but adapted from global contexts of guerrilla intervention. A likely inspiration for *Decoy*, for example, was the 1969 *Mini-Manual of the Urban Guerrilla*, authored by the Brazilian author, politician, and guerrilla fighter Carlos Marighella. Gamboa and Gronk received copies of the manual in May 1974 from Jerry Dreva, a friend and fellow artist who told them it was "must reading for subversion in the city."[70] Dreva saw utility for Asco in Marighella's attention to the uses of sabotage and misinformation as prime tools of intervention and survival. According to Marighella:

[1.3, facing page] Computer-generated beat structure, Los Angeles County Crime Map, 1973. From Phillip S. Mitchell, "Optimal Selection of Police Patrol Beats," *Journal of Criminal Law and Criminology*. Courtesy of Northwestern University Pritzker School of Law and the Journal of Criminal Law and Criminology.

> The careful reading of the press with particular attention to the organs of mass communication, the investigation of accumulated data, the transmission of news and everything of note, a persistence in being informed and in informing others . . . makes up the intricate and immensely complicated question of information which gives the urban guerrilla a decisive advantage.[71]

Decoy, of course, did not resolve the interlaced sequencing of misinformation, police reports, film, and popular culture, but did seek to alter it, if only temporarily. "Actually it was kind of interesting," Gamboa reflected later, "because at that point there was sort of a slow down and sort of a confusion and sort of a momentary peace as a result of conceptual art."[72] Nevertheless, as Chavoya somberly notes, while *Decoy* may have momentarily paused a cycle of violence, it likely prompted heightened police surveillance in the area, potentially leading to more physical and psychological violence.[73] What Chavoya describes without naming it explicitly is *aftercrimes*, an idea utilized by law enforcement when calculating beat patrols. Aftercrime refers to the expectation that a first act of violence makes the occurrence of another in its vicinity more likely.[74]

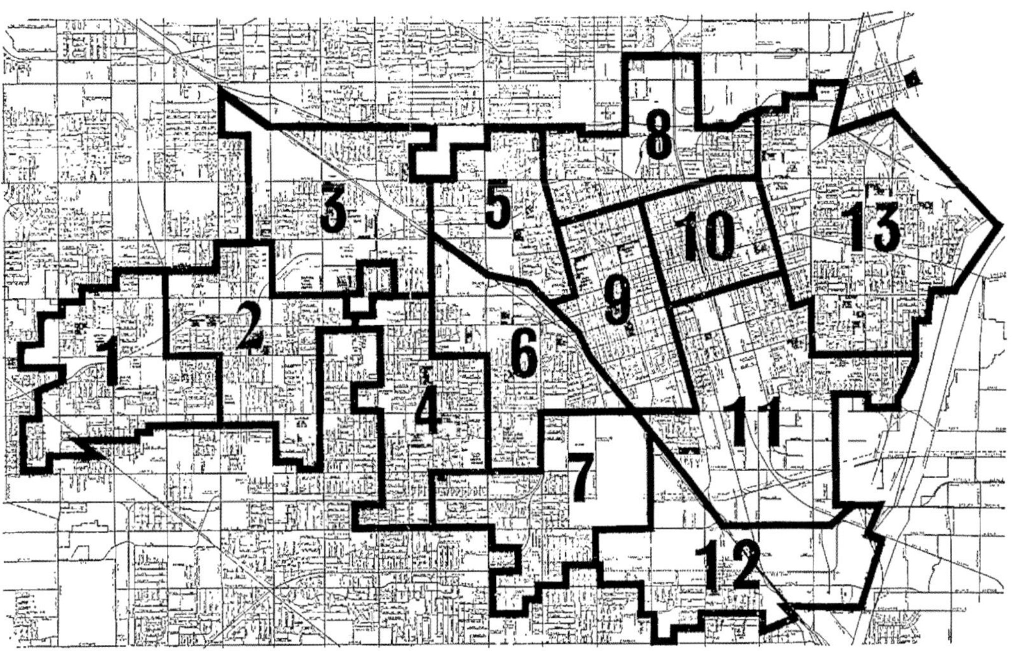

Aftercrime was an idea developed alongside the anticipation of riots that solidified in the language of the Anti-Riot Act, or Title X. This act, a rider slipped into the 1968 Civil Rights Act just before Congress voted on it, made it a felony to use "any facility of interstate or foreign commerce," whether travel, mail, or mass media, "with *intent* to incite a riot; or to organize, promote, encourage, participate in, or carry on a riot."[75] Critics quickly recognized the potential harm, arguing that the provision equated "political protest with organized violence" and would be the "foundation for a police state in America."[76] Indeed, the concept, "riot," as discussed in the introduction, focuses attention on the destruction of property and displaces important discussions about the long-standing antiblack violence and administrative governance that legalizes the disenfranchisement of Black Americans and people of color. Critics took issue with the rider's vagueness—the extent to which certain actions could be construed as *intent to incite* was left decidedly open-ended—which essentially authorized law enforcement to seek out potential rioters based on their own "reasonable suspicion," a particularly vague and biased condition. Whereas state and local laws had long covered acts of violence, this new act presented a calculated elusiveness, wherein police action required no evidence of a crime or attempted crime, just a police officer's suspicion of intent.

In anticipation of aftercrimes and "riots," the Los Angeles Police Department accumulated an "antiriot arsenal" including armored personnel carriers, .30 caliber machine guns, .41 Magnum revolvers, tear gas launchers, mace, and a smoke-screen device.[77] LAPD inspector Daryl Gates brought together antisniper and tactical operations planning units to form the special weapons and tactics (SWAT) unit.[78] As one SWAT leader stated, "Those people out there—the radicals, the revolutionaries and the cop haters—are damned good at using shotguns and bombs, and setting up ambushes. We've got to be better."[79] In 1970, Gates established the surveillance unit known as the Public Disorder Investigation Division (PDID), which authorized cops to go undercover and infiltrate activist-run organizations deemed "antiestablishment," such as the Chicano Brown Berets and Black Panthers. This unit took its cues directly from a 1968 memo sent by FBI director J. Edgar Hoover to top law enforcement officers throughout the country, urging them to "target minority nationalist movements" in "penetrative" and "aggressive" investigations.[80] Taken together, these technologies and the protocol of monitoring and "stoppages" deeply informed the punitive literacies manifest in an Asco performance staged on Whittier Boulevard, *First Supper (After a Major Riot)*.

"A Thousandth of a Second": The Pacing of Early Predictive Policing

Asco's *First Supper (After a Major Riot)*, created in 1974, materializes the logics of aftercrimes and the increasing presence of beat patrols in East Los Angeles. Like *Spray Paint LACMA* in 1972, and *Decoy Gang War Victim* earlier in 1974, the artists manifested this work through "hit-and-run" tactics. On December 24, the members of Asco briefly occupied a traffic island at Arizona Street and Whittier Boulevard in East Los Angeles. Gamboa, in his role as group documentarian, took a photograph of the piece (plate 4). In it, we see Valdez wearing a gray top hat; Humberto Sandoval, a frequent collaborator, wears a white mask and a bowler hat. Sandoval extends an arm across the small folding table, as if to toast Gronk, who wears a mask, while Herrón, to his left, leans in, raising his glass. In front of the table, a mirror carries no visible reflection, and a large baby doll lays on a blanket; the group has also hung Gronk's 1973 painting *The Truth about the Terror in Chile* from the Whittier sign.

The artists' costumes and props borrow "iconography from Dia de los Muertos" to transform the site of the traffic island into a "memorial to the dead."[81] The traffic island had been built recently, as part of the city's redevelopment plan, on the precise site where "police [had] opened fire with shotguns on an assembled crowd" three years earlier.[82] That had been a particularly violent twelve months during which police killed multiple Chicano antiwar protesters. One such event, which galvanized the artists' determination to create counternarratives, had occurred on August 29, 1970, during an antiwar demonstration organized by the National Chicano Moratorium Committee. The peaceful protest had sought to bring attention to the fact that Chicanos, as a minority group, suffered the highest death rate among US military personnel in Vietnam.[83] That morning, nearly thirty thousand people marched through East LA, from Belvedere Park to Laguna Park, where they gathered to listen to speeches and music. According to police reports, a minor disturbance along the march's route (a petty theft at a liquor store), led LA County sheriff Peter Pitchess to declare the demonstration an unlawful assembly.[84]

Before antiwar demonstrators could leave the park, however, hundreds of LAPD officers and county deputies descended in full riot gear, using riot guns, clubs, and tear gas (fig. 1.4). Their actions led to hundreds of arrests and injuries, leaving three protesters dead, including Rubén Salazar, a prominent Chicano journalist and news director for the Spanish-language TV station KMEX, who

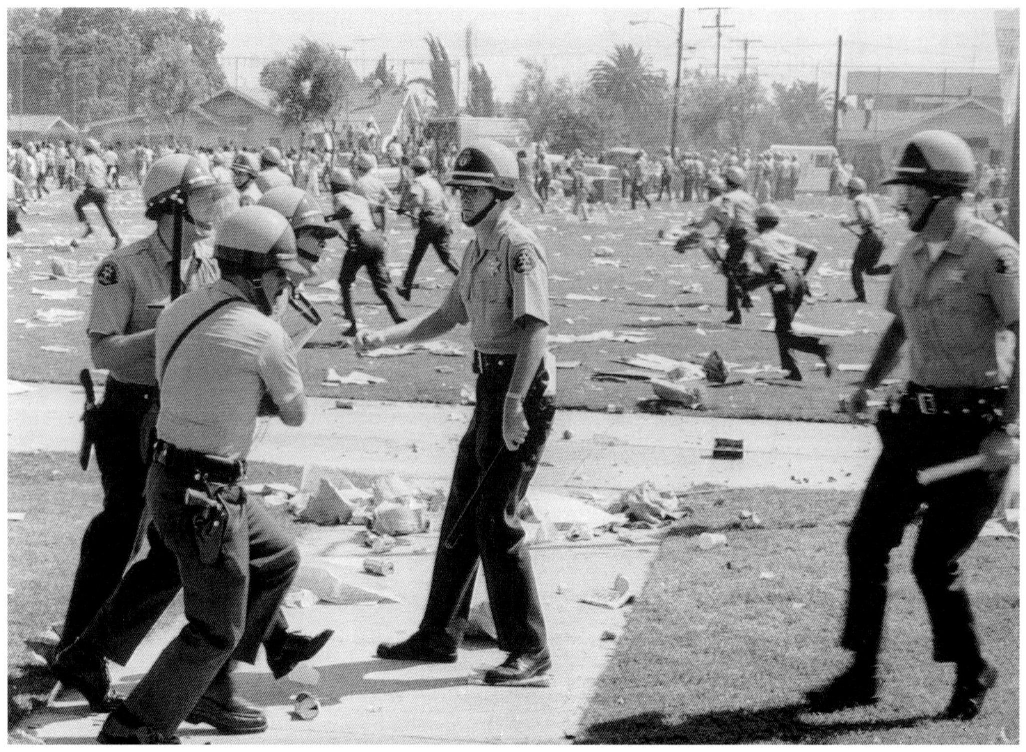

[1.4] *Police on Riotous Scene*, August 28, 1970. Archive caption: "East Los Angeles: Sheriff's Deputies make their move to disperse the crowd after being pelted with rocks and bottles following an antiwar demonstration in East Los Angeles. Violence began after police moved in to make a single arrest. Several fires were set and most windows in a shooting area were smashed. Some two dozen were injured." Black-and-white photograph. Bettmann Collection. © Associated Press via Getty Images.

had been outspoken about the LAPD chief Edward Davis's dismissal of Chicano concerns earlier that year.[85]

In the days after the violent police response to the Chicano Moratorium demonstration, skewed accounts appeared in mainstream newspapers, entirely sympathetic with the police. As one media caption, "Police on Riotous Scene," suggests, the police were there to quell unrest, words contradicted by the photograph's depiction of police running in various directions and "riotous" demonstrators nowhere to be seen. In these media accounts, Salazar's death was deemed an accident, demonstrators were blamed for the violence, and the cops were cast as victims (approximately forty had been injured). This show of bias solidified Gamboa's dedication to creating his own images as counterevidence.[86] Having experienced the Chicano Moratorium protest, Gamboa was again present when LAPD officers opened fire on another group of Chicano antiwar demonstrators, wounding ten and killing one.[87] In the *New York Times*'s coverage of that violence, Sheriff Pitchess asserted, "This was entirely a Chicano activity and they cannot *control* their own people."[88]

Labeling protesters demanding accountability as "out of control" or "bearers of chaos" positioned them rhetorically as reckless, opposed to the police and thus to law and order.[89] "After the Chicano Moratorium in 1970," Gamboa reflected,

> the cops were really framing Chicanos as being a danger to society, putting us all on a list. I would always have with me in my car maybe five or six changes of clothes, depending on where I was going, just to evade the cops. The feeling was that, because we're Chicanos, we were never allowed to hang out at all, period. But you could go somewhere and hang out for two minutes and, for those two minutes, that was the coolest place to be in all of LA.[90]

Gamboa describes the effect of this looming state violence within the work succinctly: "My concept for photography was that you only had to be in any spot for a *thousandth of a second* to make it cool—as long as you took the picture properly."[91]

These events and experiences informed Asco members' punitive literacies and underwrote their occupation of the traffic island as a kind of temporal and spatial choreography. Asco poignantly repurposed the traffic island that the county had installed to preemptively fill open spaces that might otherwise be prime sites for protest.[92] The action also invoked the idea of the island, broadly construed, within anticolonial protest: the Brown Berets had occupied Catalina Island in 1972 to draw attention to injustices and discrimination Mexican Americans faced in the US, while Native American activists had occupied Alcatraz Island for eighteen months between November 1969 and March 1971. The *First Supper* site alludes as well to the neutralized violence of municipal beautification and public safety ordinances; the Brown Berets held Catalina for three weeks until the city council enacted a camping ordinance and claimed they were violating it; similarly, the Native American activists were removed from Alcatraz under charges of trespassing. *First Supper* thus situates itself within urban planning processes meant to curtail movement, and a longer, transhistorical story of legalized displacement.

Mired within these complex conditions, Gamboa articulates one of the driving purposes for Asco's collaborations:

> A lot of our work has been pretty much one of urban survival techniques . . . in that sense of passing on ideas that would give people the idea that they could change things in their own lives and not have to be dependent on a lot of cash, or a lot of, a lot of education, really, to do a lot of things with their own life. That they weren't helpless victims in their environment. And that in itself was political in the sense that many people, where we come from, are essentially taught that they have no control over their own lives.[93]

First Supper, then, sought to refuse the "paramilitary occupation of the barrio" and the way the traffic island was designated a beautification project.[94] To reckon with this particular, seemingly mundane addition to the space of East Los Angeles, to understand its implications—a device to cover up the destruction caused by a police shooting (buildings in the area were also razed and rebuilt to conceal this lived reality)—is to see a vaster landscape of policing born out in urban renewal projects, administration, and media narratives.[95]

"Control to Burn"—Burden's False Emergencies

The aggressive policing of Chicano and Black communities in East and South Central Los Angeles, combined with urbanization and development policies aimed at securing "safety," informed the movements of artists living in these areas. These patterns also influenced, albeit inversely, the mobility of white artists in predominantly Anglo Westside areas like Santa Monica, West Hollywood, Venice, and Beverly Hills, where patrolling was laxer. Chris Burden's *Deadman* (plate 2), staged in predominantly Anglo West Hollywood, draws out this relational racial geography, though the discourse that has brought him fame pays little attention either to it or to the work's essential relation to policing.

Burden created *Deadman* during an art opening at Riko Mizuno Gallery on November 12, 1972. The gallery, at 669 La Cienega Boulevard, was not far from the Sunset Strip and upscale Beverly Hills and was already known at that time as a "seminal source for the blossoming of modernist art in Los Angeles during the sixties."[96] Burden subsequently described the work, planned with Mizuno's knowledge, and its aftermath:

> At 8pm, I lay down on La Cienega Boulevard and was covered completely with a canvas tarpaulin. Two fifteen-minute flares were placed near me to alert cars. Just before the flare extinguished, a police car arrived. I was arrested and booked for causing a false emergency to be reported. Trial took place in Beverly Hills. After three days of deliberation, the jury failed to reach a decision, and the judge dismissed the case.[97]

The authoritative language and tone of this written description—lacking emotion, striving toward objectivity—reads like an incident report.

Deadman appears frequently in exhibitions and published surveys of 1970s art and performance and body art, and features prominently in studies of Burden's oeuvre. The art historian Frazer Ward contextualizes the piece within discussions of Minimalism, consistent with the artist's intention that the work be one of "social sculpture."[98] Max Kozloff compares the disposition of the body in *Deadman* to depictions in religious art of the corpse as sacrificial lamb, while Christopher Knight celebrates Burden's body art "sculptures" for their "refusal to turn away" from the disintegration of morals in the US.[99] And yet, within the vast discourse surrounding *Deadman*, a crucial component has been entirely dismissed: Burden did not expect the police to show up.

Burden speaks to this point in a lecture delivered at the Rhode Island School of Design in 1974:

> I figured I was going to be there for ten, twelve minutes, for the length of the flares and then I would get up and leave, and that was going to be the end of the piece. It snowballed into this huge legal thing. . . . At the time I was very angry that the police came because what it did . . . the police came, then the whole thing switches to me, like you know, great, you did this piece to get arrested, and the cops are really dummies and that wasn't my intention at all. And so I felt that in a sense they destroyed the piece.[100]

Reflecting on the police's interpretation upon lifting the tarp, Burden continues, "I'm not sure they disputed the fact that I was doing a sculpture, but they did charge me with creating a false emergency. They were angry about it." In a 1979 interview, Burden reiterates the point: "*Deadman* had to do with what didn't happen. I didn't envision the police coming—that totally changed it around."[101]

The photographs documenting *Deadman*, taken by various friends, depict the work as it unfolds: two lit flares illuminate a tarp and the bulge of Burden's body curled beneath it, pressed against a parked car (plate 2). In the back-

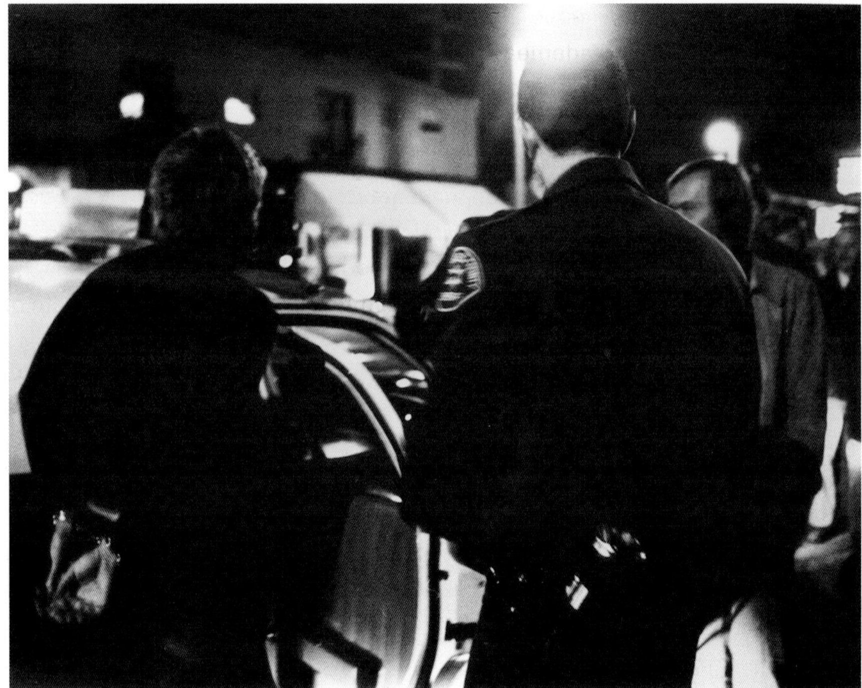

[1.5] Chris Burden, *Deadman (arrest)*, 1972. Black-and-white photograph. Documentation photo: Charles Arnoldi. Courtesy of Charles Arnoldi Studio. © 2021 Chris Burden. Licensed by the Chris Burden Estate/Artists Rights Society (ARS), New York.

ground, the gallery's large window is lit up for the opening. Silhouettes of several onlookers can be seen behind the car. Another image, taken by Chuck Arnoldi, shows part of Burden's arrest (fig. 1.5). Burden, handcuffed, stands near the open door of a police car, under the command of a uniformed white deputy. The deputy's back is turned, the sheriff's department insignia on his shoulder slightly blurred in the moment of action. Everything metallic catches light within the high-contrast image: the handcuffs, the gun in the deputy's holster, and the windshield of the police car almost shimmer, while a streetlight flares brightly over the deputy's head and more faintly illuminates what appears to be a crowd of people off to the right.

Peter Plagens, a prominent white art critic who was at the scene, recounted the moment of Burden's arrest in a story in the *New York Times*: "critic and curator step forward, tell deputy who they are, who artist is, what this is. Deputy says, everything considered, cannot lie down in middle of La Cienega Boulevard creating traffic hazard."[102] Burden wasn't charged with creating a traffic hazard or with disrupting the peace (misdemeanor crimes typically carrying minor penalties), but with having caused a false emergency to be reported.[103]

Burden's surprise and frustration with the arrival of the police at 669 La Cienega Boulevard (just six blocks, or a three-minute drive, from the West Hollywood police precinct at 720 N. San Vincente Boulevard) reveals an acute contrast between his and Asco's punitive literacies. Members of Asco expected a police presence in their East LA neighborhood, as is apparent in their anticipatory negotiation of coercive relations and Gamboa's focus on the thousandth of a second needed to document a piece and "make it cool." Burden—mere miles away in the same city—expected that police would not show up, and his exasperation when they did reflects not just their sparser Westside presence but their much more lenient treatment of white youth. His assessment suggests he had not been exposed to the constant police patrols and surveillance that figured prominently in Asco's planning—his movement had not been shaped, to recall Ahmed's words, by the possibility of being stopped and "moved in a different way."

The methods and policies developed by the LAPD—expanded surveillance, checkpoints, curfews, and early predictive policing algorithms—led to greatly increased police presence in East and South Central Los Angles, but not in predominantly white neighborhoods. Moreover, when white youth were detained, they were deemed "youth in trouble" rather than "delinquents" and returned to their parents without arrest.[104] A 1972 study, for example, reported that the West Valley area, where 95 percent of residents had Anglo surnames, had three police officers per square mile; East LA, where more than half the people had Spanish surnames, had thirteen police per square mile. Overpoliced areas, in turn, had a disproportionate number of arrests: in the category of drunk driving, for example, there were 10,000 arrests in East LA in 1972, compared to 1,500 in West LA.[105]

The largely suburban West Valley area in this study—west of the 405 expressway and north of Santa Monica and Beverly Hills—is distinct from nearby West Hollywood. But the demographic makeup of West Hollywood in the early 1970s was closer to that of the West Valley than that of East LA, as was the less aggressive policing it faced—based on the predictive logic that areas with higher past "incident loads" required greater police presence. Burden's non-anticipation of policing on a stretch of La Cienega Boulevard that operates as a kind of border between the gay and immigrant enclaves of West Hollywood was, then, reflective of several interlocking relations. While the statistics noted here are not directly comparative, they point to a widening gap in a city with a complex racial inheritance now seeking to predict criminality.

Policing and the threat of violence influenced mobilities not only within Burden's work but across the art world in Southern California, shaping professional profiles and art discourse. Decades later, John Baldessari, a white artist long active in Los Angeles, reflected on the LA scene of the 1970s and how the city's segregation had limited his knowledge of his peers and their art practices:

> It's weird—I never knew the Asco artists, for instance. I think it's due to the geography; you don't have the chance to socialize. Los Angeles is a series of city-states. There are communities here that I haven't been to even now. I was living in the Venice/Santa Monica area, and that's where most of the [white] artists were at the time. You might hear something, but I never met anybody. We all knew about Watts Towers, of course, as a landmark, but even then you were always warned about being careful when going down to see it because you're in South Central and blah-blah-blah. "You're taking your life into your own hands," they would say.[106]

"Taking your life into your own hands" is shorthand for risk work and the ways its racial implications are euphemized. Baldessari's comment frames exposure to danger as a *choice* for white artists, based on where they did or didn't go. The Watts Towers, an architectural feat created by artist Sabato Rodia with hand tools and scrap rebar between 1921 and 1954, stand to this day on a patch of land at 1765 E. 107th Street in South Central, a predominantly Black area of Los Angeles stretching from Central Avenue to Watts to the Crenshaw District. "Watts" had become shorthand for urban uprising following the unrest that occurred there in August 1965—when, after city officials had systematically shut down commercial life and displaced people with the construction of the Santa Monica Freeway, a white police officer's violent traffic stop of Marquette Frye, a twenty-one-year-old Black man, became a tipping point, leading to six days of unrest and the California Army National Guard being called in to suppress the conflict.[107]

Felker-Kantor tracks how law enforcement and politicians used the uprising in Watts to intensify police power and authority in South Central, and similarly met calls from Mexican Americans to end state-sanctioned violence in East LA with counterinsurgency campaigns implemented by the LAPD.[108] Thus, Baldessari's literacy in the punitiveness and risk structured into Watts led him to see entering the area, as a white artist, as a calculated risk—a "limit" to test. This

[1.6, facing page] "He Got Shot—For His Art," Art Section, *New York Times*, September 2, 1973. © 1973 The New York Times Company. All rights reserved. Used under license.

Art	15-16	Movies	6-8
Coins	20-21	Music	9-19
Dance	12	Photog	17
Drama	1-5	Records	18-19
Gardens	22-24	Stamps	20-21
Home	22	TV-Radio	11-14

The New York Times

Section 2

ARTS AND LEISURE

Sunday, September 2, 1973

A Psychiatric Detective Story of Infinite Skill

By WALTER KERR

LONDON

A TRUE myth is a true bind. All the facts are in, and there is no way out. Oedipus, an honorable man, can do whatever he likes to avoid fulfilling the prophecy that he will kill his father and marry his mother, but he will kill his father and marry his mother. We give assent to the unresolvable, see that it is perfectly proportioned, perfectly just, perfectly terrifying.

If there is one thing more than another that a contemporary playwright would like to do, it is to make a myth. We feel a desperate need these days for new icons, images, clothed symbols that will help us come to terms with the "dark cave of the psyche," the cave that thousands of years of reasoning haven't quite lighted after all.

*

We want a picture of ourselves that renders us whole, with all of the violent contraries and inexplicable self-betrayals locked in. Not an explanation but an intuition become flesh; not thinking, seeing. But, it turns out, myths are extraordinarily hard to make, just by the willing of it. We are used to thinking now, used to explaining before we really see, and it's not easy to wheel about and go back to magic.

The closest I have seen a contemporary play come—it is powerfully close—to reanimating the spirit of mystery that makes the stage a place of breathless discovery rather than a classroom for rational demonstration is Peter Shaffer's remarkable "Equus," now in repertory at the British National Theater. Mr. Shaffer is the author of "The Royal Hunt of the Sun," and he may have been trying for just such iconography—a portrait of the drives that lead men to crucify themselves—there. Here, I think, he has found it.

He's done it by using reason to despair of reason. We begin in what looks like a lecture lab, a handy enough arena for dissecting the brain: the center space is railed off, some members of the audience are seated above it onstage as though they'd come for a scholarly demonstration. It also looks, vaguely, like a horse-ring in which winners might be put through their paces. Then we notice that there are indeed horses about: from the rungs of steel ladders at both sides of the stage hang the silvered-frame skeletons of horses' heads. They are handsome. They are already, as John Napier has exquisitely designed them, in some way haunting.

*

A doctor is waiting for a patient, one he doesn't want to take on. He is weary and wary of tampering with the psyches of children, though that is his job. The patient is 17, a part-time stable boy. He has rammed a metal spike through the eyes of six horses. It is the gratuitous, unfathomable horror of the act that leads the doctor to accept the charge.

At once we are lured, with infinite skill, into a psychiatric detective story, the tensions of which account for half the evening's force. Clues are grudgingly, suspensefully come by. The defiant boy, blond curls framing a face of stone, won't speak, he will only mockingly hum television commercials when prodded. At last tricked into speech by adroit maneuver, he strikes a sly bargain he means to hold to. For every question of the doctor's that he answers, the doctor must answer one of his. Candor for candor, if we're going to get anywhere.

*

The process yields tantalizing bits of information. When he was a child his mother read to him—history, the New Testament, stories of horses in which horses spoke and felt. Under his mother's tutelage the boy has become religious enough to tack a cheap lithograph of the suffering Jesus, feet chained, back under the lash, to his wall. His atheist father, enraged, has torn it down and replaced it (Continued on Page 3)

I Fell in Love With Montgomery Clift

By CARYL RIVERS

Caryl Rivers, who teaches communications arts at Boston University, is the author of "Aphrodite at Mid-Century," to be published Sept. 21 by Doubleday. This article is adapted from her book.

I DID not deign to fall in with any of the boys who asked me to dance under duress and the watchful eyes of Sister Maria. Not with Richard, who was a good pitcher and who did the box step over and over again in the same spot on the brown tile floor, or with John, who was very tall and so paralyzed with fear when he approached a girl that his stomach rumbled, or with Noel, who had dimples and wavy hair and was generally proclaimed to be "cute," or with Johnny, the football player.

I was in love with the Nats' centerfielder Irv Noren, but there were others. I try to remember them all: there were more than a few, but foremost among them was Montgomery Clift in "Red River."

I was not alone. All the girls in the eighth grade fell in love with Montgomery Clift. His face had the perfection of a fragile porcelain vase; his beauty was so sensual, and at the same time so vulnerable, it was almost blinding. I think every girl who saw him in the quiet dark of a movie theater of a Saturday afternoon fell in love with Montgomery Clift, his dark eyes like the deep water of a cavern pool, holding the promise of worlds of tenderness; the straight, perfect blade of a nose that should have been the work of some sculptor the equal of Michelangelo.

There was something that happened with young girls and male movie stars, and it happened instantly, unexplicably, simultaneously to all of us, as if we were prompted by some unconscious race memory. A man who was to us no more than a flat shadow on an asbestos screen became the repository of all the dreams of all our summer nights, a tabernacle for all our unfulfilled wishes. Like our passion for the ballplayers, our love for the movie stars permitted the perfume of sexuality to drift about like a vapor, sniffed now and then but only half-recognized.

At the same time I was in love with Montgomery Clift I found the growing awareness of how people "did it" pretty revolting: all that touching and pinching and groping about. It seemed to me that if one had to "do it" after one got married, the best way was quick and efficient, sort of like the way dogs in the neighborhood did it, only they had the execrable taste to do it in the street. With me and Montgomery, it wasn't that sort of thing at all. Love with him would be long, languorous sighs, pressing close against his manly chest and telling each other all the secrets we had never told anybody, and gazing eyeball-to-eyeball, and he wouldn't think of putting his hand on my thigh. (I liked my heroes pure as the driven snow. I had just graduated to adult books after reading all the Horse books and Dog books ever written. I thought that human heroes could at least possess the virtues ascribed to "Lad, A Dog" by Albert Payson Terhune. When a protagonist in an adventure novel fell from grace by so much as unhitching a bra, I no longer admired him. I was a terrible prude.)

*

I was in love for a brief time with Robert Wagner. I went to see "With a Song in My Heart" primed to fall in love with him. Six other girls in the class saw the movie before I did and all they talked about was Robert Wagner, who had a part that lasted perhaps three minutes.

Susan Hayward was playing singer Jane Froman, and in one scene she is entertaining injured American G.I.'s in a hospital. She comes up to a shell-shocked G.I. who can neither move nor talk. He just stares up at her with spaniel eyes and a face so all-American soap-and-water perfect it made you want to cry. I did. So did millions of others. That scene made Robert Wagner a movie star.

I fell in love with James Dean, of course. He mumbled, and he was sensitive and inarticulate and so in need of Someone To Love Him. I saw "East of Eden" four times, melting to a sticky little

Continued on Page 7

Art in California

He Got Shot —For His Art

"You'll Never See My Face in Kansas City" by Chris Burden, a young California artist ... *Because everything else has been done?*

By PETER PLAGENS

LOS ANGELES.

"I know myself only insofar as I am inherent in time and in the world, that is, I know myself only in my ambiguity."

—MAURICE MERLEAU-PONTY
"The Phenomenology of Perception"

IF YOU'VE never been to Venice (. . . West, in California): it's a shank-end community of semi-dilapidated one-story brick buildings abutting freaky/proletarian sections of public beach. Pacific Ocean Park, an amusement area, burned down a long time ago and its ruins form a buffer between Venice and staid Santa Monica to the north; but the marina mentality (sailboats, stewardesses, franchise fake-elegant restaurants, and plastic singles apartments) is creeping up from the south, so Venice's days as L.A.'s bohemia may be numbered.

Under hazy, gray, indistinct skies, women looking like retired strippers somnambulate in muumuus while a distant bongo concert continues unabated, and a few artists take a break from their white studios and watch the spacey parade from walkway benches. Chris Burden, 26, lives down there in a former hotdog stand (fully converted, heavily padlocked). Burden is a Conceptual-performance artist who does *things* (an appropriately ambiguous term) often involving pain/danger to himself; although he's a product of a European childhood and high school hard by Harvard, his work, looks and mien have the same slightly sinister insouciance as the neighborhood.

William Wegman lives up the beach in Ocean Park, near the buffer zone; his work and style have a downright wholesomeness. If Burden and Wegman have anything in common besides being (Continued on Page 34)

Peter Plagens is an artist and West Coast contributing editor to Artforum.

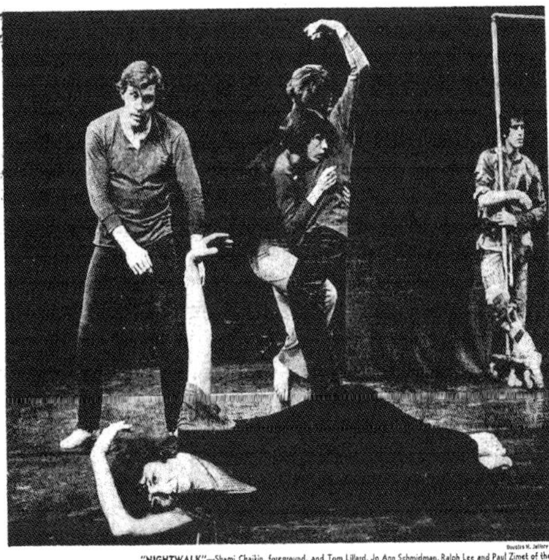

Douglas H. Jeffery

"NIGHTWALK"—Shami Chaikin, foreground, and Tom Lillard, Jo Ann Schmidman, Ralph Lee and Paul Zimet of the Open Theater ensemble portray images of disturbed sleep in the group's collective work about levels of awareness. The production, directed by Joseph Chaikin and with writing contributed by Jean-Claude van Itallie, Sam Shepard and Megan Terry, starts Saturday at St. Clement's Church, 423 W. 46th Street. The troupe's repertory runs through Oct. 13.

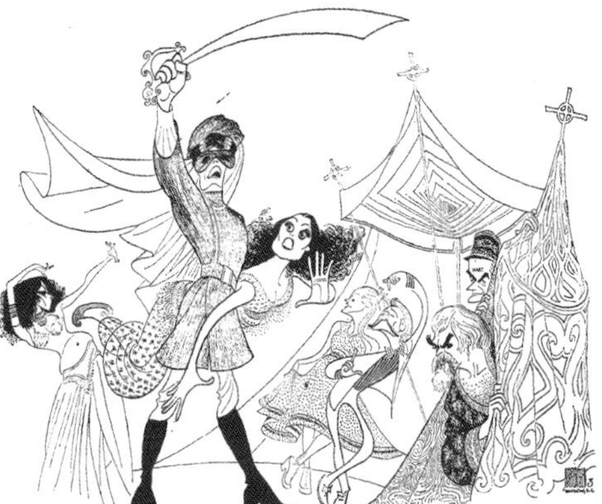

"THE DESERT SONG"—David Cryer is The Red Shadow, daring masked leader of a band of rebels in the French Morocco of 50 years ago, Chris Callan is his prisoner of love in the 1926 operetta by Sigmund Romberg. Also contributing to the doings in the dunes are Gloria Rossi, left, and Britt Swanson, Jerry Dodge, Michael Kermoyen and Sheppard Strudwick. Henry Butler staged the revival, which opens Wednesday at the Uris Theater.

THE OPENING

THE DESERT SONG—Wednesday, Uris, 6:45. An operetta, with music by Sigmund Romberg; book and lyrics by Otto Harbach, Oscar Hammerstein 2d and Frank Mandel.

conceptualization of risk-taking, based on controlled limits, diminishes the reality of artists of color who live in South Central and East LA, daily surviving the environmental racism and coercive surveillance of these government-manufactured segregated spaces.

Baldessari's recollection of LA not only speaks to the socialization of risk vis-à-vis the carving up of urban space by the police state but implicitly conjures the related lack of policing on the Westside, where Burden's *Deadman* took place. As Mitchell's recalibrated police patrol beat maps suggest, it's not just that more cops are sent to one area; it is that, conversely, fewer officers are allocated to other areas—typically areas that are predominantly white and economically advantaged areas deemed "safe." Fewer police also translate to minimized contact with the police. This territoriality indexes what art historian Thomas Crow has called Los Angeles's "semilocalized [art] scenes," wherein Spanish-speaking residential areas, in architectural historian Mike Davis's estimation, "comprise a virtually parallel urban structure—a second city."[109]

It was with these contexts in mind that the members of Asco formulated the No Movies, producing images familiar enough to be recognized as part of a larger narrative of danger, and thus to reach audiences beyond their locale, but abstract, ambiguous, and agile enough to avoid eliciting future police encounter. The pacing of being in a certain place for just one-thousandth of a second to create a photograph makes clearer the distinctive temporality and social significance of Asco's tactics and those deployed by Burden just a few miles away, and how these different but related positionalities and geographies shape art histories of risk-taking.

Mediated Risk-Taking: Anti-Riot Laws and Emergency Management

For Burden, a minimal fear of encountering police or of being arrested—manifest in his plan for *Deadman* to let the flares burn all the way down for ten to twelve minutes, and then to get up and walk away—translates directly into hypervisibility in the art world. In fact, in 1973 Burden's work is featured on the front page of the *New York Times* art section in an article by Plagens on LA art. In the accompanying image, Burden appears in a ski mask (fig. 1.6), a documentary image from his 1971 work *You'll Never See My Face in Kansas City*, for which he wore this mask for three days in both public and private spaces, culminating in a public performance in Kansas City. The image reinforces Burden's persona as a troublemaker. For one thing, it would likely have conjured global imaginaries of violence in the wake of the massacre of Israeli athletes at the 1972 Munich Olympics by the Palestinian group Black September, and after media images of Black September members wearing the same ski mask had traveled around the world.

Although Burden appears in the guise of the masked hijacker, the article makes no mention of the relation of his performance to notions of criminality, political violence, or transnational imaginaries of third-world militancy. Instead, Plagens speaks of Burden's relation to the terrain of Los Angeles, noting that his form of "conceptual-performance art" requires the city's specific "*ennui* and lack of 'battlefield feeling'" to exist.[110] Plagens's description of Los Angeles as a place known for its dreamy slowness (compared to New York City's fast-paced commerce and cultural production) also omits any mention of the escalating violence of racialized policing that reinforced segregationist urban spaces, surveillance, and punitive relations. In so doing, he disregarded the social landscape and discriminatory profiling that shaped Asco members' relationship to the art scene and its coverage.[111] Nevertheless, in his discussion of Burden's arrest and trial, Plagens mentions the national context of policing briefly, remarking that Burden had been "busted for a 1968 (year of the riots) law for knowledgeable causing-to-be-reported of a false emergency (e.g., a bomb threat)."[112]

As discussed earlier, the 1968 "year of the riots law"—the Anti-Riot Act—had been immediately criticized by liberal watchdogs as a "foundation for a police state in America." Now its ramifications for perceptions of "emergency" were central to the debate at the core of Burden's trial. Whereas California had previously punished the crime of "false report" as a misdemeanor (with a maximum sentence of one year in county jail, or a fine of up to a thousand dollars),[113] the Anti-Riot Act made it a felony (with a minimum sentence exceeding one year, and possibly including life imprisonment, as well as fines of up to $10,000).[114] Within the "false report" ordinance, the California Penal Code defines a *real* emergency, necessary for discerning *false* emergency. It determines emergency as

> any condition that results in, or could result in, the response of a public official in an authorized emergency vehicle, aircraft, or vessel, any condition that jeopardizes or could jeopardize public safety and results in, or could result in, the evacuation of any area, building, structure, vehicle, or of any other place that any individual may enter, or any situation that results in or could result in activation of [the] Emergency Alert System.[115]

While dictionary definitions generally center emergency on the experience of an unexpected, often dangerous situation that requires immediate action, within the penal code "emergency" is a tautology of the police state: an emergency happens when the emergency resources of the state are summoned. And the state is summoned when a condition occurs that requires its resources. Conversely, if emergency state funds were not deemed applicable in the event of injury, then, in the state's eyes, no emergency had occurred. Thus, Burden was not simply "busted" for a "year of the riots" law. Instead, these laws, preceding and long outliving 1968, were part of an expanding security apparatus set on anticipating tactical interventions through racialized, classist, and gendered governance. As discussed above, Asco's No Movies were also shaped, long before actions took place, by the temporality (not temporariness) of anti-riot reform, aftercrimes, and beat patrols, becoming a kind of materialized relation of time, space, and risk.

The spatiotemporal politics of policing inform Burden's trial, which took place in late January 1973 in the upper-class, predominantly white Anglo area of Beverly Hills. During the trial, two officers testified for the prosecution, offering exaggerated accounts of the number of flares, which were discredited when documentary photographs of the artwork were presented. For the defense, three individuals prominent in the art world spoke on Burden's behalf: Riko Mizuno (gallery owner), Helen Winer (*LA Times* art critic and former gallery director at Pomona College), and Jane Livingston (curator of modern art for LACMA).[116] Barbara Smith, a white artist and friend, had earlier rallied support for Burden, writing of his upcoming trial in *Artweek* and offering a set of pressing questions:

> What is the responsibility of the art gallery to the artist? And for another, to what degree should the art community or the art establishment come to the support of an artist? If no one helps Burden and he loses his case, artists will have reason to fear taking the risks that are inherent and necessary for many of the new art forms.[117]

Smith's conclusion emphasizes how the perception of risk-taking as a right of artists in the United States was one of the most important factors under consideration in Burden's trial.

In the end, Burden was acquitted. The jury voted to convict 9–3, but, Burden explained, it remained "a hung jury, which means that they couldn't come to a unanimous decision . . . the judge finally dismissed the case."[118] In short, the jury didn't agree on Burden's innocence as an artist, but eventually the case was dropped because no unanimous conclusion was reached. "I guess what shocked me," Burden reflected,

> was the kind of frenzy that the D.A. was like wanting to prosecute this. Whereas it seemed to be a pretty minor thing, you know. . . . I mean, there's something ludicrous about a three-day trial and all that energy put into trying to decide what to do about one guy who lies in a street under a tarp for 10 minutes.[119]

Plagens nuanced the artist's recollection of the hung jury, explaining, "A collector lawyer *got* him a hung jury, and when the over-zealous prosecution (for such small potatoes) called for a new trial, the judge dismissed the case."[120] Plagens's description is notable, as it emphasizes both the importance of Burden's connections and their shared sense that the authorities had overreacted in indicting and prosecuting Burden.

Burden's trial operates within the larger landscape of policing in the early 1970s. The material risks taken by Asco in works like *Spray Paint LACMA*, *Decoy*, and *First Supper (After a Major Riot)* call attention to links between urban renewal, safety discourse, and limited mobility of acute concern to Chicanx people. Burden's work likewise indelibly registers these links—but through the artist's pointed *lack* of concern with encountering the police apparatus. In her recap of the trial, Smith explains the case Burden's lawyer Jim Butler built around Burden's lack of criminal intent, arguing he had not intended either to summon the police or to be arrested. In Burden's paraphrase, his lawyer had argued that "the streets aren't made just for cars, and that *I had a right to be there*. There's no law that says you can't go out in the street and make art."[121]

What would American art history look like if Burden had been a Chicano man arrested for causing a false emergency? If he had been a Chicano man, walking around Kansas City in a ski mask for three days? Would he have been celebrated and validated on the pages of the *New York Times*? It is unlikely, given the racialized, gendered, and class politics of risk work shaping Asco's practice, that the art world would have evinced similar levels of support during his trial.

Burden's *Deadman*, made spectacular by his arrest and trial, and Asco's *Spray Paint LACMA*, a gesture immediately whitewashed from view, attest to the relational geographies bound by policing, as defined by both that which happens on the ground and that which happens in televised, mediated representations of racialized and gendered criminality. The works were both enacted in 1972 in Los Angeles, just two miles apart. While the male members of Asco tagged their signatures on LACMA's walls in response to their exclusion and a curator's presumption that all Chicanos were involved in organized crime, that museum's own curator of modern art testified on Burden's behalf during the trial, arguing for the dual seriousness and innocence of his work that had then, ironically, become the focus of a criminal trial. As Gronk explained, reflecting in the 1990s on Burden's *Deadman*, "Somebody of color, at that same time would have been implicitly told 'how dare you think you could do a performance piece by lying down in the middle of the street.' . . . Only Chris Burden can do something like that. [We, in Asco, always felt] . . . that a hierarchy did exist."[122]

The DA's drive to convict Burden also highlights approaches law enforcement officials were testing as a means of expanding their discretionary domain. Burden's acquittal was an important "win" for artists using public spaces; his court case would be studied by lawyers and judges for generations to come (see chapter 3). However, this story is part of a larger framework of policing within which Asco and Burden are situated relationally and dialectically. As the legal scholar Karen Pita Loor observes, "The rhetoric of emergency," implicated within the labor of recognizing unknown criminal intent, and preemptively containing it as a future-emergency scenario, "further serves to neutralize officials' and police's behavior that may regularly be perceived by the public and the courts as abusive and overreaching."[123] The DA's "frenzy" or "overzealousness," deemed foolish by both Burden and Plagens, takes on a more sinister meaning within the larger policing environment exposed by Asco's contemporaneous work, where the ability to define emergency, crisis, and codes of safety and order constituted a fraught battlefield.

Hostage Scenarios: Risk Work and Its Erasure

While danger is perceived to be beyond one's control, sociologist Anthony Giddens reminds us that the idea of risk is instructively future-oriented, based on a perceived ability to control and avoid unwanted outcomes. "Successful risk-takers," Giddens writes, "whether in exploration, in business, or in mountaineering, are widely admired."[124] The simultaneous rejection of Chicano artists and public legitimizing of Burden for his "daring" experimentation illuminates the privileging of white maleness at work in interpretations of Burden's transgression of legal and social boundaries.

The art world's support of Burden not only helped acquit him in criminal court but, perhaps more significantly, solidified his revered position as a leader of "risky" 1970s conceptual and performance art. The conditions of enablement that spurred Burden's practice—and their non-acknowledgement—can thus be thought of as a gendered, racial inheritance within his risk work. In keeping with the geographer and abolitionist visionary Ruth Wilson Gilmore's insightful claim that, "as every geographer knows, edges are also interfaces," the geographic punitive relations linking Burden and Asco's work emphasize the dialectical nature of their risk-taking and its embodied and juridical stakes.[125] The hierarchy remarked by Gronk meant that a different mode of decision-making was necessary for Asco, when, as Gamboa reflected, "the art was to walk away unscathed but to have touched the danger."[126]

The deep disparities born of these relations create opportunities for (protected) confrontation for Burden, while inversely shaping the forms utilized by members of Asco. This relationship is most palpable in Valdez's private ephemeral performance as a gagged and bound—but armed—Chicana woman, seen alongside Burden's *You'll Never See My Face in Kansas City* (1971) and *TV Hijack* (1972), in which he held a knife to the throat of white female curator Phyllis Lutjeans as they filmed a TV interview.

Valdez created the untitled performance piece in 1975, in her studio in her parents' garage. Gamboa shot black-and-white images documenting the work (figs. 1.7–1.8), which he later titled *Pistol Whippersnapper* when he incorporated them into a Xerox collage flyer with the same title that Asco circulated via the mail as a No Movie in 1976. In the performance, Valdez holds a plastic toy gun or, rather, her hands are held around it with tape.[127] There is ambiguity as to whether it is by choice or force. Her mouth is covered with another strip of tape. Bound and unable to speak, yet armed and confronting the camera with her eyes, Valdez occupies the paradoxical stance of victim and aggressor, challenging the discrete categories. The surviving photographs thus do not merely document a performance but are part of the performance itself. Her armed engagement with the camera cultivates a symbolic space of meditation, a condition of being seen that is an integral part of the work.

"The gun was a metaphor," Valdez says of the performance, "almost like a dare. I was so frustrated. When I looked through the lens of the camera, I was daring the world to insult me again or put me down or say something negative. 'I dare you.' It's just a silly toy gun, but 'I dare you.'" She refers, in this interview, to her sense of feeling voiceless as a young Chicana woman, expected to be seen and not heard, living in a world that fetishized a figure like the Frito Bandito. The performance was also contemporaneous with the spectacularized trial of Patricia (Patty) Hearst, the white American heiress to the Hearst publishing fortune who had been kidnapped and held for ransom in 1974, before joining her

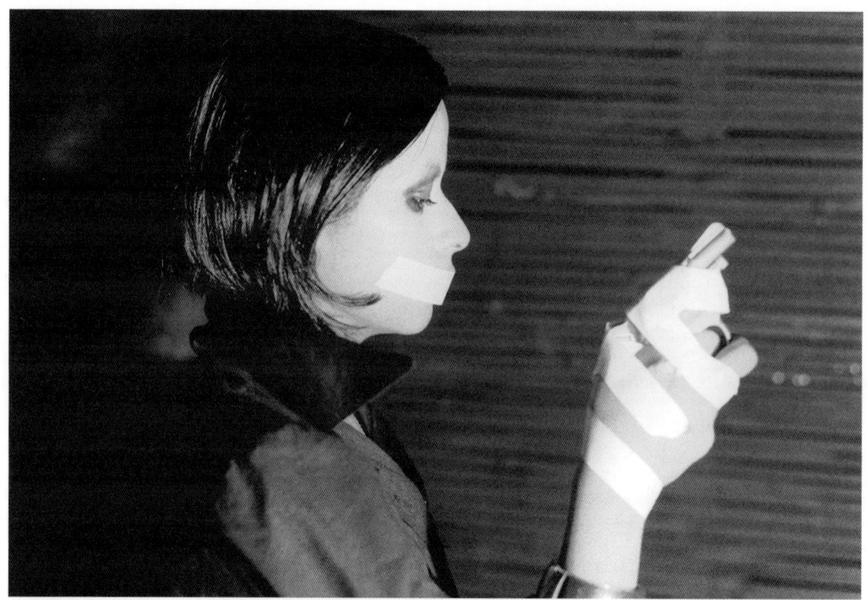

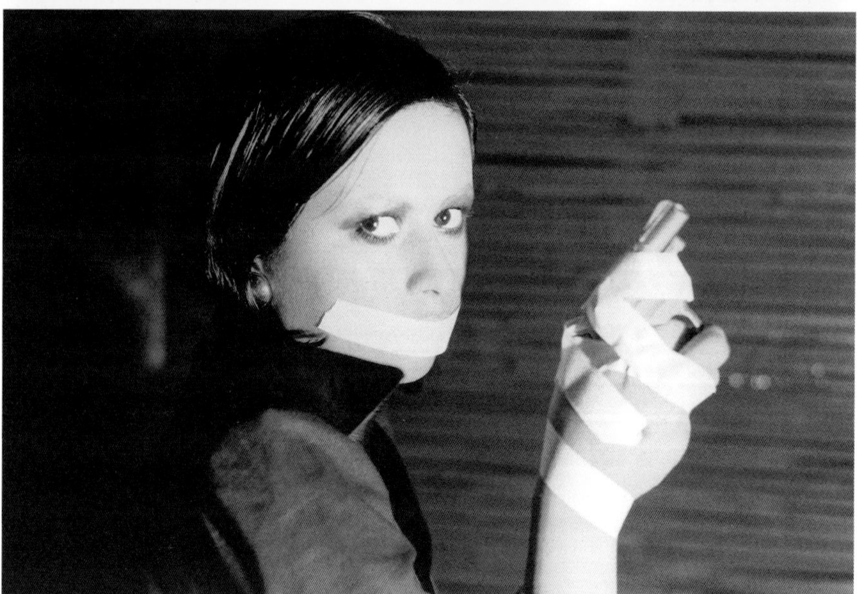

[1.7] Harry Gamboa Jr., *Pistol Whippersnapper (movement 1)*, from the Asco era, 1975. Gelatin silver print, 16 × 20 inches (40.64 × 50.8 cm). © Harry Gamboa Jr. Courtesy of the artist.

[1.8] Harry Gamboa Jr., *Pistol Whippersnapper (movement 2)*, from the Asco era, 1975. Gelatin silver print, 16 × 20 inches (40.64 × 50.8 cm). © Harry Gamboa Jr. Courtesy of the artist.

captors, the Symbionese Liberation Army, in their violent pursuit of dismantling the white capitalist patriarchy. During the trial, which was a major televised event, a grainy surveillance image of Hearst wielding a rifle during the group's 1975 holdup of the Hibernia National Bank was scrutinized again and again to determine whether Hearst had been coerced or a willing participant. The image of Hearst as an urban guerrilla also achieved mythic status as a representation of sexualized white femininity gone "bad." "I didn't think 'hostage,'" Valdez explained, in reference to being bound and gagged and to the images of Hearst then circulating widely. "I thought 'censored'"—silenced through derogatory images that obscured her perspective and diminished her ability to speak with authority.[128] Reflecting on the tension between the art of Asco and that of more traditional Chicano artists, Gronk explained, "A lot of Latino artists went back in history for imagery. We wanted to stay in the present and find our imagery as urban artists, and produce a body of work out of our sense of displacement."[129]

In contrast to work by the members of Asco, who battled the pervasive misrepresentation and ongoing censorship of Mexican Americans, Burden's *TV Hijack* suggests an artist relatively unconcerned with mediated narratives of militancy and criminality because, as a white man, such stereotypes would not be used to denigrate his character. Burden had been commissioned to create a work for the public television program in Irvine, California, but the producers had rejected every proposal he had made.[130] After agreeing to instead be interviewed, Burden held the interviewer, Phyllis Lutjeans, a curator at the Newport Art Museum, hostage during the taping. In Burden's own words, "Holding a knife to her throat, I threatened her life if the station stopped live transmission. I told her that I had planned to make her perform obscene acts. At the end of the recording, I asked for the tape of the show. I unwound the reel and destroyed the show by dousing the tape with acetone."[131] An image taken by Barbara Smith (invited, along with Gary Beydler, by Burden to be accomplices in the work's making) depicts the discomfort and apprehension in Lutjeans's face as Burden grasps at her neck (plate 5). The station manager was "irate" that the artist had destroyed the footage so it couldn't be recirculated as a primetime TV segment, but Burden faced no legal consequences for his actions.[132]

When analyzing *TV Hijack*, scholars posit this instance of hostage-taking as "a declaration of agency," an action that positions the artist as "a careful, responsible coordinator of his own performances."[133] Such readings are common, contributing to a consensus in the field that posits Burden's work as unmotivated by racial formation and aligned with riskiness and agency, overlooking as well his ready access to disparate spaces: the Irvine television studio, the street in front of Riko Mizuno Gallery for *Deadman*, F Space in Santa Ana for *Shoot*, even the front page of the *New York Times* art section.[134] As a result, Burden's privileged relation to the *work* of risk-taking and, inversely, the disproportionate praise he receives for the work's perceived riskiness become the metrics of his fame. These metrics continue to reproduce the unmarked persistence of whiteness within narratives of risk-taking in contemporary art history.

Burden had been intrigued by a much-publicized aircraft hijacking the previous year. D. B. Cooper (the alias used by an unidentified white man when he booked his flight) hijacked a Boeing 727 en route from Portland, Oregon, to Seattle, Washington. Claiming to have a bomb, he extorted $200,000 and demanded the jet be flown to Mexico, by way of Reno, Nevada. Along the way, he parachuted from the plane, evading arrest and capturing the attention of a nation. The media glamorized the highjacker, depicted in a police artist's drawing as a white man wearing sunglasses, finding in him a cinematic "James Dean" type—a look Burden seems to emulate in *TV Hijack*. Meanwhile, Mexican American men and women were demonized in news programs corroborating the narratives set forth by police about Latino delinquency; a study published in 1977 by the United States Commission on Civil Rights reported that in its media analysis, "men of Spanish origin appeared in the sample news programs *only* as criminals."[135] Even in this, Burden benefited from asymmetric opportunity.

These conditions, and this bias, are part of the story left untold when Burden's feats of agency are lauded—when he is valorized as at once ahistorical, apolitical, ethically responsible, and, always, in control. In this way, the discursive mythology of Burden as danger-seeking, which positions him as an artist attuned to but unhindered by his environment, reproduces the logics of policing that similarly insist that white men—whether artists or cops—have a right to be in and remake the city. Conditions of enablement and restriction materialize through relations of space, time, friendship, and precarity: Asco's work was often done in their parents' garages, where a certain level of respect for the space was required.

Interlaced Futures

It would be inaccurate to suggest that Burden set out to benefit from media representations of white men as "cool" or "heroic." However, the implications of these underlying factors have been systemically absent from scholarship focusing on his work, a fact that reveals the ways the structure of enablement at the core of whiteness is normalized in the making of art, as much as by the art discourse that further legitimizes it. Burden's tactics of confrontation, deployed in performances and conceptual art, reflect his presumption of safety; simultaneously, critics and art historians laud the types of risks he takes as a benchmark of danger-making. These judgments constitute an important part of risk work as a framework: whereas the work of risk entails punitive literacy, art critics and curators' simultaneous valorization of *risk* as code for one's ability to *control* vulnerability to state-sanctioned violence exacerbates asymmetrical and incommensurate relations to power and the threat of state violence. The perceived riskiness of Burden's actions was thus legitimized even as he, relative to the artists in Asco, benefited from the ways that cis-gendered straight male whiteness and patriarchal values have served as the basis of legal protections.

These dual vectors of risk work determine how and when one *shows up*—physically, emotionally, spatially, and archivally—in art history, as in American society. As Gamboa has observed, "The Chicano artist is bound and gagged across the rails of racism, flattened against the tracks of negative stereotypes, if not effaced completely."[136] Asco understood, he contends, that as Hollywood and American television "repeatedly made attempts to assassinate the image of Chicanos with cinematographic weapons. . . . Chicanos will have to shoot right back."[137]

The seemingly contradictory qualities of Valdez's performance in her family garage—armed yet positioned as a hostage—encapsulates the clashing experiences of self-preservation Valdez found in her art and in others' interpretations, which viewed her work as a sign of gendered entrapment. On the one hand, "I was very, very quiet. . . . I didn't do interviews [then]. I was very quiet. . . . I was actually trying to find out who I was in those years."[138] That experience, she says, led her to find artmaking where "nobody could censor me. I found my voice and I found freedom to do whatever I chose. It was very liberating."[139]

The charged imagery she used, however, specifically representations of bondage (which appear in a number of Asco's pieces) as symbols of sexualized female submission, caused feminist critics to reject her. Women who identified with the Chicana feminist movement rejected Valdez as passively complicit in her own objectification, merely perpetuating derogatory images of Chicana women as victims of censorship and abuse: "A lot of feminist Chicanas were really angry at me . . . they said the guys made me do it. And I'm like, 'No. No guy made me do anything.' . . . I was acting out what I was living at that time . . . that's exactly how my life was, all bound up."[140] The array of possible interpretations of Valdez's actions speak to a complex matrix of forces and regulations (from within and without) that underpin risk work: the racial, gender, class, and sexual politics of survival and growth.

Burden's ability to occupy space without much fear of legal consequences or lethal physical harm, as well as imaginaries of violence without concerns of being circumscribed within them, speaks of more than his racialized, sexualized, and gendered privileges: these calculations are manifestations of collectively managed punitive literacies and the opportunities of riskiness they afford, which commonly go unmentioned in discussions of white artists' art. It is important to note that whiteness, not to be equated with white individuals or their acts or intentions, is a system of enablement and control that reinforces white-centering exclusionary practices of land possession, resource distribution, and access to knowledge production through relations of violence that differently position people within gendered antiblack configurations of power and security.

When situated alongside nearly contemporaneous works by members of Asco, such as *Spray Paint LACMA*, *First Supper*, *Decoy*, and Gamboa's photographing of Valdez's untitled performance in her garage, it becomes clearer that Burden's *Deadman* and *TV Hijack* did not merely "test his limits," as art critics and curators have imagined but, rather, worked within conditions of gendered, classist whiteness procured as apolitical and neutral by America's governing institutions and emergency management protocols. Burden has routinely been regarded by curators, art critics, and historians as the enduring standard of the "aggressively risky" artist.[141] This chapter has sought to trouble what this label *does* in the present, when perceptions that Burden controlled his risk as a sign of his ethics of responsibility and genius remain pervasive. By rethinking the root causes of precarity in "hit and run" guerrilla tactics in art, it is possible to more effectively understand how the "spontaneous" occupation of space—sometimes with only a thousandth of a second to spare—is a relational condition that manages social difference as it secures ideas of (illusory) freedom.

[2]

Deputizing Discernment

Adrian Piper, Jean Toche, and the Politics of Loitering, 1974–1978

Amid unsuspecting pedestrians in New York City in 1970, Adrian Piper wore a shirt covered in sticky paint and a WET PAINT sign and walked through crowded commercial areas on her way to shopping at Macy's.[1] Standing beneath a NO STANDING sign, and riding a city bus, she inhabited public space with a towel stuffed in her mouth (fig. 2.1). Of this series of conceptual performances, titled *Catalysis*, Piper wrote in August 1970, "One reason for making and exhibiting a work is to induce a reaction or change in the viewer." In promoting that change, "the work is a catalytic agent," whose value "may then be measured in terms of the strength of the change [in the viewer], rather than whether the change accords positively or negatively with some aesthetic standard."[2] The strength of a viewer's response is enhanced by immediacy and the removal of mediating elements, such as an art-sanctioned context that maintains a predictable artist-viewer dynamic. Reflecting on her interest in "unobtrusively insinuating art into a nonart situation," Piper mused, "I like the idea of doing away with all discrete forms and letting art lurk in the midst of things."[3]

Scholars have retroactively described Piper's early unobtrusive, ephemeral tactics enacted in public spaces as "guerrilla performances."[4] And she did employ the term later, describing *Calling (Card) #1* and *#2* (1986–1990) as "*reactive guerrilla performances*."[5] In *Calling (Card) #1*, she created a business card to hand out at cocktail parties and dinners to simultaneously assert her Black identity (an affiliation she has since eschewed, having retired from being Black in 2012) and condemn a white person's racist remark made when they misidentified her as white.[6] With *Calling (Card) #2*, Piper rejects unsolicited advances made at bars and discos.

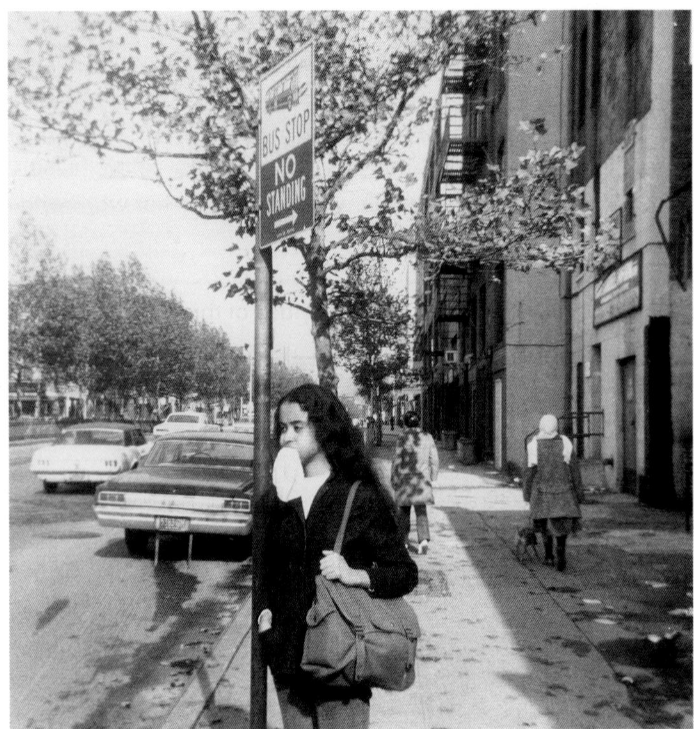

[2.1] Adrian Piper, *Catalysis IV*, 1970. Performance documentation. Five silver gelatin photographs, each 16 × 16 inches (40.6 × 40.6 cm). Detail: photograph #1 of 5. Photo: Rosemary Mayer. Collection of the Generali Foundation, Vienna; permanent loan to the Museum der Moderne Salzburg. © Adrian Piper Research Archive Foundation Berlin and Generali Foundation.

I have not seen Piper use "guerrilla" to describe or conceptualize her 1970s performance-based conceptual practice. She did, however, point in the 1970s to guerrilla theater, a related but distinct mode of public intervention through which artists such as Jean Toche had recently gained legibility, as a foil for the type of practice she was pursuing. As Piper explained in a 1972 interview with curator Lucy Lippard:

> One thing I don't do is say: "I'm doing a piece," because somehow that puts me back into the situation I'm trying to avoid. It immediately establishes an audience separation—"Now we will perform"—that destroys the whole thing. As soon as you say, this is a piece, or an experiment, or guerrilla theatre—that makes everything all right, just as set-up and expected as if you were sitting in front of a stage.[7]

One can see, based on Piper's assessment, how other artists' willingness to create or borrow from guerrilla theater (as well as direct action protest and open letter writing), by then a recognizable mode within the framework of political action and spectatorship, lent their art practice a degree of cultural familiarity. By contrast, Piper actively sought to avoid contextual references to political activism or staged performances that would pin down her work within readily recognizable situations or audience dynamics.

Chapter 2 analyzes Piper's and Jean Toche's distinctive art experiments in the mid-1970s to expand upon an essential idea of this book: that artists' anticipation and navigation of punitive contexts in their work illuminates how racialized, gendered, and sexualized structures of state power have shaped cultural production. In many ways, the tactics of persistent engagement used by Piper and by Toche could not be more different. As a white Belgian émigré in New York City, Toche actively solicited attention and vitriol from political leaders, police, and public authorities. Before arriving in the US in 1966, Toche had briefly studied law at the Université libre de Bruxelles. There, he developed a wariness of the abuse of legal rights upon discovering a "rebel" surveillance file devoted to him, which demonstrated how easily one's privacy can be violated in the name of safety. "That's when I knew," he explained, "that the government watched people. Was watching me . . . I've always been interested in contesting the law. I am impulsive by nature."[8]

In the US, Toche turned to collaborative and solo interventions that fashioned the law as a medium and situated his ephemeral art tactics within the paradigm of politicized action-taking. In 1969, as discussed in the introduction, he cofounded Guerrilla Art Action Group (GAAG) with Jon Hendricks. Together, for several decades thereafter, the artists mobilized guerrilla tactics of confrontation, sabotage, and hijacking as a conceptual art practice, conducting unannounced actions at MoMA, the Metropolitan Museum of Art, and a range of spaces; they circulated countless communiques, flyers, and postcards outlining antiwar, anticapitalist, and antiracist demands for those institutions and the art world writ large, to varying effect. For Toche, part of what was subversive about GAAG's art practice was making "planned appearances and disappearances."[9] Toche also pursued solo endeavors that heightened his visibility as a "guerrilla artist." He was purposefully combative, using words and documentation to confront what he saw as the structural forces perpetuating inequities in society—poverty, elitism, racism, and war—but also persistent, using actions that moved slowly, at the pace of civic engagement, often turning to the format of the open letter in his art.

In a piece that gained him national attention, Toche wrote an open letter on February 23, 1974, calling for the kidnapping of "museum trustees, directors, curators, benefactors . . . to be held as war hostages until a People's Court is convened, to deal specifically with the cultural crimes of the ruling class."[10] The letter was presented in solidarity with artist Tony Shafrazi's recent defacement of Pablo Picasso's painting *Guernica* at MoMA, which Toche viewed as an act of revolutionary transformation and collaboration. Rather than stage an impromptu occupation of space, Toche created a paper trail: he mailed fifty copies of his letter to critics, artists, and museum directors in the New York region. While the director of MoMA understood this to be a symbolic gesture, Met president C. Douglas Dillon, who'd received the handbill, called the FBI, leading to Toche's arrest on March 27 and a subsequent trial and court-ordered psychiatric exam.

A question drives this chapter: What can the study of differing modes of persistence, in the work of Piper and Toche, contribute to a discourse of guerrilla tactics in art that so often romanticizes fast-paced maneuvers, spontaneity, and surprise? Chapter 1 considered the relational geographies of predictive policing and anti-riot reform in Los Angeles to illuminate links between the "hit-and-run" tactics of Chris Burden and Asco. This chapter troubles the privileging of hit-and-run tactics in discussions of guerrilla art interventions by turning to work characterized by persistent staying or slow-going occupations of civic, educational, or social spaces. In keeping with the book's overarching goals, this chapter explores the interlaced realities of structural power that challenge and motivate Piper's and Toche's negotiation of forms of slowness and *in-action* in their performance-based conceptual art of the mid-1970s.

Adjacent to Toche's collaborations with Hendricks and his solo mode of open letter–writing, Piper, also active in New York City, practiced a more subtle form of persistence, exploring concepts of form and antiform, self and other, deception and legibility, abstraction and myth through actions, meta-writing, and observations. Piper was born in 1948 in New York and grew up in what she once described as "one of the very last middle-class, light-skinned black families left in our Harlem neighborhood."[11] Although her experimentation with visual art began earlier, she gained recognition in the 1960s as a conceptual artist experimenting with minimalist sculptural constructions. In the early 1970s, she began exploring performance-based situations of social alienation in public spaces, as seen in her *Catalysis* series.

As a continuation of her investment in doing away with discrete forms to create unmediated art experiences, Piper began developing *The Mythic Being*, a conceptual artwork that would manifest in various sites as a series of actions and ideas and simultaneously as sequences of images and posters, between 1973 and 1976. When Piper first began to conceptualize *The Mythic Being*, the work was about the process of letting go, and being freed of, her personal history and its materialization:

> I was trying to develop my arena by becoming an object in it. I now want to become the arena itself; I want to be, for a while, a consciousness within which I view myself and other objects. I'm thinking of a ghostly spectator, eternally viewing, taking in everything, recording and reflecting on everything, but not being an object or refraction him-herself because invisible.[12]

Between January 1973 and January 1974, Piper described altering her appearance and behavior, a process she would come to recognize during this period as the manifestation of the Mythic Being. In August 1973, for example, she donned a "short auburn wig, reflecting sunglasses, white turtleneck/shirt, black pants" to attend "public events: gallery openings, concerts, dance concerts, panels, museums, etc."[13] The prompt she set was straightforward: "Give myself in appearance and behavior to the disguise and the context in which I assume it," in order to practice "external public behavior" while maintaining "internal private mental events."[14] Soon, she referred to this altered appearance as a "witness disguise," noting a desire to take on "more 'masculine' body movements and behavior," an act that performance studies scholar Tavia Nyong'o has explored in depth as one that "extends a queer and even trans imaginary" of becoming.[15]

In a short film produced by artist Peter Kennedy, the Mythic Being appears strutting through crowded Manhattan streets (fig. 2.2). As Piper wrote in September 1973, it was her intention to use the figure to explore "identity dispersion, object dispersion/fragmentation. Transcendence of the personal" by "becoming someone else, someone without a personal history."[16] By January 1974, Piper identified the "M.B. as an alternative of myself," defining a "mythic being" as a "fictious or abstract personality that is generally part of a story or folktale used to explain or sanctify social or legal institutions or natural phenomena."[17]

In the summer of 1974, Piper moved from Manhattan to Cambridge, Massachusetts, to begin graduate study in philosophy at Harvard. Between 1974 and 1975, as she pursued her doctoral degree, the Mythic Being "cruised white women" from the steps of Widener Library near Harvard Square (fig. 2.3), "mugged" a friend and collaborator, David Auerbach, in the Cambridge Commons, and "loitered" on benches near Harvard Square. The Mythic Being also attended social gatherings, "'crashing' middle- and upper-middle-class white

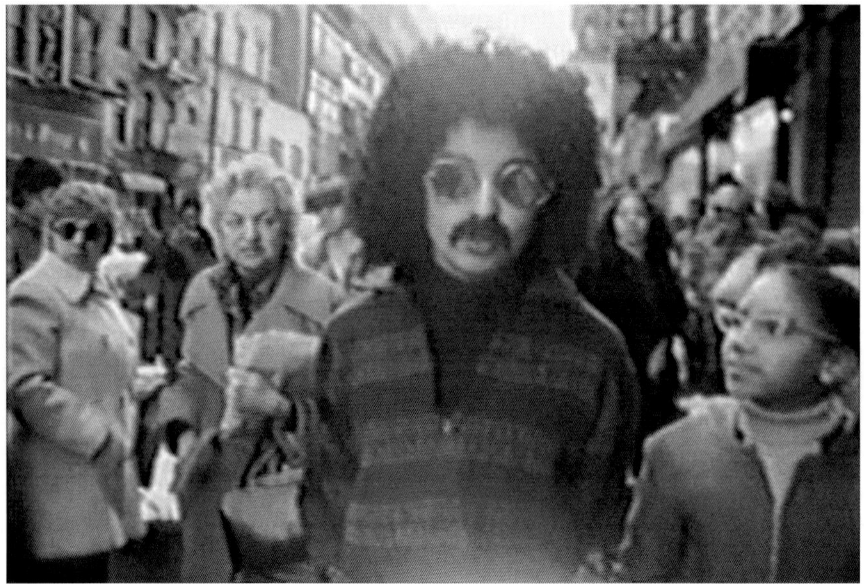

[2.2] Adrian Piper, *The Mythic Being*, 1973. Video, 8 minutes; excerpted segment from the film *Other Than Art's Sake* by Peter Kennedy. Detail: video still at 00:06:20. Collection of the Adrian Piper Research Archive (APRA) Foundation Berlin. © APRA Foundation Berlin.

[2.3, facing page] Adrian Piper, *The Mythic Being: Cruising White Woman*, 1975. Performance documentation. Three silver gelatin prints, each 8 × 10 inches (20.3 × 25.4 cm). Detail: photograph #3 of 3. Documentation photo: James Guttmann. Collection of Eileen Harris Norton. © Adrian Piper Research Archive (APRA) Foundation Berlin.

social contexts . . . (the theater, gallery openings, museums, Harvard teas, Cambridge coffee houses, etc.)."[18]

While there is no evidence that either Toche or Piper directly influenced the other, it is likely each was aware of the other's work by the mid-1970s. Both were included in the 1975 exhibition *Lives: Artists Who Deal with People's Lives (Including Their Own) as the Subject or Medium of Their Work*, organized by Jeffrey Deitch at the Fine Arts Building art space. Prior to that, Piper and Toche ran in similar circles in New York City. Toche was active within the Art Workers Coalition, which Piper joined in 1970, though her membership was short-lived.[19] And it is possible Piper would have read about Toche's 1974 arrest while flipping through the *Village Voice*—a paper she likely perused regularly, as she had begun publishing images of the Mythic Being in its ad section, roughly once a month, since September 1973.[20] Conversely, Toche, an avid reader of local news and culture magazines, may have unknowingly seen the Mythic Being staring out at him from the gallery or exhibition ads. In these instances, Toche and Piper create works that "lurk" in the midst of things—to borrow from Piper's lexicon—and animate a particular process of policing, namely the deputizing of discernment.

Deputized discernment is the name I give to the expansion of experiential risk perception developed during the 1970s as federal and state police departments "modernized" their protocols and focused attention on community relations. In response to the 1968 Kerner Report's findings on the root causes of urban uprisings in the mid- to late 1960s, a nationwide effort to "develop community support for law enforcement" reconceptualized the figure of the police officer as a maker of service work and care.[21] This initiative was part of the 1968 Omnibus Crime and Safe Streets Act—and the only recommendation, of the four provided by the Kerner Report, to be addressed. Other suggestions, historian Elizabeth Hinton notes, such as developing clearer guidelines for arrests based on the anticipation of "victimless crimes" (e.g., vagrancy) were ignored.[22] In the early 1970s, as community policing was implemented, deputized discernment conditioned people not only to "see like the state" but to know action—and, notably, slow movement, idleness, or *in-action*—from the perspective of the state.[23]

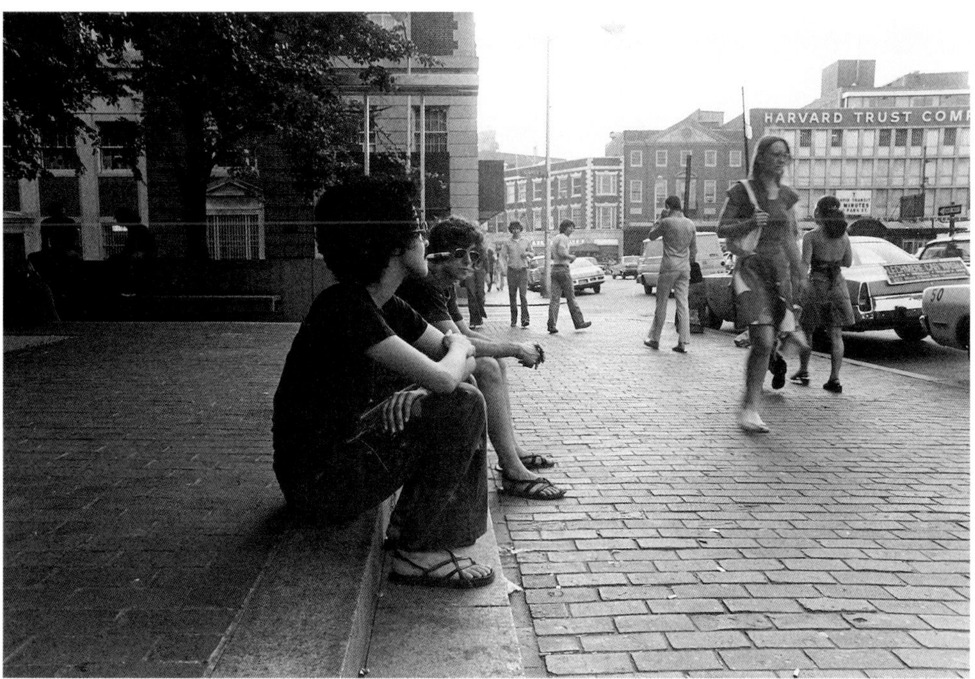

To deputize someone—to make them a deputy—is a deeply relational process. Disciplinary power held by a senior figure within an organization is transposed to a subordinate, who is thereby empowered to act, or speak, on behalf of their superior or the institution. "Deputy" designates a parliamentary representative, and it carries connotations of police power. Deputized discernment is, consequently, the present but often unnamed processes through which the logic of state governance not only becomes internalized by its denizens as a form of embodied knowledge but is communicated as an act of *punitive care*. I borrow here from queer and trans studies scholar and abolitionist theorist Ren-yo Hwang's incisive formulation of "carceral care" versus "deviant care." As Hwang writes, carceral care is enacted in carceral spaces by administrators, medical staff, and guards and exemplified by special education programs for women or in support of queer and trans inmates. Deviant care, by contrast, is a survival economy that exists as a form of support within and against these modes of institutional control presented as humanitarian penal efforts.[24] Where Hwang focuses on what happens inside the prison, the notion of punitive care helps animate the violent euphemism at work outside of prisons within the production of deputized discernment: a perceptual assessment that trains people to reproduce racial spatial orders of exclusion and control while simultaneously legitimizing them as a form of civic service.

While the state has long conditioned surveillance visuality, deputized discernment and punitive care expand in the 1970s alongside liberal reforms of police practices and the criminal code, namely the legislating of a particular class of violations known as "inchoate crimes."[25] Inchoate, meaning "in formation," indicates the anticipation of a future criminal act. Inchoate crimes, in short, are violations that have not yet occurred but might, such as conspiracy, solicitation, and loitering; they are known, more commonly in law practice, as the "crime of attempt" or, reduced further, as "criminal attempt."[26] In the wake of rebellions, government's and law enforcement's efforts to contain activists' coalitional organizing, and the perceived threat of rising crime rates, statutes regulating criminal attempt became the focus of debate and revision.

As discussed in chapter 1, the Anti-Riot Act and the case of *Terry v. Ohio* represent two factors that enhanced the power of police to act based on "reasonable suspicion." In other words, this period sees a relegitimization of police discernment based on the presumption of skillful anticipatory assessments of criminal intent *before* it manifests materially. The reliance on suspicion, with little guidance on how to evaluate it, conceals how criminalizing what has not yet happened is central to the work of the modern "racial state," defined by African American studies and criminology scholar David Theo Goldberg as "producing and reproducing, constituting, and effecting racially shaped spaces and places, groups and events, life world and possibilities, access and restrictions, inclusions and exclusions, conceptions and modes of representation."[27] Supported by both liberals and conservatives, the opportunity for local governments to expand police discretion and define both action and in-action through changes to antiloitering statutes significantly shaped movement in public and civic spaces.[28] Piper and Toche each created work during this period that provides insight into the politics of antiloitering laws, and the relations of gendered, sexualized, and racial violence concealed within policing measures presented as gestures of care-taking.

My argument does not rely on or wish to suggest any direct connection between Piper and Toche. Rather, I am drawn to the ways that each artist's turn to tactics in conceptual art practice, and specifically the notion of loitering, trouble the perceptual infrastructures of punitive contexts that produce and regulate suspicion of in-action and inscrutability. Their works thus allow us, I argue, to sit with deputized discernment, rehearsed in the perception of loitering and the scrutiny of the regulation of social space, and with how this labor grows more diffuse and abstract through liberal police reform. As artist Anthony Romero, a member of Sonic Insurgency Research Group (featured in this book's epilogue), has said of "deputized onlookers," securitization is not just about space but about listening conditioned by what the colonialist state deems too little or too much movement, noise, joy, or rest when it comes to presence in public spaces. Deputizing, he says, is a settler perspective; it is the removal of entities that threaten hegemonic power.[29] Piper and Toche's different but related engagements with the concepts of loitering and lurking illuminate a regularly overlooked complexity in the *activeness* of being still, or tactically occupying space, so often overshadowed in the glamorizing of quick or aggressive confrontations in art classified as guerrilla.

In what follows, I take up Piper's and Toche's distinctive tactical frameworks of art action in the mid-1970s, and their differing relations to the concept of "guerrilla"—Toche's claiming of it, and Piper's subtle theorizing of abstractions of hostility—to trace how each artist upsets commonly held ideas about confrontation and perception within the story of guerrilla art. To better understand the artists' negotiation of persistence and latency as a tactical maneuvering of punitiveness, this chapter analyzes Piper's 1974 *The Mythic Being: Loitering*, enacted in Cambridge, and Toche's 1974 "Open Letter to the Mayor of Boston," which involved an unexpected collaborator, the city's police chief, Robert J. diGrazia.

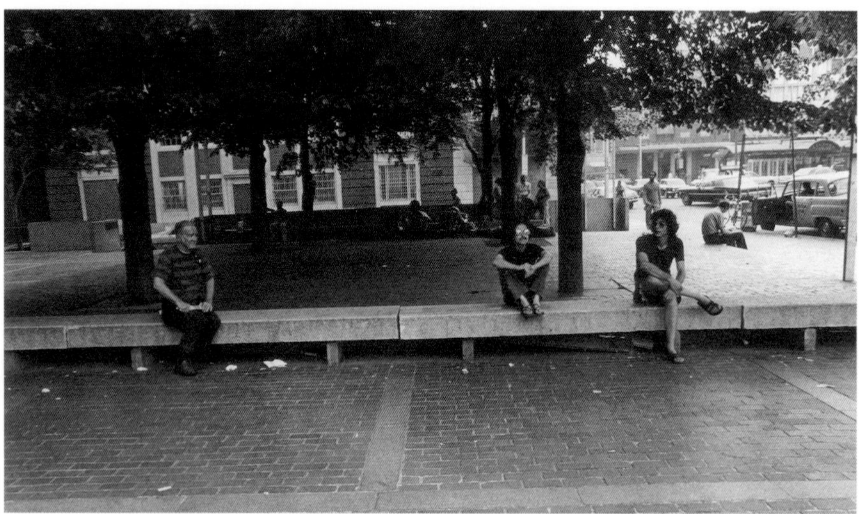

[2.4–2.5] Adrian Piper, *The Mythic Being: Loitering*, 1974. Performance documentation. Two vintage silver gelatin prints, each 8 × 10 inches. Documentation photo: James Guttmann. Collection of the Hirshhorn Museum, Washington, DC. Joseph H. Hirshhorn Purchase Fund, 2009. © Adrian Piper Research Archive (APRA) Foundation Berlin.

A note about latency and persistence: the yellowing typewritten pages comprising "Open Letter to the Mayor of Boston"—two open letters penned by Toche and two reactive letters by diGrazia—sit today in a manila folder at the Getty Research Institute in Los Angeles.[30] While numerous actions of the Guerrilla Art Action Group are represented in the group's recent anthology, this related solo effort by Toche has not yet been displayed or interpreted.[31] Similarly, Piper's Mythic Being series has received much scholarly attention, and yet the two images that constitute the photographic record of *Mythic Being: Loitering* appear relatively infrequently within this robust discourse.[32] Taken together, "Open Letter" and *Loitering*—two works that are, in distinct ways, understated within each artist's discursive footprint—raise important questions about the perception of criminalized in-action in public spaces, and how police, policy makers, artists, and citizens each, in entangled ways, navigated the resettling of punitive power through varying notions of inscrutability.

"A Status, Not a Crime"

The material record of *The Mythic Being: Loitering* consists of two black-and-white photographs taken by Piper's friend Jim Guttmann, then an aspiring pho-

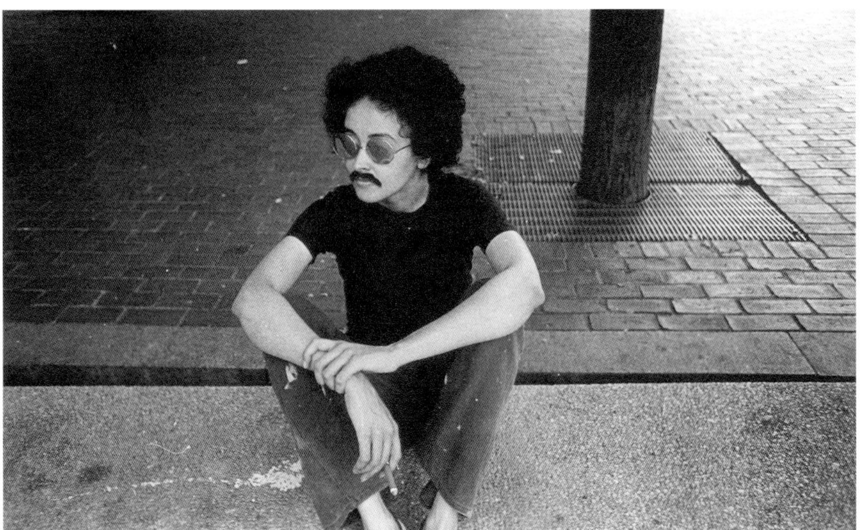

tographer and musician. The action involved Piper, transformed into the Mythic Being, sitting on a cement park bench in Harvard Square for an unspecified amount of time. The bench is in the middle of a sprawling brick plaza next to the Holyoke Center, then Harvard University's Medical Services (fig. 2.4). The Mythic Being, clad in his "witness disguise"—an Afro wig, fake mustache, large reflective sunglasses, jeans, and black T-shirt—appears sculpturelike, elbows resting lightly on knees folded up to his chest.

To the Mythic Being's left, sits a tall, white man, Auerbach, a friend and philosophy doctoral student at MIT, who would become a reoccurring participant in the Cambridge actions, including *Cruising White Women* (mentioned above, fig. 2.3) and *Getting Back*. Auerbach wears shorts, darkened sunglasses, and sandals, and sits with one leg crossed over the other. He is still, gazing beyond the Mythic Being and toward the other end of the bench where an unidentified, middle-aged white man in a striped T-shirt sits holding a rolled magazine. The Mythic Being sits closer to Auerbach but leaves enough space that passersby might think they are strangers, separate. In the second image (fig. 2.5), Guttmann focuses solely on the Mythic Being, close enough to capture the paint splatters on his pants and the cigarillo burning between his fingers.

Harvard Square, the heavily trafficked spot in Cambridge that Piper selects for the Mythic Being to loiter, is located at the busy corner of Massachusetts Avenue ("Mass Ave.") and Dunster Street, just catty-corner to the Harvard Co-op bookstore and Harvard Square subway station. Although the Red Line would later extend north to Somerville and East Arlington, in 1974 Harvard Square was the last stop, a destination populated by small, independent clothing, book, record, and craft shops, music clubs, and restaurants: Duck Soup, Café Pamplona (one of Piper's favorites), La Patisserie Française, a greasy spoon called the Tasty, the music club Passim, and a vibrant, short-lived performance venue called the Performance Center on the top floor of a commercial building still referred to as the Garage.[33] In *Loitering*, people fill the space behind the Mythic Being and Auerbach; they enter and exit the T station, while college-age adults hang out on nearby park benches. The Mythic Being looks like the other people scattered about, taking advantage of the warm weather and passing time, and yet, as the title of Piper's work suggests, the Mythic Being's *in*-action—labeled loitering by Piper—is a pathological motionlessness, potentially subject to punitive response.

Without a critical race framework, loitering might appear to be a by-product of capitalism's centuries-old insistence on temporal efficiency and productivity. *Loiter* and *lurk* have overlapping meanings and, in some dictionaries, crossed etymologies. Both connotate indolence, dawdling, or avoiding work, to which *lurk* adds a sense of furtiveness—watching from concealment or waiting in ambush. Essentially, to occupy a body deemed unproductive (or unreproductive)—not, that is, contributing to capitalist production—is defined as criminal. Within the US state's somewhat different terms of productive mobility, a loiterer is a person whose actions are illegible but must be made knowable within the structures of deputized discernment. Thus, "to loiter" has been defined as "to stand around or move slowly about; to stand idly around; to saunter; to lag behind; to linger or spend time idly."[34] Loitering also takes on a slightly more specific meaning by way of what it lacks:

> to linger or hang around in a public place or business where one has no particular or legal purpose. In many states, cities, and towns there are statutes or ordinances against loitering by which the police can arrest someone who refuses to "move along."[35]

As this definition demonstrates, loitering exists within an infrastructure that delineates who possesses a "legal purpose" to be in a particular space at any given time.

The authority to demand that someone "move along," however, encodes within it a color-blind racism in a society and culture that has, from its foundation, authorized white mobility and criminalized Black Americans' very presence. Although the origins of antiloitering laws have been traced to England's vagrancy codes, implemented to maintain control of the working class during the breakup of feudalism, loitering laws in the US were adapted to constrict the mobility of Black Americans during and after Reconstruction.[36] After the Civil War, for example, emancipated Black men and women were monitored and detained through what legal labor scholar Shirley Lung calls a "mesh of laws," such as "vagrancy, contract enforcement, anti-enticement, and emigrant-agent restrictions [that] prevailed in one form or another in the South until World War II," to ensure whites had "cheap and exploitable labor."[37]

A set of laws known as the Black Codes, enacted between 1865 and 1867, proliferated in the South, essentially making it a crime for Black people not to work under newly implemented vagrancy laws. Michelle Alexander has drawn out the connections between these vagrancy laws and convict labor laws, which simultaneously legalized hiring out detained prisoners to plantation owners and companies. Under the white supremacist logics of "Jim Crow" that followed, these laws helped legalize a new regime of enslavement in the guise of crime control.[38] These laws in turn influenced the development of modern criminality and our carceral society; they helped shape antiloitering statutes in the North during the late nineteenth century and were used as the basis for statutes against begging (because such people "lacked compulsion to work").[39] As Lung explains, "These laws formed the backbone of a coercive apparatus that sought to push Black men and women back into forced labor, reinforced by restrictions on their mobility to seek alternative employment." Collectively, vagrancy laws "empowered sheriffs and police to 'round up' and arrest Blacks who did not have labor contracts."[40] Inculcated within and against such antiblack place-making, a number of laws in the nineteenth and twentieth centuries—such as the Naturalization Act of 1870, Page Act of 1875 (not repealed until 1943), Chinese Exclusion Act of 1882, Natural Origins Act of 1924, and so on—legalized the anti-Asian exploitation and control of Chinese and Japanese immigrants, thereby further consolidating the ability to displace and constrict nonwhite bodies as a tenet of structural whiteness.[41]

These laws are not isolated instances of racism. They are part of the larger workings of racial capitalism, "an economic system through which the built environment, ideas, and knowledge, as well as sign systems and feelings, are organized into different kinds of places," as Black feminist and queer geographer Treva Ellison writes. Building upon the work of Cedric Robinson and Ruth Wilson Gilmore, Ellison explains how these different kinds of places "facilitate the extraction of surplus value, which, transformed into capital, has concentrated in the hands of white people, men, and property owners."[42] With a focus on Blackness, Ellison draws out how these relations spatialize and create "Black vulnerability" through the "legal management of harm." Through this management, the figure of the "protected citizen," dependent on "abstracting the spatial relationship between harm, violence, and multiple embodiments of blackness," emerges as a centerpiece, producing what Ellison calls a "carceral geography."[43] The idea of loitering, which relies on the classification of certain actions as "unprotectable" behavior, thus manufactures people who are "continuously out of place."[44] Given this, it's also possible to see how antiloitering laws do not reflect racial logics but *produce* racially gendered and sexualized punitive subjects through the regulation of bodies marked as inherently out of place. By conditioning people in public spaces to take part in the process of discerning inaction as criminal, the accepted concept of loitering serves to neutralize the white supremacist underpinnings of "placelessness" protected by the police.

In her book *Wayward Lives, Beautiful Experiments*, a poignant study of the policing of Black survival and the tactics used by Black women and men to enact fugitive world-making under these conditions, Saidiya Hartman explains that for Black Americans, and especially Black women, "vagrancy was a status, not a crime."[45] This *status*, she explains, is a cornerstone of antiblack racism, shaping the development of "status criminality" tethered to the status of Blackness in both public and private spaces, from the hallway of the tenement house to the hallowed halls of Congress.[46]

Hartman's consideration of vagrancy and risk-taking is instructive here. She writes specifically of risk-taking in relation to the history of antiloitering laws and the threat of being "rounded up," and centers risk-taking discourse squarely within the long arc of lawmaking historically grounded in white supremacist efforts to protect whiteness through the control and oppression of Black women and men; one way to do this was by policing Black leisure and desire entirely, reframing it as a punishable threat. As Hartman asserts, "Risk was the metric for tabulating future crimes and this foreshadowing determined the outcomes of young black women already targeted and vulnerable to myriad forms of state violence" and the enforcement of "wayward minor laws" that constricted not just the movement but the stillness (enjoyment and rest) of Black Americans, a way of bringing daily survival under the jurisdiction of police and the courts.[47] Dressed as the Mythic Being in Harvard Square, sitting quietly on a bench near Harvard's campus, Piper's experimentation with loitering is at once the artist's introspection and, I argue, a work that raises important questions about the *making* of punitive contexts in the 1970s wherein racialized and gendered inertia or in-action becomes "data" and a requisite target of deputized discernment.

To be clear, I am not suggesting that Piper created *Loitering* as a commentary on the racial roots of antivagrancy laws or their continuation into the 1970s. To the contrary, her notes tracking the evolution of *The Mythic Being* convey the work's introspective, apolitical underpinnings rooted in philosophical questions of self and other. Piper strived for the figuration of the Mythic Being to be "portable," untethered from time and place, with "no particular context or matrix in relation to which he has special significance."[48] A January 1975 note expresses concern with the figuration of the Mythic Being inevitably becoming localized and legible within a particular environment, a condition that could undermine the intentions of the piece:

> Recently, I have become more preoccupied with the iconography, with the Mythic Being as a marker, sign, or symbol of the Mythic Being himself: the abstract entity, the semifictional hero who exists partly in me and partly independent of me. I regard his image and see both that he is me and that he is completely inscrutable to me.[49]

Even as Piper's theorizing of inscrutability invited a kind of liberatory misrecognition of herself, for herself and others, the figure of the Mythic Being also, inevitably, came to operate in the world. Whereas in New York (1973–1976) the Mythic Being consisted of performances, documentary images, and ads, as well as verbal and written meta-reflections, when she left to live in Cambridge, Piper notes:

> I found the image of the Mythic Being becoming a foil for many of my fantasies of power, aggression, and secrecy: The smaller and less anonymous the environment became, the more I wanted to make an imprint on it, which I did by inviting the participation of other people and photo-documenting many of the actual street performances.[50]

Journaling in January 1976, Piper reflects on how the Mythic Being, visible by virtue of his Afro, mustache, sunglasses, and hypermasculine desire and aggression, was also legible as a "static emblem of alien confrontation . . . an abstract, generalized, faintly unholy embodiment of expressed hostility, fear, anxiety, and estrangement."[51] Years later, looking back on the work, Piper would describe the Mythic Being in terms linked with a wider international imaginary of aggression, writing that he was "my seeming opposite: a third-world, working-class, overtly hostile male."[52]

In various art-historical discussions of *The Mythic Being*, Piper's use of "third-world" to retroactively describe the Mythic Being has been addressed as a matter of ideological affiliation. The art historian John Bowles asserts that the classification as used by Piper is "more political than racial," in that the visual reference of the Afro had "assumed iconic significance among the world's youth culture and liberation movements because it had been embraced by black radicals in the late 1960s, including the Black Panthers and Ron Karenga's US Organization."[53] Elsewhere, art historian Cherise Smith emphasizes the significance of Piper's use of the term "third-world" rather than "Black," which Piper uses later in the 1990s, explaining, "Piper's word choice does double duty: it suggests a political affiliation that was popular among leftist people of color at the time, and it allows circumvention of the specifics of the persona's racial or ethnic designation."[54] Both Bowles's and Smith's analysis underscore the ways that this affiliation evokes the referential context of Black and brown power, by then synonymous in the US with the visuality of guerrilla tactics and their ethnoracial coalitional possibilities. "Third-world," associated with guerrilla insurgency, was also an object of police scrutiny.

In addition to being a political and ideological affiliation, "third-world," like "guerrilla," can be understood as a concept central to the making and shoring up of punitive relations: people who were classified thus by the government and police were aggressively surveilled. Not only that, but the FBI, law enforcement, and lawmakers seeking to contain coalitional praxis in the late 1960s and early 1970s conceptualized this conflation as a carceral object lesson. The internal reports tracking "advocates of guerrilla warfare," as well as the "wanted" list compiled by the FBI, which included Harry Gamboa Jr., alongside Angela Davis and Black Panther leaders, relied on the fantasy that one's affiliation or sympathy with third-world liberation wars was embodied, trackable, and knowable in advance.

At this time, simply wearing an Afro meant opening oneself to an increased likelihood of punitive encounter. The Afro, as historian Richard Powell recalls, was considered as "treacherous and charged" as "the African American who wore it." "It was possible," one article in *Ebony* explained, "to determine the degree of a woman's militancy by the state of her hair. Only the brave dared to 'do the thing' and naturals were encountered almost exclusively on picket lines, at civil rights meetings, and protest demonstrations."[55] When, for example, Angela Davis went underground to flee unfounded accusations of murder and conspiracy, hundreds of black women sporting large Afros like her were incorrectly identified by law enforcement as Davis and arrested.[56] In 1974, when Patty Hearst, a white woman, was a fugitive, internal FBI documentation circulated an image of her disguised in an Afro wig. The latter document indicates how visual references to gendered and sexualized Black power, enlarged through affiliation with third-world anticolonial movements had become a mythic figuration for police—one aligned with the "static emblem of alien confrontation" to borrow from Piper's theorizing of a Mythic Being—that was transferable and wearable.

Years later, in 1992, Piper changed her description of the Mythic Being from a "third-world" man, referring to him instead in a public lecture as "in drag as a young black male."[57] Uri McMillan has astutely interpretated the significance of the persona's evolution, asserting, "The Mythic Being does not represent any particular person, but is rather a fantasy, an avatar of third-world (later, black) masculinity in the national imaginary."[58] Later in the 1992 lecture, Piper speaks more directly about the racial politics at play within *The Mythic Being*, the making of which gave her insight, as a lighter-complexioned Black woman mistaken at times for white (as documented in her work, *Calling (Card) #1)*, into "what it is like for visibly black Americans to simply move through the world in any social context that is primarily populated by white people."[59] While Piper initially described her experimentation with the Mythic Being as one invested in escaping her past and becoming imperceptible to herself, the antiblack racism at work within police discernment makes legal debates of the 1970s—specifically those confronting the unconstitutionality of antiloitering laws—another generative context in which to situate *Loitering* and continue assessing the conceptual insights it has to offer today.

Inscrutability and "Plus" Laws

Indeed, Piper created *Loitering* at a time when national and statewide shifts in the social perception of idleness, and new court decisions regarding the legal definition of loitering and vagrancy in the United States, altered these concepts forever. During the 1970s, "idleness" became an increasingly loaded euphemism for the asymmetrical impacts of the high unemployment and high inflation that resulted in "stagflation." This, compounded by a shift to nonindustrial work via globalization, as Alexander notes, saw rising rates of joblessness that most heavily impacted Black men in quickly dissipating inner-city, blue-collar factory jobs.[60]

The 1974 Juvenile Justice and Delinquency Prevention Act (an amendment to the 1968 Omnibus Crime Control and Safe Streets Act), authorized heightened policing of unemployed "idle" young men—disproportionately Black—and framed them as an anticipated threat to be preemptively removed.[61] The act was the first major piece of domestic police legislation signed by Gerald Ford. As the White House deputy chief of staff, Dick Cheney, summarized in a memo to the president, "The data points out that most of our violent crime is committed by a relatively small number of individuals, and with the right kind of effort we could substantially reduce the crime rate simply by taking them off the streets."[62] The act sought to reduce racial and ethnic disparities through "data-driven approaches," but the language of dispersal ("taking them off the streets") relied upon and reinforced racist ideas of who was protectable and who was inherently out of place.

It was no coincidence that the constitutionality of laws related to police dispersal came under legal review as aggressive patrolling, boosted by funds from the federal "war on crime," occurred in cities nationwide. In the late 1960s and early 1970s, challenges to the constitutionality of local loitering and vagrancy laws reached the Supreme Court. Some, basing their claims on the due process clause of the Fourteenth Amendment, hinged on the court's "void for vagueness" doctrine. Two landmark cases in the early 1970s, in particular, changed the legal context of loitering and its discernment by police and citizens alike. In *Coates v. City of Cincinnati* (1971), the Supreme Court heard a case in which Cincinnati police had charged Dennis Coates, a Black college student, and four other students with violating an ordinance that deemed it a crime for three or more persons to gather in public "and there conduct themselves in a manner annoying to persons passing by."[63] Coates argued that "annoying" was too vague and thereby an unconstitutional infringement on his rights. Had Coates not been a Black student, it is questionable whether the gathering would have been policed at all.

In the *Coates* decision, the Supreme Court utilized the "void for vagueness" doctrine and reversed Cincinnati's 1956 law. Writing for the majority, Justice Potter Stewart noted that the ordinance violated the First Amendment rights to freedom of assembly and association, since city officials could silence expressive activities by classifying them as annoying.[64] In the second landmark case, the following year, *Papachristou v. City of Jacksonville* built off the momentum of *Coates* and redefined the labor of discerning loitering. The case is named for Margaret Papachristou, one of four defendants, all in the same car, who were arrested and charged with "prowling" under the Jacksonville, Florida, vagrancy ordinance. Papachristou was a white woman, as was the other female defendant, Betty Calloway; the other two were Black men, Eugene Eddie Melton and Leonard Johnson. The officers denied that the group's racial makeup was a factor in the arrest, yet records show that one of the arresting officers phoned Papachristou's parents on the evening of her arrest to tell them she had "been out with a negro."[65]

As in *Coates*, the Supreme Court determined that Jacksonville's ordinance was "void for vagueness." Justice William Douglas, writing for the majority, dissected the clause "wandering or strolling around from place to place without any lawful purpose or object," which lower courts had construed to include travel by car: "wandering and strolling," he wrote, "are historically part of the amenities of life as we have known them . . . [and] have been, in part, responsible for giving our people the feeling of independence and self-confidence, the feeling of creativity." Meanwhile, "the qualification 'without any lawful purpose or object' may be a trap for innocent acts."[66]

While *Papachristou* is touted as a major "win" for liberals and police reformists, the court's decision does not address the spatialized racial politics and history of antimiscegenation laws underpinning the dynamics at play in the original case. As preeminent legal scholar Dorothy Roberts explains in her canonical study "Race, Vagueness, and the Social Meaning of Order-Maintenance Policing," the parts of the Constitution that aim to protect citizens' personal liberty to move freely on the streets are typically discussed in "race-neutral terms," though in practice this vagueness can result in "a particular racial injury."[67] This original racial injury was reproduced in the months following *Papachristou* when, responding to the unconstitutional vagueness of antiloitering laws, local governments enacted "loitering *plus*" laws, statutes that claimed to narrow the definition of loitering so as to mitigate vagueness.

"Loitering plus" laws added elements intended to clarify the criminal component of motionlessness or slow-moving acts but in reality reintroduced vague delineations that further expanded unchecked police discretion. For example, New York state implemented four such laws, declaring, "A person is guilty of loitering when he: 1. Loiters, remains or wanders about in a public place for the purpose of begging; 2. Loiters or remains in a public place for the purpose of gambling with cards, dice, or other gambling paraphernalia; 3. Loiters or remains in a public place for the purpose of engaging or soliciting another person to engage, in oral sexual conduct . . . or 4. Being masked or in any manner disguised by unusual or unnatural attire or facial alteration, loiterers, remain or congregate in a public place with other persons so masked and disguised."[68]

The first clause criminalizes poverty (as a threat to the members and functionality of capitalist society); the second, leisure and opportunism (the kind that operates outside the holdings of the state and its capitalist structures); the third, sex work, desire, and enjoyment (as a threat to conventional structures of heterosexual reproduction—the emphasis on "oral sex" was also a way of criminalizing cruising sites and queer intimacy); and the last, inscrutability, whether expressed individually or as part of a gathering of similarly "unnatural" people. Conversely, certain people and behaviors—legible as white and middle class, and hetero-masculine or feminine—are afforded the right to be in place even when out of place. These laws presume to define loitering itself more concretely but expand police discretion to define as criminal individuals with perceived intentions of begging, gambling, cruising, sex, or, in the fourth statute, simply being illegible or suspicious: "unnatural."[69]

As Roberts explains, "Vague laws are likely to be imposed upon disempowered racial groups, and may not be experienced by privileged groups at all. This racial discrimination, then, is an integral part of the law's due process violation and a central reason for limiting police discretion."[70] "The point of vague loitering laws," she writes—and not a mere by-product—is that

> they permit the police to haul off the streets people who *look* suspicious even though they have committed no criminal conduct. . . . Loitering laws inevitably involve judgments about people's criminal propensity. They embody legislative predictions about the likelihood that people engaged in certain activities, bearing certain characteristics, or belonging to certain groups will engage in criminal activity.[71]

In succinct summary, Roberts spells out the ultimate goal of antiloitering laws: "removing crime-prone people from the streets before they have a chance to break the law."[72] Tellingly, mechanisms of accountability for the policing of inchoate crimes were, and remain, woefully inadequate. In the 1970s, as "plus laws" were introduced, courts did not formulate guidelines for the evaluation of suspicion or whether such circumstances "warrant alarm for the safety of persons or property."[73] As late as 2005, a report found that no major study in the field of criminology had yet analyzed *how* police develop and define suspicion despite its centrality to policing.[74]

It is unclear whether Massachusetts adapted its own set of "plus" laws; if it opted to establish regulations like New York's, Piper's *Loitering* transgresses at least one of them, namely the ban on unnaturalness. In a "witness disguise," Piper lurks—to use her term—in an unobtrusive artwork wherein she aims to become unrecognizable to herself and others. But also, I suggest, she lurks within the contradictions of coming to know and recognize loitering itself. Viewers of these black-and-white images, I propose, are positioned simultaneously as the eyes of the state and as potential collaborators, like Auerbach and Guttmann, in Piper's philosophical explorations. Viewers are invited to sweep the scene, thereby also inhabiting a position of lingering, becoming a person who could be seen as staying in-active for too long and told to "move on." In effect, viewers are asked to

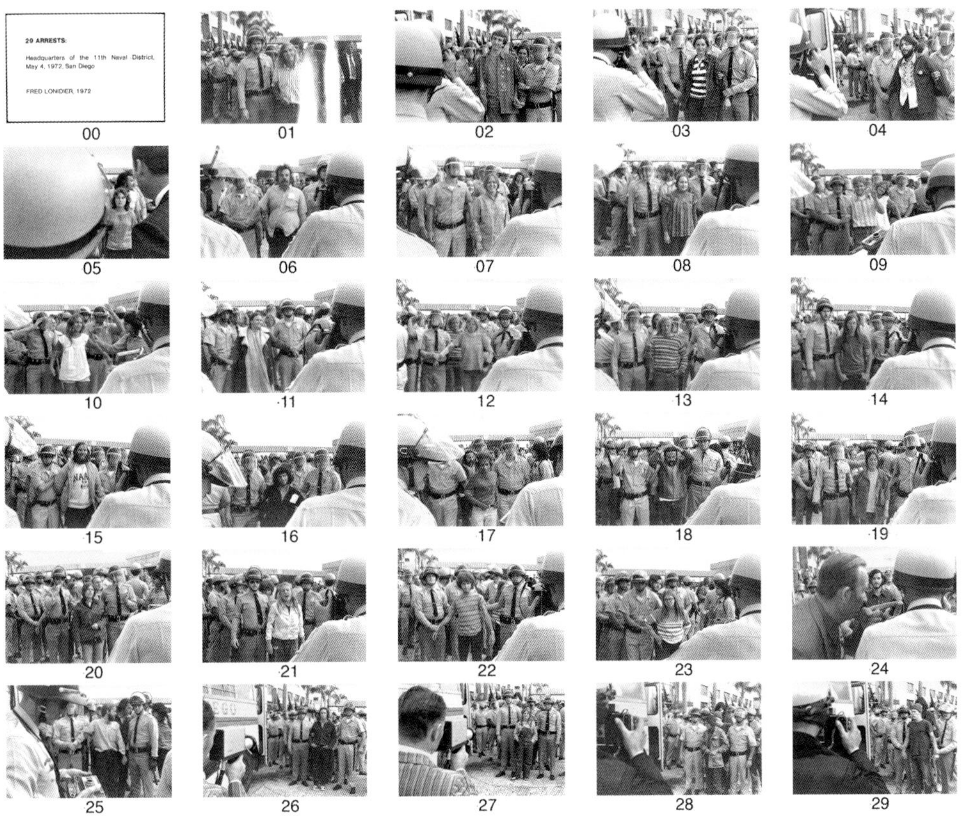

[2.6] Fred Lonidier, *29 Arrests: Headquarters of the 11th Naval District, May 4, 1972, San Diego*, 1972. Black-and-white photographs. © Fred Lonidier. Courtesy of the artist.

imagine not only the loitering practiced by the Mythic Being but to internalize *punitive care*, enacted in the name of public safety. In turn, this kind of looking solicits imaginings of what "safe" or "protected" forms of stillness are vis-à-vis motionlessness deemed potentially criminal.[75]

A deceptively simple question arises: what do we *see* when we look at Piper's *Loitering*? Art historically, these images operate in dialogue with conceptual photography emerging during the 1970s, in particular a strain wherein artists such as Hans Haacke, Asco, Martha Rosler, Allan Sekula, Fred Lonidier, and others sought to unseat the assumed objectivity of visual evidence, archives, and governance. Lonidier's *29 Arrests: Headquarters of the 11th Naval District, May 4, 1972* (fig. 2.6) offers a compelling example. While attending an antiwar Moratorium protest staged in San Diego, Lonidier saw that an officer was photographing the arrests of protestors and decided to make his own images, standing directly behind him, replicating his line of vision. The protesters in these photos had blocked the entrance to the naval headquarters, and when they did not move they were arrested by a majority-white group of officers on charges of trespassing on federal property, unlawful assembly, and failure to disperse.

In Lonidier's photographs, the "riot" helmet of the officer taking the photos serves as a recurring visual anchor. In ten of the twenty-nine photographs, the person being arrested smiles, locking eyes with Lonidier and not the officer in front of him. Whereas punitive encounters at civil rights and antiwar protests composed predominantly of people of color typically resulted in aggressive arrests if not lethal police violence (as documented with the 1970 National Chicano Moratorium, discussed in chapter 1), the officers at the naval headquarters show great restraint. As Huffa Frobes-Cross asserts, Lonidier reclaimed the photographic gaze of the police and its archive by creating a counterarchive. By "undermining the representational authority of the police," he humanized the protesters, and presented their plight to a more sympathetic audience (the images appeared soon after in Lonidier's MFA thesis show at the University of California, San Diego).[76] Like Lonidier's series, Piper's *Loitering* records deputized vision, but it offers a different lesson in perception: there are no officers in the scene and no arrests recorded; instead, the *absent presence* of these markers and the invitation to look for future criminality collapse the labor of discerning loitering with the act of unseeing the police (normalizing their abundant lurking).

It is worth noting that Piper's subtle loitering in a witness disguise went unnoticed and unregistered in Cambridge. Jim Guttmann, the work's documentary photographer, recalls, "No one said anything to us" and "we didn't make a big deal out of what we were doing."[77] Nevertheless, the presence of police in Harvard Square, was known and expected. Guttmann recalls one officer, referred to as "Benny the Cop," who was in his face whenever he, an aspiring musician, busked in the area.[78] This was part of the political life of a musician and, for that matter, of a visual artist experimenting with public space; at the time, Guttman explains, there was no formal way to get a permit or to request permission to make art in public space. With the introduction of a permit process in the late 1970s, the definition of loitering, and its relation to artmaking, would again change. The documentary images of *Loitering* occupy a particular moment, a post-*Papachristou*, pre-permit notion of lurking.

Within surveilled spaces that make and protect whiteness, sitting, being still, and occupying space are not—for people who are visibly Black, Asian, brown,

Indigenous, or nonwhite and racially ambiguous—neutral acts; they're what Black studies scholar La Merr Jurelle Bruce describes as "radical inertia." Bruce ruminates on loitering as a strategy of refusing the very structures of formlessness or aimlessness weaponized against Black and brown people. Dictionaries, he notes, define "loiter" as "to remain in an area for *no obvious reason*" or "to linger aimlessly or *as if* aimless." "Both definitions," he observes, "hold that loitering *appears* to lack purpose, but the *appearance* of aimlessness might conceal a truth of deliberation, strategy, and care."[79] Piper's *Loitering*, as an exercise in witnessing the misrecognition of oneself, contests the aimlessness ascribed to the action of "being out of place." The Mythic Being's act is productive, not aimless, creating a paradoxical relation of pathologized in-action; it draws out the ideological criminalizing of in-action by reflecting on the regulation of space, subject formation, and intention.

Bruce incisively proposes a "praxis of loitering: a willful, ethical, critical, radical inertia when the anti-black officer barks 'keep it moving'; or the gentrifying sign reads 'no loitering'; or the right-wing cable news pundit insists that you just 'get over' and 'move past' the still-unfurling devastation of chattel slavery and Jim Crow." I am reminded of *Catalysis* (fig. 2.1): how Piper stands beneath a NO STANDING sign in New York City with a protruding towel stuffed in her mouth, a leather purse casually slung over her shoulder. Her act of standing and inhabiting this space in the city, deemed "out of place" by the sign above her, underscores architectures of belonging and dispossession. Bruce explains that "radical inertia" is a loitering that

> queers and signifies upon the legal category of 'vagrancy,' which was enshrined in (anti-)Black Codes throughout the US South after the Civil War. . . . Whereas fugitivity, wandering, waywardness, and derangement are modes of *motion* defying modern mandates for 'proper' movement, loitering is slowness or *stillness* that violates said mandates. The fugitive goes when told to stay, while the loiterer stays when told to go.[80]

Borrowing from Bruce, it is possible to see how Piper signifies upon the seeming stability of a visual field that would allow police officers to discern her forms of in-action as a threat; how stillness is a form of movement critical to the making of risk perception in art and America.

Antiloitering laws can be understood, then, as shorthand for the state's preemptive framing of in- or underaction as a criminal unproductivity. The antiloitering perception is also a learned deputized discernment: an attunement to the threshold of too little or too much action in race- and gender-neutral terms of nuisance, safety, and order. Moreover, to be able to discern what is active or radical inertia within the seeming nonaction in the documentary images of Piper's work is thus to be (or become) literate in deputized discernment.

If loitering, as a concept, trains people to perceive in-action through punitive relations, then Piper's work offers a look at deputized discernment itself, and enlists viewers as co-conveners. *Loitering*, I want to suggest, provides not a panoptic gaze (the all-seeing state internalized) but a furtive portrait of the making of relational punitive literacies that expand outward, and ripple across time (never fixed, but constantly changing based on one's sense of being in or out of place). As such, it helps draw out the pathologizing of in-action and the routinized production of "reasonable suspicion" that presents a productive challenge to readings of tactics that only look at the individual, and the temporariness of the action, rather than the referential field of coming to know being in or out of place. As Piper shared in a 1990 interview, sometimes her Harvard colleagues passed her in the street while she was the Mythic Being but didn't *see* her: "People don't see except what they're trained to perceive as familiar."[81] Alongside Toche's "Open Letter," discussed in the following section, *Loitering* animates the ways that literacy in punitiveness—specifically within moments of self-making and estrangement—is itself conceptual, performative, and collectively managed.

Toche and diGrazia's Exchange: Discernment as Skill

Throughout the month of October 1974, artist Jean Toche and Boston police chief Robert diGrazia created a conceptual work that bridged mail art, revolutionary communiques, police work, and civic engagement. The exchange began on October 8, when Toche sent an open letter to the US attorney general in response to a horrific act of racial violence. A day earlier, Andre Yvon Jean-Louis, a thirty-three-year-old Black Haitian Bostonian, had been assaulted by a group of white men and women protesting the racial integration of Boston's schools.

Jean-Louis, on his way to pick up his wife from work, was stuck in a traffic jam on Dorchester Street.[82] Nearby, white protesters had gathered at the intersection near South Boston's Old Colony housing project, angry about the racial integration of black and white students. Southie—"97% Irish and 100% white"—was, as a report in the Weather Underground's clandestine paper *Osawatomie* put it, "the nerve center of the racist movement. Along Broadway, Southie's main street, are the offices of the American Nazi Party, the White People's National Socialist Party, and the South Boston Information Center. One window has a poster which says, 'Stop the Black Terror from Roxbury.'"[83] The white demonstrators surrounded Jean-Louis's car, rocked it from side to side, and when he ran from the vehicle, pursued and brutally beat him. Police officers at the scene fired warning shots to disperse the attack.[84]

This kind of assault had become common across Boston since September, following US district judge Arthur Garrity's order in June that Boston racially integrate its public schools at the start of the upcoming school year.[85] Boston school administrators immediately began the process of busing approximately eighteen thousand students to new schools; students from the largely Black areas of Roxbury and Mattapan were sent to the mostly white neighborhoods of South Boston ("Southie") and Hyde Park, and vice versa. In 1973, even before Garrity's mandate, white women in South Boston had organized under the name Restore Our Alienated Rights (ROAR) in anticipation of a court order. At ROAR demonstrations, white women and men carried signs—"Whites Have Rights"—and some even wore white berets, appropriating the symbolism of Black and brown liberation that was by then highly visible in the United States.[86]

On September 12, the opening day of school in Southie, hundreds of white demonstrators, including children and their parents, pelted a caravan of twenty school buses carrying Black students from Roxbury with rocks. Regina Williams, a young Black student who had been on one of these buses, described the scene as a "war zone."[87] One police officer, witnessing the deployment of the Tactical Police Force to quell protests, called Southie and Roxbury "a scene of open guerrilla warfare," and others deemed the conflict a "second Vietnam."[88] Inside the schools, the relations of violence manifest in the whiteness of the space itself, rendered visible in a poignant press photograph taken of Valerie Banks seated amid a sea of empty chairs on September 12, 1974 (fig. 2.7). She was the only student to show up for her geography class on the first day of school at South Boston High School; the empty chairs as a metonymic form materialize the exclusionary sociospatial field of whiteness that renders bodies in and out of place through the antiblack withholding of time and resources. Here, her sitting inhabits a radical inertia. The image provides a portrait of the ways that logics of whiteness produce instances of racialized "idleness" or "motionlessness," as part of its perceived "right" to order space and time.

The turmoil and violence weren't unique to Boston. "Busing is a political time bomb," one reporter wrote in 1974, as integration mandates and protests took place across the country—from New York, Providence, and Trenton to Pontiac, Detroit, Denver, and Pasadena.[89] "Busing," Nikole Hannah-Jones explains incisively, is a "race-neutral euphemism" for something that was anything but neutral: white opposition to integration, which by definition ignored the structural violence of resource hoarding and exclusionary practices upon which the protests rested.[90] The issue was not merely the busing of students from one neighborhood to another, but the court-ordered action to break the educational caste system. As reflected in the press photo of Banks, this issue would not be resolved once white students, who felt they had a right to boycott the very presence of Black students ("restore our alienated rights" was the chant)—again took their seats.[91] Moreover, when classes resumed, daily school activities would be monitored by armed state police officers who occupied the school for three years. The prolonged presence of law enforcement, of course, did not translate into a safe space. As one reporter covering Boston school integration observed in antiquated language, "Police called in to protect the Blacks have either stood *idly by* or attacked the Blacks."[92]

It was precisely the inadequate efforts of the police to protect Black citizens that Toche set out to address in his tactical conceptual work. In his open letter, Toche condemned the Boston police for racism and inaction. He mailed his statement to attorney general William Saxbe and sent carbon copies to the Boston mayor Kevin White and diGrazia, the police commissioner. It's unclear what Toche expected to happen, but it probably came as an exciting surprise when, a few days later, diGrazia wrote back.

DiGrazia's reply to Toche, dated October 11, is laced with venom: "I received a copy of the contemptible lie which you forwarded to the Attorney General of the United States, in which you recounted an incident that never happened."[93] In just a few sentences, diGrazia dismisses Toche's accusation that he and other police officers covered anything up; he reverses the blame, decrying "blatant lies such as yours which fan the flames of hatred." "You are free to do your dirty work," he asserts, "simply because you are in a country which is strong enough to harbor thousands of your ilk without fear of the harm you can do."

There are two significant things to consider about this and a subsequent round of letters between Toche, an artist, and diGrazia, a police commissioner: (1) the exchange provides a rare firsthand look into the labor of deputized discernment that links artists and police and (2) that the dialogue manifests at all is in large part due to diGrazia's role as a liberal, reformist police commissioner tasked with modernizing Boston's police force. As

[2.7, facing page] Peter Bregg, black-and-white photograph, 1974. As a 2019 caption explained, "Valerie Banks was the only student to show up for her geography class at South Boston High School in 1974 on the first day of court-ordered busing" (Nikole Hannah-Jones, "It Was Never about Busing," *New York Times*, July 19, 2019). © AP Photo.

such, the guerrilla art action that constitutes "Open Letter" embodies two questions crucial to both artistic production and police reform in the mid-1970s: who holds the skills to determine both violence and accountability, and who decides when risk management is artful or a threat?

DiGrazia's counteraccusation implicitly culls from the rhetoric of vermin and infestation, suggesting that Toche's efforts are purposeless, unproductive, and aimless—a mode of loitering—and that his criticism can be tolerated because America is a "free country" but ultimately is unacceptable. Similarly, when Toche was arrested the previous March, he was told by the FBI driver, "Listen boy, if you want to stay in this country, you better start making some money."[94] Echoing this same line of reasoning, diGrazia closes his first letter by attacking what he perceives to be Toche's inadequate production: "If you, as an artist, mirror Nature in the same manner that you depict America, your works must really be something to behold. Go back to your garret."[95] Because it was written on official Boston Police Department letterhead, the letter became a matter of public record rather than private correspondence.

Upon receiving diGrazia's letter, Toche penned a second open letter,

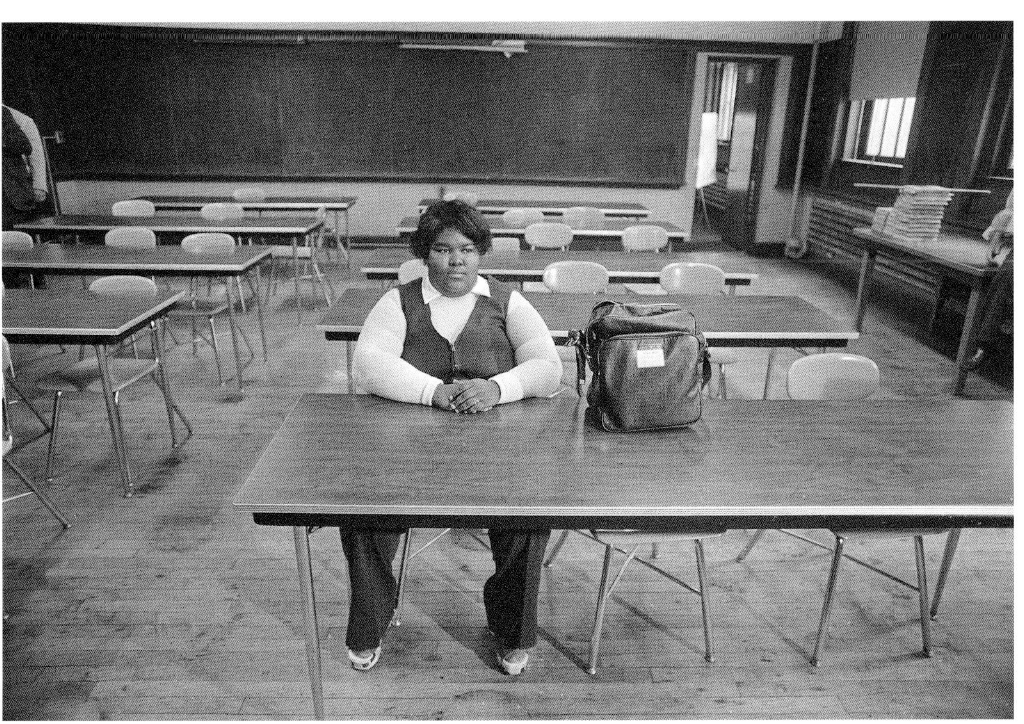

dated October 21 and this time addressed to the police chief's direct supervisor, Mayor White (fig. 2.8). In three terse, numbered points typed on a single page, Toche supports his headline demand for "THE IMMEDIATE RESIGNATION OR FIRING OF BOSTON'S POLICE COMMISSIONER, ROBERT J. diGRAZIA, FOR COVERING UP A RECENT RACIAL INCIDENT IN BOSTON, IN WHICH A WHITE MOB VICIOUSLY ATTACKED A BLACK PERSON."[96] He opens his case with two definitions of "lynch," cited to *Webster's Third New International Dictionary*. The first, "to beat or otherwise do physical violence to by mob action," clearly encompasses the violence described in his second exhibit, a block quote from an article in the most recent *Newsweek*, laying the ground for its describing Jean-Louis's attackers as a "old-time Southern lynch mob with a Boston accent" and undercutting potential objections to linking the violent tactics of Jim Crow–era white supremacists and antibusing vigilantes.[97] Toche closes with the flat denial from diGrazia's October 11 note: "AN INCIDENT THAT NEVER HAPPENED."

DiGrazia's second and final rebuttal arrives quickly. Dated October 23, it makes a pointed effort to undermine Toche's credibility as a discerner of evidence. On a single typed page, again on official letterhead (fig. 2.9), the police chief mockingly adds "Very" to the phrase "Dissident Artist," with which Toche had signed his letter. DiGrazia leads off with two stanzas from a poem by Rudyard Kipling, then writes:

> Your chiaroscuro is showing. Do your concepts of Dark and Light, Black and White, and Things as They Are, ever clash? . . . Your linear perspective and depth perception could also use sharpening. Canvases cry for those kinds of things. Language should be adorned with veracity, its style supported by conclusiveness and an accuracy that may exclude incorrectness, and a sagacity whereby a proper discrimination, or lack of discrimination is attained.[98]

By wielding terms from the bedrock of Western art history — *chiaroscuro, linear perspective, depth perception, canvases, style* — diGrazia positions himself as an authority able to leverage the interpretation of art within the realm of police work and risk perception. In some ways, his letter is the inverse of Toche's strategic use of authorized sources as "evidence." Whereas Toche mobilizes authorial voices (a dictionary definition, the news) to unseat diGrazia, the police commissioner turns to various forms of art making, such as poetry and painting commissions, to refute Toche's artistic authority and assert his own. With sarcastic panache, diGrazia encloses an embroidered police badge, explaining, "I appreciate your

OPEN LETTER TO:
The Mayor of Boston,
Boston, Mass.

October 21, 1974.

A CALL FOR THE IMMEDIATE RESIGNATION OR FIRING OF BOSTON'S POLICE COMMISSIONER, ROBERT J. diGRAZIA, FOR COVERING UP A RECENT RACIAL INCIDENT IN BOSTON, IN WHICH A WHITE MOB VICIOUSLY ATTACKED A BLACK PERSON.

1 - A DEFINITION:
lynch: a) to beat or otherwise do physical violence to by mob action.
b) to hang or otherwise kill by mob action in punishment of a presumed crime or offense.
(Webster Third New International Dictionary)

2 - A QUOTE FROM NEWSWEEK, OCTOBER 21, 1974:
"It was an old-time Southern lynch mob with a Boston accent. Spilling out of a South Boston rally, to protest the court-directed busing of Boston's school-children, the crowd of angry whites spotted Jean-Louis Yvon, a 33-year-old black Haitian immigrant on his way to pick up his wife from work. Chanting and yelling, the whites surrounded Yvon's car and began rocking it, trying to open the doors. Next they smashed the windows, pulled the frantic black man to the street and starting beating him. Yvon broke free and began to run - only to be caught by other whites. One belted him with a club; another kicked him in the groin and boasted: "I showed that nigger, didn't I?"

3 - A QUOTE FROM BOSTON'S POLICE COMMISSIONER ROBERT J. diGRAZIA, IN A LETTER TO JEAN TOCHE OF OCTOBER 11, 1974:

"AN INCIDENT THAT NEVER HAPPENED".

(Robert diGrazia's letter was in answer to a letter written by Jean Toche to the Attorney General of the United States to protest this Boston's lynching, letter dated October 8, 1974)

Jean Toche

Jean Toche,
Dissident artist.
730 Bay Street,
Staten Island,
New York 10304.

[2.8] Jean Toche, "Open Letter to the Mayor of Boston." Jean Brown Papers, GAAG files; 2016.M.14. Box 23, folder 10, October 21, 1974. Typewritten letter on paper. © Manuela Gandini. Courtesy of Getty Research Institute.

Boston Police

Office of the Commissioner
154 Berkeley Street
Boston, Massachusetts 02116
617-536-6700 Emergency 911

October 23, 1974

Ms. Jean Toche
Very Dissident Artist
730 Bay Street
Staten Island, New York

Dear Ms. Toche:

When Earth's last picture is painted, and the tubes are
twisted and dried,
When the oldest colors have faded, and the youngest
critic has died,
We shall rest, and faith, we shall need it -- lie down
for an eon or two,
Till the Master of All Good Workmen shall put us to
work anew.

And only the Master shall praise us, and only the Mas-
ter shall blame;
And no one shall work for money, and no one shall work
for fame;
But each for the joy of the working, and each, in his
separate star,
Shall draw the Thing as he sees it for the God of
Things as They Are!

Ms. Toche, your chiaroscuro is showing. Do your concepts of Dark and Light, Black and White, and Things as They Are, ever clash?

Your linear perspective and depth perception could also use sharpening. Canvases cry for those things. Language should be adorned with veracity, its style supported by conclusiveness and an accuracy that may exclude incorrectness, and a sagacity whereby a proper discrimination, or lack of discrimination is attained.

I appreciate your concern for my employment status. As a token forwarded herewith is the artistic patch which saved the life of Jean-Louis Yvon, a life worth saving. If you wish to paint it lifesize, you have my permission.

Your patron,

Robert J. diGrazia
Police Commissioner

RJdG:jl

[2.9] Robert J. diGrazia, letter to Jean Toche, "Open Letter" series. Jean Brown Papers, GAAG files; 2016.M.14. Box 23, folder 10, October 23, 1974. Typewritten letter on Boston Police letterhead paper. Courtesy of Getty Research Institute and Jon Hendricks.

concern for my employment status. As a token forwarded herewith is the artistic patch which saved the life of Jean-Louis Yvon, a life worth saving. If you wish to paint it lifesize, you have my permission." He then signs off, "Your patron."[99] By framing the police badge as an "artistic patch," diGrazia playfully suggests that police work, mimetically embodied by the patch, is an artful labor too.

This exchange between diGrazia and Toche records a minor history of encounter. For both participants the stakes were small. Each wrote with a sense of immunity from a "safe" position, the white police commissioner and the white dissenting artist—Toche with little expectation that diGrazia would retaliate, and diGrazia with little worry that he would be fired on account of an artist's rebukes. Yet the (unknowingly) coauthored conceptual artwork provides unique insights into the practice of scrutiny for both police and artists. I noted that "Open Letter" exists *because* of diGrazia's commitment to a liberal, reformist policing philosophy. As such, this collaboration offers a record of the ways that the making of punitive literacy occurs not just between law enforcement and civilians but through internal debates within police departments about the management of punitiveness itself, as it stretches across and even blurs dichotomies of civilian and police, artist and audience.

Reform and Risk

Almost always, when the conflict between policing and artists is mentioned in art-historical studies, the focus remains on physical violence and conflict. But there are many ways that police encounter, constrict, and deputize people in the US, as we saw in the conceptual exploration of lurking and loitering in Piper's work. In Toche and diGrazia's correspondence, we find a different kind of example of how police reform translates into an ever-expanding field of police presence, police discretion, and police vision. In the 1970s, this expansion was framed by the government as an act of progressive caretaking.

Mayor White had hired diGrazia in 1972 with the express mandate to reform the Boston Police Department (BPD). The BDP was known as a notoriously "old, conservative, Irish" force, regarded by experts in the federal government and in private foundations "as one of the worst police departments in the nation."[100] In many ways, Boston was the prototype of police conservativism: the oldest municipal police department in the United States and the city in which the Patrolmen's Association formed in the mid-1960s, in response to officers' sense of "increased public hostility towards the police."[101] Despite being one of the largest and longest-running forces, it was dysfunctional: "an average of 200 calls for help went unanswered during *each* eight-hour shift (or 600 calls each day)."[102]

DiGrazia, a young, self-described "liberal" cop of Italian descent, arrived in Boston by way of Novato, California, where he'd had risen from officer to police chief in the early 1960s, and then St. Louis County in Missouri, where he served as commissioner from 1970 to 1972 and gained national recognition for modernizing the department. He was seen as part of an "upstart generation" professionalizing police departments with "liberal law-and-order" across the country; his cohort included Darryl Gates of Los Angeles and Clarence Kelley of Kansas City (who in 1973 became FBI chief under President Nixon).[103]

Upon his arrival in Boston, diGrazia created an unprecedented Special Investigation Unit to look into police corruption. His stated goals were "implementing an ombudsman system to monitor police activities; and developing a self-administered, modern, concise code of ethics for police officers."[104] DiGrazia told his officers that their role was to not only "serve and protect" but to be "social workers"; he also argued that "criminal codes had to be simplified, and unenforceable laws, especially those dealing with 'victimless crimes' such as loitering, had to be repealed so that patrolmen would not be tempted to circumvent these laws via the 'pay-off' route."[105]

DiGrazia's philosophy affronted many officers, who had made gains through collective bargaining as the Boston police union evolved. The union had succeeded, for example, in securing time-and-a-half pay, with a three-hour minimum, for all court appearances. That meant officers could supplement their income by arresting people who would require a court appearance—precisely the kind of behavior diGrazia sought to eliminate. As a result, the conservative majority of Boston patrolmen hired a high-powered attorney, Frank McGee, to challenge each of diGrazia's reforms.[106] Even as diGrazia raised the ire of conservatives, advocates of transparency and fairness remained skeptical of his commitment to racial equity. Artist Dana Chandler, then a professor of art at Simmons College in Boston, recalls, "If you were Black in Boston, you knew diGrazia. He wasn't as bad as the Los Angeles chief of police during Watts, but he was a typical white police chief. In any urban area in the USA, Black folks were the 'other.'"[107]

It is unlikely Toche knew of diGrazia's reformist objectives or the growing tensions between him and the police force when he called for his firing. Nevertheless, Toche's open letters, accusing the BDP of inadequate action and diGrazia of covering up the facts of the assault on Yvon, challenged the very code of ethics, and the praxis of social work, that diGrazia was working to promote. He, like many liberal police commissioners around the country, sought to develop a public-facing persona that would make the modernizing of the police visible and well received. The goal was to appear transparent and attuned to local communities while staking a claim to "risk communication," what legal criminology scholars Richard Ericson and Kevin Haggerty have identified as a form of performative labor that became "central" to all aspects of police work, starting in the 1960s and 1970s.[108] In Ericson and Haggerty's estimation, police predominantly operate as "knowledge workers engaged in the production and distribution of knowledge of risk."[109] Even more important, however, is the way this work is made legible to those outside the police department.

In their landmark publication *Policing the Risk Society*, Ericson and Haggerty explain that "the police engage in *numerous* kinds of institutionalized *publicity* that make their work an exercise in high visibility. As risk communicators to various institutional audiences, the police not only distribute knowledge widely but also make their own actions highly visible in producing that knowledge."[110] Television was one way to accomplish this task; police representatives appeared publicly with greater frequency than had been the case during the urban uprisings that defined the 1960s.[111] DiGrazia embraced this component of police work, what criminal justice scholar Jarret Lovell calls "the art of impression management through media services."[112] He and his command staff held frequent press conferences and television briefings, modeling his belief that they should be "visible and accessible to the public, to the news media, and most importantly, to every member of the police department . . . to communicate directly with the people they service and demonstrate to the community their willingness to meet problems with total openness and candor."[113]

In a photo published in the *Boston Globe* in February 1976 (fig. 2.10), diGrazia, in tweed jacket and dark tie, sits at the center of a long table strewn with microphones, as well as baseball bats, bottles, and wooden planks. Some of the objects have been tagged—transformed into evidence. The objects had been used as weapons by antibusing protesters during a "rock-throwing melee that took place in South Boston," in which seven civilians and seventy police officers were injured and thirteen people arrested. DiGrazia is flanked by his department's highest-ranking officers, all in uniforms adorned with the police patch diGrazia had mailed to Toche. To his right sit Captain Fred Connolly of the Tactical Police Force and Deputy Superintendent Lawrence Quinlan, and to his left sit Superintendent Joseph Jordan and Captain Morris Allen. In the background, an American and a Boston flag frame a map of the city's various police jurisdictions.

Press conferences like this, Lovell explains (citing the dramaturgical anal-

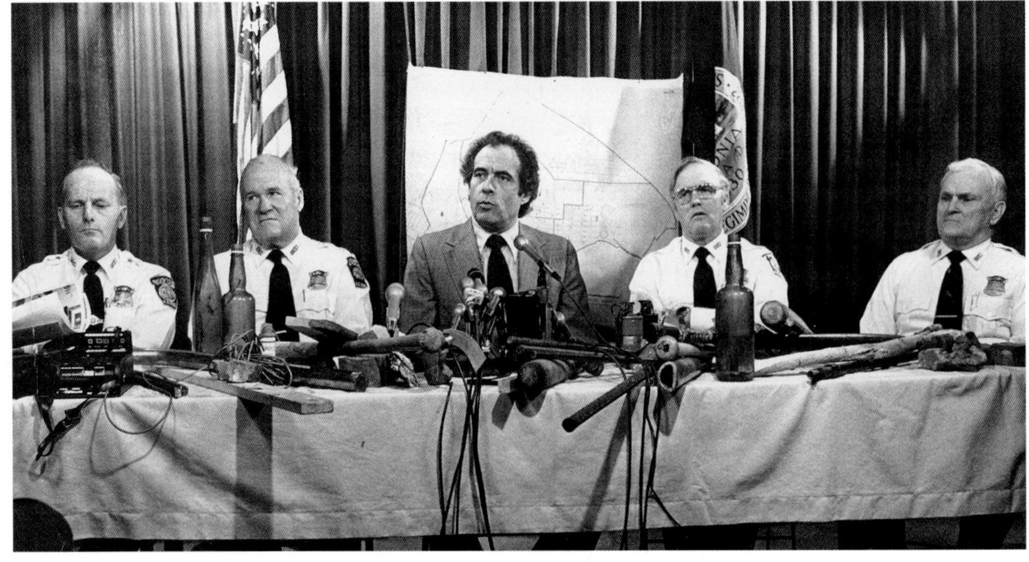

[2.10] Bill Ryerson, "Press Conference on South Boston Melee," 1976. Black-and-white photograph. Archive caption: "Boston, MA—February 16: From left, Captain Fred Connolly of the Tactical Patrol Force, Deputy Superintendent Lawrence Quinlan, Boston Police Commissioner Robert diGrazia, Superintendent Joseph Jordan and Captain Morris Allen hold a press conference at Boston Police Department headquarters on February 16, 1976, regarding a rock-throwing melee that took place in South Boston where 13 people were arrested and at least seven civilians and 70 police officers were injured. Leaders of the antibusing movement in South Boston said the confrontation resulted from police overreaction to what was intended as a peaceful march." © The Boston Globe via Getty Images.

ysis of Peter Manning) became a way for the police to "create the appearance of control" and to "dramatize their effectiveness." "They use props," he writes, "such as published crime statistics, for the purpose of a dramatic presentation of their performance outcome."[114] Or, in this case, the map behind the panel and the weapons on the table, was detritus collected and categorized by the police professionals, thereby transformed into punitive "facts." The press image —with its lineup of white, middle-aged men—stages an implicitly racialized performance, presenting the "look" of risk communication and order by way of who is positioned as an authority. The panel is itself an emblem of deputized discernment that links the press conference to the jury and the job interview.[115] The press conference reinforces deputized forms of collecting evidence and positions this kind of looking as an act that citizens can and should rely on. It also presents the work of analysis—of finding evidence and meticulously tagging it, often behind closed doors—along with the labor of answering questions, as a choreographed staging of policing as service.

Toche's letters threaten the transparency that diGrazia's police reform philosophy relied upon. He challenges diGrazia's capability to act with skilled discernment and his judgment concerning events in Boston. DiGrazia, inversely, seeks to portray Toche as an inadequate witness, a failed translator of American events. DiGrazia suggests that his colleagues (to whom he sent carbon copies) should recognize Toche as a nonauthority due to his inadequate artistic skill. And he fastidiously reasserts his own authority as an artisan or patron of risk assessment. The exchange between diGrazia and Toche reveals the low, almost inaudible scale of debate, at times internal and private, through which methods of risk communication come into being.

Turning back to Piper's *Loitering* and the ways it reveals the unseeing of police presence, whether motionless or active, as criminal, Toche's criticism of diGrazia offers another point of entry into the concept of loitering itself: Toche implicitly suggests that it is the police force that loiters within society—and is a criminal element. This idea is further borne out in a collaborative work Toche created with Hendricks a few years later. In it, they explicitly turn to the subject of loitering and white-collar crime. On February 2, 1978, while the US Senate was debating a new criminal code reform bill, Toche and Hendricks printed a communique-style statement, headed *Forwords!* (fig. 2.11), in which they pose the provocative question "Who are the loiterers we need protection from?" They reverse the top-down logic of deputized discernment and counter that the true threat is the "political johns." In the list that follows, they call out various Johns as loiterers who loot the "have-nots." Included in the list are specific people, such as the New York mayors Edward "John" Koch, Abraham "John" Beame, and John (his actual name) Lindsay, as well as generalized positions of authority, such as "John Cop," and "John Judge." At the top of the statement, the artists point to the larger implications of loitering: "The anti-loitering law is a threat to us all, a threat to our freedoms to stand on a street corner dressed the way we want saying what we want to whom we want to say it to."

Pointedly, *Forwords!* lists as a loiterer C. "John" Douglas Dillon, the president of the Metropolitan Museum, who in 1974 had reported Toche to the FBI. As mentioned at the start of the chapter, Toche had mailed handbills to, among others, art museum directors in New York City, calling for the kidnapping of MoMA personnel following the arrest of artist Tony Shafrazi. When Toche was arrested he was ordered to undergo psychiatric testing to determine his sanity (data that would remain part of his permanent record). In fact, the district court order for

FORWORDS!

February 2, 1978

The anti-loitering law is a threat to all of us,
a threat to our freedom to stand on a street corner
dressed the way we want saying what we want
to whom we want to say it to.

WHO ARE THE LOITERERS WE NEED PROTECTION FROM?

Is it a church worker who has the guts
to go out on the streets to practice what she preaches
and give counseling to women where they work?

Or is it the political johns
who earn their power and their loot
raping the have-nots
in order to add to the piles
they've already got:

JOHN ROCKEFELLER,
JOHN CAREY,
JOHN CARTER,
JOHN BEAME,
JOHN KOCH,
JOHN LINDSAY,
JOHN PALEY,
C. JOHN DILLON,
JOHN MARCHI,
JOHN MOYNIHAN,
JOHN McCALL,
JOHN NADLER,
JOHN BLACKSTEIN,
JOHN GOLDIN,
JOHN L. HUNT,
JOHN MORGENTHAU,
JOHN COP,
JOHN JUDGE,
AND JOHN, HIS GRACE, CARDINAL COOK,

and all the other johns
who never pay for their tricks.

Jon Hendricks Jean Toche

FORWORDS!, *488 Greenwich Street, New York, N. Y. 10013*

[2.11] Jon Hendricks and Jean Toche, *Forwords!*, 1978. Jean Brown papers. Courtesy of Getty Research Institute and Jon Hendricks. © Jean Toche and Jon Hendricks.

the examination was issued on October 8, 1974—the precise date Toche submitted his first open letter regarding Jean-Louis and diGrazia.[116]

It is important to note that Toche knows he is under FBI investigation for criminal attempt when he pens his open letters to the attorney general and the mayor of Boston—actions that predictably attract further attention from authorities. While these events may appear to have little to do with one another, the fact that Toche engaged in the public critique of diGrazia's discernment while his own—his ability to understand his actions—was being evaluated by the state points, in the very least, to the ways in which the right to define irrationality and disorderliness was a powerful device.

Though he was arrested for soliciting a (symbolic) political kidnapping, Toche was ultimately charged under 18 US Code § 876, "mailing threatening communications." Although he went to trial and was eventually acquitted in 1975, it was not without a fight. Writing for an affidavit prepared by Amnesty International in May 1974, months ahead of the court-ordered psychiatric exam, the white feminist curator and art critic Lucy R. Lippard situates Toche's handbills as part of the Guerrilla Art Action Group's art oeuvre, explaining that the artists' choice of forms that blur lines of art and militancy was part of the work's misrecognition by the authorities:

> The fact that they [Toche and Hendricks] use a broadly accessible framework—a simple, xeroxed sheet—is perhaps why they have provoked fear on the part of the authorities. Were the same thing said in oil on canvas or in cut-out metal sculpture, their "art content" would be more obvious and would inspire an entirely different reaction.[117]

Lippard's astute observation underscores how the *forms* of address used to convey a message trigger aesthetic judgment that relies on a knowledge of art history intertwined with iconographies of protest and militancy.

Echoing Lippard's assessment, sixteen artists supporting Toche published an open letter in *Artforum* in November 1974 demanding that the order for a psychiatric exam and the charges both be dropped: "The arrest of Jean Toche was essentially a political act," they state. Their critique of the charges against Toche positions Dillon, the Met president (1970–1977), as someone abusing the deputizing of discernment to censor artists:

> The Director of the Metropolitan Museum of Art must have known, as did the art world as a whole, that the call for kidnapping could not have been

> anything but symbolic in essence. It was made in a public letter, against an unspecified number of people of various categories. We believe that Mr. Dillon acted not against a real threat, but against a statement he must have understood to be metaphoric, in an act of vengeance against an artist who for years played a role in the antiwar movement and the movement for artists' rights vis-à-vis the establishment and the museum hierarchies.[118]

The open letter conflates Dillon's role as museum president with the position of museum director (then held by Thomas Hoving), suggesting that these positions of authority were seen as interchangeable, if not easily confused. Nevertheless, for either an art museum director or president, coordinating with security and law enforcement, the FBI, and the police contributes to the making of deputized discernment. In Dillon's case, the credentials he brought to his position likely intensified the FBI's swift attention.

Prior to his museum work, Dillon had served as the fifty-seventh secretary of the treasury from 1961 to 1965, and as a member of the executive committee of the National Security Council during the Cuban Missile Crisis. Given these connections, his assessment of Toche was likely boosted by previous decisions he'd been privy to as part of the national security state. Through this example, it is possible to see how the perceived borders between cultural production, international relations, and securitization constantly blur—and how Toche's publicized self-identification as a *guerrilla* artist positioned him as policeable entity.

Redeputizing Risk

A key claim in this chapter has been that perceptions of both lurking and loitering—whether expressed within or used to interpret Piper's and Toche's artwork—have much to teach us about the deputizing of discernment mobilized by police, judges, museum leaders, and policy makers in the mid-1970s, and about how punitive contexts and legal concepts shape the aesthetic decisions made by artists. Toche's correspondence with diGrazia is a study in deputized discernment as *work* that relies upon the bridging of aesthetic and punitive forms. Their exchange exposes a debate about who possesses the adequate skills—authorized looking and knowing—to determine the details of events within a punitive society, and how ideas of liberal, leftist care appear as a device for both artist and police commissioner. When Toche and diGrazia argue about culpability within violence, they do so by assessing scrutiny and an ability to turn events into evidence as artful skills.

Piper's work, I argue, also invites audiences to consider the making of punitive literacy. In *Loitering*, I've contended, Piper offers us a way to look at deputized discernment by theorizing abstractions of hostility that are central to policing and part of debates within legal review. She redeputizes vision by soliciting viewers to perceive the Mythic Being as a loiterer, engaging them in a slow-going viewership that renders them potentially culpable as loiterers too: it's a positionality that requires relational duration and entangled punitive literacies. Piper's *Loitering* thereby conceptualizes, among other things, the sociality of risk that is part of cultivating one's sense of being in or out of place, inviting contemporary viewers of the work to consider what it is we can and can't know when perceiving inertia in a punitive context. While theorizing the various possibilities of transcendence in the Mythic Being, Piper's work also makes clearer that becoming literate in loitering is a process of coming to know and manage inscrutability.

Within these structures, the seeming nonaction perceived within *Loitering* might be read as "low risk." However, this definition of risk relies on the notion that risk-taking is voluntary and deviant rather than imposed, necessary, and imperceptible when done to survive the forms of "protection" that rely upon the eradication of one's own stilled presence in a particular setting. Piper's work translates the ability to theorize loitering, and the perception of in-action, not as a matter merely of self-exploration or legal status but as an existential struggle in hegemonic white, capitalist spaces. Together, Piper's and Toche's works allow for a study in deputized discernment as a complex process through which people are taught and conditioned to know modes of spatial occupation (of both in-action and action) in service of the state's scripting of progressive (punitive) care.

[3]

Rethinking Endurance

Pope.L, Tehching Hsieh, and Surviving Safety, 1978–1982

In the few existing documentary photographs of Pope.L's 1978 performance *Times Square Crawl*, we mostly see the artist from behind: a young Black man wearing a dark business suit and leather shoes crawls on his hand and knees along the crowded sidewalks and crosswalks of Times Square. As he moves forward, pressing his open palms and knees onto the cement and pavement, the high sun casts his shadow alongside. Pope.L follows the rules of traffic, remaining within the crosswalk's white painted lines, while cars wait for the light to turn. A rectangle of bright yellow fabric affixed to the back of his suit jacket communicates "caution" in the language of traffic safety (plate 6).

Pope.L intended the crawl as a "symbolic action" that would reorient passersby to the "spectacle of bodies lying on the ground," a commentary on the increasing numbers of unhoused people visible on the streets of the city.[1] In selecting business attire associated with managerial and professional workers, he also aimed to address the social inequities that persist even when Black Americans begin to accumulate wealth. In an interview with curator Lowery Stokes Sims, Pope.L explained, "In our society, masculinity is measured in presence. However, no matter how much presence the BAM [the artist's abbreviation for the black male body] contrives, it will continue to be marked as a lack."[2] During *Times Square Crawl* Pope.L temporarily "gave up his verticality," as he put it, and slowly crawled on all fours through the area then known as "the Deuce." This stretch of 42nd Street and Broadway between Seventh and Eighth Avenues, dubbed "the sleaziest block in America" by *Rolling Stone*, was known for its sex shops; theaters screening porn, Blaxploitation, and Kung Fu films; and sex workers and drug dealers working the street. Police monitored the cross-class and racially diverse crowds of tourists, street hawkers, and commuters present each day.

Throughout the 1970s and early 1980s the area was targeted for "urban revitalization" efforts as a succession of politicians sought to "clean up" the "deviance" of its growing porn and gay sex culture and the "wayward youth," simultaneously passing city ordinances authorizing police to forcibly detain individuals deemed "disorderly."[3] *Times Square Crawl* was personal for Pope.L: soon after graduating from Montclair State University in 1978, he experienced homelessness, sleeping at NYU's Loeb Student Center.[4] During his childhood, he'd also witnessed several family members living in and out of shelters.

At some point during his crawl in Times Square, Pope.L encounters a police officer. In the documentary image, we see Pope.L as he reaches the sidewalk, and a white-presenting policeman intervening (plate 7). The officer, caught in profile, stands at the edge of the street, just off the curb and the crosswalk, his hat tucked beneath one arm, a billy club hanging from his belt. The officer leans down and presses a hand against the artist's right shoulder. But no arrest ensues: crawling is not a criminal offense. As Pope.L would later describe his encounter with the officer, "He thought I was inebriated, or crazy, or both. *I wasn't loitering. I was actually moving.*"[5] Pope.L's attention to the specificity of this movement conveys both an understanding of traffic flows and a knowledge of vagrancy and antiloitering laws used to remove people (differently positioned by white supremacist and gendered antiblack structures of governance) from public spaces.

Pope.L's contemporary Tehching Hsieh also anticipated punitive relations, and also encountered New York City police officers in the process of making his conceptual and performance-based works. In 1978, as Pope.L crawled through Times Square, Hsieh created a work that outed himself as an undocumented Chinese immigrant. After leaving Taiwan, his country of origin, Hsieh had arrived on a freighter and jumped ship when it docked in Philadelphia in 1974. Since then, he had lived in Manhattan's Tribeca neighborhood, another area targeted by the city for urban renewal. As an expression of his intense anticipation of punitive encounter, he created *Wanted by U.S. Immigration Service* (fig. 3.1).

On the document, a conceptual self-portrait modeled on wanted posters and intake forms for processing immigrants, he disclosed his full name, "Hsieh Teh-Ching," and announced his crime: "Illegal Entry, without visa," retroactively dated it to July 13, 1974, the day of his arrival.[6] In the high-contrast black-and-white photograph, he appears with buzzed hair, wearing a white button-up shirt and a tie. At the bottom of the page, his fingerprints fill two rows of boxes. Part conceptual artwork, part pseudolegal document, Hsieh's disclosure of his undocumented status plays with the state's procedure for authenticating these facts.

WANTED BY

U.S. IMMIGRATION SERVICE

Date : July 13, 1974

Name : Hsieh Teh-Ching

Photo take in 1974

DESCRIPTION

Age : 24 Born 12/31/1950

Eyes : Black

Hair : Black

Weight : 115 Lb.

Heigh : 5'3"

Race : Oriental

Nationality : Chinese

OCCUPATION : Seaman

Hsieh Teh-Ching

VIOLATION : Illegal Entry, without visa

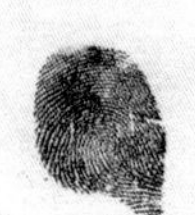

1 R.Thumb	2 R.Index	3 R.Middle	4 R.Ring	5 R.Little
1 L.Thumb	2 L.Index	3 L.Middle	4 L.Ring	5 L.Little

please call: 212-349-8735

[3.1] Tehching Hsieh, *Wanted by U.S. Immigration Service*, 1978. Printed paper. © Tehching Hsieh. Courtesy of the artist and the Gilbert and Lila Silverman Collection.

Unlike fingerprints taken for official intake forms created during the process of detainment (through intimate, routinized touching between a sanctioned state agent and the person being documented), his fingerprints constitute a record of as yet unrealized physical contact with the state. This condition, as chronicler of Hsieh's work Joan Kee observes, amplifies the underlying anxiety of a "wanted" poster, namely, the state's limited ability to locate or discipline him—to hold him.[7] Below the fingerprints is a direct, then-active telephone number for the New York City Immigration service office and the artist's request, "please call," conscripting readers as would-be agents of state surveillance.[8] Hsieh created *Wanted* in 1978 as an expression of "always thinking [that the] immigration service wanted me," but he did not, at that time, choose to circulate the poster.[9] Four years later, when his fear of arrest was realized, the poster was on view for the first time.

In February 1982, Hsieh was told by a building manager to vacate the doorway of a private apartment building at 34 Hubert Street in Tribeca where he had been sitting, reading, and drinking tea.[10] When Hsieh refused, the building manager, one Mr. Van Campbell, allegedly threw Hsieh's backpack—which contained all of his valuables, including his camera—and brandished an iron rod at him.[11] In self-defense, Hsieh fought back with nunchakus he was carrying before leaving the premises. Months later, on May 3, he crossed paths with Van Campbell again, this time while walking around the Lower East Side with his friend the artist Claire Fergusson, who was carrying a camera. Upon seeing Hsieh, Van Campbell called over a police officer, accusing the artist of "damaging [his] knuckles" with "a pair of chukka sticks," a weapon that had been outlawed in New York state since 1974.[12] Two more officers arrived and arrested him on charges of possession of an illegal weapon and second-degree assault while Fergusson snapped photos (fig. 3.2).

In one photo, Hsieh looks at Fergusson from within a circle of three male officers. In the images that follow, Hsieh is pulled and even carried by the police officers up the precinct's steps. Hsieh's anguish, which is palpable as he struggles to resist arrest, is largely due to his commitment to a durational performance piece he had begun in September 1981. Hsieh initiated *One Year Performance, 1981–1982*, informally titled, *Outdoor Piece*, dedicating himself to following a set of self-imposed rules for twelve consecutive months (fig. 3.3): "I shall stay OUTDOORS for one year, never go inside. I shall not go into a building, subway, train, car, airplane, ship, cave, tent. I shall have a sleeping bag." This work, like *Wanted*, grew from his feelings of isolation and the fear that he dealt with daily, as he sought to evade capture and deportation. Detainment would not only disrupt his commitment to remaining outdoors but potentially expose him to surveillance by Immigration Services and to deportation. Despite his initial efforts to resist, the officers succeed in bringing Hsieh into the jailhouse, where he was held for fifteen hours before being released. He later faced two court hearings in June 1982.

Pope.L's *Times Square Crawl* (1978) and Hsieh's *Wanted* (1978/1982) and *Outdoor Piece* (1981–1982) have become well-known examples of each artist's oeuvre, and of what is often called "endurance art." This chapter takes up the works made by these contemporaries in New York City to cross-examine the artists' tactical decisions and the specificity of the punitive relations shaping their work and its reception. Despite the artists' run-ins with police, little attention has been paid to the role and implications of punitive ordinances and their enforcement in these works' formal qualities, or to how relations of punitiveness have informed aesthetic and material notions of endurance itself in art and American society. Building upon the previous chapters, which considered the relation between guerrilla tactics in art, anti-riot policy, and post-riot cities, this chapter examines how shifting ideas of endurance—articulated through the racialized, ethnonational, and gendered policing of self-defense and resourcefulness in the fiscal crisis moment—underwrite the maturation of guerrilla tactics in art as it gains institutional traction, in both exhibitions and court trials, in the late 1970s and early 1980s. This chapter also criticizes the widespread tendency in art discourse to leave discussions of punitiveness out of "endurance art."

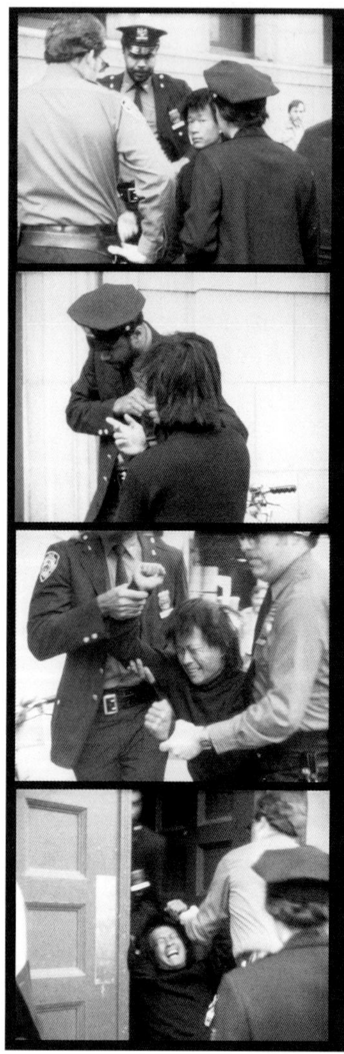

In the period considered in chapters 1 and 2, the early to mid-1970s, artists' experimentations with embodied "hit and run" tactics in art were just becoming legible. Within the story of punitive literacy told across this book, this chapter focuses on a significant turning point in the history of guerrilla tactics in art in the US, namely, the late 1970s and early 1980s, when artists' use of tactics in art had accrued a certain level of legibility thanks in part to

September 26, 1981

STATEMENT

I, Tehching Hsieh, plan to do a one year performance piece.

I shall stay OUTDOORS for one year, never go inside.

I shall not go in to a building, subway, train, car, airplane, ship, cave, tent.

I shall have a sleeping bag.

The performance shall begin on September 26, 1981 at 2 P.M. and continue until September 26, 1982 at 2 P.M.

Tehching Hsieh

Tehching Hsieh

New York City

[3.2, facing page] Tehching Hsieh, *One Year Performance 1981–1982,* Arrested, May 3, 1982. Black-and-white photograph. © Tehching Hsieh. Courtesy of the artist and the Gilbert and Lila Silverman Collection.

[3.3] Tehching Hsieh, *One Year Performance 1981–1982,* Statement, September 1981. Printed paper. © Tehching Hsieh. Courtesy of the artist and the Gilbert and Lila Silverman Collection.

citation of these earlier precedents. I argue that this period marks a historically unprecedented turn toward the *citation* of these earlier tactics: a moment when the legal horizons of tactics in art were legitimized in courts and in the emergent field of art law, and were brought to art-viewing audiences via exhibitions, such as *Illegal America*, aiming to conceptualize risk-taking in art—all of which drew upon earlier precedents while laying a framework for assessing risk that has remained in place for subsequent generations. This history conjures, thus, both meanings of the word *citation*: as an act of homage in art history, and as the procedure of serving court proceedings on an individual, instructing them to attend and become legible before the law.

Endurance as Political Discourse

Pope.L earned his title of "endurance artist" through his numerous crawls. In each crawl, starting with his first one, *Times Square Crawl*, Pope.L responds to a particular sociopolitical context. In New York City, he enacted *Tompkins Square Crawl* in 1991, crawling in a wool suit alongside the park where a protest had turned into a police raid resulting in the forceful removal of unhoused people and, for a time, the closure of the park. Between 2001 and 2009, he staged one of his most arduous crawls, *Great White Way*, crawling the length of Broadway, from Liberty Island to the South Bronx, intermittently over the course of nine years. While the work began before 9/11, it became infused with "legacies of attack," security infrastructure, and imaginaries of superheroism when his route took him past the site formerly occupied by the Twin Towers.[13]

Pope.L almost always encounters law enforcement during these actions. During *Tompkins Square Crawl*, for example, a Black resident, initially concerned for his well-being, grew angry when he realized that Pope.L intended to continue defiling himself, dragging himself through the street belly-down in a military crawl (plate 8).[14] The resident called over a police officer, and the confrontation ultimately ended the piece early. In *Great White Way*, two National Park Service troopers on Liberty Island ordered Pope.L back onto the ferry, and a police officer at Ground Zero "forced him to stand up," declaring "You need a permit for this!" before relenting.[15] Over the years, Pope.L has explored the possibilities of crawling in numerous American cities, as well as Berlin, Amsterdam, Budapest, Prague, Madrid, and Tokyo, while simultaneously working across other mediums, including painting, sculpture, installation, text-based work, performance, video, and scripts. In 2019, he returned to New York City, on the occasion of his multivenue retrospective, hosted by the Whitney Museum of American

Art and MoMA, to enact *Conquest*, a large group crawl, involving 140 blindfolded volunteers, each crawling with one shoe missing and a flashlight, from the West Village's John A. Seravalli Playground to Union Square.[16] In each iteration, the meanings of his crawling has shifted based on the particular place, police involvement, politics, and historical context.

In contrast to Pope.L's crawls that garnered attention from passersby and police, Hsieh gained notoriety for his self-imposed feats of endurance in private spaces, as well as public performances that allowed him to blend into the background of daily events. While living outdoors for a year in *Outdoor Piece*, he was described by several art historians as "invisible in plain sight." Frazer Ward noted, for example, that the artist utilized the anonymity of the street to invert his trackability as an undocumented immigrant.[17] *Outdoor Piece* was the third in a sequence of five yearlong durational pieces staged between 1978 and 1986.

In each yearlong work, Hsieh specified a set of rules requiring methodical, repetitive disciplinary actions, subjecting himself to isolation and extreme self-monitoring as he explored psychological and physical expressions of exile and anxiety, as well as meditative self-perseverance. For the first piece, *One Year Performance 1978–1979*, known informally as *Cage Piece*, he constructed, in his Soho loft, an 11.5-by-9-by-8-foot wooden cage, in which he stayed for a year, from September 1978 to September 1979.[18] During that time, he committed to isolation suggestive of penal solitary confinement, pledging not to speak, read, listen to the radio, or write. Once a day, his loftmate, Chen Wei Kuong, removed his waste, brought him food, and took a documentary photograph that would later constitute the visual archive of the work. The following year, Hsieh executed *Time Clock Piece*, punching in on a time clock installed in his loft every hour on the hour for a year—a discipline that led to intense sleep deprivation and temporal incoherence, again akin to a form of temporal punishment typically used on incarcerated people.[19] *Outdoor Piece* followed as the third in the sequence. Each of these yearlong performances was rooted in Hsieh's experience as an undocumented immigrant, a powerful meditation on the unique legal status of persons who are constantly committing their crime and continually aware of the possibility of being caught "in the act."[20]

In many ways *Wanted*, Hsieh's fingerprinted poster was a prototype for the artist's ensuing yearlong performances. The document, which compressed four years he'd spent living in America and fearing deportation, was created in May 1978, just a few months before his first such performance, *Cage Piece*. As noted above, Hsieh did not publicly share the poster at that time. *Wanted* was too risky to circulate initially. Nationally, the "hunt" for undocumented Asians in the US, as Kee explains, was heightened by a "new racial pressure brought to bear as the devastation wreaked by the Vietnam War led to an influx of refugees from Indochina."[21] In New York, in particular, local politicians and the media were taking note in May 1978 of the "swelling" number of applications to the New York City Office of Immigration.[22] In 1978, Hsieh had adopted the Americanized name of "Sam" to disguise his identity and was working as a dishwasher and cleaner at a restaurant in Chinatown that was frequently raided by immigration officials.[23] Only years later, in 1982, while living on the streets for *Outdoor Piece*, did Hsieh publicly display *Wanted* in *Illegal America*, an exhibition exploring criminality and art, curated by Jeanette Ingberman at Franklin Furnace (112 Franklin Street) in Tribeca. Reflecting on his body of work in 1983, Ingberman conceived of the following equation for Hsieh's practice: "body resistance + mind resistance = endurance."[24]

"Endurance" is a generative, albeit problematic, term with a convoluted history. "Endurance art," sometimes also referred to as "masochistic art," typically indexes performance or body-based art in which injury, self-harm, and pain are organizing elements.[25] When Pope.L and Hsieh began exploring psychologically and physically challenging durational works, an art-world discourse had only recently formalized the links between performance art, risk, and danger. The 1975 show *Bodyworks*, at Chicago's Museum of Contemporary Art, was the first museum exhibition of durational performance art testing the bounds of permissibility through self-harm, danger, and spectatorship. In Ingberman's estimation, it was also the first show to bring the "validity of the genre" into a "legal perspective"—providing lawyers with a framework in which to begin considering liabilities and the need for new policies in tort and criminal law.[26] In other words, the exhibition became a vehicle through which artists experimenting with their bodies as mediums were legitimized as valid artists whose legal trespass might thereafter be recognized as a form of legitimate cultural expression in both art and law.

In 1978, the Italy-based contemporary art magazine *Flash Art* published a groundbreaking themed issue, "Danger in Art," which further shored up the work's validity. The issue surveyed cis-gendered, heterosexual white men and women, namely Chris Burden, Marina Abramović, and Vito Acconci, who had inflicted self-injury in the name of artistic production since the early 1970s. In François Pluchart's contribution to the issue, "Risk as the Practice of Thought," he documents Burden's *Shoot*, printing images of Burden just before the gun is fired and of his puffy bullet wound, thereby bringing the work to an international audience. Though endurance of pain was discussed in the article in universalist terms, this discourse ultimately relies upon the culturally conditioned idea of "physical vigor," a concept mired in the construction of white cis-gendered heterosexual masculinity. As historian Gail Bederman demonstrates, centuries of historical processes—including art-historical representations of strength and willfulness—construct the white male body as a metonym for power. Herein, "superior manhood," Bederman asserts, is developed as an inherited white racial attribute.[27]

In the late 1970s, bodybuilding gained unprecedented appeal. And as Richard Dyer in his larger study of imaging whiteness states succinctly, "bodybuilding in popular culture articulates white masculinity."[28] In the art world, the links between the ideology of imperialist strength and power long embedded within the history of classical sculpture were put on display in 1976 when the Whitney hosted a one-night exhibition titled *Articulate Muscle: The Male Body in Art*. The show featured three white male "Mr. Universe" bodybuilders, including a young Arnold Schwarzenegger. While organizers anticipated only three hundred attendees, the event attracted more than five thousand visitors. Long lines wrapped around the block, and a standing-room-only crowd overwhelmed the museum space. During the event, a panel of well-known art critics and curators discussed the (white) male body as a classical art form. Meanwhile, the bodybuilders, on rotating circular pedestals, struck poses reminiscent of classical and more recent sculpture, such as Rodin's *The Thinker*. In figure 3.4, the densely packed spectators, beyond just enjoying an entertaining event, are learning how to see and evaluate the performance of physical endurance—how to recognize it as a form with a cultural history legitimized through centuries of idealized white masculinity.

In many ways, this image of Schwarzenegger displaying his physique on a rotating pedestal exemplifies how endurance is seen and discussed in art history: decontextualized from its social environment, the focus entirely on titillating muscles construed as personal accomplishments, with no consideration of white racial politics. Underlying this decontextualization in 1976, national anxieties about the defeat in Vietnam mobilized the obsessive need for visual white male strength. "Given the valorization of the soldier that began in the decades *after* the Vietnam War ended," Paul Achter observes, "as well as the increasing use of protroop arguments in political discourse during the last decade, war rhetoric is now heavily invested in rhetorics of the warrior's body."[29] The event's title, *Articulate Muscle*, suggestively invokes the ways bodies "speak" through physique, training, and endurance, from within a deterritorialized, whitened,

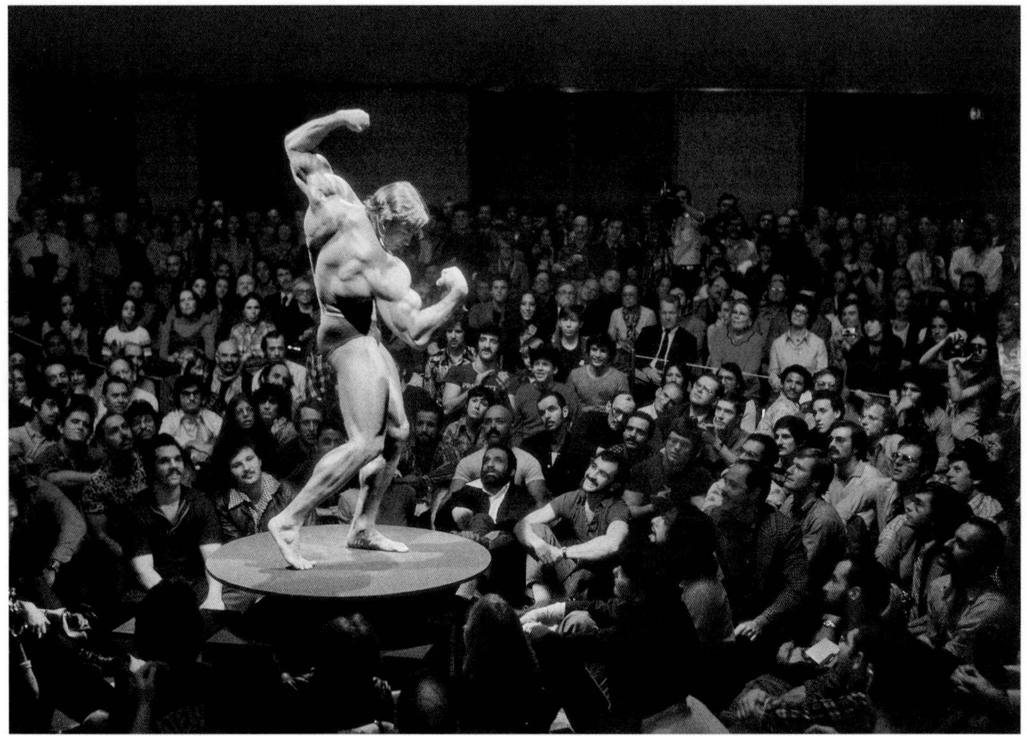

[3.4] Elliot Erwin/Magnum Photos, Arnold Schwarzenegger during the opening of *Articulate Muscle: The Male Body in Art* at the Whitney Museum of American Art, February 25, 1976. Color photograph. © Erwin Elliot/Magnum Photos.

and ahistorical space. While endurance training and danger-seeking was made legible through such white-centering platforms of fitness culture and the art world, Pope.L and Hsieh's exploration of durational feats that attract punitive attention draws out the realities of working within a racialized and gendered field of action-taking.

In her book *Performing Endurance*, Lara Shalson provides an insightful recontextualization of the idea and history of "endurance" in art, troubling its social underpinnings. Surveying the meanings ascribed to endurance in art, she notes that it is typically associated with experiences of pain and personal risk and cited in describing physically and psychologically difficult, durational situations. Shalson incisively pushes against the centering of suffering and theorizes that to endure is to both "*do something*" and to have "*undergone*" something; it is this *doing* and *undergoing* that generates a politically and socially *relational* form of endurance, one that exceeds the individual and their agency.[30]

As mentioned in chapter 1, curator Valerie Cassel Oliver writes, astutely, of the links between radical Black performance artists' navigation of public space and Chris Burden's unawareness of his privileged white male positionality:

> For Burden, who is white, these actions were apparently aimed at testing his own physical limits as well as the limits of what might constitute artistic expression. For black artists, however, the social and political aspects of endurance-based performance are inescapable, specifically because the black body has particular meanings and a particular history in the Americas.[31]

Taken together, Pope.L and Hsieh's "endurance" works of the late 1970s and early 1980s draw out the *relationality* of endurance—of doing and undergoing—and how it differently positions artists and their audiences vis-à-vis ideas of safety and the need for protection or self-defense. Pope.L and Hsieh's works differently negotiate survival techniques in art at a time when a number of policies and ordinances criminalizing certain forms of survival were being implemented in New York City, as well as nationwide: anti-riot urbanization (chapter 1), antiloitering laws (chapter 2), and bans on public intoxication and activities associated with poverty and being unhoused: public urination, sleeping, sitting, waiting.

The perception of thriving Chinese American urban communities was also mobilized in this period in support of the argument that welfare benefits and public services associated in popular discourse with historically disenfranchised Black and brown people should be cut.[32] Under these conditions, certain modes of *enduring* were legitimized, namely, those that upheld conceptualizations of agency and resourcefulness rooted in the maintenance of whiteness and masculinity. Meanwhile, behaviors and maneuvers used to survive these structures were deemed excessive, criminal, or threatening by policy makers, politicians, and pundits.

As these examples demonstrate, racial formation—always inflected by class, gender, and sexual orientation—operates not by way of binaries but through interlocking processes of oppression and their rationalized neutralization, relations made increasingly legible following the coining in 1989 of "intersectionality" by legal scholar, Kimberlé Crenshaw.[33] At the crossroads of labor, crime, immigration, race, and citizenship, the race-neutral use of the term "endurance" to describe artists' work belies an infrastructure of whitened ideas of fitness and self-defense that makes some people recognizable as fit for citizenship through degrees of assimilation, and Black and brown people a threat to these structures. In the late 1970s and early 1980s, the incommensurate but entangled matrices of racism, white ascendancy, and capitalism were central to what Black studies scholar George Lipsitz has named a white "patriotic revival of the post-Vietnam era," giving way to a "new warrior" culture in the US.[34] As Lipsitz explains, "The 'white' identity conditioned to fear the Asian 'menace' owes it origins to the history of anti-Indian, anti-Black, and anti-Mexican racism at home as well as to anti-Arab and anti-Latino racisms shaped by military struggles overseas and by condescending cultural stereotypes at home."[35] The way these tropes of endurance are extended in ostensibly race-neutral, yet deeply racialized, policies of urban development, antipoverty, citizenship, and upward mobility is of utmost importance for reckoning with what, precisely, is endured in Pope.L and Hsieh's durational works.

Through attention to the complex, multidimensional contexts in which ideas of endurance and national safety become interlaced, Pope.L and Hsieh's tactics differently anticipate how laws enforce not only the "right way" to survive but the "right way" to be an American.[36] In the following sections, I provide close readings of Pope.L's *Times Square Crawl* and Hsieh's *Wanted* and *Outdoor Piece* to analyze how each artist engages with personal and state-sanctioned risk management defined by his surroundings; how their work negotiates changing federal and state policies indicative of larger shifts within concepts of work ethic, citizenry, and self-defense; and the distinct but related histories of cross-racialization normalized through safety discourse, part of both policing and emergent art law policies of the late 1970s and early 1980s. As I've argued throughout this book, artists' turn to specific tactics offers a record of their punitive literacy and its sociality. This is not to suggest that these concerns were the most important factors at play in the work for the artists, nor that these artists were the only ones troubling the use of public space in performance-based works beyond art-sanctioned spaces—a number of artists walked, fell, loitered, hauled, stalked, vended, and sat in public at this time in their art experimentation.[37] Thus, while acknowledging that punitiveness is just one force impacting the creation and interpretation of these works, I want to consider Pope.L and Hsieh's pieces as entangled aesthetic responses to urban policing protocols. When taken together, Pope.L's and Hsieh's tactics reveal how structures of policing enacted in the name of *safety* become something that the most vulnerable denizens of the city, and the art world, actively and tactically survive and endure.

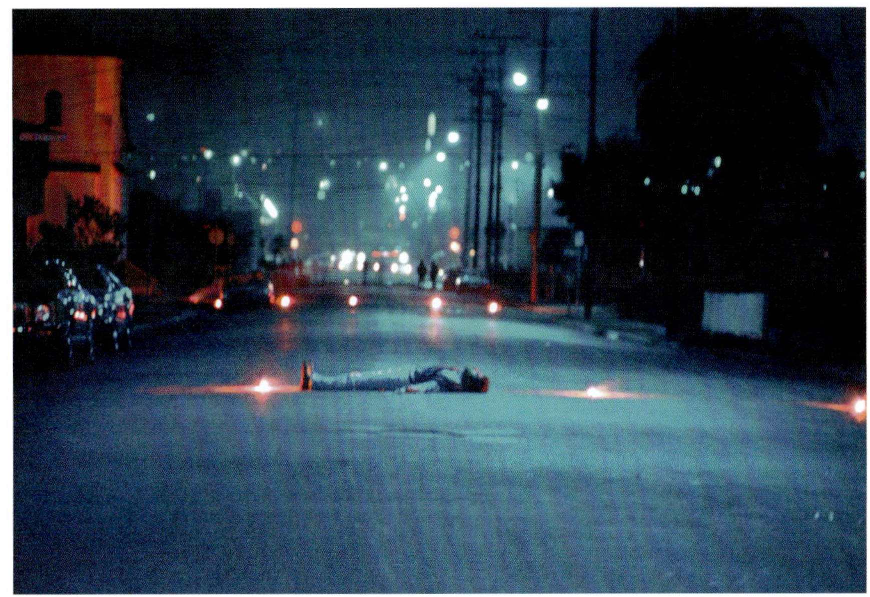

[Plate 1] Harry Gamboa Jr., *Decoy Gang War Victim*, 1974. Chromogenic Color Print. © Harry Gamboa Jr. Courtesy of the artist.

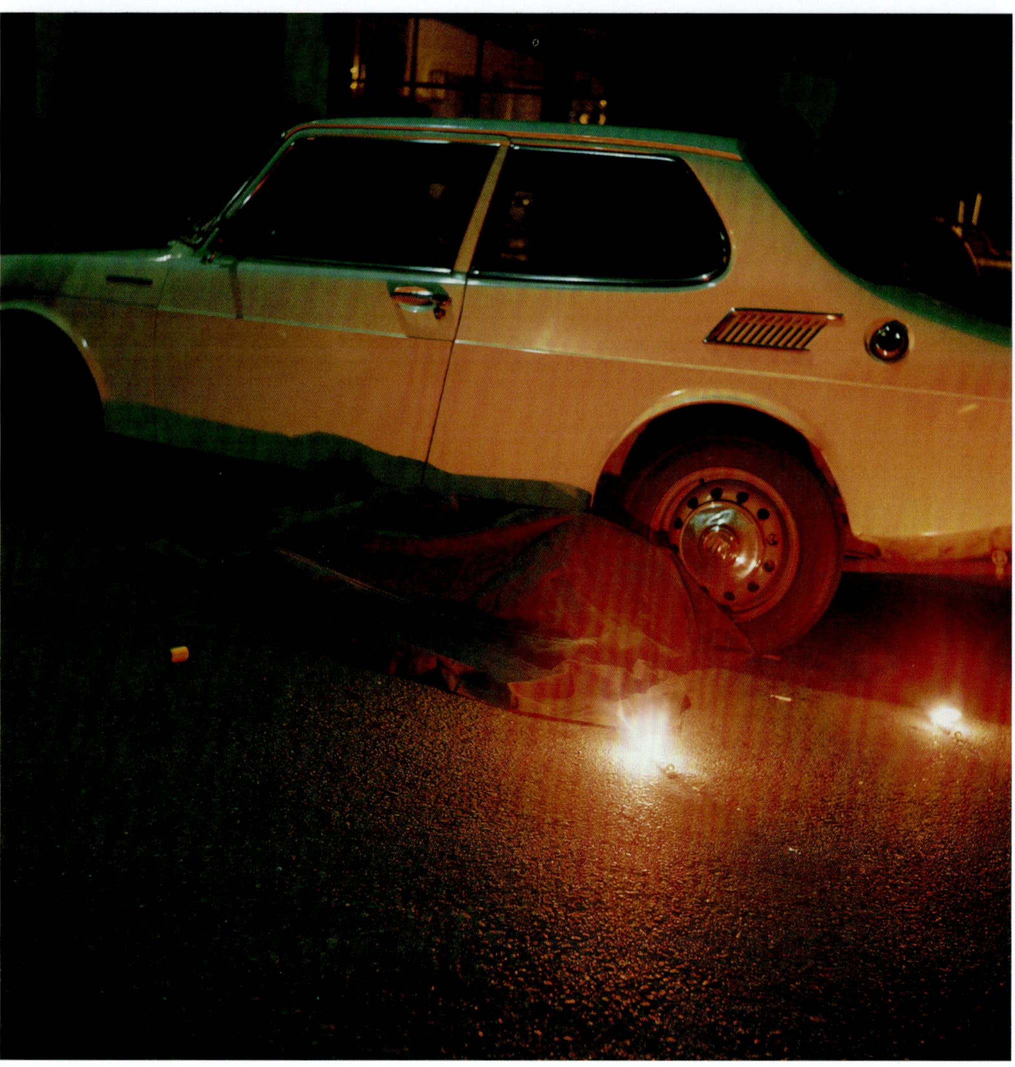

[Plate 2] Chris Burden, *Deadman*, November 12, 1972. Color photograph. Documentation photo: Gary Beydler. © 2021 Chris Burden. Licensed by the Chris Burden Estate/Artists Rights Society (ARS), New York.

[Plate 3, facing page, top] Harry Gamboa Jr., *Spray Paint LACMA*, 1972. Color photograph. © Harry Gamboa Jr. Courtesy of the artist.

[Plate 4, facing page, bottom] Harry Gamboa Jr., *First Supper (After a Major Riot)*, 1974. Color photograph. Performers (*left to right*): Patssi Valdez, Humberto Sandoval, Willie Herrón III, and Glugio "Gronk" Nicandro. © Harry Gamboa Jr. Courtesy of the artist.

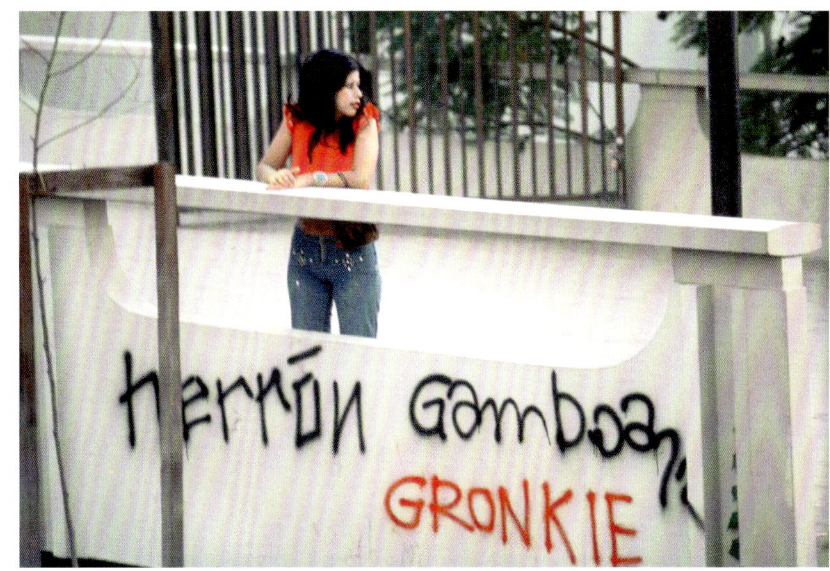
herrón gamboa
GRONKIE

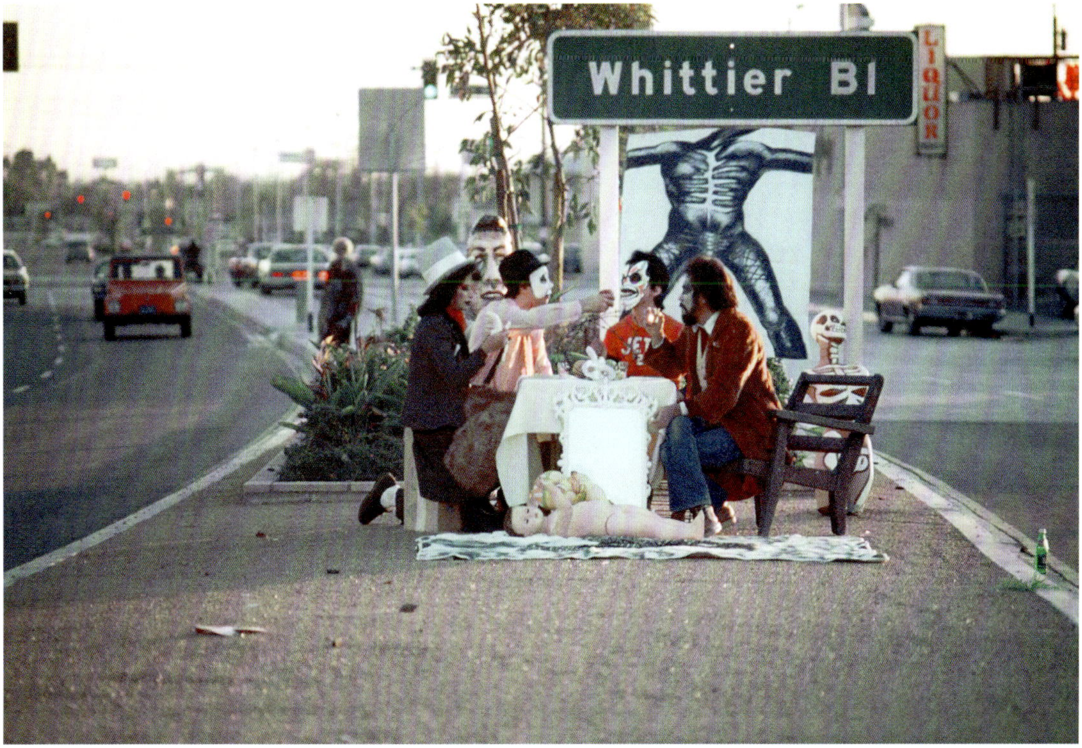

Whittier Bl
LIQUOR

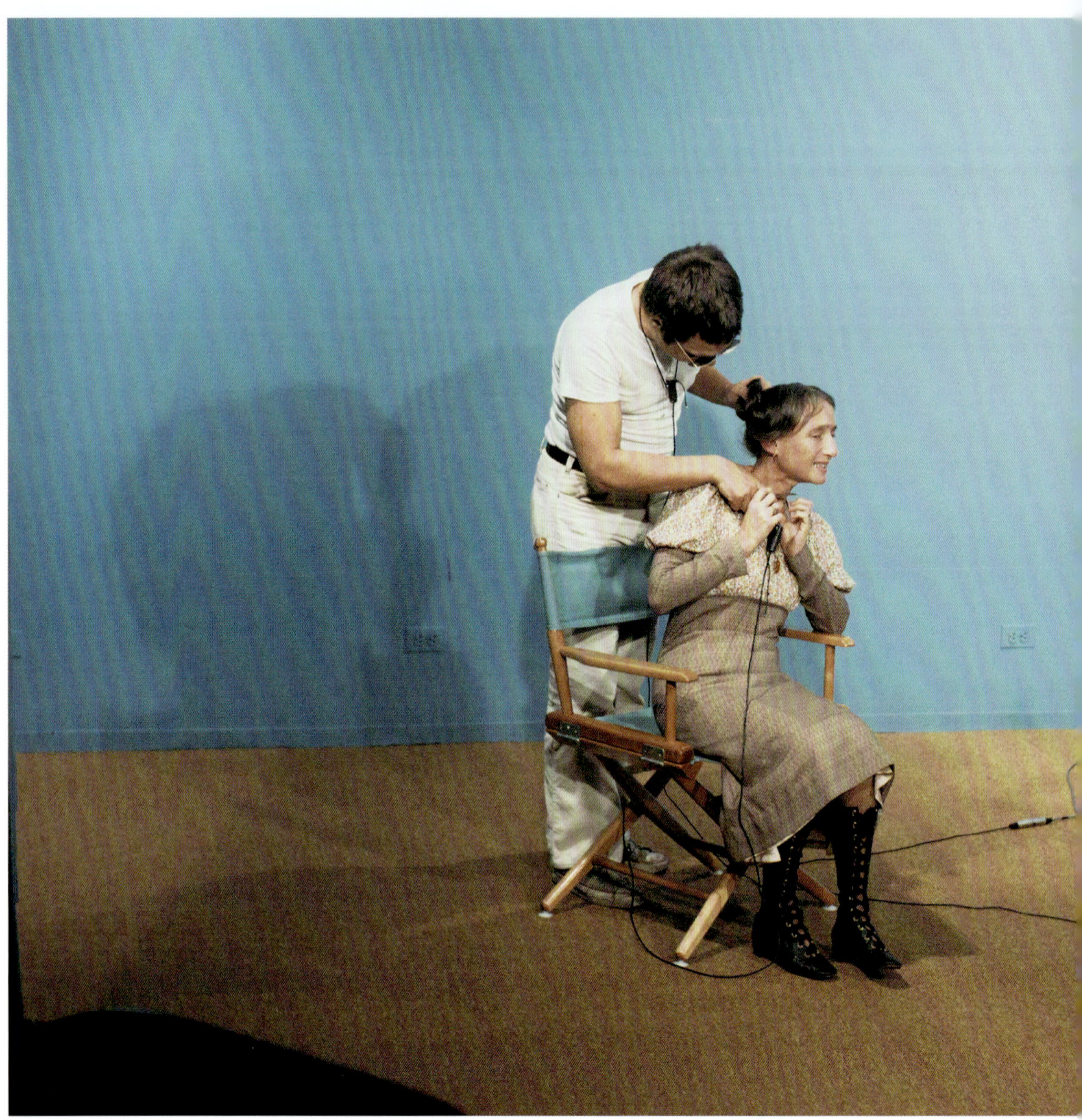

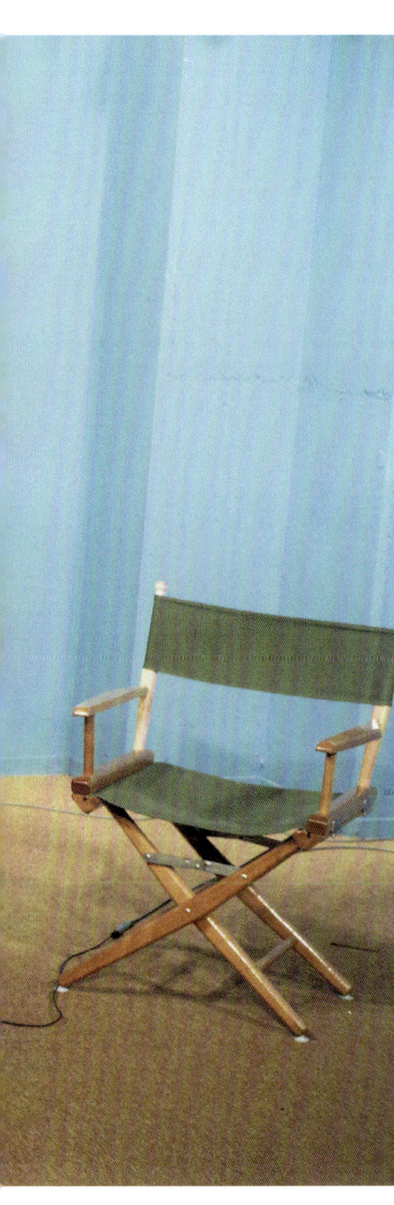

[Plate 5] Chris Burden, *TV Hijack*, 1972. Color photograph.

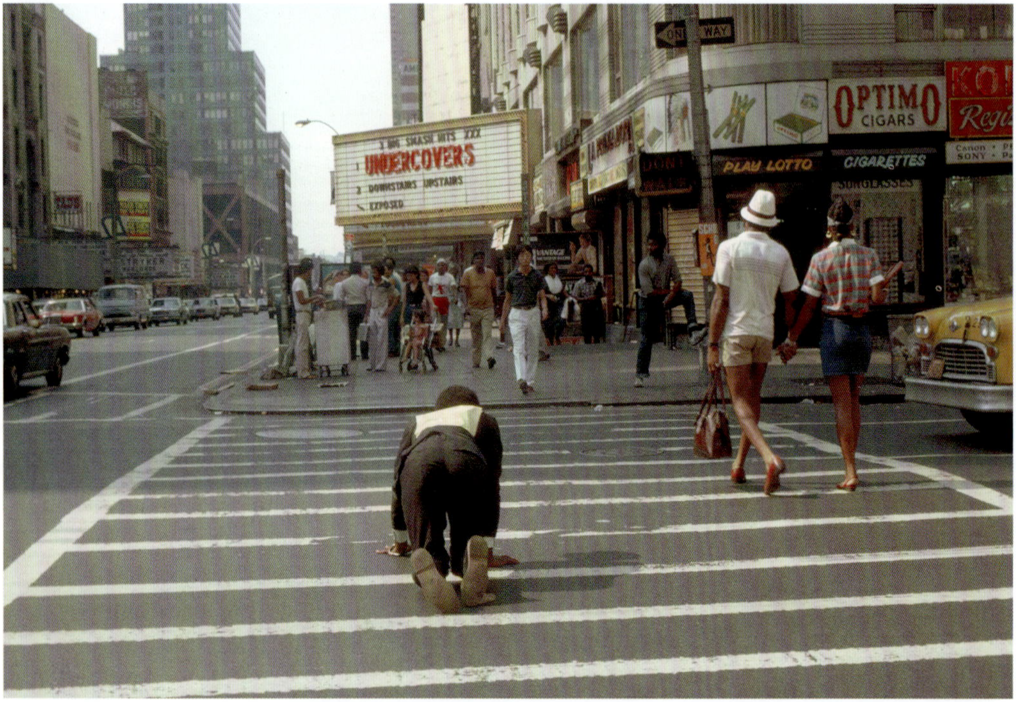
3 BIG SMASH HITS XXX
UNDERCOVERS
DOWNSTAIRS UPSTAIRS
EXPOSED
OPTIMO
CIGARS
PLAY LOTTO
CIGARETTES

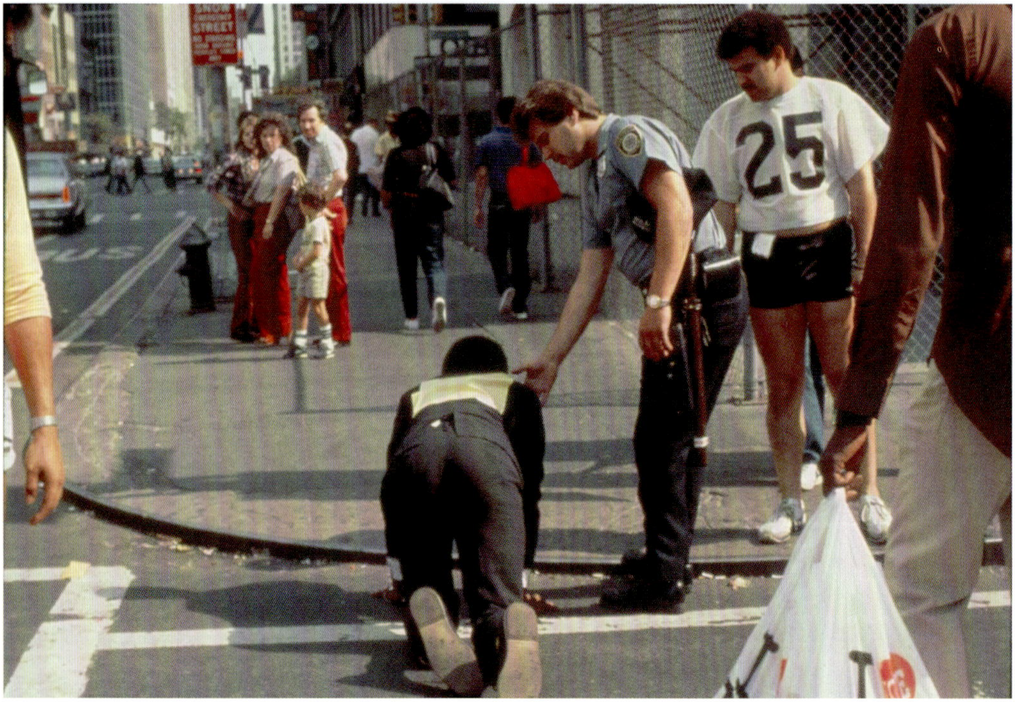
25

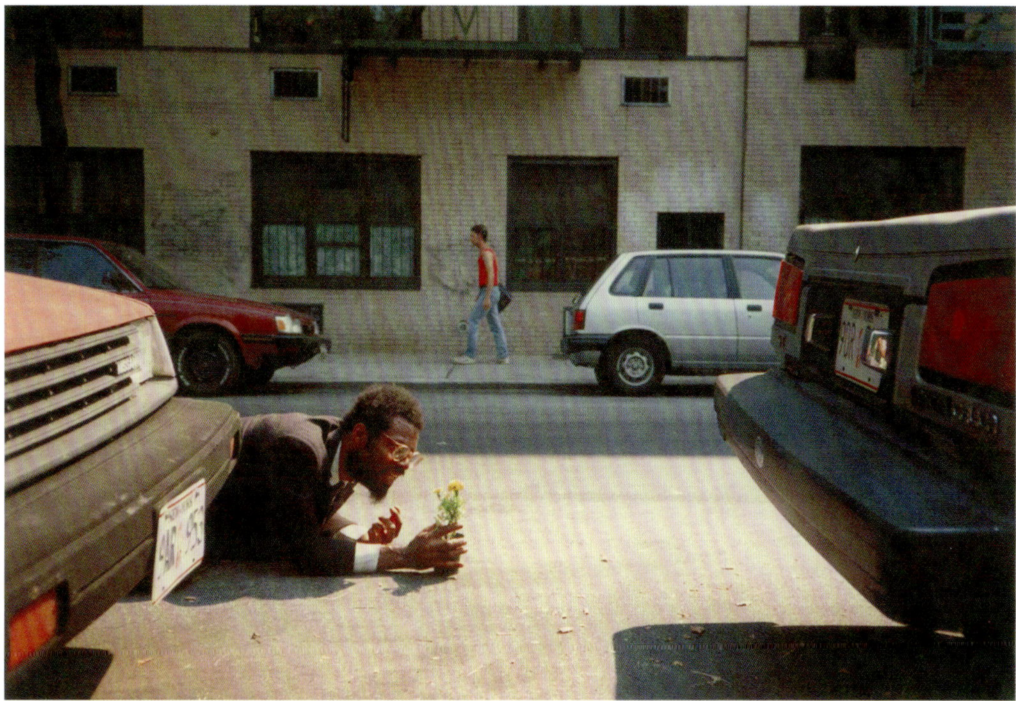

[Plates 6 and 7, facing page] Pope.L, *Times Square Crawl a.k.a. Meditation Square Pieces*, 1978. Digital C-prints on gold fiber silk paper, each 10 × 15 inches. © Pope.L.Courtesy of the artist and Mitchell-Innes & Nash, New York.

[Plate 8] Pope.L, *How Much Is the Nigger in the Window a.k.a. Tompkins Square Crawl*, 1991. Digital C-prints on gold fiber silk paper, each 10 × 15 inches. © Pope.L. Courtesy of the artist and Mitchell-Innes & Nash, New York.

GUERRILLA GIRLS REVIEW THE WHITNEY.

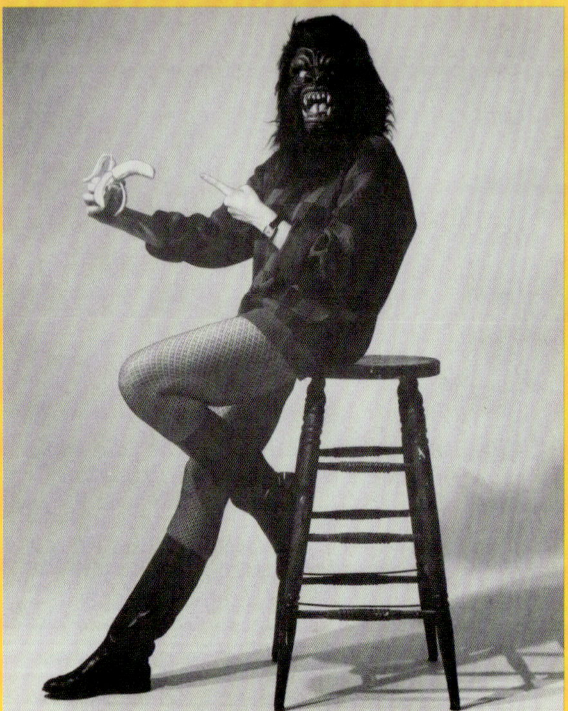

APRIL 16-MAY 17 1987

Opening Thurs April 16 6-8 PM Gallery open Thurs-Sun 12-6 PM

THE CLOCKTOWER

108 Leonard St, NY 212 233-1096

The Institute for Art and Urban Resources, 46-01 21st St, Long Island City, NY 11101

The Clocktower facility is owned by the City of New York. Its operations are supported in part by a grant from the Department of Cultural Affairs, City of New York: Diane Coffey, Commissioner; David Dinkins, President, Borough of Manhattan

[**Plate 9, facing page**] Guerrilla Girls, *Guerrilla Girls Review the Whitney*, 1987. Poster. © Guerrilla Girls. Courtesy of guerrillagirls.com.

[**Plate 10**] Art v War, *Art v War at Whitney Museum*, December 2018. Color photograph. © Cindy Trinh. Courtesy of the artist.

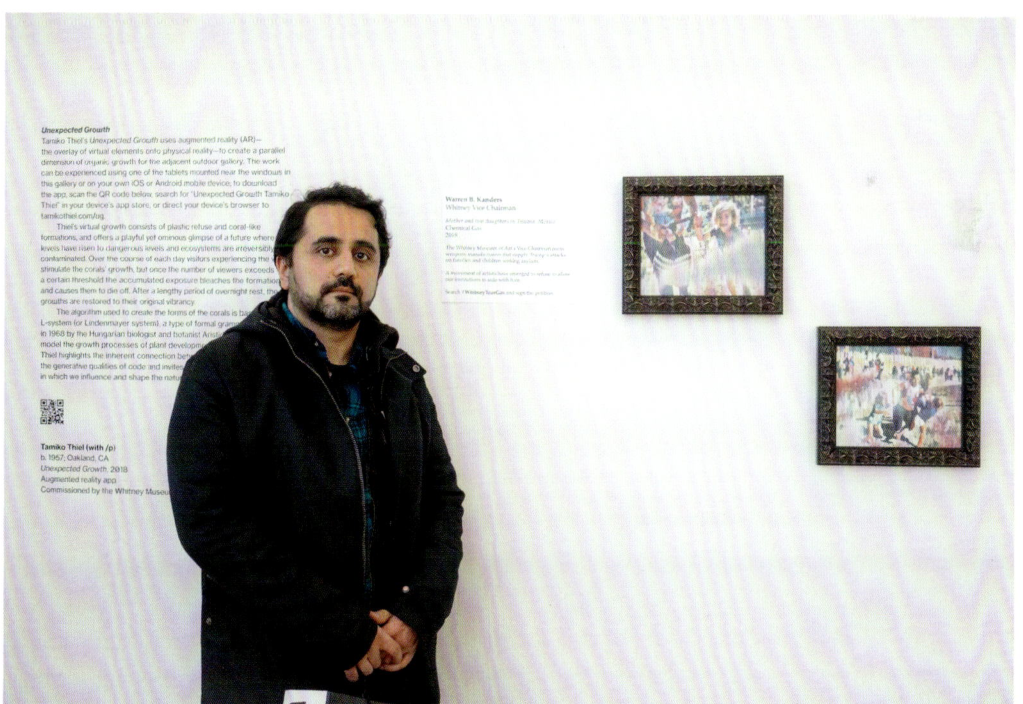

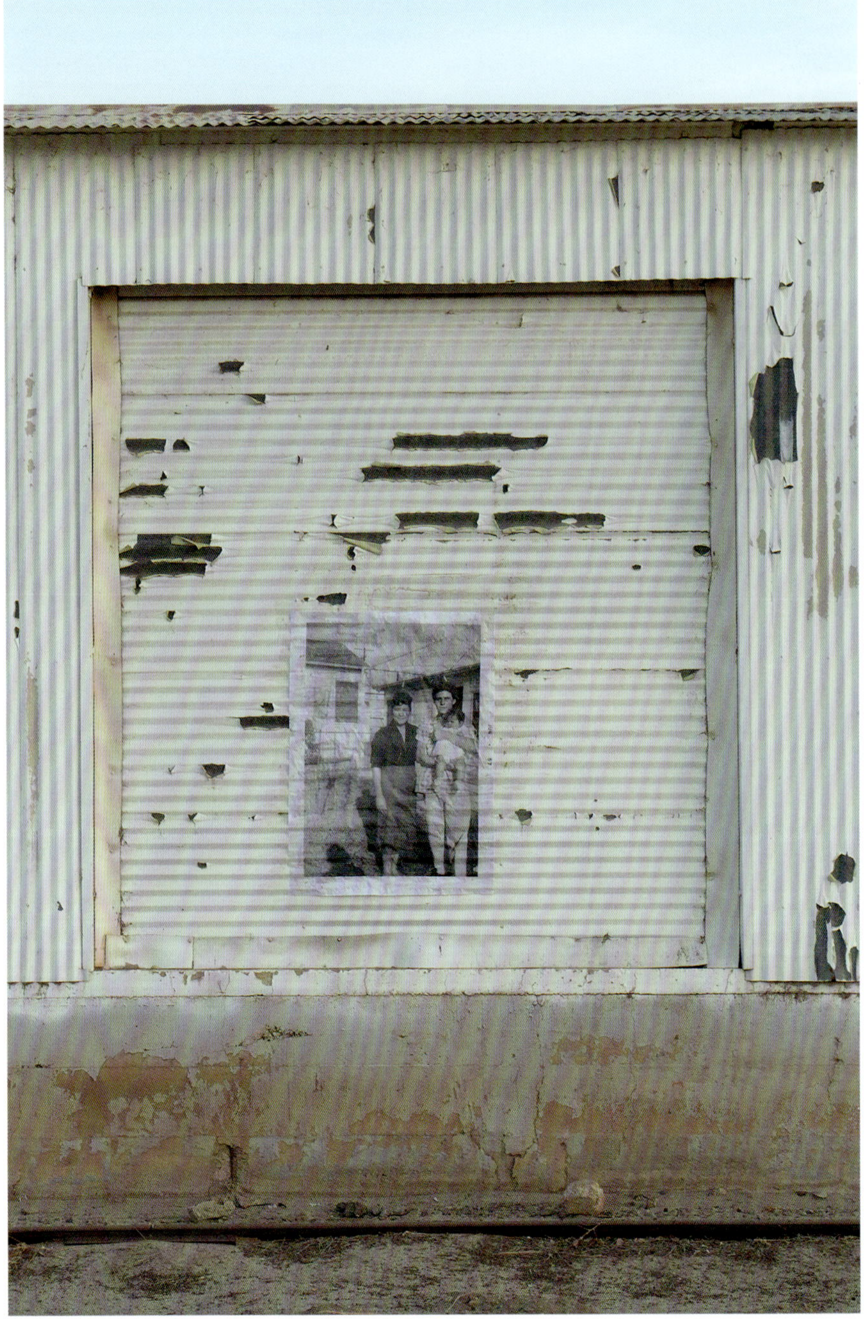

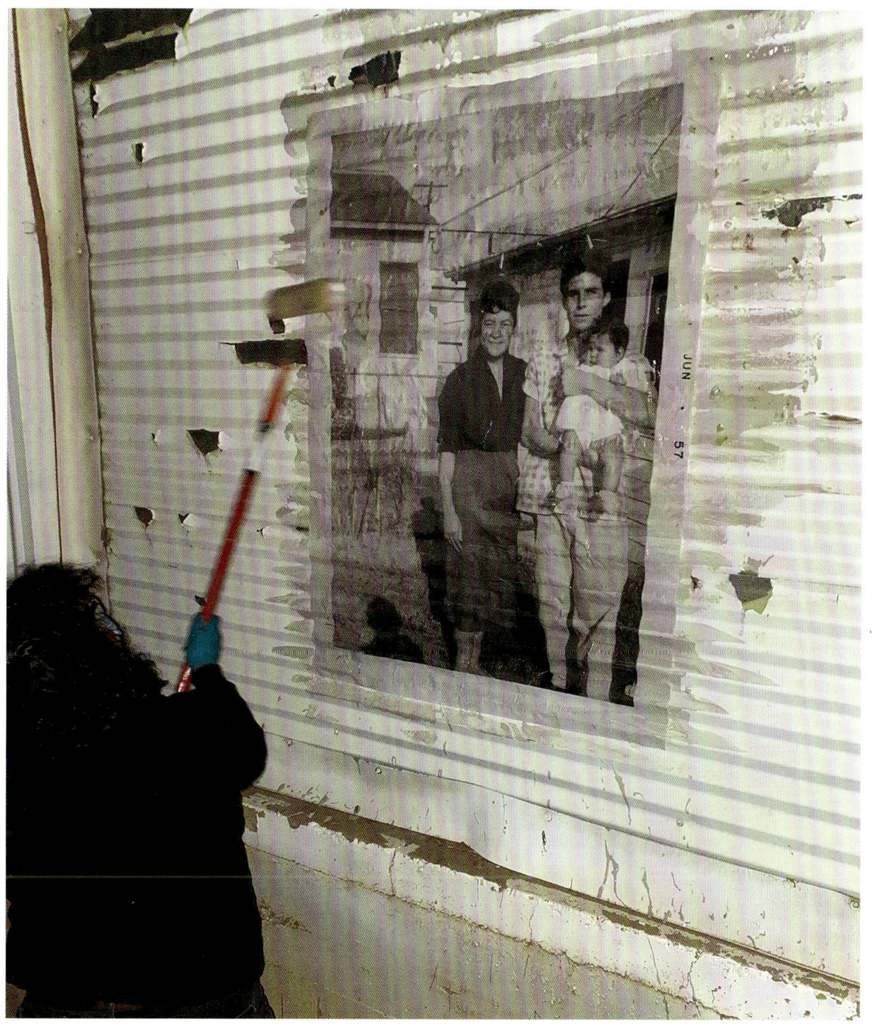

[Plate 11, facing page] Amina Cruz, *Nana, Grandpa y Chita* (original photo June 1957), from the series *me & mine & you & yours,* December 2020. Photograph, wheat-paste. 52 × 38 cm. Courtesy of the artist.

[Plate 12] Amina Cruz, installation of *Nana, Grandpa y Chita* (original photo June 1957), from the series *me & mine & you & yours,* December 2020. Color photograph. Courtesy of the artist.

Pope.L's Crawls: A Prevarication with Lawfare

Although Pope.L staged his first crawl—titled in full, *Meditation Square Pieces a.k.a. Gutter Pieces a.k.a Times Square Crawl*—in 1978, he had been thinking about the street as a framework for creative expression long before.[38] Born in Newark, New Jersey, to William Pope and Lucille Lancaster, Pope.L—a name he chose that combines his father's surname and his mother's last initial—grew up during the 1950s and 1960s on New York's Lower East Side in a family life filled with art, language, and books that also suffered from financial and emotional instability exacerbated by addiction and incarceration.[39] During his youth, Pope.L used "to blow up stuff and break into things and get hauled into jail by the police."[40] "I thought it was exciting," he recalls. "I wanted to forget. Now I crawl to remember. But then I wanted the tension. I wanted attention." Pope.L also articulates the ongoing effect of punitive pressures on the decisions he makes when he crawls in public:

> I fear the transitions, the disruption. And cops, you know, cops and black people—even if they're black cops. But the more I think about why I shouldn't do it, the more I realize that I should. When I was younger and always in crisis, I was always afraid. By going out and constructing crime scenarios in the street, I could construct my fear. I could put it in a framework that made sense to me, and I could control it. I was pretty good at constructing these scenarios and getting away with it.[41]

Pope.L's naming of "getting away with it" entails literacy in the larger scene, beyond a moment of encounter with the state, and an ability to construct a crime scenario that is predictable and therefore controllable.

Punitiveness on the street is learned not just through encounters with police but through exposure to polices and surveillance of one's interior life and spaces. Poignantly, Pope.L cites his mother's navigation of the administration of welfare policy, wherein surveillance occurs in both public and private spaces, as one of his earliest lessons in the tactical necessary of surviving punitive relations. Thinking back, he describes "welfare people" at his childhood home, "showing up whenever," as "the institutional forms I remember first." Pope.L identifies his mother's readiness to perform in front of social workers as an early part of his own education in performance and institutional critique: "It's something I learned to do with institutions . . . prevaricate, lie."[42] Crawling can be thought of as Pope.L's prevarication with the institution of safety.

When Pope.L crawled through Times Square, his encounter with the police officer was not a question of *if* but *when*. That year, 1978, this area recorded the most felony and net crime complaints in the entire city.[43] The concentration of incidents was indicative of the great number of police patrol units active in the vicinity. Times Square had become a widely politicized site of "urban renewal" and "clean up," and inhumane treatment of people on the street had worsened under city ordinances passed in the name of beautification, commerce, and public safety. Between 1972 and 1978, a number of laws allocated more police to the swiftly changing commercial area of Times Square, while economic policies simultaneously incentivized real estate moguls to displace and close its many sex shops, hourly motels, and theaters.[44]

In 1972, for example, Mayor John Lindsay initiated the federally funded Midtown Project, creating two new superprecincts within the police department—Midtown North and Midtown South—to "fight crime and disorder" in "high profile areas" between 30th to 60th Streets from the Hudson River to the East River, including Times Square.[45] Lindsay's successor, Abraham Beame, expanded the Midtown Project. Under his watch, in 1973 the new cadre of superprecinct officers arrested 1,945 people for direct solicitation of prostitution and 400 "johns" for patronizing streetwalkers in Times Square. Beame also deployed another special task force, the Mayor's Office of Midtown Enforcement, to secure the area's real estate to "good commercial uses."[46] As the policing increased and arrests continued, Times Square crystallized as a political platform for pushing a moralizing profile. On April 29, 1976, Beame, along with a group of state senators, staged a televised rally at the Majestic Theater in Times Square calling for a crackdown on loitering and sex work.[47] In his speech, Beame asked the audience to support a new bill before the state legislature that would mandate jail sentences of up to ninety days for prostitutes and allow police to arrest pimps for loitering.[48]

The succession of politicians targeting Times Square continued. In 1977, when Edward Koch took office, he too focused on Times Square, establishing his own Midtown policing program, called Operation Crossroads, which expanded Beame's work and deployed "eighty *additional* uniformed and twenty-five plainclothes officers in the area bounded by West 40th Street, West 50th Street, Broadway, and Ninth Avenue."[49] As police historian Themis Chronopoulos has observed, Koch was trying to "make New Yorkers feel safer by flooding high-profile areas [i.e., Times Square] with police officers."[50] During this time, the city also used Section 8 funds intended for the poor to provide upper-class amenities to nonpoor groups in the massive real estate development just beside Times Square known as Manhattan Plaza.[51]

Mayor Koch's expansion of police forces occurred in tandem with new tax incentives for developers seeking to convert single-room occupancy hotels (SROs) into luxury condominiums, accelerating gentrification.[52] The state's incentivizing of developers coincided with the systemic defunding and dismantling of SROs across the city. Whereas in 1960, there were 129,000 such units, by 1978, when Pope.L crawled, the number had fallen to 25,000.[53] Simultaneously, mental health institutions were defunded, increasing the need for SROs. The burden on these already diminished facilities worsened their disrepair and overcrowding even as the gap between rents and income for the poorest households increased in the wake of the mid-1970s fiscal crisis. As art historian Rosalyn Deutsche explains, this was a problem throughout the city: for example, a $3.6 million restoration project in Union Square displaced a large population of unhoused people, while the number of lower-priced units in New York declined more than 60 percent between 1975 and 1981, exacerbating the issue of public space and who it belonged to.[54]

Taken together, these conditions limited affordable housing, disproportionately affecting larger number of Black and brown lower-income citizens, long disenfranchised through patterned racial (dis)inheritance. Between 1978 and 1988, more than a hundred thousand blue-collar jobs in the city were lost while over twice that many were gained in finance, insurance, and other business industries.[55] While these shifts contributed to a larger underclass with higher unemployment rates that impacted Black and Chicano communities with the greatest force, gentrification and rising rent in previously low-income neighborhood simultaneously created an upsurge of evictions and homelessness among these same communities.[56]

Nevertheless, narratives in the media celebrated those doing the gentrifying. Political geographer Neil Smith identifies the romanticizing of masculinized endurance underwriting discourses of urban renewal, explaining, "Gentrification only appears to result from the heroic conquest of hostile environments by individual 'pioneers.'" In truth, he writes, "it is apparent that where the 'urban pioneers' venture, the banks, real-estate companies, the state or other collective economic actors have generally gone before. In this context it may be more appropriate to view the James Rouse Company not as the *John Wayne* but as the Wells Fargo of gentrification."[57] Rather than rebuild or reinvest in SROs, which would give relief to the rising number of people facing eviction and poverty,

Koch authorized extrajudicial confinement of people sleeping or living on the streets, permitting police to forcibly detain anyone they believed to be a threat to themselves or others.[58] Through this extension of antivagrancy laws and the role of the police as social workers (discussed in chapter 2), an officer's assessment of "self-neglect" and "mental hygiene" was authorized as grounds for a criminal offense.

Because crime maps were still hand-drawn in New York City, there are no easily accessible records of police beats. In their absence, the documentary images of Pope.L crawling through Times Square record a path shaped by experiments in the hyperpolicing of public space. One photo shows Pope.L crossing Eighth Avenue, crawling in the direction of the Rialto II theater (plate 6). He had likely just passed the Crossroads building on 42nd Street, where, the summer before, a new police substation had recently replaced a pornographic bookstore on the first floor. The substation was justified as a way to serve wayward youth—another instance of the nationwide trend of cultivating policing as caretaking—concealing its primary function of surveillance.

The block Pope.L is approaching features in images created by Fernando Natalici (shot, also in 1978, on the same street from the adjacent corner) and Scott McPartland, whose April 1970 photograph (fig. 3.5) appears to have taken just a few feet from where Ellen LaForge later stood while documenting Pope.L's crawl.[59] Natalici's image shows the density of marquees on both sides of the street and the rush of people. It also captures the range of films being screened: amid the many XXX-rated offerings are survival films such as *Avalanche* and *Survive!*—the latter a 1976 Mexican thriller about survivors of a Uruguayan air force crash who must ultimately contemplate cannibalism. There were, as well, reportedly "hundreds of kung fu movies . . . hitting the Deuce each year, and each grindhouse worked them into their fare."[60] In McPartland's image, a large banner that is washed out by glaring sunlight in LaForge's documentary image is legible: "Welcome to 42 St."

Just beyond the Rialto II theater, Pope.L's crawl would have taken him past the 42nd Street subway entrance, followed by the infamous grindhouse theaters (the Empire, Lyric, and Apollo) as well as the Elk (360 W. 42nd Street), known for its pay-by-the-hour rooms—all spaces under constant police surveillance. Further along, it is likely Pope.L crawled by the Port Authority Bus Terminal, then newly renovated. This terminal was, according to police reports, "home" to many unhoused people, leading to its heavy surveillance by the Port Authority police—another security force that was part of the various mayors' Midtown programs. Pope.L's crawl indexes a temporality and mobility inherently informed

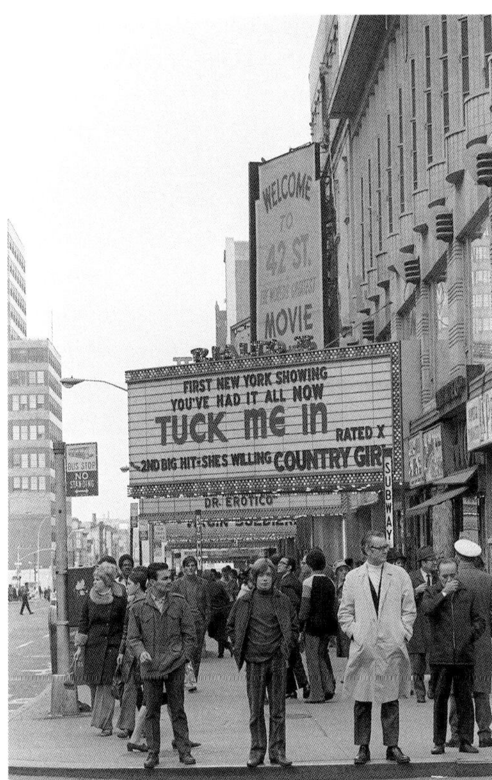

[3.5] Scott McPartland, 42nd Street Times Square, New York—Adult Movie Theaters, 1970. Archive caption: "1st April 1970: Pedestrians walk under the many adult movie theater marquees showing pornographic films lining 42nd Street in the heart of Times Square, New York." Photo by Walter Leporati. © Getty Images.

by the anticipation of police presence. The artist's run-in with the officer documents precisely *this* landscape and its punitive relations.

In interpretations of Pope.L's work, scholars tend to prioritize his description of crawling as a symbolic act. Darby English, for example, writes:

> When he started doing crawls in the late 1970s, Pope.L wanted to commit symbolic actions that could generate images of a contradiction that he knows intimately: between the image of the homeless person as evacuated of subjectivity and "the history of skills and knowledge," his restorative term for an image of the homeless subject around the competing images that converge in the production of any social idea.[61]

The "power of the crawl" by a Black man in a suit, English asserts, lies in how the movement "*symbolically* appropriates a public space" in an "act of evidencing unrealized potential" while "throwing light on the deterring forces themselves."[62] Thinking about the specificity of the crawl in relation to symbolic notions of work, English pinpoints the subversiveness in Pope.L's crawling as his "commitment to nonfunctional labor," which he argues "aestheticize[s] dispossession."[63]

Following English, André Lepecki and Tiffany Barber have each situated crawling as a symbolic reference to irregular or limited mobility that denaturalizes the order of the capitalist state. Lepecki poetically describes Pope.L's crawling as "a clumsy temporality" that metaphorically reveals "cracks" in our "kinetic assumptions related to ideological, racial, and gendered mechanisms of urban belonging, circulation, and abjection." He also sees the larger implications of this symbolic movement, asserting that "any politics of the ground is not only a political topography, but it is also a political kinesis."[64] Barber likewise recognizes metaphors of "abjection" and "powerlessness" in the crawl, but ultimately sees that the "metaphor of invisibility is not solely about homelessness or race bodies as invisible, but also the pervasiveness and the normalization of race as an ordering system that Pope.L responds to in his practice."[65] Barber concludes that Pope.L's "*choosing* to crawl becomes a project of recovery and resistance," wherein his "restricted mobility" as "performed abjection" intervenes in proslavery constructions of black masculinity and "deconstructs ideological myths of racial hierarchies."[66]

Each of these assessments of the symbolic reclaiming of space in Pope.L's crawling brings a significant layer of meaning to the work. And yet the scholarly focus on the metaphorical has perhaps steered too much attention away from the punitive relations structuring crawling and its initial reception. English even warns of an overreliance on the symbolic, writing, "As the crawls make painfully clear, to aestheticize dispossession is not necessarily to metaphorize it or to make it pretty."[67] Picking up on English's caution, and expanding upon Lepecki's notion of "political kinesis," I want to suspend the symbolic momentarily and consider the ways that crawling responds directly to its punitive context: how Pope.L's crawls are calibrated to the policing of both stillness and excessive movement of minoritized subjects in New York City urban policy specifically, while navigating prevailing notions of endurance circumscribed by white-centering political and aesthetic discourses of fitness, value, and self-defense more broadly.

Pope.L's crawl as a Black man in a business suit through Times Square in 1978 occupies intermeshing contexts of safety and the securitization of space. As critical theorist and abolitionist Jackie Wang asserts:

The urban landscape is organized according to a spatial politics of safety. Bodies that arouse feelings of fear, disgust, rage, guilt, or even discomfort must be made disposable and targeted for removal in order to secure a sense of safety for whites. . . . The visibility of poor black bodies (as well as certain nonblack people of color, trans people, homeless people, differently abled people, and so forth) induces anxiety, so these bodies must be contained, controlled, and removed.[68]

The formal aspects of Pope.L crawling, in this light, manifest as a kind of tactical self-defense calibrated to the desires motivating the work: a need to draw attention to the bodies in the street, while bracing against the unregulated discretion of police to interpret disorderliness and enforce laws of removal, which were designed, from the start, to differently police the mobility of Black, brown, Indigenous, and Asian people while enabling and prioritizing whiteness. The latter intensifies a process known as *lawfare*.

If law can be understood as a set of rules legitimized by a state and its institutions, lawfare is the messy, unwritten, but lived realities of how the laws are enforced by those in power. The term "lawfare" emerged in the 1970s but came into popular use in 2001, whereafter it was commonly defined by military strategists as the purposeful use of laws as a corollary or supplement to asymmetrical "kinetic warfare" waged against nations.[69] For example, the legal management of trade sanctions or land possession may be used to deter or undermine another nation's military action or access to weapons, demanding compliance. However, as the abolitionist geographer Ruth Wilson Gilmore explains, lawfare is not merely a part of international relations but a central component of policing and governance in the United States through which laws legitimize, abstract, and legalize the way the state and its disciplinary police force wage warfare against the most vulnerable through legalized methods they call risk management.[70] Pope.L's crawling is indicative of the conditional enforcement of such governance: how certain people are removed from view in the name of order.[71] Thus, as geographer and leisure studies scholar Rasul Mowatt elucidates, "Lawfare either is the enabling of force to be performed legally or the provision of alternative non-force methods" used to criminalize modes of surviving the state.[72]

Times Square is not just a site where the police remove or discipline those perceived to be unhoused individuals, sex workers, and drug dealers. It is also a site where risk communication was observed and consolidated, and where adaptation of law(fare) from other urban contexts was tested before being implemented elsewhere. Returning to the image documenting Pope.L's encounter with a police officer (plate 7), punitive contact occurs not just in the police officer's physical touch but in the ways people on the street turn to see what is happening. Several passersby take in the scene. One man, visible on the image's left edge, casts a backward glance as he continues forward, while another man in black shorts and a sports jersey pauses just behind the cop to watch. Nearby, a group of white pedestrians in matching rust-colored pants stand in a cluster, the adults locking eyes on Pope.L while a young child looks away. The decision to pause, stare, or keep walking shapes the performance as it unfolds. It signals toward the sociality of risk communication—the varying ways people respond to a crime scenario—as the artist and the officer address one another.

The crawl, as a form not explicitly identified within punitive ordinances, aids Pope.L in his maneuvers through the policing laboratory of Times Square. Significantly, Koch's efforts in Times Square borrowed from punitive ordinances enacted in other cities. Phoenix, Arizona, for example, passed "anti–Skid Row" zoning that disallowed the construction of shelters and food kitchens downtown and declared sleeping or lying down on public property illegal. Another Phoenix ordinance even determined that garbage was public property so that picking through trash cans could be cited as theft.[73] Likewise, Beame's 1976 press conference in Times Square referenced a Milwaukee city ordinance, then only nine months old, that allowed police to arrest a woman if she made a minimum of four contacts with men (the ordinance didn't provide a definition of "contacts").[74] These city statutes, passed in the 1970s to outlaw survival economies generated by the state's patterned and historical disenfranchisement of Black Americans, expanded the discretion of the police in the name of public safety. The policing tested in Times Square, and implemented statewide, operates as part of a national program of lawfare to gradually deny the unhoused *habeas corpus* or due process. Under these conditions, the population of people experiencing criminalized precarity in New York multiplied. Unhoused people congregated in parks, while law enforcement officials were ordered to maintain curfews and enforce ordinances that outlawed camping.[75]

Within a punitive environment, Pope.L's crawling is at once symbolic and tactical; it is a prevarication with risk communication. Because the form of the crawl is not immediately recognizable as either lawful or lawless, it bends toward both while challenging the binary. It makes passersby and police slow down since they do not know how to read the action punitively. The crawl is therefore specific in its disruption and confusion of binaries—productive and not-productive, moving and not-moving, threatening and not-threatening—that hold the punitive space together and make the management of "safety" feasible. The crawl operates in the gray area of each classification. It is an extralegal form; it is not illegal to crawl, but crawling offers movement that flirts with enforceable dichotomies of order and disorder. Pope.L wears a yellow patch communicating "caution" and "slowness" to commuters, thereby making himself visible to others who are also literate in the state- and culture-sanctioned mobility of city spaces and traffic flows. Instead, it is the police officer who stops traffic, who halts movement and flow. Pope.L's precise description of *Times Square Crawl* as "not loitering" but "actually moving" thereby portends a specific action attuned to the gray space of legal frameworks used by police and citizens to manage both the private and public spaces.

Crawling engages with a particular tactical history: the state's use of economic development initiatives to legalize nonaccountability toward vulnerable populations, while criminalizing their forms of survival. The efforts of urban renewal around New York City's 42nd Street at Times Square, writes historian David Church, "were often veiled attempts to gentrify these areas by forcing out minorities such as the African American audiences who later made 1970s blaxploitation and kung-fu films so successful in grind houses." "42nd Development Project's urban renewal plans aimed to 'move out lower-income citizens and taxpayers and to replace them with more affluent ones'" and, he asserts, also resulted in displacing the possibility of future contact and networking among cross-class, cross-racial, and queer populations.[76] Redevelopment opened spaces up to white professional classes.[77] This was a death knell for interracial, cross-class, and queer sociality. In this decimation, Samuel Delaney writes, "a complex of social practices . . . dies."[78] Summarizing Delaney's argument regarding policing, the repression of sexual desire and queer sociality, and gentrification in Times Square, Jack Halberstam posits that the mobilizing of "logics of safety" were ultimately "deployed to justify the destruction of an intricate subcultural system."[79]

Pope.L's crawl through Times Square in 1978 may not have set out to theorize punitive literacy, but his work nevertheless articulates the relational specificity of a set of interrelated modes of survival and self-defense then under assault through the state's wielding of public safety policy. In this context, a Black man crawling in a suit is a form that responds aesthetically and legally to the crime scenario in the street and the ways this scenario activates site-specific risk perception; its challenge to the classification of lawful and lawless acts underscores the state's and citizens' *labor* of managing distinctions between orderliness and disorderliness. Possibilities of lawlessness reside within the crawl, an action that is neither illegal nor threatening but nonetheless suspect. Within Times

Square in 1978, specifically, Pope.L's work offers insight into the criminalizing of urban tactical survival itself, as an intensely local, as well as national and transnational, contemporary and transhistorical process. *Times Square Crawl* underscores how low-tech self-defense and survival of the street was targeted through lawfare, how urban renewal policies and politicians seeking to "clean up" did so by forcefully removing individuals *as well as* the forms of social interaction, pleasure, and tactical knowledge they deemed a threat to the "safety" of commercial revenue.

Looking back on this period, Pope.L explains:

> When I work in the street, I wear a suit and I enter into the paranoia and anxiety that comes with an intimate relationship with the street. That fear. That freedom. I don't want to speak for street people or in the name of street people. I want to poetically recreate street images and experiences that reconfigures the troublesome feelings we all go through when we encounter these "sides" in the street. I want to renew that troublesome spirit. Make it more difficult to be denied. I want people—even if it's only the policemen who arrest me, especially policemen—to experience my contradiction.[80]

Pope.L's reflection draws attention to the centrality of the police, not as a byproduct of the work but as a primary consideration and audience. In this sense, the specificity of crawling takes up the punitive site as a primary scene. As Pope.L has asserted:

> It's not just crawling, it was also *where* you crawled. As soon as you go outside, there's this issue of where are you in space and who owns that space. So, I realized that I was setting up a tension when I crawled about being in space, and how you're located in that space, and how you're supposed to behave in that space, and who can own that space, and how *you* can own it.[81]

Hsieh's Survival Tactics

While the principal connective tissue between Pope.L and Hsieh may appear to be their durational street works, self-imposed feats, or a theorizing of nonfunctional labor, I find a key link to be their shared interest in survival tactics defined by, and in response to, city ordinances outlawing certain forms of self-defense, and how this becomes a choreography—a specific relational form—within their endurance works. The kinds of risk work that underpin their tactics in art reveal the overlooked aspects of lawfare functioning within discussions of endurance in art. In their different but related forms of movement, preparation, and documentation, we can better understand how ideas of "endurance" emerge through infrastructures of safety deeply informed by norms of white cis-gendered masculinity.

Hsieh's relation to discipline and endurance training was born of his experience in the Taiwanese army. Before coming to the US, Hsieh began painting. He dropped out of high school in 1967 and joined the army in 1970. Following his three-year compulsory service, Hsieh had his first solo art show at the gallery of the American News Bureau in Taiwan, displaying paintings, such as *Paint (dot) Red Repetitions*, indicative of his experience with arduous, disciplined tasks.[82] In this work, for example, Hsieh created a thirty-sheet sketchbook filled with grids of red painted dots, each page similar but no two pages exactly alike. The work expressed the rote tedium of tasks such as those he'd experienced in the army through aesthetic gestures of repetition, while the grid of ovals conjures the visual domain of fingerprints taken at a police precinct. "In Taiwan, I spend three years in the army. Every day is very long, very boring. One year performance not long compared to three in army."[83]

In preparation for his year outdoors in Manhattan, Hsieh saved up money, subsisting on the rent he collected for subletting his loft and money he received from his parents.[84] He also did a test-run on the streets. "I must be very careful, very organized to be safe," he told Ingberman and her collaborator, the artist and curator Papo Colo. "I always test a piece first to see if it is possible for me to do it. I do it for one week."[85] Anticipating conflict and violence on the street, Hsieh strategically carried with him nunchakus for self-protection, as well as a sleeping bag and one knapsack containing essential clothing, a flashlight, and a radio. Yet, despite his preparation for the bending of the law, art critics debate whether Hsieh's labor in *Outdoor Piece* falls on the side of, or against, the word of the law.

Misrecognition or diminishment of Hsieh's punitive literacy has shaped assessments of *Outdoor Piece*. In one exemplary article published in *Art in America* in the summer of 1982, art critic Barry Kahn describes Hsieh's movement through Manhattan as "wanderings" similar to those of "Christian martyrs or the solitude of Buddhist monks," a reference meant to conjure the iconography of saints celebrated for their passive endurance of physical and mental challenges.[86] Kahn's reference, steeped in Christian iconography of pain, deems Hsieh's endurance dignified, timeless, and ahistorical. His depiction of Hsieh as

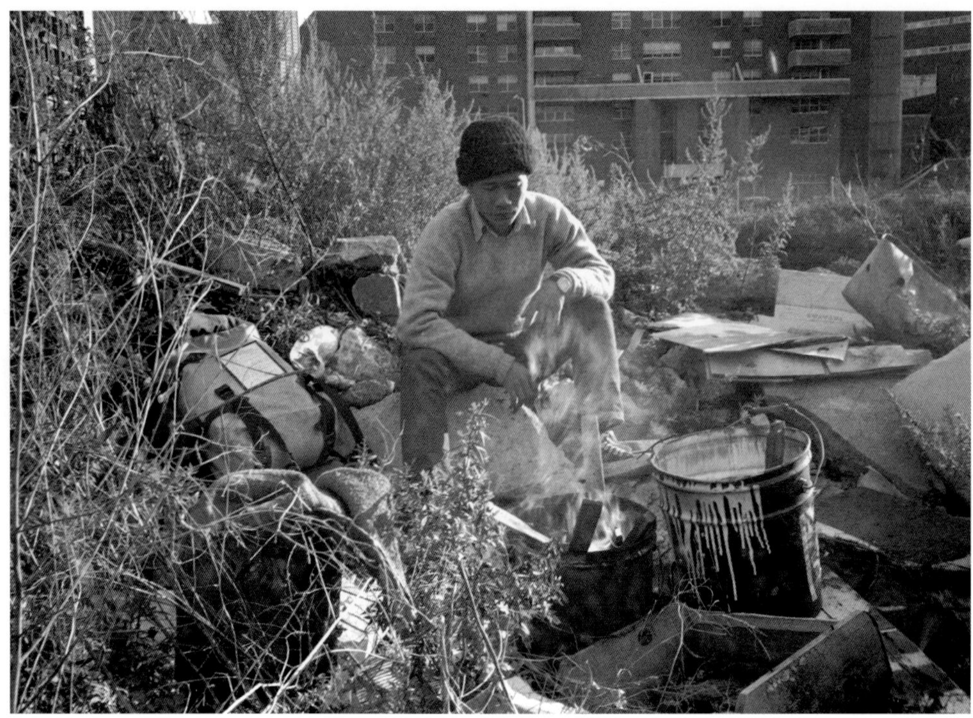

a *wanderer* renders invisible the *work* of his risk-taking, negating the way the piece records the artist's tactical knowledge of place.

Hsieh doesn't merely "wander" but strategically moves with tactical foresight attuned to his terrain, and he meticulously documents this labor. As Shalson notes, Hsieh risked fines or jail time every time he peed or defecated outside — relieving oneself publicly was punishable by a fine of up to $250 or ten days in jail under the state's sanitation code.[87] This meant that Hsieh selected locations — and a choreography of daily living — in response to, among other things, punitive horizons of encounter. As he moved from place to place, Hsieh carried a camera to document his activities and a blank set of maps, one for each day, upon which to record his maneuvers. In images he created with a tripod, we see Hsieh drinking coffee in an abandoned chair, reading a book on a stoop, bathing in a fire hydrant, and warming himself by a fire he built (another act punishable by heavy fines) (fig. 3.6). In the latter image, and many of the others, Hsieh's backpack faces the camera, his statement of intention on view in the plastic window of the bag. The scene, like many of the photographs, suggests

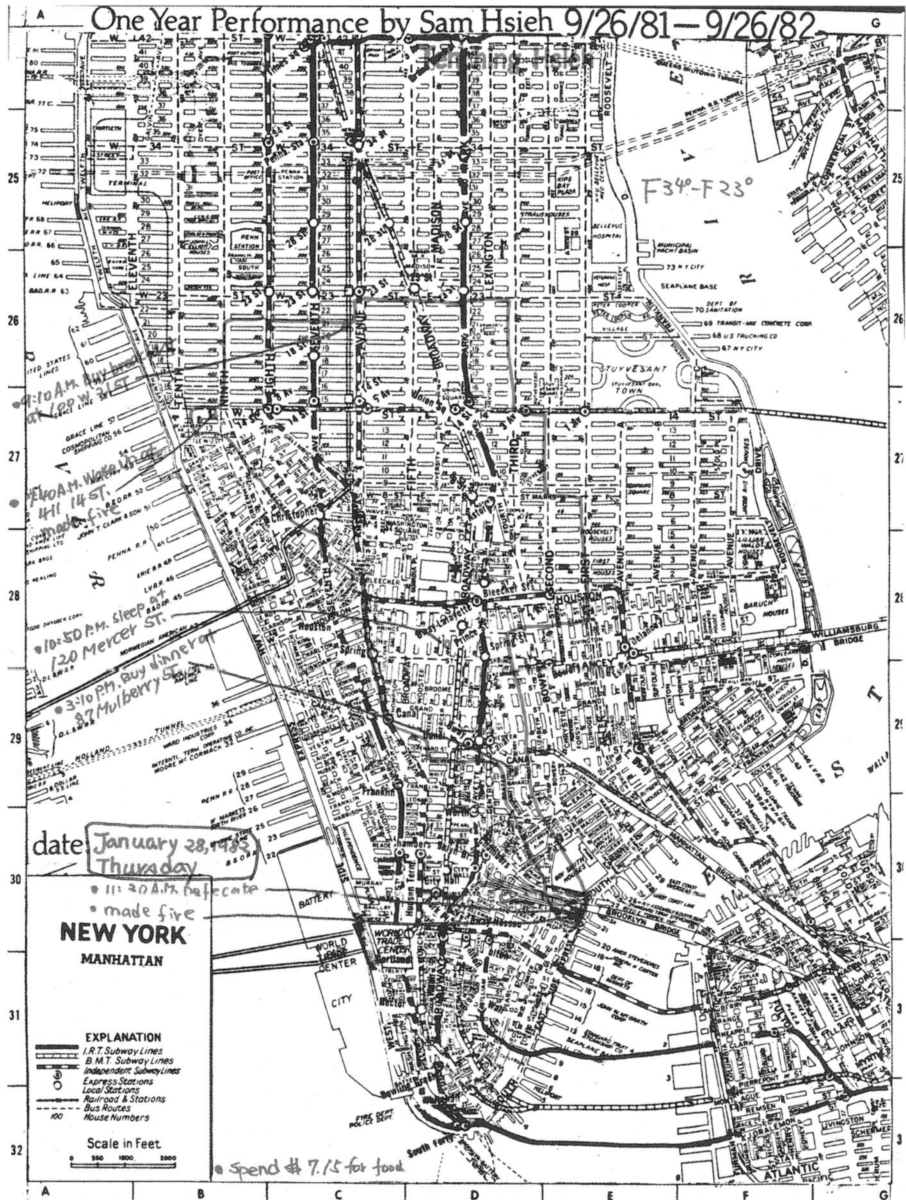

[3.6, facing page] Tehching Hsieh, *One Year Performance 1981–1982,* Life Images. Black-and-white photograph. © Tehching Hsieh. Courtesy of the artist and the Gilbert and Lila Silverman Collection.

[3.7] Tehching Hsieh, *One Year Performance 1981–1982,* Daily map. Printed paper. © Tehching Hsieh. Courtesy of the artist and the Gilbert and Lila Silverman Collection.

that Hsieh sought out spaces isolated from possible intruders or police enforcing laws against fires and sleeping outside.

On the daily maps, Hsieh marks his walking path in red pen, and notes locations where he slept, ate, and defecated, as well as the day's high and low temperature, how much he spent on meals, and what friends he saw. During the colder months, the maps also record where, exactly, he built fires for warmth, as seen on January 28, 1982 (fig. 3.7). We see from the maps that Hsieh does not wander aimlessly, nor does he move all over Manhattan. He tends to stay in and around Chinatown, Tribeca, and Soho. He routinely buys meals at 190 Hester Street and 117 Mott Street in Chinatown, as a typical map, dated April 19, 1982, conveys. The maps also reveal that Hsieh stayed away from Times Square, an ongoing battleground of urban renewal and a site of increasingly zero-tolerance policing. As Simon Wu observes in his assessment of Hsieh's piece, "It doesn't seem that Hsieh felt all that safe during his performance. He carried around those nunchucks in his backpack. His favorite places to sleep were the small parks of SoHo or a drained public pool where he could minimize unwanted disturbances." For Wu, this work by Hsieh can be understood as "a screen on which Asian American experience, carceral politics, and intersecting and sometimes conflictual race and class solidarities are crystalized across time and space."[88]

By and large, Hsieh stays in areas with which he is familiar, areas, too, where he has developed relationships with people in the food industry and in the art world. He hangs around Tribeca, not far from his loft. He frequents sites where he might expect a measure of safety. For example, Hsieh's map from July 2, 1982, indicates that he likely showed up for the opening of the exhibition *Public Vision* at White Columns; his red line passes directly by the gallery, located at 325 Spring Street, that evening, and suggests that he slept nearby that night. In fact, he often slept in this area, and in recurring spots, frequenting doorways at 96 Greene Street and 12 Wooster Place (the latter, the home of James Wentzy, a friend and sporadic photographer of *Outdoor Piece*). He also held planned meetings with Ingerbman, negotiating the terms of his upcoming Franklin Furnace exhibition "from the stoop" of the gallery.[89] Notably, his map from June 12, 1982, reveals that his route syncs up with the Rally for Nuclear Disarmament, a march supported by many artists and involving an estimated one million people—the largest antiwar demonstration in US history at that time—that culminated in Central Park.

These glimpses into the social life of living outside for a year demonstrate that Hsieh remained inside the art scene, mingling with curators and artists and witnessing new work being made and performed. His familiarity with the areas that were part of his typical routine also indicates an attention to safety; staying where he was known by business owners and other regulars was an important precaution given the policing, and coded lawfare, enacted against unhoused people. Hsieh's itineracy is thus paradoxically structured; it is repetitive and organized by a deep, almost durable sense of place-making, and evinces his risk-averse anticipation of possible violence or punitive encounter. In this light, *Outdoor Piece* materializes a territorial intelligence resonant with Pope.L's mode of crawling, as a form attuned to the punitive structure of one's surroundings.

Times Square, Chinatown, and Tribeca operated as different kinds of policing zones during this period. Facing a fiscal crisis, New York City began cutting its police department at unprecedented rates. The number of officers working in the Lower East Side, for example, dropped by a third between 1976 and 1984, from 733 officers to 492.[90] As the New York City Police Department was systematically gutted, the agency looked for other ways to maintain its control, especially in places, like Times Square, deemed a crime "hot spot."[91] "Hot-spot" status in itself "targets" particular people; the space and its disproportionate coverage in the media thereby serves as a way for the state to reinforce and sharpen who "it exacts policing and carceral harm on and [to create] spaces and people that are inherently criminal" just for being present.[92]

Policing in hot spots is dialectically related to that in other parts of the city. New York City's Chinatown has a relevant history, not only in terms of community identity, but as another, adjacent punitive context. In the mid-1950s, community leaders had concluded that ridding their neighborhood of delinquency would help them achieve full citizenship and promote "pro-Chinese attitudes." *Chinese World* editor Dai-ming Lee advised, "If we give the police the cooperation they seek, hoodlumism can be eliminated and Chinatown can be made a truly model area."[93] In the midst of a perceived (and media-amplified) juvenile delinquency crisis in the 1960s and 1970s, Chinese American leaders appropriated the "nondelinquency" trope by mandating courteousness and a "law-abiding spirit."[94]

During the mid-1960s, the idea of an innate Asiatic "nondelinquency" became a foil used by politicians and reporters to categorically demonize Black and brown Americans, who had long been overpoliced and portrayed in the media as perpetrators of violence. The idea of a "model minority" garnered unprecedented attention in a 1966 *U.S. News and World Report*, aligning, not coincidentally with the founding of the Black Panther Party for Self-Defense. The report found that one minority population, "the nation's 300,000 Chinese-Americans, is winning wealth and respect by dint of its own hard work," and set this accomplishment as a foil against which to admonish Black Americans for civil rights protests.[95] That same year, the *New York Times* praised Japanese Americans' dedication to "education, low crime rates, and strong family values," again using Black Americans who have failed to "properly assimilate" as a point of comparison.[96] It wasn't just that the lumped-together Asiatic "model minority" enacted "quiet dignity" and "hard work," but that their lifestyle, perceived to be committed to a traditional nuclear family, was framed thereafter as a "preventive" to juvenile delinquency insofar as it was "anti-slum," thereby reinforcing the idea that areas of cities predominantly populated by Black and Latinx communities were innately inclined to criminality.[97]

In the late 1970s, Ronald Reagan, the former California governor campaigning for president, praised "rugged individualism, hard work, thrift, traditional morality, and stable family life," juxtaposing it with an idea that the recent "drift and disaster" was caused by the "riots, assassinations, and domestic strife" of the 1960s era.[98] Without mentioning race or gender, Reagan invoked a racialized, sexualized, classist discourse of efficiency wherein the higher Black unemployment rate was compared to the rising financial success of Asian Americans. Through these seemingly race-neutral evocations, historian Ellen Wu explains, the combination of "Japanese and Chinese American racialization" and "racial liberalism" shaped "conditions of black citizenship" through the theorizing of endurance and delinquency.[99] In Reagan's equation of "hard work," endurance becomes a mark of moral success detached from the racialized, structural inequities that create asymmetrical access to resources, and yet he specifically singled out users of welfare programs as a key source of the nation's weakness.[100]

The perception of Chinatown as anti-slum affected the kinds of policing that occurred there. Conversely, Times Square, an area associated with Black and Latinx populations, and sex industries framed as an assault on the nuclear family, was continually hyperpoliced well into the mid-1980s, serving as a hub for policing experimentation. Furthermore, between Pope.L's *Times Square Crawl* in 1978 and Hsieh's 1981 experiment in living on the streets of Manhattan, litigation had deepened police discretion to disperse and remove people: the 1979 ruling in *Callahan v. Carey* determined that the city was responsible for providing shelter to unhoused men. While this landmark decision led to an expansion of emergency resources, the funding of temporary housing did not alter the structural problems that continued to generate an unhoused population. Meanwhile, Mayor Koch disliked the "right to shelter" and fought to deepen a zero-tolerance response to disorderly living.

In March 1981, in the name of public health and safety, Koch authorized police to forcibly hospitalize endangered unhoused individuals for seventy-two hours by deeming them mentally unfit.[101] The criteria for assessing "endangerment" and mental "unfitness" were left entirely to police discretion, much as the Milwaukee city ordinance had left "contact" undefined. Hsieh's avoidance of Times Square suggests awareness of these interconnected geographies—how the targeting of one area consolidates its profile of disorderliness relative to other, more orderly and civil parts of the city. Hsieh's maps, then, become poignant portraits of his literacy in punitiveness and risk when we attend to both where he did and where he *did not* go, as he calculated his own safety vis-à-vis the normalized violence of the city's "safety" protocol and lawfare.

While Pope.L explored "not loitering" but "actually moving" in the hyperlocal context of Times Square, Hsieh navigated both local antiloitering and antivagrancy laws and, on a national scale, perceptions of "loitering" as the crime of undocumented immigrants. In a telling revelation of how Hsieh's sense of security changed between 1978 and 1982, the artist circulated his *Wanted by U.S. Immigration Service* poster in the exhibition *Illegal America* while enacting *Outdoor Piece*. As mentioned above, the stakes were too high in 1978, when *Wanted* was conceived, to circulate the work, which disclosed his full name, photo, and fingerprints. In 1982, the statement Hsieh displayed in *Illegal America* (fig. 3.8) makes clear the overlap of *Wanted* and *Outdoor Piece*: he asserts that *Wanted* will begin on February 10, 1982, and continue until March 6, 1982, the nearly one-month duration of the run of *Illegal America* overlapping with his year outside. The fusion of these works provides crucial, albeit previously overlooked entry into Hsieh's risk work—how his living on the streets mitigates some of the fears at work in *Wanted*, while its logic of transparency and documentation inadvertently legitimizes *Outdoor Piece* for art critics and lawyers.

This reciprocal relation between Hsieh's *Wanted* and *Outdoor Piece* has been overlooked in the vast discourse on Hsieh's durational performance work. But *Outdoor Piece* makes possible the public display of Hsieh's *Wanted* piece while, conversely, the public display of *Wanted* contributes to the artist's acquittal in court when later arrested while living on the streets. The public viewing of *Wanted* and the making of *Outdoor Piece* articulate a particular formation of punitive literacy, articulated across the two contemporaneous—and codetermined—pieces. For *Outdoor Piece*, Hsieh leaves his home for a year. He also forgoes work in business spaces, like the Chinatown restaurant where he had worked as a dishwasher, that are vulnerable to INS raids. He thus becomes less trackable. When asked whether living outdoors made it easier for immigration official to find him, Hsieh replied slyly, "I was living on the street during

February, 1982

STATEMENT

I, Sam Hsieh, did the piece WANTED BY IMMIGRATION SERVICE in May 1978.

I shall publish my WANTED poster in the exhibition ILLEGAL AMERICA at Franklin Furnace in New York.

If someone should see me, please call the Immigration Service at 212-349-8735.

The WANTED piece shall begin on February 10 and continue until March 6, 1982.

Sam Hsieh

Sam Hsieh

New York City

[3.8] Tehching Hsieh, *Wanted*, 1978/1982, Statement. Printed paper. © Tehching Hsieh. Courtesy of the artist and the Gilbert and Lila Silverman Collection.

the time the 'Wanted' poster was exhibited in a group show. No officer came to find me."[102]

In *Wanted*, Hsieh reverses the tradition of "paper sons," a long prehistory to the "model minority" myth in the US in which Chinese immigrants fabricated paper trails with upstanding fictional names, employment records, and transcripts to counter surveillance and anti-Chinese sentiment.[103] Instead, Hsieh announces his criminal status and discloses his real name and likeness, preempting deportation. In so doing, he also disrupts and denies the antiblackness that operates within the upholding of a model minority mythology by refusing to play the part of a "model" citizen—a figuration at the center of racialized notions of innocence and self-efficiency.[104] Like Pope.L, who prevaricates with the institution of risk communication, in *Wanted*, Hsieh prevaricates with the institutionalized ideas of ascertaining illegality as an individualized unit of recognition. He calls attention to the network of relations that make possible the very idea of illegal personhood.

Notably, *Wanted* circulated not only within the exhibition space but internationally when, in May 1982, it was chosen as the representative image to accompany a review of *Illegal America* published in *Artforum*, an international venue for contemporary art coverage. In its printed circulation beyond the US, *Wanted* raises a different specter of criminality—reaching a much larger audience in a form that outruns state fingerprinting: in its diminished size and quality, Hsieh's fingerprints become unreadable, legible only as tiny spots of black ink. Furthermore, as the artwork selected as the "face" of an exhibition titled *Illegal America*, Hsieh's wantedness becomes a fraught stand-in for structures of illegality in the US. Its circulation also belies a significant change from Hsieh's earlier discomfort with circulating the poster: "Regarding the poster shown on *Artforum*, I was doing my third one-year performance," he explains. "Although I was still illegal, psychologically I wasn't afraid, I wasn't worried about having my image circulated."[105] The canonizing of guerrilla tactics in performance and conceptual art helped usher in this shift, as prior experimentations offered a record of citational practice. Part of this sense of security came from having been accepted by curators like Ingberman and art critics like Kahn, but part came from the expanded legal imagination interwoven with these acts.

Hsieh's trial corroborates his sense of risk and safety, his sentencing marking a new phase in the legal perception of tactical works as well as risk assessment of art among lawyers and judges. As mentioned earlier, Hsieh was arrested on charges of assault and possession of an illegal weapon—nunchakus, which had been banned in New York state since 1974 due to the government's fear of the kung fu "craze." During Hsieh's two hearings in June 1982, the presiding judges, Rose McBrien and Martin Erdmann, allowed Hsieh to remain outside on the sidewalk. As Hsieh's lawyer explained to him via walkie-talkie, the judges "accepted that you're a *serious artist* and that this is your piece that you're doing, and he understands that you can't come into court, consistent with the integrity of your art."[106] Erdmann had read a story about Hsieh's durational endurance works by the economist Kathleen Hughes in the *Wall Street Journal*, in which she interviewed gallerist Leo Castelli. Hsieh's yearlong endurance performances were not "avant-garde," Castelli told her. "Performance art (expressing ideas by using the body rather than by creating an object) became a legitimate art form in New York in the 1960s, by such people as Chris Burden, who had himself shot in the arm."[107]

In his ruling, Judge Erdmann reduced the charges against Hsieh from second-degree assault and possession of an illegal weapon to the comparatively minor disorderly conduct. Hsieh pleaded guilty to this offense and was sentenced by Judge McBrien to "time served" —the fifteen hours he had spent in jail in May. The following week, the *New York Post* ran a story on the verdict. The tone of the article, as suggested by its title, "Gotta Have Art, Says Judge with a Heart," was playful and light. To legitimize Hsieh's practice, the reporter quoted from the "respected art gallery owner Leo Castelli," who said that "Hsieh's performance art, as it's known, is a legitimate art form using the body rather than creating an image."[108] Judge Erdmann also remarked, "These days anything is art. Staying outside may be art. I'm getting old and nothing surprises me."[109]

The outcome of Hsieh's trial, and the legitimization of his artwork, marks a moment when lawyers, judges, and volunteer legal counsel recognized the deployment of tactics in artwork as "serious" art. When Burden was acquitted in 1972 for a traffic violation and causing a false emergency to be called in (as discussed in chapter 1), it had not been because the judge or jury found that he was making "serious" art. It was instead due to a hung jury, as well as the art world rallying behind him. The Volunteer Lawyers for the Arts had suggested, for example, that "Burden's only defense is to plead insanity," since they didn't "believe his work is art." As Ingberman noted in her research on art and criminality, the Volunteer Lawyers "really think that [Burden] must be unstable to perform such acts," an idea that had changed by the 1980s, as indexed by Hsieh's trial.[110] While Burden had largely abandoned his "hit and run" tactics and more confrontational art of the 1970s, his sculptural experiments and installation art of the 1980s were received within the antecedent of his famed danger-seeking profile.

The judges' acceptance of Hsieh's actions as art and reduction of the charges against him rest precisely on the canonizing of (the white-centering risk work of) tactics within conceptual and performance art. Hsieh's court case provides a record of the clear legal perception of such experimental works as viable forms of cultural production, and how this opinion was cultivated through the legal precedent set by artists' earlier arrests. Hsieh's commitment to contracts was a form of self-determination, rendered possible through his mobilizing of forms legible within legal contexts, as Kee has discussed. For Hsieh, who would not receive amnesty until 1988, the enactment of fluency in conceptualism, seen as legitimate and relevant, was another kind of collateral, a form of punitive literacy, that contributed to his strategy of survival. Significantly, as Kee notes, Hsieh's status as a landlord also played a role in his trial, where it was used to "refute in court any accusations that he was a permanent vagrant (then the definition of a homeless person)."[111]

But who is a "permanent vagrant" in the punitive structures of America? As discussed in the previous chapter, the making of bodies that are permanently "out of place" is not just a legal definition of "homeless person" but a social status within the visual field of Indigenous land dispossession and racial capitalism and its antiblack foundations, which shape different but entangled anti-Asian regulations of labor and personhood. What is achieved in the outcome of Hsieh's trial may thus be a "win" for conceptual art, but one iterative of a "structural adjustment," a "kind of 'whitening' effect" that maintains vagrancy as a settler colonialist and antiblack category through race-neutral terms.[112]

Hsieh's own vulnerability within, and navigation of, the punitive-legal apparatus shows how incommensurate yet entangled relations of gendered and racialized risk inform artistic production and its reception. Not coincidentally, the verdict in Hsieh's trial recuperates his "disorderly conduct" as orderly within the purview of art discourse's citation of riskiness, as well as in the newly established guidelines of art law, published in John Merryman and Albert Elsen's 1979 volume *Law, Ethics, and the Visual Arts: Cases and Materials.* The text was the first to directly address danger and liability in performance and conceptual-based works.[113] A foundational text in the newly defined subfield of art law, the book was the product of a class at Stanford, cotaught by Merryman, a law professor, and Elsen, a professor of modern art. It assembled case studies, evidentiary texts, and "teaching questions" for law students, as well as a previously unpublished 1977 essay by Bruce E. Mitchell, "Body Art: A Legal Policy Analysis."

Mitchell's recommendations for the treatment of "dangerous pieces" draw upon court transcripts and ethical dilemmas raised by the preceding decade's "high-risk art," highlighting work by white male artists, with the cases of Burden's *Deadman* (1972) and Toche's open letter in defense of Tony Shafrazi (1974) as two significant examples.[114] Mitchell identifies a "lack of identifiable standards" for assessing body art or performance art, and sets out to establish guidelines for "maximizing balance between artistic freedom and the public interest in minimizing exposure to unwanted and unnecessary harm."[115] He presents two modes for recognizing the value of body art: "the artist as citizen" and "the artist as hero." Of the latter category, he writes, "The artist, like mythological Prometheus, risks the sin of hubris to go one step beyond the established order; to steal fire from the gods in order to enlighten mankind."[116]

In Mitchell's estimation, such heroics can be validated by the white, male artist's demonstrable minimizing of risk, maximizing of safeguards, and transparency, precautions that could provide a basis for legal immunity for artists as "cultural heroes": "If there is full disclosure of the risks involved in the piece, and the conscious or even perhaps written consent of the parties, then a no-fault immunity would be appropriate among the group."[117] He follows these notes with a final recommendation: "Art galleries and museums need to become more conscious of their potential legal liability," and might consider having the "artist post a bond, taking out insurance on the artist's life or their premises, or obtain written agreements of disclaimer from liability."[118] Given the political framework of endurance and risk, Mitchell's discussion of performance art liability in relationship to "heroism" in his recommendations for policy are especially haunting. Far from neutral, heroism is an idea that reifies notions of power entrenched in histories of hypermasculine whiteness, strength, and idealized citizenship. Mitchell concludes, "perhaps the artist as hero becomes the artist as martyr" in the next iteration of body art.[119]

Xeroxed pages from Mitchell's essay appear in Ingberman's curatorial files for *Illegal America*, indicating its influence on the exhibition and her prior research. The show grew from scholarship Ingberman completed for her art history dissertation, titled "Art and the Law in 20th Century America." It's therefore likely that Mitchell's text was on Ingberman's mind when she and her partner, Papo Colo, interviewed Hsieh in 1983 about his endurance works. They ask, "Do you feel that you are creating a hero aesthetic with the kind of work you do, or that you are being some kind of martyr?"[120] Hsieh answers, "Hero doctrine is a public thought. I am not interested. This is just a personal expression, a new way to be creative. I just try to touch my limit, to see what point I can reach." As Hsieh's and Pope.L's tactics of risk-taking in art demonstrate, however, touching limits isn't a personal venture but one embedded within political and aesthetic frameworks of social control.

Against the backdrop of emergent art law and its reliance on notions of citizen and hero, Hsieh's contract for *Outdoor Piece* (a form he also used in *Cage Piece* and *Time Clock Piece*), delineating what he plans to do, puts the project in compliance with cutting-edge risk work when it comes to performance and guerrilla art. "Full disclosure," performed by the contract he carried with him at all times (always pictured in the plastic pocket of his backpack), is ostensibly a form of ensuring legal credence in the eyes of those interpreting art law. *Wanted*, however, performs a kind of disclosure that complicates this ethical stance: the disclosure of "illegal entry" is lawful in its transparency but simultaneously discloses a potential exemption from the notation of "artist as citizen" upon which Mitchell bases his policy analysis. What this highlights, in part, is the limitations at the core of art law when its discourse is solely informed by the risk-taking and court records of white, heterosexual, cis-gendered men; the ensuing evaluation of resourcefulness, and risk itself, then remains interred within neutralized horizons of enablement. When it is possible to be deemed "illegal" without breaking any law, the ongoing misrecognition of risk, as that of surviving the laws meant to exterminate and delegitimize certain modes of survival, will continue to distort narratives of resourcefulness unattuned to racial formation, anti-immigration lawfare, and policing.

Exhibiting Punitive Literacy

Illegal America is important for its role in canonizing guerrilla tactics in art. It is also a time capsule, documenting the legal understandings of tactical art as it was gaining such recognition in the late 1970s and early 1980s.[121] Hsieh was one of thirty artists included in the show, all of whom either had been charged with crimes or had tested the bounds of crimes ranging from treason to copyright infringement, obscenity and indecent exposure to trespass and destruction of private property. The exhibition was the first to survey the global phenomenon of artists' engagement with illegality, showing US-based artists such as Hsieh, Chris Burden, Guerrilla Art Action Group, Vito Acconci, and Dennis Oppenheim alongside Viennese Action artists and Japanese avant-garde artist Gempei Akasegawa. It was also the first exhibition to survey the aesthetic manifestation of artists' varying punitive literacies. The show's title, *Illegal America*, is a double entendre. It suggests that America itself is a criminal aberration, while also positing America as a leader in surveilling and defining the contours of an increasingly carceral state.

The ways in which Hsieh's *Wanted* is addressed in reviews of *Illegal Amer-*

ica reveal the whitewashing at work in skepticism surrounding the *rigor* of risk-taking in the works. In the *Artforum* review that reproduced Hsieh's piece, art critic Kate Linker is broadly dismissive of Ingberman's vision and the works in the show: "What it adds up to is a colossal display of political impotence." Of the artists, she says, "Many have legitimized their actions through the confines of the gallery, using its space as a shelter for illegality." Some of the works "seem directed more toward publicity than toward public provocation; they are careerist documents." She specifically calls out Burden and Hsieh:

> What beyond narcissism and esthetic definition could motivate Chris Burden's silly gesture of sending a toy plane with a joint attached over the Mexican border? Similarly, Sam Hsieh's printed statement (using this show as his platform) that he has been living in the United States as an illegal immigrant seems tied more to personal needs than to valid political ends.[122]

Linker's dismissal flattens important distinction between these actions, rendering comparable Burden's 1978 piece *Coals to Newcastle*, when he playfully (as a white male citizen) sent drugs over the California–Mexico border, and Hsieh's vulnerability to arrest and deportation, which motivated him to create his work. Simultaneously, Linker views Hsieh's gesture of self-exposure, disclosure, and conceptual temporal durational work—the collapse of years of stress and anxiety into a single document—as one of "personal needs" without political ends.

Hsieh's *Wanted* poster, however, exceeds a personal action and instead summons both historical and contemporary relations of anti-Asian and anti-Chinese violence. His gesture signals to a long history (dating at least to the 1875 Page Act and the Chinese Exclusion Act) of Chinese and Japanese immigrants to the United States being lumped together and deemed a threat to the work ethic and resourcefulness of the "true" (that is, white) American due to their supposed eagerness to take low-paying jobs.[123] Hsieh's astute positionality as "wanted" and at the same time "feared" is itself a material risk, one rendered violently tangible in the murder of Vincent Chin in June 1982, during the year Hsieh was living outdoors. Chin was brutally beaten outside a bar in Detroit by two white autoworkers, Ronald Ebens and Michael Nitz, and died a few days later.

At trial, Ebens and Nitz claimed self-defense, citing their recent layoffs from the Chrysler plant, which they blamed on jobs being exported to Japan and on the success of Asian Americans in the domestic auto industry. This, they argued, justified their assault on Chin, a Chinese American man whom they mistook as Japanese American.[124] The case underscores the implications of literacy in risk. Hsieh faced a possible sentence of one to five years in prison for the mere possession of nunchakus (associated with Asian as well as Afro-Asian martial self-defense). Meanwhile, Ebens and Nitz received only probation and a fine for the murder of an Asian American man; neither spent one day in jail.[125]

Like Linker's review, John Perreault's take on *Illegal America*, "Crimes of the Art," published in the *Soho News* in March 1982, evacuates the work of its social stakes. Perreault, too, sees the gestures and actions represented in the show as manifestations of "bourgeois individualism" that romanticize the artist as criminal. Echoing Linker, Perreault refers to Hsieh's *Wanted* as motivated by "psychological necessity." He asks wryly, "Is this kind of art—as someone said of Streetworks in the '60s—a training for guerrilla warfare?"[126] Perreault's question is striking for the way it addresses, across generations, the entanglements of tactics in art and tactics of subversion and shows how the forms of the 1960s were understood and recognized in the 1980s. This periodization loses, however, precisely what had emerged during the 1970s: literacy attuned to changing and expanding punitive relations. The works on display in *Illegal America* may not be training for guerrilla warfare but, rather, a foretelling of artists' recognition and negotiation of lawfare—the gray area galvanizing governance and sociality.

Ultimately, Perreault's inattention to the diverse punitive contexts underwriting these actions leads to his dismissing them wholesale through the lens of class: "It is probably exciting for a middle-class person to be arrested, or at least to experience the paranoia-rush of fearing arrest. How much is initiated by genuine politics or aesthetic exploration? Does breaking the law really challenge the oppressors?" By presuming all artists to be middle class, his review conceals and erases the wider sociality of risk-taking and what the knowledge of lawfare requires; how it is not universally held, but differently learned, conditioned, and survived by artists variably vulnerable to state-sanctioned measures of safety and citizenry. From this limited perspective of "genuine politics," Perreault concludes, "In retrospect, withdrawal from the system and from society—becoming a criminal—results in non-risk isolation."[127]

The Colorblindness of "Non-Risk Isolation"

The authority to determine what constitutes "valid political ends" in tactics—and the presumed risk involved—sits at the core of a problem that emerges in reviews of *Illegal America*, a problem that has shaped subsequent colorblind narrations of tactics in art. Both Linker's and Perreault's reviews of the exhibition communicate a sense that these art forms are rendered "non-risk" because of the "security of art." But art only provides securitization in ways that reproduce the racialized structures of property relations, fitness, and self-defense in society, each codifying an underlying privileging of whiteness. Hsieh's trial makes this clear in 1982. His charges are reduced because his lawyers can prove that he is not a "permanent vagrant": he has a mailing address and is, in fact, a landlord subletting his loft. His form of surviving the criminalizing of undocumented status subversively manifests in the hyperdocumentation of action by then accepted as a legitimate, respected form of artmaking in the legal eye, through its association with artists like Burden and Toche, written into legal precedent. As the court judge said during Hsieh's trial, "Anything can be art these days." But this reference to "anything" again relies on a limited set of credentials and standards of risk-taking, codified in exhibitions and law books wherein the people "breaking the law" are white men and women.

As noted above, Pope.L was not arrested for crawling. This non-arrest matters: his action did not enter into legal discourse, and was not available as a historic case study for Mitchell, who argued that the most "disturbing examples" in art law are the "ones which threw the art/law equilibrium into upheaval, and consequently must be the core of the restructuring of that equilibrium."[128] And yet Pope.L's tactical crawling, as a form of strategic resourcefulness, exquisitely reveals the impossibility of an art/law equilibrium that registers as "safety" for all. Importantly, Pope.L's crawling shapes the discourse of guerrilla tactics in art in its *absence* from art law—its noninclusion. His non-arrest provides an adjacent sociolegal form: Pope.L's work is not a precedent to be cited by judges and lawyers, but this *lack* of legal citation, due to the material consequences of both art and law's selective protections, offers a glimpse of a shadow archive of guerrilla tactics—the forms that evade structures of containment but in so doing remain undertheorized. This is also how the normalized whiteness of the law figures the discourse of deviance in art; what is legible as criminality obscures the lawfare that all artists navigate from their varied positions of vulnerability.

If *Times Square Crawl*—or, as discussed in previous chapters, Adrian Piper's *Mythic Being: Loitering* or Asco's *Spray Paint LACMA*—had been included in *Illegal America*, would it have been dismissed as non-risk too? Would Pope.L's movement through Times Square (or Piper's stillness in Cambridge, or Asco's swiftness in East LA) be seen as "narcissistic" or "careerist" because arrest was evaded? This logic conceals the risk work of tactical intelligence attuned to punitive relations and law(fare), how the crawl is attuned to the punitive contexts and sociality of risk communication. One need only think for a moment of the lethal material consequences of a Black man or woman being stopped for a suspected "traffic violation" — how these moments of citation, which have led to countless deaths of Black Americans at the hand of police officers, are also one of the main ways that the carceral state expands its visual and material hold of individuals through a criminal database that keeps and shares reports with employers, landlords, insurance companies, and schools in the name of public safety.[129]

Contact with the punitive state — citation — differently informs the look and manifestation of endurance in society, as in art: for Hsieh to protect himself, he created a meticulously documented archive of his conceptual art actions that positions him as a denizen of the art world; alternatively, Pope.L, differently positioned to state-sanctioned violence in punitive America, enacted an action illegible within laws of dispersal and removal. "Arrest," Allan Feldman once wrote, "is the political art of individualizing disorder."[130] It is an operation that normalizes the structures of state containment enacted upon people and conceals their distinctive but entangled vulnerabilities.

One of the goals of this chapter (and the other chapters within this book), then, has been to push against the individualizing impulse within arrests that have shaped art discourse; to instead study artists' punitive literacy as a vector that informs how each, differently marginalized by and distinctly vulnerable to state-sanctioned violence, maneuvers through "safety." Ultimately, the ways Pope.L and Hsieh differently anticipate and navigate city ordinances of removal and displacement in and across Manhattan in the late 1970s and early 1980s draws attention to the granular level of block-by-block knowledge of enduring punitiveness, as well as the fashioning of safety intertwined with economic and material dimensions of endurance not captured by a criminal-legal conception of security and risk.[131] Their aesthetic responses to these conditions make clearer that what is being endured is not only gendered racism, the criminalizing of poverty, or xenophobia relative to whiteness, but the intersecting discourses of public safety, urban control, and tactics in art.

[4]

"¿Why *Won't* You See Us?"

The Guerrilla Girls, PESTS, and the Limits of Anonymity, 1985–1987

In a black-and-white photograph at the center of the bright yellow poster, a pale-skinned woman in a short sweater dress sits upon a wooden stool, her long legs clad in tall black boots and fishnet stockings (plate 9). Her identity is concealed by the large gorilla mask, its toothy mouth gaping as if caught in midroar. The woman points a judgmental finger at the half-peeled banana in her other hand. The poster promotes *Banana Report*, the analytic exhibition, held in April and May 1987 at the Clocktower, that critiqued the overwhelmingly white and male-dominated selection of contemporary artists then on display in the Whitney Biennial.[1] This poster is also recognizable today as an iconic image made by the Guerrilla Girls, a feminist collective of anonymous artists and curators that formed in 1985 to criticize sexism and racism in the New York art world.

The idea for the Guerrilla Girls' formation emerged in June 1984 in response to their experiences protesting the lack of women artists included in the Museum of Modern Art's *International Survey of Contemporary Painting and Sculpture*. On June 15, 1984, the Women's Caucus for the Arts held a demonstration outside the museum; women marched in a picket line, carrying signs decrying how only 19 out of the 169 artists included in the show were women, and all were white.[2] Afterward, dissatisfied with the lack of attention given to their protest, seven of the participating white women artists and curators sought to find new methods for effecting change. They soon after claimed the mantle of the Guerrilla Girls, translating calculations of gender imbalance in art exhibitions and collections—what they called "weenie counts" and "banana counts"—into striking posters they began wheat-pasting around Soho and the East Village in the spring of 1985.[3] To maintain their anonymity, members wore gorilla masks when in public, and adopted the names of deceased women artists

GUERRILLA GIRLS' 1986 REPORT CARD

GALLERY	NO. OF WOMEN 1985-6	NO. OF WOMEN 1986-7	REMARKS
Blum Helman	1	1	No improvement
Mary Boone	0	0	Boy crazy
Grace Borgenicht	0	0	Lacks initiative
Diane Brown	0	2	Could do even better
Leo Castelli	4	3	Not paying attention
Charles Cowles	2	2	Needs work
Marisa del Rey	0	0	No progress
Allan Frumkin	1	1	Doesn't follow directions
Marian Goodman	0	1	Keep trying
Pat Hearn	0	0	Delinquent
Marlborough	2	1	Failing
Oil & Steel	0	1	Underachiever
Pace	2	2	Working below capacity
Tony Shafrazi	0	1	Still unsatisfactory
Sperone Westwater	0	0	Unforgivable
Edward Thorp	1	4	Making excellant progress
Washburn	1	1	Unacceptable

A PUBLIC SERVICE MESSAGE FROM **GUERRILLA GIRLS** CONSCIENCE OF THE ART WORLD

[4.1] Guerrilla Girls, *Guerrilla Girls' 1986 Report Card*, 1986. Poster. Copyright © Guerrilla Girls. Courtesy of guerrillagirls.com.

as aliases. "We had to have a new image and a new kind of language to appeal to a younger generation of women," says "Liubov Popova," or L. P., a founding member, presumably white (who later left the group).[4] The artist-activists who remain active today have aimed to "make feminism fashionable again."[5] The posters they created presented damning percentages in tandem with pithy, often acerbic questions and other text. One iconic example, an art gallery "report card" issued in 1987, tabulated the lack of progress blue-chip New York galleries had made during the previous two years in representing women artists. Galleries such as Mary Boone, Leo Castelli, Marlborough, Pace, and Marian Goodman, among others, were deemed "boy crazy," "failing," "delinquent," and "unforgivable" (fig. 4.1).

The Guerrilla Girls' characteristic mode of criticism—public appearances in gorilla masks, bright, pithy posters and billboards, and playful, almost slapstick symbolism—provides salient critiques of cultural power structures in the art world, alongside public service announcements that address legislation ranging from reproductive rights to war budget spending. Because of its ability to attract attention and galvanize discussion with a statistical approach to critique, and its theatrical style of intervention, the group has become a favored example in art history of feminist intervention since the mid-1980s. As art historian Anna Chave noted in 2011, "A signal fact of the Guerrilla Girls' existence is how much in demand they proved to be, and how long that demand endured, not only in the United States, but abroad."[6]

Today, the Guerrilla Girls' national and international profile continues to grow. The group has been the focus of exhibitions in museums, galleries, and universities, in the US and numerous other countries, from Japan and Indonesia to Brazil, and all over Europe; in addition to these temporary displays, a number of large collecting institutions, such as the Smithsonian American Art Museum, Walker Art Center, and Metropolitan Museum of Art, have acquired their posters, while the Getty Research Institute acquired the group's papers in 2009. The group has further widened its audience by taking to social media, maintaining active Facebook and Twitter accounts that call out the art world's ongoing racism, xenophobia, and sexism, and inviting others to join the dialogue and participate in similar lobbying efforts. In 2020, the group celebrated their thirty-five-plus years of art and activism with the publication of a comprehensive book, *Guerrilla Girls: The Art of Behaving Badly*. Given the visibility and longevity of their contributions, the Guerrilla Girls has become one of the primary points of reference, if not *the* primary point, for the concept of "guerrilla" in art.

Like any group with a large public following and platform, the Guerrilla Girls have received their fair share of criticism. One of the larger critiques concerns the group's predominantly white leadership and membership, as well as its initial primary focus on sexism, which deemed racism secondary. In the past, women of color who joined the group (maintaining their anonymity) have also commented on the group's costuming and the ways it traffics in racist imaginaries. The Guerrilla Girl known as "Alma Thomas" once told an interviewer, "The mask becomes a physical and psychological burden at times, limiting our functions. It doesn't dictate our behavior, but it affects our bodies and minds. As an African American, when I put on the mask, I look the way some people see me every day, unconsciously."[7]

Although, as art historian Elizabeth Hess explains, "racial assumptions" about the meaning of the gorilla mask were "entirely unintended," its racist associations have also been mentioned by "Julia de Burgos," a Latina member of the Guerrilla Girls, who confided, "I never wanted to wear the mask," which "had such a terrible connotation for black women," but "you had to go along, okay?"[8] "De Burgos" emphasized that "the very fact that they felt comfortable using this gorilla mask was part of the White privilege." If it had been up to her, the group's stylization would have been "something like a female Che [Guevara] kind of thing . . . towards more of the Latin American guerrilla."[9] According to another member, "Gertrude Stein," the group has only belatedly addressed the structural whiteness of its organizing:

> One of the most critical recurring issues was the lack of diversity in the group. The Guerrilla Girls was founded by seven white women, and honestly, we did not have many artists of color as members for many years. Artists of color who joined the Guerrilla Girls often left after a few meetings because they could sense the unspoken hierarchy in the group; multiple women of color could not find a place and left to start their own organizations.[10]

PESTS, an anonymous group of Black, Latinx, and Asian-American women artists and curators, is one such organization.[11] Howardena Pindell, a Black member of the Guerrilla Girls, left the group in December 1986 to start PESTS—a role she kept secret for decades until confirming her leadership in 2020—due to frustrations with the Guerrilla Girls prioritizing of gender inequity in ways that discounted its intersections with racial discrimination.[12] As Pindell reflected in 2020, when she brought up the topic of racism with fellow Guerrilla Girl members, she was repeatedly told to "please be cooperative" or that racial bias was "just politics," beyond the scope of the group's aims.[13]

A December 1986 letter from Pindell, then working as a curator at the Museum of Modern Art, to Martha Wilson, one of the Guerrilla Girls' original leaders, confirms Pindell's founding of PESTS, and outlines an urgent but neglected problem: "This is the letter and list that I have sent to all alternative spaces, museums and the establishment art publications. As you can see, I am trying to address this issue [of racism] as best I can, but I cannot do it alone—that is why I started P_____."[14] The attached letter draws attention to a worrying development:

> In recent months I have become more fully aware of a trend in the established art world of museums, galleries and art publications. There is a *moving away* from low token inclusion of artists of color in art world activities

> and *moving toward* a bare-minimal tokenism or complete exclusion. This exclusion and limited tokenism is a total distortion which misrepresents the broad multicultural, multiethnic character of the art world.[15]

The consequences of this censorship manifests in another December 1986 letter written to the Guerrilla Girls by L. P. Her critique of the Guerrilla Girls echoed Pindell's and would soon lead to her own departure: "Please read at next meeting?" she begins: "I don't agree that we lose our 'focus' by taking on racism. In my opinion, it would be a mistake to be a one-issue group. What's important is to make connections—that sexism and racism inevitably go hand-in-glove."[16]

PESTS formed to counteract the censorship and erasure they and other artists of color experienced due to systemic racism embedded within the New York art world. PESTS combined images, statistics, and text to visualize the gendered racial inequities of the art world. On the front of one of their PESTS STRIP newsletters, from 1987, the words "We Serve Whites Only" appear in elegant cursive script at the top of an elongated page bearing a black-and-white image of a lavish place setting (fig. 4.2). The table arrangement promises a seat in a premier restaurant: a white porcelain dish on a white tablecloth, replete with glass ash tray, bud vase, and crystal goblet. Instead of food items, however, the menu below lists art galleries commonly touted as blue-chip venues: Gracie Mansion, Leo Castelli, Marian Goodman, Mary Boone, Paula Cooper, Pace/MacGill, and thirty-three others. These spaces share a unifying exclusionary practice. Within the drawing, a folded note atop the dish announces that "The Following New York City Galleries Are 100% White"—a status left unnamed in the Guerrilla Girls' critiques of the same galleries' gender imbalance in their 1986 public panel hosted by Cooper Union, and corresponding posters, *Hidden Agender: An Evening with Critics* and *Passing the Bucks: An Evening with Art Dealers*.

The newsletter's back page extends the exposé of the mainstream New York art world's whitewashed "tastes" (fig. 4.3). Beneath an image of a silver tureen, the menu of *Artists Du Jour* presents the percentages of white artists at another twenty-five galleries: 95% Charles Gowles. 94% Ronald Feldman. 93% Holly Solomon. 84% Sidney Janis, Bernice Steinbaum. Both pages cite the source of the statistics: "Taken from *Art in America* Annual 87–88." This informational campaign, visualizing the whiteness of those with a seat at the proverbial table in the New York art scene, exemplifies PESTS' efforts in its newsletter to "publicize the myopia of the art establishment."[17]

[4.2, facing page] PESTS newsletter, vol.1, no.3, *We Serve Whites Only*, 1987. Black-and-white Xerox. © PESTS. Courtesy of Getty Research Institute (2008.M.14).

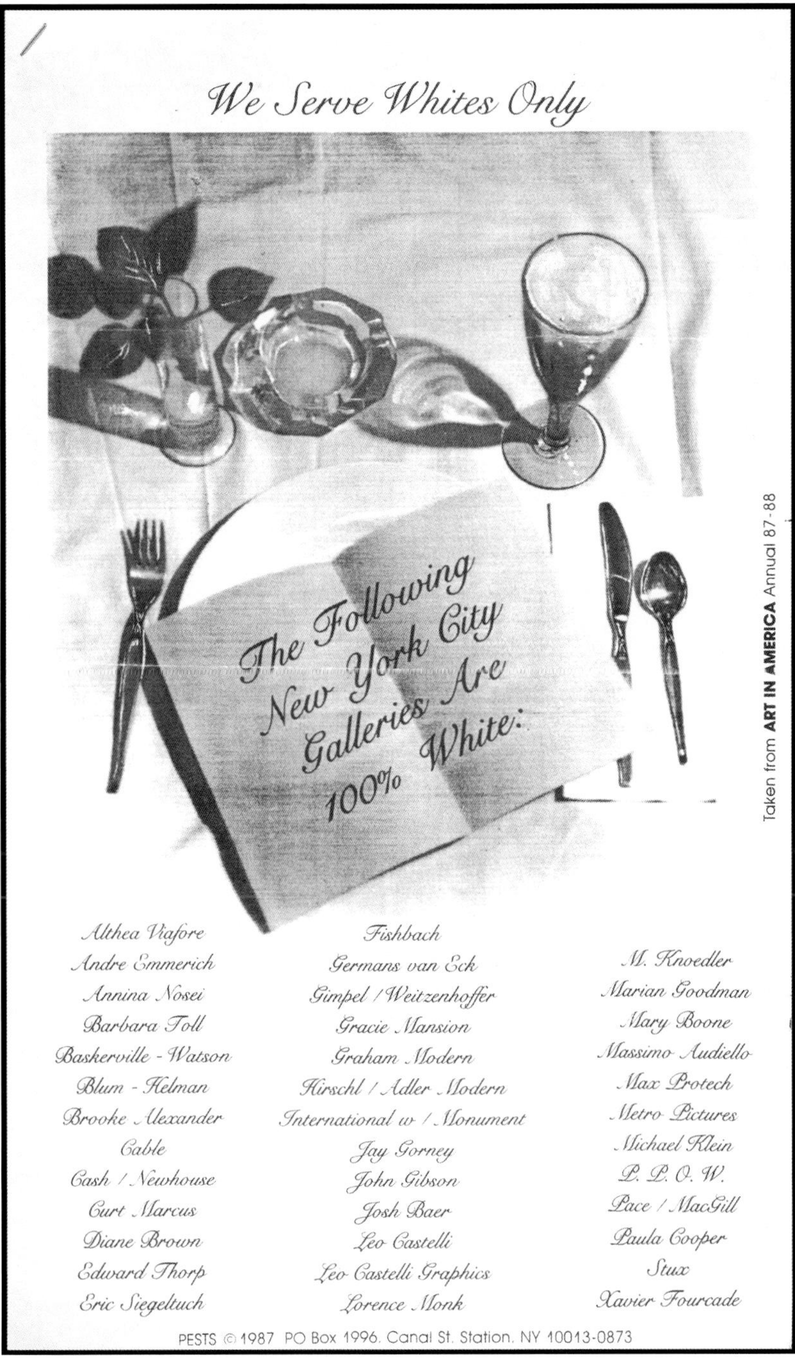
We Serve Whites Only
The Following New York City Galleries Are 100% White:
Taken from ART IN AMERICA Annual 87-88
Althea Viafore
Andre Emmerich
Annina Nosei
Barbara Toll
Baskerville - Watson
Blum - Helman
Brooke Alexander
Cable
Cash / Newhouse
Curt Marcus
Diane Brown
Edward Thorp
Eric Siegeltuch
Fishbach
Germans van Eck
Gimpel / Weitzenhoffer
Gracie Mansion
Graham Modern
Hirschl / Adler Modern
International w / Monument
Jay Gorney
John Gibson
Josh Baer
Leo Castelli
Leo Castelli Graphics
Lorence Monk
M. Knoedler
Marian Goodman
Mary Boone
Massimo Audiello
Max Protech
Metro Pictures
Michael Klein
P. P. O. W.
Pace / MacGill
Paula Cooper
Stux
Xavier Fourcade
PESTS © 1987 PO Box 1996. Canal St. Station. NY 10013-0873

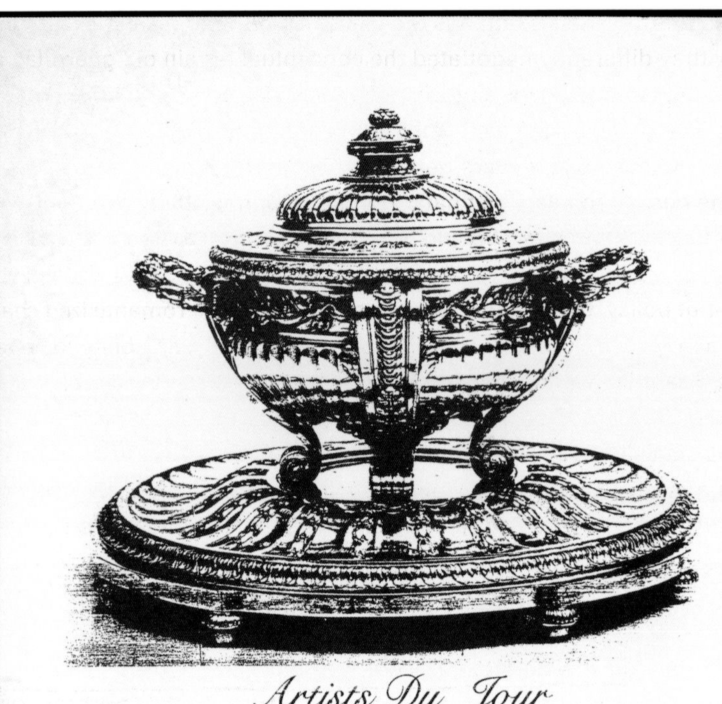

Artists Du Jour

95%
Charles Cowles

94%
Ronald Feldman
Allan Frumkin
Sperone Westwater
John Weber

93%
Louis K. Meisel
Holly Solomon

92%
Barbara Gladstone
Phyliss Kind
M13
Salander O'Reilly
Pace

91%
David McKee
Postmasters
Anita Shapolsky

89%
O.K. Harris
Maeght - Lelong

86%
Rosa Esman

84%
Sidney Janis
Bernice Steinbaum

82%
Marlborough

80%
Sharpe

75%
Nancy Hoffman
Pat Hearn

69%
Semaphore

Taken from **ART IN AMERICA** Annual 87-88

This chapter cross-examines the tactics of the Guerrilla Girls and PESTS and how they differently negotiated the conceptual terrain of "guerrilla" as it evolved alongside relevant historic, technological, and political events. The Guerrilla Girls gained immediate and lasting notoriety. PESTS was little known and active for only a few years between 1986 and 1989, succumbing by the end of the decade to a lack of financial support and visibility. While previous chapters have tracked artists' deployment of various tactics in conceptual and performance-based practice amid changing policing landscapes, urbanization, and anti-riot policy, this chapter turns to one of the more romanticized characteristics of a guerrilla fighter: tactical anonymity, namely, an ability to "attack" and then disappear without leaving tracks.

In studies of the Guerrilla Girls and PESTS, the use of anonymity is taken at face value. Moreover, when the two groups are discussed in tandem, their methods are, at best, seen as comparable models of an avant-garde agitprop—"agitational propaganda"—that surged nationwide in the 1980s alongside appropriation art, exemplified by John Fekner and Jenny Holzer, and the work of HIV/AIDS activist groups such as the AIDS Coalition to Unleash Power (ACT-UP) and Gran Fury who merged "spectacle and activism."[18] Elsewhere, PESTS's work is positioned as a derivative of the Guerrilla Girls—"using similar guerrilla tactics, including posters, a *Peststrip* newsletter, and the beginnings of a direct lobbying effort."[19] While the Guerrilla Girls and PESTS share an aesthetic of graphics, statistical quantification, and printed materials, this chapter seeks to name and analyze what, I argue, is an irreducibly different calculation of risk work within each group's distinctive use of anonymity.

Anonymity, from the Latin for "nameless," is often applied to "a person who is unnamed, unidentified, unknown, unspecified, undesignated, unseen or unacknowledged."[20] And yet, as informatics and media studies scholar Jacquelyn Burkell has argued, "anonymity is not an all or nothing condition."[21] Burkell breaks anonymity into three types, with different purposes and outcomes: "identity protection (withholding of name or other unique identifiers); visual anonymity (being unseen by communication partners); and action anonymity (keeping the content or even the existence of actions unavailable to others)."[22] This typology is useful for reconsidering the risk work of artists differently oriented to anonymity, when taken in tandem with performance studies scholar Jasbir Puar's contention that the very expectation of, or belief in, the possibility of privacy is a privileged position.

As Puar explains, the belief in privacy neutralizes the

[**4.3, facing page**] PESTS newsletter, vol 1, no. 3, *Artists du Jour*, 1987. Black-and-white Xerox. © PESTS. Courtesy of Getty Research Institute (2008.M.14).

disproportionate effects of invasive surveillance on the domestic and interior lives of Black and brown people in the United States, and specifically individuals whose bodies and words come to be inculcated within government-generated imaginaries of militancy, violence, and terror: "Without an intersectional analysis . . . the private is naturalized as a given refuge from state scrutiny," an idea that extends to the notions of privacy that sit within universalized considerations of anonymity as well.[23] Taken together, these arguments reveal the nuanced range of relations within anonymity, informed by racialized, sexualized, and gendered ideas of (un)safety in American society.

This chapter proceeds from this point of departure: anonymity is not universal in a carceral state that racializes, genders, and sexualizes spontaneity (chapter 1), in-action (chapter 2), and endurance (chapter 3). To be sure, the Guerrilla Girls and PESTS were each aware of the risks they sought to evade by turning to anonymity. The Guerrilla Girls, for example, agreed from the beginning that to oppose the cult of personality that surrounded women artists, masked anonymity was key. As Guerrilla Girl "Rosalba Carriera" told *Artworld*, "When we attack something, we want what we're saying to be heard, not who's saying it."[24] Relatedly, PESTS never once made a public appearance; their anonymous practice exists entirely in posters, stickers, and newsletters.

What remains overlooked is how a heteronormative white raciality of misbehavior informs the Guerrilla Girls' famed anonymity; how it functions vis-à-vis imaginaries of violence through which Black and brown women artists have been policed; and how, relatedly, these conditions shape the actions and sustained (in)visibility of PESTS. To explore these interlaced relations, I draw here upon a long line of feminist and queer of color theory scholars, from Puar to Cynthia Enloe to Alison Howell, who have published widely on the interwoven conceptualizations of aggression that emerge at the intersection of militarism, feminism, heterosexuality, neoliberal capital, and a cultural conditioning of ideas of action and innocence.[25] In this body of work, links between representations of gender and sexuality in cultural production and war industries provide an expanded definition of policing and the violence of administrative work and lobbying efforts.[26]

Building upon their research, this chapter, like its predecessors, seeks to challenge our received histories of guerrilla tactics in art: What cultural and political *work* does the Guerrilla Girls' and PESTS' deployment of anonymity do, and *for whom*, in the mid- to late 1980s? How does the artists' use of tactics perceived as "guerrilla" or "clandestine" coalesce with the simultaneous rebranding of guerrilla as counterinsurgency by Reagan's administration? And with national debates about the discernment of racial bias and hate crimes? To attend to these concerns, this chapter tracks how "guerrilla," as a concept, continues to mutate throughout the decade, while becoming synonymous in the art world with the Guerrilla Girls and the marketability of their stylized tactics of misbehaving. Furthermore, while both the Guerrilla Girls and PESTS embraced playfulness and biting sarcasm as a tactical intervention, and both utilized familiar, legitimized forms of critique—humor, report cards, statistics, and advertising—the cross-analysis that follows considers how the strategies each group used carried real, incommensurate material risks of retribution. I argue that their distinct modes of anonymity reveal their differing sense of risk work, informed by the spatialized racial, sexual, and gender politics of punitive relations sustained both within and beyond the art world. As such, this chapter confronts how the conflation of their tactics has not only erased each groups' specific literacies in risk-taking, but has also become part of an oversimplification in American art wherein celebratory stories of feminist resistance foreclose antiracist modes of accountability in coalitional praxis.

Beyond Agitprop: The Guerrilla Girls as a "Terrorist Feminist Organization"

The Guerrilla Girls became art-world celebrities almost immediately for their clandestinely pasted posters that sought, as the group proclaimed, to be the "Conscience of the Art World."[27] The simple designs, using the authoritative language of "cold facts" associated with business consumer reports, also made use of the new practice of "guerrilla marketing," a term coined in 1983 by Jay Levinson in a book of the same name. Levinson outlined how advertisers could appropriate the appeal of graffiti art to sell corporate messages and merchandise.[28] The Guerrilla Girls' spin on this strategy, marked by stylized humor and sexual innuendo, captured the attention of the art-world leaders whose names were disapprovingly featured on the group's broadside "report cards" and exhibition reviews. In their earliest days, these posters were displayed in specific sites; it was important that the messages not only reach the people in positions of relative power in the art world, but arm others with the statistics and information that could potentially disrupt the narratives of progress celebrated by art-world leaders.

Recalling their earliest interventions in 1985, members of the Guerrilla Girls explain, "Whenever we would put up new posters, we would lurk on the streets nearby, overhear what people had to say and get ideas for the next ones."[29] This spatiotemporal specificity is often lost when Guerrilla Girls' posters are reproduced in art-historical texts or exhibitions as clean, decontextualized

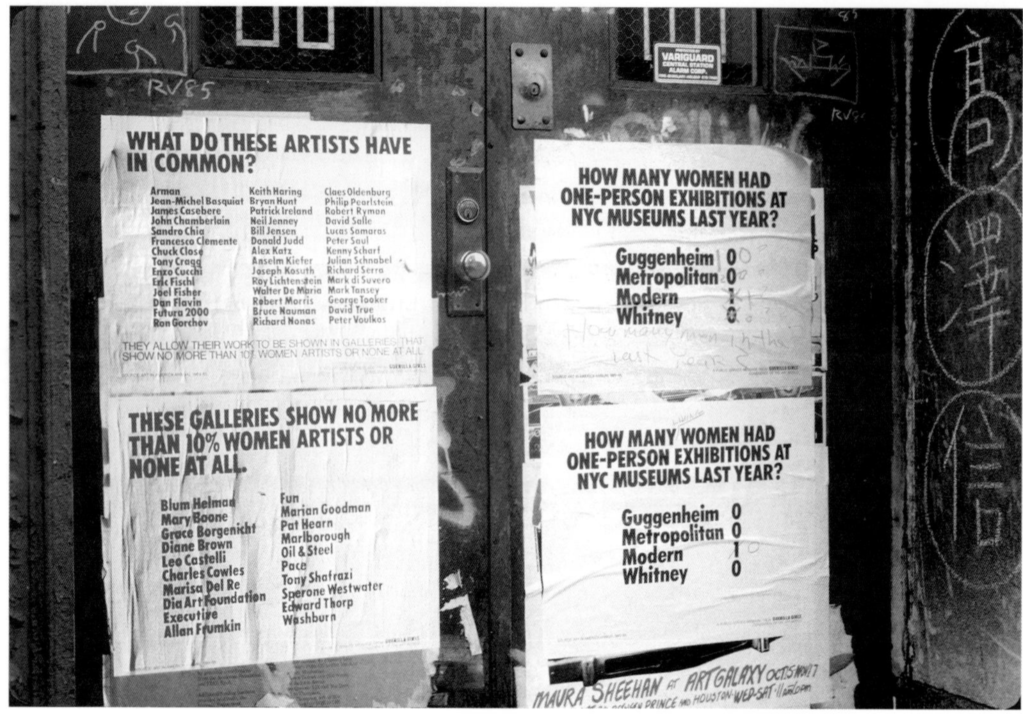

[4.4] Guerrilla Girls, Guerrilla Girls First Poster Campaign, New York City, 1985. (Individual poster titles: *How Many Women Had One-Person Exhibitions at NYC Art Museums Last Year?*, 1985; *What Do These Artists Have in Common?*, 1985; *These Galleries Show No More Than 10% Women Artists or None at All*, 1985. Offset prints.) Color photograph. © Guerrilla Girls. Courtesy of guerrillagirls.com.

images. As depicted in a documentary photograph dated to 1985 (fig. 4.4), the posters were intended as sites of contact and participatory activation. Here, four posters appear on a set of metal doors next to Chinese characters tagging individuals' names in blue chalk; a publicity poster for Maura Sheehan's exhibition at Art Galaxy peeks out just below. Passersby have written with faint blue and red pen on the posters, updating numbers, modifying wordings, and scribbling their own questions—someone has added "living" to the lower right poster, for example, altering the question and affecting the (even more egregious) outcome.

Placing these four posters in proximity to the Soho and East Village galleries meant the Guerrilla Girls risked confronting those the posters accused of the sexism. They also anticipated possible run-ins with the police. Members did not wear masks when they wheat-pasted—from midnight to 3 a.m. on Friday nights, so that the posters would greet art collectors and gallery staff first thing on Saturday morning.[30] As "Jane Bowles" recalls, "It was like this really kind of exciting, illicit kind of thing . . . you know, watching out for the police; it was very scary . . . but it was a lot of fun."[31] During those early years of postering, New York City's expanding punitive paradigm was evolving under a "broken windows" approach formulated by leading American social scientists James Q. Wilson and George Kelling in 1982 in a landmark article published in the *Atlantic*. Their theory of crime promoted aggressive arrests for minor offenses based on the idea that small, visible signs of disorder (like a broken window or discarded syringe), were gateways to cascading criminal activities.[32]

In 1985, the punitive risks associated with wheat-pasting and writing in chalk on a city wall were still relatively low in comparison with, say, graffiti. New York City had recently banned the sale of aerosol spray paint and indelible markers more than half an inch wide to anyone under 18. Graffiti writers could face a $500 fine, jail time of up to three months, or both.[33] While postering did not carry these penalties, the greater scrutiny paid to the streets and exterior walls was part of the group's calculus. In a sense, the temporal and spatial coordinates of the poster reflect, in part, the predominantly white group's punitive literacy as it bridged the policing active in the gallery district, art gallery hours of business, and, increasingly, the physical response to postering that occurred in conjunction with the aggressive surveillance of graffiti writing. As Mira Schor reflected in 1990, Guerrilla Girl posters stayed up for a maximum of "two or three days . . . on regularly trafficked streets in SoHo," noting how they get "ripped up and disappear (out of anger, obsessive architecture hygiene, or desire to own the posters)."[34]

In addition to the posters, which garnered attention on the street, the messaging of the Guerrilla Girls expanded by way of the group's catchy play with metaphors of militancy, which seduced art writers and news reporters. A news report in the *Village Voice*, published around the time the first posters appeared, situates the stakes of the wheat-pasted interventions undertaken by the new collective: "The Guerrilla Girls think things are so bad for women in the Reagan years that they have to use 'shock-tactics' to wake people up, or so they say."[35] Indeed, the Guerrilla Girls received a great deal of media and press coverage for their "shock-tactics," both literal and figurative. Dinah Prince, in one of the first published articles about the group, explained that the Guerrilla Girls intended to stage a "friendly though earnest revolution." Distinguishing them from feminist guerrillas, she mused lightheartedly, "They do not pack AK-47's. They don't build bombs in their basements. But they *are* the Guerrilla Girls. And, they do

PALLADIUM
EXHIBITION
OCTOBER 17, 1985

ALICE ADAMS
JERRI ALLYN
LAURIE ANDERSON
ELEANOR ANTIN
IDA APPLEBROOG
ALICE AYCOCK
JENNIFER BARTLETT
DARA BIRNBAUM
LYNDA BENGLIS
LOUISE BOURGEOIS
STEPHANIE BRODY LEDERMAN
JOAN BROWN
VIVIAN BROWNE
MARINA CAPPELLETTO
CYNTHIA CARLSON
LENORA CHAMPAGNE
PETAH COYNE
DONNA DENNIS
SANDY DE SANDO
JANE DICKSON
MARY BETH EDELSON
LAUREN EWING
JACKIE FERRARA
KAREN FINLEY
JANET FISH
ILONA GRANET
DENISE GREEN
VANALYNE GREEN
HARMONY HAMMOND
DONNA HENES
JULIA HEYWARD
CANDACE HILL-MONTGOMERY
KAY HINES
NANCY HOLT
JENNY HOLZER
VALERIE JAUDON
JOYCE KOZLOFF
JILL KROESEN
CHERYL LAEMMLE
ELLEN LANYON
LOUISE LAWLER
KAREN LAWRIE
ANN LEDA
R.T.LIVINGSTON
JOAN LOGUE
BONNIE LUCAS
LISA LYON
DOREEN MCCARTHY
MELISSA MEYER
MARY MISS
ELIZABETH MURRAY
PATSY NORVELLE
HELEN OJI
PAT OLESKO
HOWARDINA PINDELL
LADY PINK
JUDY PFAFF
BARBARA QUINN
MARCIA RESNICK
FAITH RINGGOLD
IRIS ROSE
ERIKA ROTHENBERG
CHRISTY RUPP
ALISON SAAR
MIRIAM SHAPIRO
JOAN SEMMEL
BONNIE SHERK
CINDY SHERMAN
HOLLIS SIGLER
SANDY SKOGLUND
ALEXIS SMITH
KIKI SMITH
JOAN SNYDER
NANCY SPERO
PAT STEIR
MAY STEVENS
REDY STORY
MICHELLE STUART
MIERLE LADERMAN UKELES
MIA WESTERLUND
HANNAH WILKE
NINA YANKOWITZ
BRAHNA YASSKY
JERILEA ZEMPEL
BARBARA ZUCKER
RHONDA ZWILLINGER
LIST INCOMPLETE

GUERILLAS GIRLS REMINDS
YOU THAT MANY GREAT WOMEN
ARTISTS ARE NOT IN THIS SHOW

ONE HUNDRED TWENTY-SIX EAST FOURTEENTH STREET NEW YORK CITY 212-473-7171

Exhibition Curated By
GUERRILLA GIRLS
The Women Artists Terrorist Organization

[**4.5**] Guerrilla Girls, *Palladium Will Apologize to Women Artists*, 1985. Exhibition poster. © Guerrilla Girls. Courtesy of guerrillagirls.com.

want to cause trouble." As one group member quoted in the article explained, "We have a sense of humor. We're sort of turning anger into fun."[36]

As is widely shared in accounts of the group's formation, the Guerrilla Girls' visual pun on "guerrilla" began when a member misspelled the word as "gorilla" and the idea for their signature costume was born. Less known or remarked upon is that the Guerrilla Girls also self-identified for a short time as "The Women Artists Terrorist Organization."[37] This label appeared on the October 1985 poster promoting an exhibition the group was invited to curate at the Palladium, a nightclub used as an alternative art space (fig. 4.5). The exhibition included 150 works of art by eighty-five women artists.[38] Even though the Guerrilla Girls would stop using the word "terrorist" by 1987, its use in media coverage before then helped bring attention to their messages and objectives.

In a representative example, art critic Paul Taylor's written coverage of the Guerrilla Girls in 1987 articulated a framework of militancy in which to situate the group's emerging practice. Looking to an international nexus of information warfare and surveillance, he writes, "As propagandists their methods recall everything from Radio Free America to the Red Brigade, and they try to make the impression, like Big Brother himself, that they are everywhere—with spies in high and mighty places like art magazines."[39] These connections were enhanced by the Guerrilla Girls' performative play with the masculinist iconography of the anticolonial urban guerrilla: in 1986, members of the group spoke publicly as part of the "Anger Panel" at the College Art Association conference, appearing in black leather jackets reminiscent of the Black Panthers and Young Lords of the 1960s and 1970s, while also wearing gorilla masks. Following their diatribe against art-world sexism, they received a standing ovation, and various invitations to speak nationwide.[40] While the leather jackets and claims to be feminist guerrillas and terrorists were received as "earnest" acts of transgressive "infiltration," it is difficult to believe that a group like PESTS, made up of women of color, performing these same symbolic gestures—masked or not—would have received such a warm welcome given the entangled histories of Black and brown men and women's very presence being treated as a threat to white hegemonic power, and the fact that groups such as the Black Panthers and Young Lords had made demands for equity that challenged white hegemonic power.[41]

Whereas Prince and Taylor offer loose associations between the Guerrilla Girls and a larger culture of warfare and surveillance, some writers found a special resonance in the language of militancy and terrorism. In March 1986, a reporter for the *Philadelphia Inquirer*, Stephan Salisbury, announced the Guerrilla Girls' upcoming visit to Philadelphia in an article titled "Getting Militant about Women's Art." Referring to the group as a "women artists' terrorist organization," he describes their meteoric rise via the visual symbolism of guerrilla warfare: "In the last several months, the Guerrilla Girls have emerged from the jungle of the art world to do the unspeakable, the unheard of, the one really unfair thing in that genteel realm. They named names."[42]

In his article, Salisbury interviews Judith Stein, assistant curator at the Pennsylvania Academy of Fine Arts, who explains:

> [The Guerrilla Girls] have co-opted—as I see it—or raided the language of terrorism without themselves intending to do bodily harm to people or to art. The only harm they intend, the damage they hope to inflict, is on sexism by raising awareness and consciousness. To me, that's humorous. . . . Yes, there will be groups who protest this kind of thing, but the Guerrilla Girls have a freshness about them in their tactics. They're using street posters and anonymity, which is very provocative for people.[43]

Although Stein is aware that the Guerrilla Girls' sense of humor will not appeal to everyone, her assessment of the "freshness" of their maneuvers leaves untroubled the political history of the tactics that bolsters the group's provocativeness. To accomplish their "raid" on the "language of terrorism" successfully and safely, the Guerrilla Girls mobilize a particular mode of literacy in both punitiveness and risk: they acknowledge a need for masking as a way to protect their professional careers and identities and, at the same time, benefit from the comedic distance they can leverage that distinguishes them from "serious" groups and individuals perceived by government officials and police as threats to public safety.

Although many New York art critics and curators found the group's use of guerrilla and terrorist rhetoric refreshing in its unabashed sexualizing of feminist critique and defanged militancy, the white feminist art critic Lucy Lippard offered a less enthusiastic perspective. In her review of the 1985 Palladium show, she rebukes the group's self-branding, particularly its use of the word "terrorist." "It's become post-punk cute to be a terrorist," she quips. Moreover, "the Reagan administration already calls us that, and it lets state terrorists off the hook to be coy about it."[44] Lippard's criticism of the Guerrilla Girls offers a generative point of entry into how the group's self-promotion vis-à-vis "terrorist" and "guerrilla" problematically leveraged international imaginaries of violence through which the aggressive policing of Black and brown people had been justified both domestically and internationally.

Guerrillas and Terrorists

I do not want to exaggerate the connection between the Guerrilla Girls' adopting the words "guerrilla" and "terrorist" in their critiques of the art world and the actions of armed, militant revolutionaries then targeted or supported by the government. The Guerrilla Girls were never, and are not today, affiliated with a larger militant movement. They did (and do), however, benefit from the evolving cultural cachet of imaginaries of militancy summoned by these terms. In keeping with the book's focus on the gendered and sexualized racial politics of risk work, I find it pertinent to consider how the Guerrilla Girls' decision to deploy these concepts is a manifestation of members' distinctive and, at times, conflicting literacies in punitiveness. Relatedly, I am concerned with the impact that the group's decisions and reception have had on art discourse that uncritically valorizes its tactics.

In the late 1970s and early 1980s, the term "guerrilla" was used somewhat interchangeably with "terrorist."[45] But as Puar reminds us, "guerrillas and terrorists have vastly different national and racial valences, the former bringing to mind the phantasmatic landscapes of Central and South America, and the latter, the enduring legacy of Orientalist imaginaries."[46] In his 1985 State of the Union address, Reagan advocated support for "freedom fighters" to oppose the spread of communism by "terrorists," adamantly insisting that, while each used a wide range of guerrilla tactics, the freedom fighters' tactics were distinct from the terrorists'. Rejecting the widely held view that the US should stay out of overseas conflicts—sometimes called "Vietnam syndrome"—he declared, "Support for freedom fighters is self-defense." This "counterinsurgency" model, also known as "low-intensity conflict," came to be known as the Reagan Doctrine and promoted, among other things, US efforts to overthrow Nicaragua's revolutionary government by organizing and financing an army of anti-Sandinista *contra-revolucionarios* ("contras").[47]

The Guerrilla Girls adapted the loaded meaning of "freedom fighters" for the purpose of mobilizing critiques of the art world's inequities. As one group member explained, "in terms of the double meaning of the word—'gorilla,' the animal, and 'guerrilla,' the action. We spell it like the freedom fighters but then we wear gorilla masks, so that it works imagistically. It's very effective."[48] They publicly claimed the labels "guerrilla" and "terrorist" at a particular juncture: the Reagan administration denounced guerrilla tactics as un-American even as it repackaged them for American use as anti-insurgency "low intensity conflict"—and sought to erase the use of "guerrilla" to describe its own actions and national security protocol. These ideas were created and circulated through the State Department's Office of Public Diplomacy for Latin America and the Caribbean (S/LPD), which Reagan had established during his first term. The agency, whose work expanded in the mid-1980s, circulated pro-contra literature to college libraries and scholars, journalists, religious organizations, conservative lobbyists, and members of Congress in an effort to shape public interpretations of guerrilla militancy.[49]

The media's depiction of "guerrillas" in Central America helped the government "marketize" American counterinsurgency and build support for the US-backed fight against the Sandinista Front for National Liberation (FSLN), which had come to power in Nicaragua in 1979 after overthrowing dictator Anastasio Somoza Debayle. While sending millions of dollars in weapons to the contras, Reagan lambasted critics of his actions as communists and endeavored to "bolster the official portrait of the contras as freedom fighters" to make them "palatable" to Congress, as national security archivist and activist Peter Kornbluh puts it. "The administration also turned to high-profile public relations firms to project the new image of the contras and to lobby Congress to restore funding for CIA operations."[50]

In the midst of Reagan's publicity campaign, the Guerrilla Girls' use of "guerrilla" and "terrorist" in the cultural sphere gained them attention. In fact, US discussions of terrorism reached a fever pitch just seven days before their 1985 Palladium exhibition—the publicity poster promoting the group as the Women Artists Terrorist Organization—was set to open. The MS *Achille Lauro*, an Italian cruise ship en route from Alexandria to Ashdod, Israel, was hijacked near the coast of Egypt by four men representing the Palestine Liberation Front, who demanded the release of several Palestinians from Israeli prisons. Leon Klinghoffer, a sixty-nine-year-old American Jewish man aboard the ship, was murdered by the hijackers. In response, Reagan authorized US military forces to intercept an aircraft transporting the *Achille Lauro* hijackers—designated "terrorists" by the US government—in international airspace, then handed them over to the Italian government for prosecution. In a press statement issued on October 10, White House spokesperson Larry M. Speakes reiterated the President's desire to "emphasize once again that the international scourge of terrorism can only be stamped out if each member of the community of civilized nations meets its responsibility squarely. . . . We cannot tolerate terrorism in any form."[51]

The Guerrilla Girls' papers, housed at the Getty Research Institute, reveal a more introspective consideration of the stakes of using such concepts. Even a year later, in December 1986, members still voiced concern about the group's use of the word "terrorist," as well as the loaded nature of "guerrilla." In a note addressed to the larger group, L. P. expresses concern about the group's self-branding:

> I think we have to be very sensitive about wording. . . . Somehow a press-release or something went out around the Palladium show calling us a "terrorist group" and the next week there was Achille Lauro, and we were all very embarrassed. We vowed to be more careful in the future.[52]

The significance of the *Achille Lauro* hijacking for the Guerrilla Girls demonstrates how the larger context of international politics informed their punitive literacies: as events unfolded, they responded, and decided which kinds of wordplay were acceptable—"guerrilla"—and which were too controversial. The "embarrassment" belies a fraught relation. Part of what made these words polemical was the ethnonational racialized, sexualized, and gendered politics of domestic and global insurgency inscribed within them.

Looming large was the fear of terrorism taking root in the US. Take, for example, how the same issue of the *Philadelphia Inquirer* that covered the Guerrilla Girls in 1986 also reprinted a report on terrorism from the *Dallas Morning News*. Its author wrote:

> Many Americans are beginning to wonder: Can [terrorism] happen here? The answer, experts on terrorism suggest, is that while our geographical isolation makes us less vulnerable, and while the government is fully on guard against such attacks, it is just about impossible to foil a truly committed terrorist. . . . "We have to always presume that it is possible," said Oliver "Buck" Revell, the FBI's executive assistant director who is the top spokesman on terrorism. "We always have to prepare for it and work to prevent . . . Middle East–style terrorism from migrating to the U.S."[53]

This idea of "Middle East–style terrorism" being imported to the United States resonates with and reproduces the same logic applied in the 1960s and 1970s to descriptions of *guerrilla*, wherein these tactics were strategically tied by politicians and security officials to *foreign* agents of invasion (as discussed in the introduction). The spatializing of these modes of action, located as "here" versus "elsewhere," is a device used by the government to justify demarcating war zones at home and abroad. Less than a decade after the war in Vietnam, the US's fetishizing of "Middle East-style terrorism" also reinforces an American exceptionalism that distinguishes its use of weapons such as napalm and Agent Orange on Vietnamese civilians from the repertoire of terrorist violence.

Whereas the figuration of the "guerrilla" in the late 1960s conjured anticolonial liberation tactics in Africa, Latin America, and Vietnam, by the 1980s, "terrorist" was used in the US as shorthand for tactics associated with Arab-Muslim actions, a message boosted by coverage of the 444-day Iran hostage crisis (1979–1980). As film and media studies scholar Sohail Daulatzai asserts, the "Black criminal" (linked, in part, with the criminalizing of Black discontent and militant resistance to white supremacy) and the Arab and "Muslim terrorist" came to serve as the two defining, and entangled, threats within US state formation.[54] Complicating this, Puar has written at length about the figuration of the "monstrous terrorist" that arises through racialized homophobic instantiations of a "failed masculinity," wherein the terrorist as a "queer transgressive subject" not only threatens the idealized white heteronormative nation-state but becomes an organizing feature of it.[55]

Adding to this duality of "Black criminal" and "monstrous terrorist," it is important to note the fomentation of a white nationalist movement in the 1970s and 1980s — largely organized by white male army veterans trained in counterinsurgency tactics in Vietnam, and expanded by white women's successful recruitment strategies.[56] Across the US, white nationalist groups emboldened by Reagan's calls for "freedom fighters" to defend the US from communist invasion in its "own backyard" mobilized against people of color, Jews, and queer communities.[57] As historian Kathleen Belew notes in her extensive research on the reinvention of white nationalism in the 1970s and 1980s, "Even if federal agents and a few journalists were aware of the white power movement, the mainstream public continued to see most white power violence as the work of errant madmen," giving rise to the phrase "lone wolf," which was "employed increasingly in the 1980s and 1990s to describe white power activists," and remains in wide use today.[58]

Within these overlaid contexts, the Guerrilla Girls' cultural mobilization of "terrorist," and its interchangeable use with "guerrilla" in 1985 and 1986, is only possible as an "earnest" or "humorous" gesture when rebranded as an innocuous (read: cis-gendered, heterosexual, white or white-adjacent) feminist theatricalization of militancy within the majority-white art world. This figure was also set against another foil: the "female terrorist" then becoming, as Amanda Third asserts, a "preoccupation for governments, law enforcement agencies, and popular culture more generally in the Western world."[59] In the context of South and Central America, these stories extended back at least to the 1950s and 1960s, gaining attention with the success of the Cuban revolution and the guerrilla movements it helped inspire, such as the Popular Liberation Army (EPL) in Colombia.[60] Notably, the Guerrilla Girls' performative harnessing of a playful, "earnest" type of militancy occurs contemporaneously with the increased celebrity of Nora Astorga, a Nicaraguan feminist known as a guerrilla fighter turned diplomat whose public persona was used by the US government to undercut her negotiating power.

Astorga had become a controversial figure in the US, known for her undercover role in the notorious 1978 Sandinista operation dubbed "El Perro." According to the US media, she "lured" General Reynaldo Perez Vega ("el Perro"), the deputy commander of Somoza's national guard, to her apartment for sex, where she and other FSLN operatives killed him.[61] In 1984, when Astorga became a Nicaraguan representative to the United Nations, the American media cast her as an "inspiration for the New Woman."[62] As one admirer, quoted in a *Washington Post* article swooned, Astorga "is the most exciting modern female revolutionary around."[63] Buried within the hype, the American press mobilized ideas of *guerrilla* through the Sandinistas in Nicaragua, as well as the Revolutionary Armed Forces of Colombia (FARQ), as if to narrate the "right way" for indigenous people in South and Central America to liberate themselves from US-backed dictatorships.[64] It is within this context that the Guerrilla Girls' use of "guerrilla" and "terrorist" is read as "new" and "refreshing" by art critics and curators. Arguably, this "freshness" is encoded with the idiomatic connotations of guerrilla in the US mediated by domestic representations of the guerrilla feminists, both at home and abroad.

It is worth noting that the Guerrilla Girls did more than utilize the latter term symbolically; they also considered historic representations of guerrilla actions as a model to be adapted organizationally. In 1985, one member wrote in an internal document regarding solicitation of new members, "We should create a structure in which many women could participate. I especially love Ann's idea about all the interconnected cells (like in the *Battle of Algiers*)."[65] The implementation of a "cell" structure can be tracked in the group's recruitment efforts, as recorded in a 1986 letter of solicitation seeking membership across the country: "We are writing to you because we would like to encourage women artists in other cities to begin Guerrilla Girl cells. We're enclosing examples of things we've done, as well as press clips showing the range of responses we've had."[66] It is precisely these actions, which art historian Josephine Withers identifies as "guerrilla tactics" and "hit-and-run tactics," that allowed the group to become "highly visible in the New York City and national art press." As Withers notes, "*New York Magazine*—always on the lookout for trendsetters—in 1987 saw them as one of the four powers-that-be in the art world."[67]

As these various examples suggest, the Guerrilla Girls' turn to terms and tactics associated with imaginaries of violence and war to bolster the attention garnered by their posters, exhibition, and public programs was an integral part of their organizing as well as their initial brokering of cultural power. Thus, despite the members' identities remaining hidden on account of the gorilla masks, the pale skin of the seven white founders was legible in public events and publicity photos. Additionally, "Alma Thomas," one of the few Black members during this early period, has acknowledged that due to her lighter complexion audiences could not tell that she was Black when she was masked, and that when she told them, they didn't believe her.[68] Finally, while there may have been queer members of the Guerrilla Girls, the underrepresentation of lesbian, gay, and transgendered artists, and the ways this inequity intersects with sexism and racism in museum exhibitions and collections, does not appear to have been an issue publicly addressed in the Guerrilla Girls' calculations or posters.[69] To be clear: there is not an expectation that any group—especially one doing the laborious work of statistical tabulations in minutes stolen between full-time jobs, child care, and art-making—can or should account for all instances of inequity; the concern here, instead, is that the group's gender-conforming, heterosexual, and often white-centering critiques of art-world sexism and racism limns their anonymity and, again, is arguably part of what permits their use of "guerrilla" and "terrorist" to be perceived as a generative and nonthreatening gesture.

It is this gendered, sexualized, and racialized relationship to anonymity that occurs in the midst of the government's ongoing yet heightened surveillance of people sympathetic with guerrilla revolutions in Central and South America and the expansion of policing through a "broken windows" paradigm. Moreover, Reagan's neglect of AIDS, and the pathologizing of HIV as a gay disease, was constructed through media stories that linked the virus with connotations of communist guerrilla invasion: in an issue of *Time* from November 3, 1986, a photograph of HIV entering a Helper T cell provided a visualization of the "disease of the century."[70] The virus was framed as an "alien" or "foreign agent" of death and destruction. In another instance, HIV was also spoken of as "the stranger in our house," as the ultimate outsider—the elusive enemy lurking within.[71]

These contexts do not diminish the Guerrilla Girls' contributions to the art world and the trenchant observations they've made about sexism and racism, but instead clarify some of the circumstantial factors that enabled the Guerrilla Girls' meteoric ascent to media and art-world visibility. Even though its use was short-lived, their deployment of the word "terrorist" alongside "guerrilla," and the attention it garnered for the group, evidences that the members' symbolic harnessing of tactics of intervention were never fully divorced from domestic and international discourses then gaining visibility, nor from punitive urban contexts where mobility was under heightened surveillance.

Indeed, the Guerrilla Girls eventually abandoned impromptu wheat-pasting to instead book more engagements on campuses and in museums, because, as one member explained, "it got harder and harder for us to poster. . . . The police became more attentive."[72] This acknowledgment of increasing police scrutiny both reflects members' punitive literacy and indexes an important shift in the arc of the city's intensification of broken-windows policing. As mentioned earlier, this paradigm, which pursued minor offenses, was incrementally implemented throughout the 1980s, becoming a cornerstone of police philosophy by the early 1990s.

In a society that prioritizes heteronormative whiteness—and in which straight white women, in particular, are seen as vessels of prototypical innocence and vulnerability—the impact of this kind of policing is never evenly distributed. As Black studies scholar Erica Edwards underscores, Reagan's "War on Drugs" further "rationalized the intense, militarized policing of everyday Black life."[73] Diverging from the common use of the phrase "long war on terror" to describe the nation's righteous fight for democracy, Edwards instead calls out the "war on terror" as the four centuries of domestic antiblack terror enacted upon Black women's bodies, physically, psychologically, and ideologically, and exported by the US in the name of its imperial antiblack designs. PESTS' members' differing relations to anonymity during this same period, discussed in the following sections, inculcates the enduring presence of racist colonialist policing in its many forms, revealing how their tactics and critiques, perceived as the same as the Guerrilla Girls', interject distinctive challenges to hegemonic power structures in the art world and American society.

PESTS' Swarm: "Keeping the Records Straight"

The Guerrilla Girls sought to maintain anonymity while appearing in public wearing eye-catching gorilla masks; accepting invitations to curate exhibitions and speak at universities, museums, and conferences; and organizing their own speaker programs, which continue to this day. PESTS, by contrast, was resolutely committed to an anonymity unaccommodating of spectacle. PESTS never convened or spoke publicly. Nor did PESTS use the language of militancy in self-promotion. As Pindell explains:

> The concept of "guerrilla" was different for PESTS. PESTS didn't physically go out publicly in disguise. No one knew who we were. We had a P.O. Box for the newsletter. Everything was anonymous. I shouldn't even talk about it, but I don't know how to speak about it any other way.[74]

PESTS' avoidance of public appearances meant not just that they remained anonymous but also that they were not offered interviews or paid speaking engagements. Consequently, the group received sparse financial support, relying entirely on donations. As noted in one of their two newsletters, PESTS STRIP, "This newsletter has burned all of our financial bridges. If you'd like to keep our antennae out of the water, send us a donation. It'll be put to good use."[75]

The emphatically *public* anonymity and theatrical appropriation of militancy that the Guerrilla Girls harnessed did not serve PESTS. In a letter of solicitation dated December 1986 (fig. 4.6), PESTS announced the group's purpose and goals: "Observations have led us to feel that it is time to reverse *art world apartheid*, which misrepresents a multiethnic and multiracial culture." By the mid-1980s, anti-apartheid movements, both in South Africa and in the US, were gaining momentum as well as increasing attention in the art world.[76] While situating

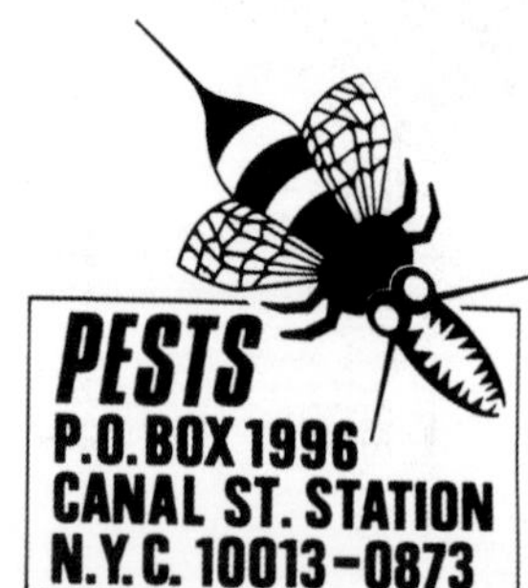

December 6, 1986

How often do you see a one-person show by an artist of color?

Have you ever wished that the art world was more informed and knowledgeable about works created by **artists of color**? Observations have led us to feel that it is time to reverse **art world apartheid**, which misrepresents a multiethnic and multiracial culture.

PESTS, an anonymous artists organization aims to publicize the myopia of the art establishment. Through our future activities we plan to generate positive interest in **artists of color**, overriding past neglect and misrepresentation.

Our immediate goals are to publicize the serious ommission and de facto censorship practiced by galleries, museums and art publications. As a person of conscience, you must have reflected on these issues and wished you had been presented with a broader and more accurate view.

Support your local PESTS activities!

We need your help now, no matter how smalll the contribution!

We plan to bug the art world!

Please send check or money order to:

PESTS
P.O.Box 1996
Canal Street Station
New York, N.Y. 10013-0873

Thank you for your support!

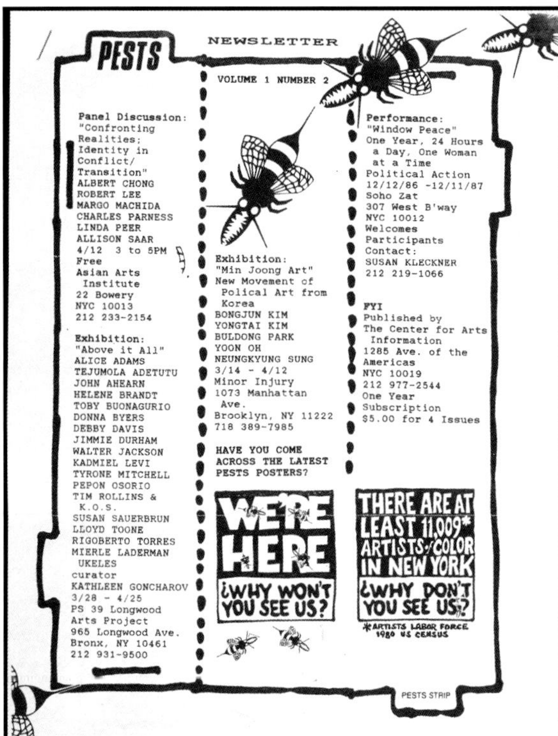

PESTS NEWSLETTER

VOLUME 1 NUMBER 2

Panel Discussion:
"Confronting Realities; Identity in Conflict/ Transition"
ALBERT CHONG
ROBERT LEE
MARGO MACHIDA
CHARLES PARNESS
LINDA PEER
ALLISON SAAR
4/12 3 to 5PM
Free
Asian Arts Institute
22 Bowery
NYC 10013
212 233-2154

Exhibition:
"Above it All"
ALICE ADAMS
TEJUMOLA ADETUTU
JOHN AHEARN
HELENE BRANDT
TOBY BUONAGURIO
DONNA BYERS
DEBBY DAVIS
JIMMIE DURHAM
WALTER JACKSON
KADMIEL LEVI
TYRONE MITCHELL
PEPON OSORIO
TIM ROLLINS & K.O.S.
SUSAN SAUERBRUN
LLOYD TOONE
RIGOBERTO TORRES
MIERLE LADERMAN UKELES
curator
KATHLEEN GONCHAROV
3/28 - 4/25
PS 39 Longwood Arts Project
965 Longwood Ave.
Bronx, NY 10461
212 931-9500

Exhibition:
"Min Joong Art"
New Movement of Polical Art from Korea
BONGJUN KIM
YONGTAI KIM
BULDONG PARK
YOON OH
NEUNGKYUNG SUNG
3/14 - 4/12
Minor Injury
1073 Manhattan Ave.
Brooklyn, NY 11222
718 389-7985

HAVE YOU COME ACROSS THE LATEST PESTS POSTERS?

Performance:
"Window Peace"
One Year, 24 Hours a Day, One Woman at a Time
Political Action
12/12/86 -12/11/87
Soho Zat
307 West B'way
NYC 10012
Welcomes Participants
Contact:
SUSAN KLECKNER
212 219-1066

FYI
Published by
The Center for Arts Information
1285 Ave. of the Americas
NYC 10019
212 977-2544
One Year Subscription
$5.00 for 4 Issues

PESTS STRIP

[**4.6, facing page**] PESTS, letter of solicitation, December 6, 1986. Printed paper. © PESTS. Courtesy of Getty Research Institute (2008.M.14).

[**4.7**] PESTS newsletter, vol. 1, no. 2, pg. 1, "PESTS STRIP," 1987. Black-and-white printed paper. © PESTS. Courtesy of Getty Research Institute (2008.M.14).

the American art world within an international context of racial oppression, PESTS encouraged potential supporters to reflect on the normalizing of bias and misrepresentation: "Have you ever wished that the art world was more informed and knowledgeable about works created by *artists of color*?" And it promised action: the group's "immediate goals are to publicize the serious omission and de facto censorship practiced by galleries, museums and art publications."[77]

PESTS' posters, plastered around Soho and reproduced on the front page of their second PESTS STRIP newsletter, demanded acknowledgment of statistical ratios of underrepresentation, but went further. As suggested by Pindell's note to Martha Wilson, the poster campaign confronted the art world's *distorted* representation of men and women artists of color: "WE ARE NOT EXOTIC. WE ARE NOT PRIMITIVE. WE ARE NOT INVISIBLE. WE ARE NOT FEW IN NUMBER. WE ARE ARTISTS. 'Just like your gifted white boys.'" In another poster, the group explains part of the cognitive dissonance of racism: "¿WHAT IS TOKENISM / WHEN YOU'VE SEEN ONE ARTIST OF COLOR BUT THINK YOU'VE SEEN TEN." Distinct from the cutesy cursive of the Guerrilla Girls' report cards

[4.8] Guerrilla Girls, *You're Seeing Less Than Half the Picture*, 1989. Poster. © Guerrilla Girls. Courtesy of guerrillagirls.com.

or their business-adjacent font (Futura Extrabold Condensed), PESTS' posters used handcrafted white block lettering, almost as if pressurized against a black ground punctuated with buzzing bugs.[78] Pindell recalls putting the posters up around Soho with just one other PESTS member: "Many people didn't want to join; they didn't want to get caught."[79]

In two more posters, reproduced in miniature within the group's newsletter, PESTS uses data from the Artists Labor Force 1980 US Census to quantify not the absence but the abundance of artists of color, while also posing the problem as questions: "WE'RE HERE / ¿WHY *WON'T* YOU SEE US?" and "THERE ARE AT LEAST 11,009 ARTISTS OF COLOR IN NEW YORK / ¿WHY *DON'T* YOU SEE US?" (fig. 4.7).[80] While the upside-down question mark, borrowed from Spanish, notably implies a bilingual speaker, PESTS' questioning also offers a useful counterpart, if not rejoinder, to one of the Guerrilla Girls' posters criticizing sexism and racism. In a 1989 poster, the Guerrilla Girls assert, "YOU'RE SEEING LESS THAN HALF THE PICTURE / WITHOUT THE VISION OF WOMEN ARTISTS AND ARTISTS OF COLOR" (fig. 4.8). The first phrase, running vertically down the right side of the poster, sits beside a stretch of empty white space. The visual messaging of the poster presents a blank space where the missing "visions" can be projected, to complete the picture, or withheld, a present absence.

Juxtaposed with PESTS' calculations, however, this offering—to fill the other half of the picture—is revealed as a small and inadequate landing pad for the abundant buzzing of "at least 11,009 artists of color in New York." Rather than make spaces for balanced ratios, PESTS calls in its newsletter for action that aims to dismantle this limiting "picture" of the art-world structure altogether: "HELP US COMBAT THE NARROW VISION RAMPANT IN THE VISUAL ARTS. PLEASE SEND US ANNOUNCEMENTS AND PRESS RELEASES FOR EXHIBITIONS THAT YOU FEEL ARE BIASED AND/OR COLORLESS." PESTS endeavors, thus, to challenge the positivist idea at work within statistical findings, that what you see is what you see—and poses, instead, harder-to-quantify questions: *Why won't you see us?* Simultaneously, the group's solicitation of "biased and/or colorless" events pointedly addresses its primary audience: people of color whose labor and work is not being seen by the art world. In this request, PESTS both validates and grows its web of makers.

PESTS' newsletters promote the hyperpresence of a diverse multiethnic, multigenerational network of artists and institutions, both through the content they provide and the graphic design choices made. Dense columns offer information about upcoming projects and programming at venues across the country: for example, LA's Museum of African American Art and Shifflet Gallery, Miami-Dade Community City College Art Gallery, N'Namdi Gallery in Detroit, and in New York, Ceres Gallery, Liz Harris Gallery, AIR Gallery, the Native American Museum, Jamaica Arts Center, El Museo del Barrio, and more. Even the composition of its newsletters suggests a swarm of data: one can move up and down and around, rather than reading left to right, to gather pertinent information. PESTS thus provided a counterarchive that materialized buzzing activity that *already existed* but was regularly excluded from what it called "Manestreem Nus."[81] PESTS, performance studies scholar Uri McMillan has incisively recognized, "acted as insurgent political agents interrupting the status quo," while Pindell, as a leader within the group, enacted a "performance of Invisible Art World Instigator."[82]

Whereas the Guerrilla Girls initially gained media attention and speaking invitations through their symbolic use of guerrilla warfare and terrorism, PESTS' actions are attuned to the heightened risks of mobilizing critiques of the hegemonic white art world within an American society that has long censored and violently eradicated Black and Latinx individuals who voice dissent.

The second PESTS STRIP newsletter, for example, publicized an upcoming lecture by Esther Parada, "Art, Photography, and Representation of Other," at the International Center of Photography.[83] By this time, Parada was well known for *C/Overt Ideology: Two Images of Revolution*, a conceptual photo book exposing the Reagan administration's media campaign to unlearn and repackage notions of guerrilla warfare and American-backed terrorism in Nicaragua. PESTS promoted the event at a time when, as Kornbluh reports, "FBI agents visited more than a hundred citizens who had traveled to Nicaragua or attended public forums critical of the administration," while the FBI questioned and intimidated critics of US policy in order to silence public dissenters.[84] The newsletter also promoted exhibitions, such as *Outside Cuba*, hosted by the Zimmerli Art Museum, featuring artists of the Cuban diaspora at a time when US–Cuban national relations were deteriorating, and *Up South*, a show animating the racism of the Northeast. Together, these examples make clearer how a group of anonymous women of color calling out the racial apartheid in the art world, and supporting artists critical of America's history of war and slavery, might attract the punitive gaze of the state as well as that of the art world.

In papers uncovered in the Spelman College archives by Erica Edwards, Toni Cade Bambara wrote saliently about the specific material risks that Black women cultural workers took on in the 1980s when laboring as "image makers" and "image resurrectionists." They were embroiled, she writes, in a "minute by minute battle over who will define/depict/disseminate," tirelessly challenging the "state's culture brokers" who "would appropriate our tongues." As an indicator of the stakes of this action, Bambara expressly situated these makers as "combatants" whose act of "simply keeping the records straight" turned their fact-keeping into a kind of "para-military affair."[85]

Considering these factors, it is fitting that PESTS chose for its group symbol a cartoonish drawing of a fantastical bug. Part hornet, part scorpion, this image (which also circulated as stickers clandestinely posted around the city) can be understood as a subtle negotiation of the risk work inherent to critiquing intermeshing systems of oppression as women artists of color. Notably, this "pest" operates on quite a different symbolic register than words such as "guerrilla" or "terrorist"; the buzz of a bug avoids associations with a militant threat and, for the same reasons, does not muster the visual appeal or art-world attention that self-proclaimed white feminist terrorist artists do. Additionally, the metaphorical stickiness of a PEST STRIP was useful given another of PESTS' goals: catching the difficult-to-evidence, impossible-to-quantify distortions of the work of artists and curators of color in the art world.

The Problem of Distortion: Horizons of Bias and Risk Law

PESTS' critique of the politics of distortion at work in the art world put pressure on the recruitment of whiteness that underwrites the presumed objectivity of ratios of underrepresentation. In an introductory essay for a 1987–1988 exhibition of art by multiracial women, Pindell writes, "Being a woman of color, I have experienced directly the omission and underrepresentation of works by women of color." More than this, she adds:

> I have also noted how people of color, their history and culture are being appropriated, *distorted* and used as images and points of focus by white artists while artist of color are excluded from "speaking" visually, interpreting themselves on the same platform.[86]

In alignment with Pindell's observation, PESTS enlisted newsletter readers to help them set benchmarks of tokenism that would clarify how distortive racial and ethnic bias begins in overlooked interactions and spaces, long before the exhibition or collection. In an exemplary instance from 1987, PESTS issued a caustically witty call for nominations for the "First Annual Pests Awards" (fig. 4.9):

> Criteria is open—there's so much myopia in the art world that it shouldn't be hard to come up with the names of a few idiots who, for example, are so Euro-centric that they insist on ascribing atavistic yearnings to your work so they won't have [to] see it on the same level as the half-baked jokers they currently admire. Nominate that dealer who came to your studio looking for something "funky", "folksy", "self-taught", "primitive" or "wild". Honor the sensitive curator who wanted so much for you to paint coconuts & palm trees. What about the fool who claims to know you so well but refers to you by the name of another person of color and don't forget the ones that can't deal with you if you aren't obsequious and speak in monosylables [*sic*].[87]

In listing these "award-winning" acts of distortion and misrecognition, PESTS names the normalized aggressions used by white curators and artists to exoticize, produce, censor, and diminish the taxing discrimination experienced by women of color artists.

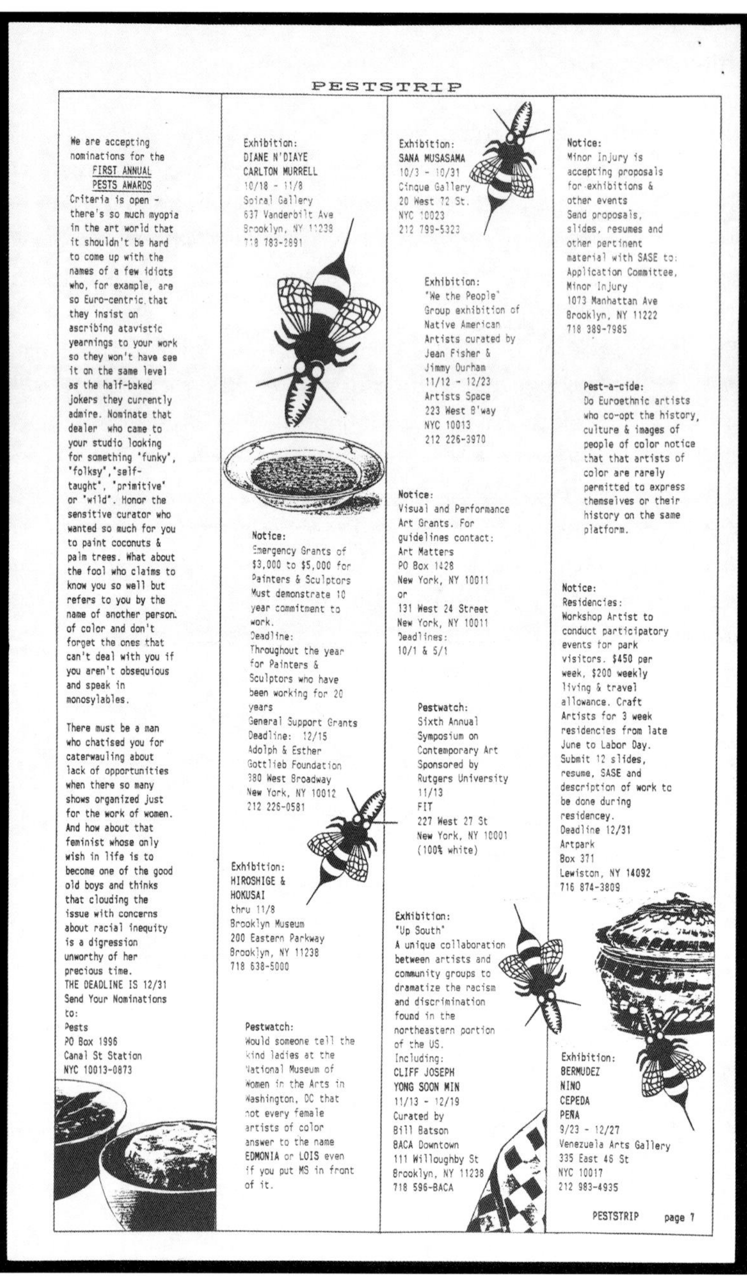

PESTSTRIP

We are accepting nominations for the FIRST ANNUAL PESTS AWARDS
Criteria is open - there's so much myopia in the art world that it shouldn't be hard to come up with the names of a few idiots who, for example, are so Euro-centric that they insist on ascribing atavistic yearnings to your work so they won't have see it on the same level as the half-baked jokers they currently admire. Nominate that dealer who came to your studio looking for something "funky", "folksy", "self-taught", "primitive" or "wild". Honor the sensitive curator who wanted so much for you to paint coconuts & palm trees. What about the fool who claims to know you so well but refers to you by the name of another person of color and don't forget the ones that can't deal with you if you aren't obsequious and speak in monosylables.

There must be a man who chatised you for caterwauling about lack of opportunities when there so many shows organized just for the work of women. And how about that feminist whose only wish in life is to become one of the good old boys and thinks that clouding the issue with concerns about racial inequity is a digression unworthy of her precious time.
THE DEADLINE IS 12/31
Send Your Nominations to:
Pests
PO Box 1996
Canal St Station
NYC 10013-0873

Exhibition:
DIANE N'DIAYE
CARLTON MURRELL
10/18 - 11/8
Soiral Gallery
637 Vanderbilt Ave
Brooklyn, NY 11238
718 783-2891

Notice:
Emergency Grants of $3,000 to $5,000 for Painters & Sculptors
Must demonstrate 10 year commitment to work.
Deadline:
Throughout the year for Painters & Sculptors who have been working for 20 years
General Support Grants
Deadline: 12/15
Adolph & Esther Gottlieb Foundation
380 West Broadway
New York, NY 10012
212 226-0581

Exhibition:
HIROSHIGE & HOKUSAI
thru 11/8
Brooklyn Museum
200 Eastern Parkway
Brooklyn, NY 11238
718 638-5000

Pestwatch:
Would someone tell the kind ladies at the National Museum of Women in the Arts in Washington, DC that not every female artists of color answer to the name EDMONIA or LOIS even if you put MS in front of it.

Exhibition:
SANA MUSASAMA
10/3 - 10/31
Cinque Gallery
20 West 72 St.
NYC 10023
212 799-5323

Exhibition:
"We the People"
Group exhibition of Native American Artists curated by Jean Fisher & Jimmy Durham
11/12 - 12/23
Artists Space
223 West B'way
NYC 10013
212 226-3970

Notice:
Visual and Performance Art Grants. For guidelines contact:
Art Matters
PO Box 1428
New York, NY 10011
or
131 West 24 Street
New York, NY 10011
Deadlines:
10/1 & 5/1

Pestwatch:
Sixth Annual Symposium on Contemporary Art
Sponsored by Rutgers University
11/13
FIT
227 West 27 St
New York, NY 10001
(100% white)

Exhibition:
"Up South"
A unique collaboration between artists and community groups to dramatize the racism and discrimination found in the northeastern portion of the US.
Including:
CLIFF JOSEPH
YONG SOON MIN
11/13 - 12/19
Curated by
Bill Batson
BACA Downtown
111 Willoughby St
Brooklyn, NY 11238
718 596-BACA

Notice:
Minor Injury is accepting proposals for exhibitions & other events
Send proposals, slides, resumes and other pertinent material with SASE to:
Application Committee,
Minor Injury
1073 Manhattan Ave
Brooklyn, NY 11222
718 389-7985

Pest-a-cide:
Do Euroethnic artists who co-opt the history, culture & images of people of color notice that that artists of color are rarely permitted to express themselves or their history on the same platform.

Notice:
Residencies:
Workshop Artist to conduct participatory events for park visitors. $450 per week, $200 weekly living & travel allowance. Craft Artists for 3 week residencies from late June to Labor Day.
Submit 12 slides, resume, SASE and description of work to be done during residencey.
Deadline 12/31
Artpark
Box 371
Lewiston, NY 14092
716 874-3809

Exhibition:
BERMUDEZ
NINO
CEPEDA
PEÑA
9/23 - 12/27
Venezuela Arts Gallery
335 East 46 St
NYC 10017
212 983-4935

PESTSTRIP page 7

[4.9] PESTS newsletter, vol. 1, no. 3, page 7, "PESTS STRIP," Fall/Winter 1987. Black-and-white printed paper. © PESTS. Courtesy of Getty Research Institute (2008.M.14).

In the announcement's second paragraph, PESTS turns directly to the labor of distortion that white curators, artists, and activists continue to participate in:

> There must be a man who chatised [*sic*] you for caterwauling about lack of opportunities when there are so many shows organized just for the work of women. And how about that feminist whose only wish in life is to become one of the good old boys and thinks that clouding the issue with concerns about racial inequity is a digression unworthy of her precious time.

Here PESTS calls out the Guerrilla Girls, recipients that year of a Susan B. Anthony award—who, even in their progressive critique, primarily of gendered and secondarily of racialized hierarchies of power, did not recognize the scope and scale of structural racism within their own risk-taking and their own organization.[88] As PESTS suggests, the distortion—the unseeing and dismissal—of women artists of color in the art world occurs through overtly racist exclusionary decisions, as well as within the fight for race-neutral gender equality and the changing status of bias in emergent liberal policies. Like the Guerrilla Girls, PESTS does not appear to have collected data on the bias toward, and misrecognition of, queer of color women or men artists. It focused instead on racialized gender politics.

Not coincidentally, the Guerrilla Girls' and PESTS' differing engagements with inequity in the art world in the mid- to late 1980s unfolded at the same time as a legal review of changes in the recognition of discrimination, and the documentation of and liability for bias, within corporations and institutions.[89] The problem, legal expert Michael Selmi explains, is that "the Court has not modified the case law to take into account the changed nature of discrimination but instead remains tied to doctrinal methods of proof that largely fail to capture more subtle forms of discrimination."[90] Selmi makes a point of articulating the limitations of antidiscrimination rulings under Title VII (the rider in the Civil Rights Act of 1964 prohibiting employment discrimination) that are based on statistics of underrepresentation.

While statistical proof of workforce underrepresentation could be used to establish an intent to discriminate, such rulings made it harder to prove discrimination beyond quantifiable numbers.[91] In his discussion of "bias-motivated violence" within the context of transphobic discrimination, legal scholar and trans activist Dean Spade puts the problem another way: a "perpetrator based" understanding of "what constitutes violation, of what can be recognized as oppression, serves to naturalize and affirm the neutrality of the status quo."[92] In other words, as Spade asserts, we have to "resist individualization and intentionality as key elements of identifying oppression."[93] Both the Guerrilla Girls and PESTS utilize the tactic of "naming names" in the artworld. But the PEST STRIPS—as messier, spatialized webs, buzzing and thriving—complicate the mechanisms that produce "big names" in the first place, thereby offering one such contestation of individualization and intention. They also evidence how ethnoracial, ethnonational solidarities already exist but are rendered unseen when they exceed, and thereby defy, the controlled (read: extractive, limited) space provided to them within neoliberal metrics of "diversity and inclusion." As Puar has insightfully asserted, "Multiculturalism is the accomplice to the ascendancy of whiteness, reproducing the biopolitical mandate to live through the proper population statistics."[94]

The distinctions this chapter traces between the Guerrilla Girls' and PESTS' models of critique are even more revealing when contextualized within larger legal discussions regarding racial bias and its tabulation then in the national dialogue and in the courts—the formulation of the Hate Crime Statistics Act in 1985, for example, created to track "hate" but in a way that has served to further neutralize the bias at work within the collection and reporting of such data.[95] Under these conditions, when ratios and statistics are legitimized as the acceptable way to record the problem of inequity, they become the means for the solution. Statistics of inequity, while revelatory and potentially part of a path toward change-making, do not, however, adequately challenge institutional power dynamics and punitive relations in which violations often outstrip the seeable and quantifiable.

In a 1988 essay likely published around the time PESTS ended its data-collecting and printing efforts due to a lack of funds, Pindell laments how the "co-option" of activist groups, "being transformed by the dominant culture into something trendy or chic," was undermining the work at hand. The work of these groups was further exacerbated by monetary factors reinscribed by white-centering relations of resource distribution: "Funding sources that would possibly fund a Guerrilla Girls' action, because of their reputation for dealing with white women's issues are reluctant to fund a group like PESTS which deals with race." Her conclusion: "The art/culture industry specializes in a form of insider trading which, on the institutional level, is too often supported by our tax dollars. We must ask questions, we must empower ourselves to challenge the system and ourselves."[96] Within the rhetorical questions posed by PESTS—*Why don't you see us? Why won't you see us?*—sit others: *What are you not willing to give up?* And perhaps a more self-directed consideration for its primary audience: *Do we see us?* PESTS' challenge, inscribed within these questions, is to reckon with, and hold accountable, the white racist art world while refusing the limits of its narrow and distortive terms, advocacy, and questions.

Post-Script: Policeable Anonymity

While the preceding chapters have largely focused on artists' performance-based conceptual works, this chapter has been decidedly more disembodied. The focus has been on clandestine graphic posters and written critiques, groups of largely unidentified artists and curators, and the politics of symbolic and semantic militancy and its discursive afterlives. As a result, it may seem that the physicality of punitive relations is less of a concern; however, what is at stake here is inextricably bound up in the ways people move through space and are stopped, constricted, and held up. In this telling of the making of guerrilla tactics in coalitional art praxis of the 1980s, at issue is not only what constitutes anti-racist intersectional methodology but which models of activism and resistance become legitimized and which are undermined and erased entirely when punitive relations are pushed to the edges of art-historical inquiries.

PESTS was not able to rely on the same white privilege and punitive relations as the Guerrilla Girls; its members worked within the limits of a white supremacist framework of presumed aggression and hostility that differently positioned them in relation to antiblack and xenophobic state-sanctioned violence and censorship, as well as discussions of bias in the art world. While PESTS sought to widen its network of allies and accomplices, the Guerrilla Girls' goal was to gain "more access" to the system of the art world by critiquing the gender imbalance in its exhibition record, as "opposed to breaking down the system."[97] This assimilationist logic is distinct from that adopted by PESTS, which called into view the vast and diverse multiethnic network of artists that already questioned the hegemonic white structure of the art world—and yet were refused official recognition as such. Under these conditions, PESTS' anonymity was a tactical maneuver of incalculable importance—one that is still in effect today, with Pindell as the only publicly, yet ever-hesitant, confirmed member of the group.

Interestingly, "anonymity" itself, and how to punitively maintain it, was an important topic of debate for the Guerrilla Girls. "Notes for Guerrilla Girls big meeting," a handwritten list from 1985 includes the following prompt: "Discuss anonymity, perhaps even a way to 'punish offenders.'"[98] *Anonymity* is the only word underlined on a page that lists some eight other topics for consideration, including publicity, recruitment, legal actions, and public talks, thereby underscoring its significance—as well as the need for disciplinary oversight. The need to establish rules for punishing those who did not strictly adhere to anonymity underscores that some members in the group were less concerned about the possible implications of identification. Notably, the group's relationship to anonymity has continued to change. What began as a protective measure later mutates into a "burden" for members whose careers would have benefited from the group's accrued fame.[99] As Guerrilla Girl "Käthe Kollowitz" says of anonymity in a 2020 interview:

> We wanted to create the idea that we are everywhere, and we are listening. We could be working at the MoMA or even at Leo Castelli's gallery. We wanted to create this idea that the art world was being watched, surveilled, and scrutinized. Anonymity has protected us, but now I'm not sure anyone cares any more who we are. It has changed.[100]

The protection afforded by anonymity complicates the subtitle given to this interview, "We upend the art world's notion of what's good and what's right," which testifies to the ways the Guerrilla Girls' mode of "bad behavior" continues to be used as a standard of protest—one that leaves untroubled the asymmetries of risk work through which their boisterous "badness" and access to anonymity is made possible. To be sure, the Guerrilla Girls' prominent place within the pantheon of feminist art making has been hard-earned through the immense work members have done to educate audiences about the inequities animated within art exhibitions, museums, and collecting practice. At the same time, the continued lack of attention in art-historical discourse to *how* the Guerrilla Girls initially mobilized ideas of militancy, terrorism, and the representation of misbehaving continues to foster a selective memory that *unsees* PESTS' crucial critiques of such white-centering approaches, and *distorts* its broad-scale efforts.

What would the history of the guerrilla tactic in art look like today if the interventions of the Guerrilla Girls and PESTS were routinely taught and exhibited as an interlaced story? What kinds of antiracist feminist politics would be amplified? What examples of collectively managed distortions would become recognizable with renewed attention to the processes that sanitize and conceal relational adjacencies to violence and power? What kinds of political possibilities for art might we then come to know? And, following PESTS' instructive questioning: what is *not* being said in the stories told again and again in the canon of American art? Who is telling these stories? Who is (not) listening? This chapter was written with an eye for honoring the complexity of the Guerrilla Girls' and PESTS' actions, and what these ideas of action *do* and for whom, then and now.

Epilogue

At the Edges of Guerrilla

Risk Work tells just one possible story about the intersection of tactics, art, punitiveness, risk, and governance in the United States. The chapters of this book have sought to bring into focus a matrix of relations that constitute the interlaced *making* of art and the *making* of risk. How artists who use guerrilla tactics come up on, and against, and *with* newly conceived punitive structures as they take shape on local, federal, and international scales. By focusing on punitive literacies, the social, penal, and juridical infrastructures that have shaped tactical art emerge as a structural form. At the same time, this book set out to understand the political history of guerrilla tactics in US-based art produced during the 1970s and 1980s—weighing the social, pedagogical, and juridical imaginings of the mythic scale of a coming guerrilla war, and artists' evocations of guerrilla, alongside the ways this notion of action-taking was used by politicians and policy makers to expand and cement gendered, racialized, sexualized, and xenophobic risk management across the country.

There are many more stories to tell to continue to understand the history of the romanticizing of tactics in art and its political implications: through queer of color critiques challenging the reifying of the heterosexual masculinist gaze of tactics leveraged by straight men and women in performance-based art; critical trans studies assessments of the racialized transphobic and homophobic metrics that underwrite a romanticizing of sexualized modes of confrontation, and the risk work that emerges in response; critical disability studies' questioning of the ocularcentric methods through which tactics in art have been classified and archived as well as disrupted and disassembled; nuanced accounts of gendered colorism within artist collectives and solidarity building movements; and so on.

This coming-to-know how risk, and thereby vulnerability, is made and described is a labor of perceiving the limited narratives of agency and resourcefulness and pushing past them: the history of guerrilla tactics in art in the US is, at its base, the history of artists—as well as curators, lawyers, police, and urban planners—negotiating, altering, and reimagining possible ways of being in relation through acts of anticipation, research, intimacy, and preemptive planning, all while navigating an asymmetrical, ever-evolving apparatus of policing and surveillance. As a structural and aesthetic form, the naming of punitive literacy aims to provide a jumping-off point for resisting limiting frames of individualistic agency, violation, or reactive response that have foreclosed upon more generative analyses of the sociality of tactics in art. Through this analytic, artists' decisions to act—or not act—under conditions of punitiveness, racial capitalism, and surveillance reveal how the collectively managed making of risk limns the maintenance, and potential dismantling of intertwined power relations.

The label "guerrilla" continues to appear in art discourse in the twenty-first century. In December 2018, activist and artist Rafael Shimunov, along with members of his newly formed art collective Art v War, created an unannounced, unauthorized installation at the Whitney Museum of American Art in New York City. An online article describes the "guerrilla-style installation of painting" in an area on the museum's fourth floor where Shimunov had noticed there was "little security detail or surveillance." The exhibit, *Mother with Daughters in Tear Gas*, consisted of two small, framed works, along with wall text that credited the works to "Warren B. Kanders" and listed only one material: "Chemical Gas."[1]

The paintings reproduced news images, taken by Reuters photojournalist Kim Kyung-Hoon, of families being sprayed with tear gas at the US–Mexico border near Tijuana on November 25, 2018. One shows Maria Meza, a mother from Honduras, attempting to cross the border with her twin five-year-old daughters.[2] Tear gas cannisters, shot from the US side at the migrants, hit the sandy bank below the barbed-wire fence, forming a cloud behind them, as Meza pulls her daughters away and people in the background begin to run. Tear gas—like rubber bullets, used as a "nonlethal" alternative by anti-riot police—is itself an act of punitive abstraction; commonly thought of as a dissipating gas that merely creates blurred vision, its effects can in fact be permanent, even fatal if too much is inhaled.

Shimunov acted in solidarity with museum staff demanding that Warren B. Kanders resign from his position as vice chairman of the Whitney's board of trustees. It had come to light that Safariland, a company of which Kanders was

CEO, had manufactured the tear gas used by US border agents on the asylum-seekers near Tijuana. Kanders had been CEO since 2012, during which time Safariland had expanded its merchandise line of police body armor, tear gas hand grenades, and firearms, becoming a leading international supplier of law enforcement and military supplies. When the image of Meza and her children circulated worldwide in November 2018, Whitney Museum staff, many of whom had friends and relatives directly affected by Trump's immigration policies and the weaponry produced by Safariland, composed and shared a letter demanding Kanders's resignation; he and his company were benefiting from the violent containment of demonstrators and refugees, they argued, and his presence on its board made the museum complicit.

Tear gas made and marketed by Safariland was used not only on migrant asylum seekers at the US–Mexico border but also, as the open letter asserted, on the "mostly-Indigenous Water Protectors" protesting the Standing Rock Dakota Access Pipeline, and "mostly-POC protestors" in Ferguson, Palestine, Egypt, and Puerto Rico.[3] As the open letter made the rounds, an artist-led organization, Decolonize This Place, staged a demonstration in the museum's lobby, burning sage until the smoke detectors went off, to symbolize the toxic gas used on protesters at the border. The fire department was summoned, but no arrests ensued as the activist-artists left the space. Shimunov, a refugee from Uzbekistan, felt moved to do something to help publicize the staff protests. He was also disgusted with the museum, which had recently received critical acclaim for an exhibition of Indigenous Latinx practices yet defended Kanders's continued presence on its board.

To create the paintings for *Mother with Daughters in Tear Gas*, Shimunov printed the original press photographs on canvas board and altered them with oil paint. To hang them in the museum, he relied on his punitive literacy: having researched the museum's security policies online, he scaled the panels to just within the size of items that can be carried into the Whitney without inspection. As a further precaution, he carried the paintings, wrapped in blue tissue paper in a shopping bag, telling security guards they were a birthday gift for his mother, which he figured would deter them from wanting to unwrap them.[4] In a photograph taken by Art v War collaborator Cindy Trinh, Shimunov stands beside the installation, looking straight into the camera, his hands gently clasped, his winter coat slightly unzipped, the gift bag in his hands just visible at the bottom of the frame (plate 10). The image circulated on Twitter and other social media and was reproduced in news articles describing the installation.

As art discourses expand in necessary ways to illuminate the interlacing conditions of oppression, the ongoing use of "guerrilla" to describe actions of intervention sheds light on longer lineages of action-taking, while simultaneously concealing important relations of power. Labeling Shimunov's installation a "guerrilla" art exhibition does, on the one hand, generate context for his gesture, situating him within what has become a canonical, collected history. The poetics of Art v War furtively installing paintings at one New York art museum nearly fifty years after Toche and Hendricks removed a painting from another in their "Malevich" action is striking, suggesting that not much has changed. On the other hand, the application of "guerrilla" elides the structural logic of policing in favor of glamorizing the artist's spontaneity and activism. Here, the notion of "guerrilla" is a flattened placeholder that effaces the social factors of Shimunov's specific positioning in relation to the surveillance state, museum apparatus, and use of Twitter and other social media to disseminate information about his act.

Within the news coverage of his installation, Shimunov's observation that there was "little security detail or surveillance" on the Whitney's fourth floor meaningfully articulates his response to the securitization of the museum space. Art museums employ a large and ever-growing number of private security personnel, their hiring managed by private companies such as Securitas; security staff tend to be part-time, hourly employees without benefits—and to make up the largest number of people of color hired in art museums.[5] Whereas guards manned museum galleries in the late 1960s and early 1970s, today's art museum security practices also include video surveillance, motion detectors, intruder alarms, and metal-detector scanning, among other physical security devices. As art museums have grown in scale and number in the US, so too has their punitive footprint: large-scale museums contract labor with local police.

Amid calls nationwide for cultural institutions to divest from working with police, art museums have remained largely silent about their own privatized security apparatus. Instead, a trend is emerging, wherein curators invite museum security guards to curate temporary exhibitions or to lead tours.[6] In a sense, these shows and tours amount to nothing more than white carceral art-world theater: without changes in hiring practices and health care benefits for security staff, invitations to part-time employees to serve on museum advisory boards, or plans for museums to address the punitive logics of their gallery spaces, serve only to reinforce the assumed necessity of hyperpoliced spaces in art museums, while performatively achieving "points" under the rhetoric of diversity and inclusion initiatives. Through the museum's own savvy punitive literacy, these programs stage a vanishing act of sorts: they promote the assumption that guards bring "new perspectives"—those of "officer-curators"—as if museum curators did not also conceive their exhibitions as they do within the calculus of security politics, insurance, and perspectives shaped by guarding and being guarded.[7]

The realities of an expanding carceral society, recumbent with racial capitalism and managed precarity, raises a series of nested questions that push beyond the study of conceptual and performance art labeled guerrilla: How are art experiences and security infrastructures already entangled? How have cultural narratives of threat and safety become central to being together in front of, or behind, art experiences? Who decides when an action becomes threatening? What does accountability to the punitive histories of American culture look like in art history? And what, alternatively, would the headline covering Shimunov's installation, and the discourse it might initiate, begin to address or anticipate if his work were not called a "guerrilla art exhibition" but a form of "punitive literacy," or some other classification that focuses attention on the collective practices of policing and not solely on the gesture of resistance? What kinds of research, artmaking, and discourse might emerge if archives and databases organized art using searchable keywords like "punitive art," "securitization," or "carcerality" alongside "guerrilla," "protest," or "activism"? What interlaced relations would materialize?

The concept "guerrilla" as a method of art intervention is still meaningful, yet its horizons are limited in today's America when its naming forecloses upon more critical engagement with the root causes of its formation, and artists' and audiences' complex understanding of punitive encounters. Our critical vocabularies need to evolve, to keep up with risk work and museal as well as global imaginaries of policing. Setting an example, in *The Militant Image Reader*, a 2015 text expanding upon the exhibition *The Militant Image: Picturing What Is Already Going On, or the Poetics of the Militant Image*, staged by the Vienna- and Vancouver-based collective Urban Subjects, Stefan Romer challenges the quick use of "militancy" when looking for strategies of refusal. "Instead of recuperating *the militant* and *revolution*," he makes an argument "against the term *militancy*," the goal being instead to "envision a new and different (dis) order of images from out of the old humanist production of pictures."[8] Similarly, the work ahead for renarrating guerrilla tactics in art of the past and present, so as to alter its horizons of possibility in the future, would benefit from a critical vocabulary trained more explicitly on the ongoing neutralizing of the carceral context writ large.

+ + +

At the time of this writing, the United States faces intertwined pandemics: the global crisis created by the spread of COVID-19 and a belated reckoning with the epidemic proportions of structural racism and antiblack police terror perpetuated by white supremacist logics of privilege and the protection of property and extractive labor conditions. Under these circumstances, the framework of risk work becomes even more pronounced, as the conditions of coercive containment continue to evolve and intensify.

While the book focuses on the period of the 1960s to the 1980s, this is a cross-generational story whose implications become even more pronounced with historical distance. In many ways, the subsequent careers of several of the artists considered here offer insights into the different ways risk work in an evolving security state brings artists into the limelight or, conversely, keeps them out of sight. For example, Jean Toche lived off the grid in his Staten Island home until his death in 2018 at the age of eighty-six. Fearing electronic surveillance, he never obtained an email address.[9] Instead, he used an unlisted telephone number and continued to conduct ephemeral guerrilla campaigns through the mail until the end of his life. Despite being acquitted in his 1975 trial, the arrest and prosecution intimidated him; he changed his cavalier relationship to risk-taking, and shifted away from performance-based interventions to mail art. As Toche explained to me during an interview in 2014:

> You see, when you're arrested it becomes your occupation to get out of being investigated. That's how they detain you, really, by giving you these tasks that distract you from the real issues at hand. After the trial, even though I had won, I was told by [the lawyer, Michael] Ratner to stay away from the art world to avoid future incarceration. In this way, the outcome of the case affected my first amendment rights. To be able to say something, you have to be able to see something, and I was no longer allowed, so to speak, to see things in the art world, or to participate.[10]

Toche's articulation frames policing as structural and durational, rather than momentary and confrontational, revealing how exposure to even the threat of state violence alters actions that manifest as an aesthetics of intervention.

In November 2014, I received one of Toche's guerrilla art pieces in the mail, a few months after interviewing him about his experiences during the 1970s and 1980s. In the one-page xeroxed flyer, he wrote in penned cursive, "The artist was found dead on arrival at the art opening of 'relevancy' at a New York City museum. 'Improperly packed' said one of the supervisors." The piece refers to his fleeting reemergence in New York after many decades of self-imposed exile: in the fall of 2013 he visited a friend's opening but left early, feeling paranoid that security guards were watching him, and at the same time remorseful that no one else seemed to know who he was.[11]

Like Toche, Asco and PESTS, groups differently positioned by policing in and beyond the art world, remain understudied. Asco disbanded in the mid-1980s due to personal differences and interests. Its four original members, Patssi Valdez, Harry Gamboa Jr., Gronk, and Willie Herrón, have each continued to produce art, working in more traditional mediums of painting, sculpture, installation, and conceptual photography. Each has presented solo exhibitions in Europe and the US. Yet even as the group has gained attention in landmark exhibitions hosted by the Getty's Pacific Standard Time initiative, landing a detail of *Decoy* on the cover of *Artforum* in 2011, museum acquisitions of their work remain nil.[12] As for PESTS, the group's cofounder, Howardena Pindell, has recently been the focus of large-scale museum exhibitions and scholarly studies, yet within these shows discussion of PESTS has been minimal, likely due to her belated, and ever-wary, public acknowledgment of her role in the group.[13]

In perhaps the most eye-opening example of how punitive relations continue to hold and position artists, Adrian Piper learned in 2006 that she'd been identified as a "suspicious traveler" on the US Transportation Security Administration watch list.[14] The "no-fly list" is a small subset of the US Government Terrorist Screening Database, established in 2002 in the aftermath of 9/11 and, as noted by its critics, typically used to restrict the mobility and movement of political activists. With this knowledge, Piper, who was on unpaid leave in Berlin at the time, refused to return to the United States while listed as a "suspicious traveler," leading Wellesley College to forcibly terminate her tenured full professorship.[15] But, as Hawa Allen writes in a review of Piper's memoir addressing why she left and why she stays away from the US, Piper had known what it meant to be seen as a "suspicious person" long before appearing on the watch list.[16] Indeed, her work from the 1970s maneuvered through imaginaries of innocence and aggression—the very horizons of abstracted hostility that inculcated various meanings for her during the making of the *Mythic Being*.

Mis/Periodizing Risk

Piper's presence on the US no-fly list and her subsequent restricted travel reemphasizes how the "symbolic" register of artmaking does not exempt artists, especially women of color and historically minoritized individuals, from state scrutiny and containment. One more recent prismatic moment within state scrutiny is that of 9/11 and the ensuing "War on Terror" as a focus of politics, culture, and art. Punishments for political dissidents' tactics of intervention have intensified, essentially placing political dissent into "a new category of domestic terrorism."[17] For example, under the Patriot Act, signed by President George W. Bush in response to the attacks, "mail fraud (a crime typically used against activists when other avenues of arrest fail) has gone from a maximum of five years to twenty," a change that, had it been the case in the 1970s, would have significantly altered the stakes for Toche and Asco's use of the mail.

During the writing of this book, I have observed that one of the effects of the events of 9/11 and the War on Terror has been a mis/periodizing of histories of risk-taking that unremembers the significance of prior racialized and gendered counterinsurgency and lawfare, and the preceding "punitive turns" of the twentieth century. In effect, the emphasis on the figure of the terrorist and its related surveillance infrastructure that emerge after 9/11 makes it difficult to recognize significant palimpsestic links across cross-generational tactical stories of punitive literacy. Historical accounts of insurgent tactics in society post-2001 often lose sight of the continuities within criminal code reform, urban renewal, and policing practices of the Cold War period, and how anticipations of guerrilla warfare that developed across the mid- to late twentieth century make possible the conditions of surveillance and containment in the 2000s.[18]

In Bush's 2002 State of the Union Address, Sara Ahmed observes a call for "the transformation of democratic citizenship into policing," when he said, "And as government works to secure our homeland, America will continue to depend on the eyes and ears of alert citizens" — always keeping watch for suspicious others.[19] Ahmed directly references Ulrich Beck's 1986 ideas about "risk society," asserting that, "insofar as we do not know what forms others may take, those who fail to materialize in the forms that are lived as norms, *the politics of continual surveillance of emergent forms is sustained as an ongoing project of survival*."[20]

The security-marketing slogan "If You See Something, Say Something™," appearing in the country's airports, bus stations, schools, and hospitals, was originally disseminated by New York City's Metropolitan Transportation Authority. In 2010, the MTA licensed the slogan to the federal Department of Homeland Security.[21] Although the slogan may seem like a unique innovation linked with a post-9/11 moment, the work of artists in the 1970s and 1980s offers an archive of the incremental deputizing of discernment and its negotiation, visually, materially, legally, and socially. As police historian Stuart Schrader estimates, "Since the 1970s another period in the evolution of policing has been upon us, one that scholars have yet to identify and name."[22] This understudied period, Schrader explains, has seen shifts from managerial to entrepreneurial goals for police, whereby commissioners and law enforcement officers transition from foot soldiers carrying out orders of the state to self-proclaimed "artists" of scrutiny and risk communication with lobbying power in the name of modern reform and community relations. The period between the mid-1960s and mid-1980s—not coincidentally, the time when artists developed an unprecedented array of guerrilla tactics in art—remains a critical period for understanding the infrastructure of policing today.

A second possible reason the significance of the punitive turn and its relationship with art-making has been understudied—in addition to the impact of a post-9/11 discourse of counterinsurgency and policing—is the misperiodizing of predictive policing that emerges in the hype surrounding algorithmic technologies. The origin myth of predictive policing in criminology tends to trace its development to New York and the use of CompStat (computer statistics) under transit police officer Jack Maple in the 1990s, then its formalization in Los Angeles and Santa Cruz, California, in the early 2000s under the leadership of police chief William Bratton (previously in New York)—a story that conceals the impact of its earlier iterations in the 1970s.[23] Instead, the software PredPol, which launched in Santa Cruz in 2009, has been viewed as the progenitor of predictive policing, having steadily become the ubiquitous tool used by police in American cities. Police departments purchase the expensive software, which takes as its template the beat patrol algorithms (discussed in chapter 1) that in the early 1970s mined data on past crimes; fed them into an algorithm that consider location, timing, and incident load; and then specified which city blocks police should target.[24] With PredPol, updates to these crime maps occur daily, if not hourly.

This pattern of predictive analytics, Andrew Ferguson explains, follows the same structure wherever it's implemented: "invention first, then adoption, and finally assessment only after the fact."[25] Given the delay in assessment (as well as the limitations of assessment, largely self-conducted by law enforcement), artists' attunement to the incremental changes in an area through the manifestation of punitive literacy in art provides an invaluable counterarchive of assessment in the moment and durationally across time and space. An additional challenge now lies in also engaging with the ways that those who create and manage software like PredPol are not outside of aesthetics and visual studies but are at times a creative force within it (for example, Larry Samuels, named PredPol's CEO in 2012, was previously employed by Atari and Creative Labs).[26]

In *Carceral Capitalism*, scholar-activist-poet Jackie Wang reflects on the expansion of a "carceral apparatus," namely how "invisible forms of power are circulating all around us, circumscribing and sorting us into invisible cells that confine us sometimes without our knowing. Perhaps an invisible cell could be described as a carceral apparatus that does not control or confine populations by housing them in physical structures."[27] In dialogue with Wang's focus on the dematerialization of monitoring, political theorist and carceral geographer Brian Jefferson notes another factor that further expands the scope of this carceral apparatus: the deputizing of citizens' *metadata*.

Jefferson describes the impact of technology such as cell phones in what he calls "human dronification," which he defines as "the transformation of civic subjects into a flexible configuration of sentinels."[28] In other words, crowdsourced wireless technologies—such as smart phones, laptops, and Apple watches—geocode movement, and this information becomes part of the punitive network tracking individuals. In tandem with geocoded movement made available in real time, Jefferson notes how police information has become available online through incident report posting as a gesture of "governmental transparency." As Jefferson reflects, "The democraticization of police data allows for the democraticization of racialized policing."[29]

Recognizing the Non-Event of Punitiveness

If the risk work of artists active in the 1970s and 1980s, and the legacies of their art experimentation, provides an archive of how previously implemented racialized and gendered infrastructures of policing and monitoring remain in place, then the work ahead requires reckoning with how these forms are repurposed and extended within changing punitive contexts today, so as to more effectively identify and dismantle them. The crime maps of the 1970s—studied and made the basis of early predictive policing, as documented across the works of Asco and Burden—are the same ones that are later factored into the "objective" algorithms used in predictive policing in the present. Today, as Jefferson explains, "predictive policing identifies entire demographics and neighborhoods as criminally predisposed" with a goal of "permanent supervision."[30]

Los Angeles, the "home" of predictive policing, has only intensified its surveillance grid and police power: every mayor since the late 1980s has sought to increase the LAPD's budget, while gentrification, property values, and urban development have continued to exacerbate environmental racism.[31] For fiscal year 2022–2023, within the LAPD budget ($1.88 billion), nearly half (roughly $909.66 million) is spent on patrolling "field forces" versus specialized investigations, traffic control, custody, training, and tech support. With a population of roughly four million people, there are approximately ten thousand officers.[32] Of course, people living in LA experience the impact of these realities differently through the vectors of racialized gendered violence, the criminalizing of poverty, and the ongoing prioritizing of whiteness as a protected status. In 2019, according to the Sentencing Project's tabulation of 2022 census data, California incarcerated nine Black people for each white person incarcerated (per 100,000 residents).[33] Los Angeles County, in particular, operates the largest jail system in the United States, but it tends to incarcerate people from just a few neighborhoods—East LA among them.[34]

LA-based conceptual photographer Amina Cruz, whose family ties to East LA date back to the 1960s, considers the affective forms of punitive literacy in unassuming site-specific installations. In her larger practice, Cruz turns to the photographic documentation of queer brown punk life in the United States, Peru, Colombia, and Mexico. In 2021, Cruz began creating a series, *me & mine & you & yours*, in urban and rural environments that explores her family's photo archives and deploys a knowledge of risk-taking shaped by the laws of the 1970s and 1980s. The wheat-pasted photographic interventions began in Arvin, California, just outside of Bakersfield, where her grandparents, Luis and Nellie, met in the 1950s while laboring as Mexican migrant farm workers on what was then the DiGiorgio Farms. Cruz returned to those fields and warehouses, which have since been sold to smaller companies, to clandestinely paste large photographs (both black-and-white and color) of her elders.

In one of the images, Cruz's grandparents smile for a candid portrait in June 1957, holding Chita (Veronica; Chita was her nickname), the firstborn of their eight children and later Cruz's aunt (plate 11). The trio, encased by the frame of a house at the DiGiorgio Farms migrant camp, face into the sun, their long shadows stretching behind them on the grass of the yard; in the foreground, the photographer's silhouette hugs the image's bottom left edge. The work, titled *Nana, Grandpa, y Chita*, ripples across the corrugated metal of the warehouse where her Nana used to pack fruit. This was the third image of several that went up that night (when they all went up).

In her placement of these images, Cruz reinserts family image-memories into the space of labor as a gesture of desire, a ritual. It was important to put the photographs up in the spaces where her elders worked: her grandfather in the fields, and her Nana in the packing warehouses of Arvin. The images, each roughly three by four feet, are meant to be seen at a distance. From far away, the paint chipping off above looks like redactions on a page. These surfaces evoke tactile memories: by retaining the white margin bearing the date stamp "Jun 57," the image brings together seemingly contradictory scales of intimacy and of handling; the processing and printing of analog film, juxtaposed to the eroding, rippling surface of the metal siding. Timing matters in the site-specific installation itself: it was meaningful to post the photographs as the sun was coming up (Cruz began at 4 a.m.), so that the first light touched them and they would be in place when the present workers—their intended and ideal audience—arrived at the fields and factories.[35]

Cruz's series and its placement resonate within the longer history of artists' interventions in public space discussed in this book. And here, too, Cruz mobilizes her punitive literacy. For example, she attends to the incremental distinctions between misdemeanor and felony that have been assigned to mark-making within Southern California. Cruz reflects on how tagging with spray paint went from a misdemeanor to a felony in California—with penalties of up to a year in jail and a fine of one to five thousand dollars—part of the state's effort to restrict the expression of gangs and graffiti writers.[36] It is worth noting that Asco's *Spray Paint LACMA*, staged in 1972 in LA, wasn't yet the felony it would be today. Cruz knows this history; she has researched consequences in advance, and wheat-pastes because it carries a lower likelihood of arrest and material loss.

The change from misdemeanor to felony for graffiti wasn't limited to California but a nationwide trend implemented state by state between the late 1980s and early 1990s. Lavie Raven, an artist active in Chicago in the 1980s, remembers the impact of this change: "I know people that got arrested twenty times [in the 1980s] and were still out doing graffiti. In 1993, the State of Illinois turned graffiti into a felony," heightening the consequences for this form of expression.[37] Graffiti made after 1993 in Chicago, then, one could reflect, entails a different kind of risk work than prior graffiti—especially as states such as New York and California also began adopting "three-strikes" laws in the early 1990s, making twenty-five years to life the mandatory sentence upon conviction of a third felony. At this time, twenty-eight states have adopted "three-strikes" laws.

In Cruz's hands, punitive literacy becomes an ethical tool. She tells friends who assist in wheat-pasting what the punitive risks are before they join, and what the consequences could mean long-term. In Arvin, a friend joins Cruz to help get the work up and document it (plate 12). Cruz's awareness of possible arrest educates and extends the punitive literacies of her collaborators; it also relies upon her collaborators' own literacies and openness to being exposed to a run-in with police. It is an aesthetic practice mired in social relations and cross-generational tactics, but also one that showcases how artists today benefit from knowledge of performance-based conceptual art's legacies of risk work *and* their intersection with evolving punitive literacy. Cruz wants to expand the series of photographic interventions in East LA—in and around Ditman Avenue where her grandparents bought their home in 1969—but hasn't yet, the material consequences much higher there than in Arvin.

In the aftermath of Minneapolis police officer Derek Chauvin's murder of George Floyd in May 2020, and the proliferation of demonstrations that followed, amplifying the messages of Black Lives Matter, public spaces and expressions of protest nationwide have come under heightened punitive scrutiny. In 2021, for example, thirty-four state legislatures increased the repercussions for behavior perceived by the police as "riotous."[38] The most aggressive of the resulting bills was Florida's Combating Public Disorder Act, championed and signed into law by Republican governor Ron DeSantis, which created new and increased punishments for protesters (later blocked by a judge).[39] Section 2 of the law, for example, addressed road obstruction, while another section established new felonies, punishable up to ten years in prison, for destroying or demolishing a memorial, plaque, flag, or object that commemorates "historical people or events," here criminalizing the removal or defacement of monuments to the Confederacy.[40]

These bills, arts writer Joy Harris observes, "threaten the work of social practice artists" whose use of "spontaneity and incalculability provide the ground for new ways of acting in concert."[41] She recognizes a need for policing, since "businesses, homeowners, bystanders, and passersby should be protected from harassment, violence, and destruction of property," and believes "optimistically" that heightened risk assessment "could incentivize local officials to work more closely with artists." "Still," Harris observes, "it seems that the law's increased penalties in the context of social practice art pose problems because of their impact *on* spontaneity, participation, and enforcement."[42]

As *Risk Work* has sought to demonstrate, however, an artist's spontaneity in public space is not made possible by more restrained policing, but is itself a form that actively negotiates punitive relations and the ways they are collectively *managed*, indeed how punitiveness organizes sociality, based on one's degree of exposure to state violence. To continue to situate spontaneity in art termed "social practice," or "guerrilla" for that matter, as inherently progressive, or readily available under "kinder" partnerships with the police, obscures the ways that mobility itself is produced by and through the asymmetrical threat of carceral geographies and punitive care. This kind of liberal desire for better policing potentially plays into what scholars have named "carceral humanism." With this approach, explains carceral abolitionist and scholar of queer and trans studies Ren-yo Hwang, the best hope is the reform and further re-entrenchment of police power since it presupposes the inevitability of the police structure.[43] If liberal critiques of aggressive policing track the implications for art history but leave the long, violent history of criminalizing Black and brown mobility and the underpolicing of whiteness unnamed, such interpretations of artists' tactics produce a carceral formalism that normalizes punitive encounter.

Finally, as laws, public policy, and policing change and require altered risk perception, a critical vocabulary attuned to how the carceral apparatus colonizes *feeling* becomes expedient. The artist collective Sonic Insurgency Research Group (SIRG) works in this vein. The group is comprised of three artists, Josh Rios, Anthony Romero, and Matt Joynt, based in Chicago and Boston. SIRG thinks about the relationship of sonics and policing through "research-based performance and exhibition practice" that, as its members write, "examines normalized associations between criminality and sound, silencing as a form of social control and voicing as a form of social resistance."[44] For example, in a digital zine exploring spatialized power, Joynt and Rios theorized the police siren in the following terms: "It is a political sound within a hermeneutics of surveillance. It is not the police per say. But it is not a sign of their absence either. It is an odd index of an imminent arrival. . . . It sonically occupies social space via speculation. . . . It both produces and marks the impending."[45]

In their conceptualization of the siren as a sensorial extension of state power, the artists give voice to an important reality: that the work of punitive literacy is embodied and conditioned through physical, affective, and psychological exposure—and increasingly so. The technology of sirens has continued to evolve. In the art collective's research, they've found that in 2007, Federal Signal Corporation released "the Rumbler," a suboctave frequency siren—using subwoofers designed for dance floors in the 1960s—that can be felt in the body and heard through walls.[46] In their text, Joynt and Rios assert, "Afterall, the siren does not signify safety, but a precarious event, a coming encounter, in which black and brown people must successfully predict and manage the racial imagination of the police." They conclude that the siren not only "demobilizes by inviting the signification of hard power (militarized violence) among populations most affected by hyper-policing," but that this "event is a non-event. It polices by mere suggestion."[47] Artists engaged with tactics that materialize the fraught relations between state power, aesthetics, and knowledge production are theorists of the non-event. At its core, then, the history of art doesn't merely tell a story about modes of intervention; it creates and maintains relations of power and vulnerability by mere suggestion, in its siren call, a coming encounter.

Acknowledgments

I am humbled by the number of people I have to thank, who helped make this book a reality and whose presence in my life indelibly shaped its formulation. I want first to acknowledge and honor the artists whose risk-taking makes this story possible. I hold a special place of gratitude for Harry Gamboa Jr., Patssi Valdez, Dana Chandler, Jean Toche, Jon Hendricks, Howardena Pindell, PESTS, Gronk, Willie Herrón, Inverna Lockpez, Tehching Hsieh, the Guerrilla Girls, Adrian Piper, Jim Guttmann, Amina Cruz, Pope.L, Chris Burden, Fred Lonidier, Cindy Trinh, and Rafael Shimunov. Thank you for sharing your reflections, images, and insights. Additionally, I'm grateful to Michael Ratner, the lawyer who represented Toche and cofounded the Center for Constitutional Rights in New York City.

This book has benefited from a great deal of mentoring and support over the years. At the top of this list are the professors who were a critical part of my doctoral training at Northwestern University. To my original readers—Huey Copeland, Hannah Feldman, Krista Thompson, and Ramón Rivera-Servera—thank you for giving your time and insight to this project early on. Your own work has deeply enriched my understanding of art, theory, and the stakes of writing about artistic interventions and social justice. I am especially indebted to Huey, my stellar doctoral advisor: I am deeply grateful for your incisive questions, advocacy, infectious energy, and mentoring, which has sustained me at every stage of this process. Your brilliance and generosity have taught me more than I can ever say. I am also thankful for the support and guidance of Hollis Clayson, Jesús Escobar, Rob Linrothe, Kate Masur, Ivy Wilson, Dilip Gaonkar, and Soyini Madison, who were important influences during my doctoral studies. I also wish to thank my esteemed master's degree mentors at George Washington University—Alexander Dumbadze, Bibiana Obler, Lilian Robinson, and

Ami Lynch—and fantastic undergraduate mentors at Washington University in St. Louis: Joseph Lowenstein, Elizabeth Childs, John Klein, and Angela Miller. The imaginativeness and intentionality of each of these exceptional teachers has been invaluable.

Across my scholarly studies at Wash U, GW, and Northwestern, I've had the great fortune of growing intellectually alongside a truly luminous group of peers who have remained wonderful friends and collaborators. My deepest thanks to Jordan Amirkhani, Lindsay Amini, Kemi Adeyemi, Dan Paz, Colleen Daniher, Brynn Hatton, Emma Chubb, Beatrice Choi, Aileen Robinson, Anndrea Mathers, Dwayne Mann, Brian Jordan Jefferson, Liza Oliver, Nick Miller, Antawan Byrd, David Molina, Linde Murugan, Grace Deveney, Josh Honn, Perry Altman, Matthew Seymour, Michelle Smirnova, Tien Tran, Elliot Heilman, and Kathleen Tahk. My special thanks to AB Brown, Jasmine Jamillah Mahmoud, Delia Solomons, Tara Rodman, Erin Reitz, and Jordana Cox; your thoughtful intellectual engagement with various parts of this text, and the emotional support you each provided buoyed me during the most critical moments. And to Emilie Boone, my weekly accountability partner and dear friend, I am eternally grateful for the ways you've helped me prioritize care and celebrate milestones, large and small. Finally, in memory of Rhonda Saad, I offer thanks and admiration.

My colleagues at Indiana University and in the wider Bloomington community have been equally instrumental to this book and my trajectory as a scholar and a teacher. My deep gratitude goes to Dina Okamoto, Michelle Moyd, Freda Fair, Cara Caddoo, Alberto Varon, Maria Abegunde Hamilton, Ellen Wu, Liza Black, Micol Seigel, Walton Muyumba, Rasul Mowatt, Rebecca Fasman, Lauren Richman, Kristin Chuang, Judy Rodriguez, Meredith Lee, Shane Vogel, James Nakagawa, Malcolm Mobutu Smith, Vivek Vellanki, Betsy Stirratt, Carmen Henne-Ochoa, Artemis Brod, Federica Carugati, Stephanie DeBoer, Carmel Curtis, Jessica Eaglin, Andres Guzman, Ishan Ashutosh, Sonia Song-Ha Lee, Sarah Martin, Phoebe Wolfskill, Joanna Woronkowicz, Stephen Deusner, Andrew Grodner, Chris Pelton, Mary Craig, Markus Vodosek, Ryan Powell, and Tim Bell. I'm humbled by your kindness, meals, collaborations, and comradery. A special note of appreciation goes to Elizabeth Claffey—our walks, brainstorming sessions, and laugh breaks have nurtured my heart and research. Thank you for being a constant source of tender love and fierce support.

In the art history department, I am grateful for the support of Diane Reilly, Bret Rothstien, Sarah Bassett, Bárbaro Martinez-Ruiz, Maria Domene-Danés, Michelle Facos, Cordula Grewe, Giles Knox, Jeffrey Saletnik, Andre Molotiu, and Julie Van Voorhis, and am especially thankful for the invaluable insights into the book-writing process shared by Margaret Graves and Melody Barnett Deusner. To the members of IU's writing groups, run under the steadfast leadership of Laura Plummer, thank you for making my experience of completing a book one of community. And for my students, from whom I have learned so much and gained a wealth of energy and inspiration, special thanks go to Milly Cai, Claire L'Heureux, Destini Ross, Rachel Kabukala, Jesse Lanay Moore, Hoda Nedaeifar, Anne Mahady, Joey Quiñones, Aaron Ellis, Chaeri Lee, MaryClare Pappas, Yalie Kamara, Mehru Athar, Justin Carney, Andrew Wang, Colbie Symone Cooke, Liliana Guzman, Kaela Laughlin, and Adam Pease.

I have also been extremely lucky to develop my research investments within the creative intellectual spaces of museums, exhibition projects, and artist residencies. I'm grateful to Tom Colley, Abina Manning, and Ruth Hodgins of the Video Data Bank; to Lynn Russell, Diane Arkin, David Gariff, Arlette Raspberry, Wilford Scott, Eric Denker, and Liz Diament at the National Gallery of Art; and to Naomi Beckwith, Michael Darling, and Joey Orr at the Museum of Contemporary Art Chicago. I am especially appreciative of Marjorie Susman and her named curatorial fellowship at the MCA, which allowed me to curate the exhibition *The Making of a Fugitive* (2016), where I developed research questions that became central to this book. Through my curatorial endeavors, I have also had the privilege of coming to learn from visionary artists and curators—Hương Ngô, Allison Glenn, zakkiyyah najeebah dumas o'neal, Teresa E. Silva, Nyugen Smith, and Josh T. Franco, among others. To my first artist-curator family in DC—my fellow museum security guards at the Phillips Collection and Ding Ren, an early artist-collaborator—I'm also grateful.

During the revision and production process of this book I have received incredible editorial and image research assistance. This book has benefited immensely from the astute consideration of David Lobenstine, as well as my marvelous research assistant, Destini Ross. Thank you, both, for bringing care, humor, and an unparalleled attention to detail while working with me on the final phase of this project. At the University of Chicago Press, I was extremely lucky to work under the expert eye of senior editor Susan Bielstein, her editorial assistant Dylan Montanari, and the editorial expertise of Joel Score. I also gained crucial image permissions expertise from IU's head copyright consultant, Nazareth Pantaloni III, and benefited from the excellent administrative support offered by the art history department's Doug Case, Alexandra Burlingame, Amelia Berry, and Calvin Caskey.

Funding for the research and writing of this book was generously provided by a number of sources, including the Henry Luce Foundation and American

Council of Learned Societies; Northwestern's Buffett Center for International Studies and Graduate Research Grant; the Smithsonian American Art Museum; and the Georgia O'Keeffe Museum Center for American Modernism. Publication was also made possible in part by a generous gift from Elizabeth Warnock to the Department of Art History at Northwestern University, and by the IU Presidential Arts and Humanities and College Arts and Humanities Institute.

Over the years, I have had the pleasure of workshopping portions of this book project with supportive audiences at the American Studies Association, the College Arts Association, the Centre for American Art at the Courtauld Gallery, the Georgia O'Keeffe Museum, the School for Visual of Arts, the National Women's Studies Association, and the Smithsonian American Art Museum. I am grateful to my hosts, colleagues, and audiences for their engagement and feedback in each of these venues. Among those who organized or participated in these conference panels, programs, archive visits, and fellowships, I want to extend special thanks to Eumie Imm Stroukoff, Chon Noriega, Tom Day, Mark Tribe, Amelia Goerlitz, Melissa Ho, Frazer Ward, Ananda Cohen-Caponte, Lee Ann Custer, Christine Garnier, Dina Murokh, Ana Cristina Perry, Caroline Riley, and Olivia Young. I also received invaluable guidance regarding legal discourse from Jarryd Paige, Nicole Arrow, and Jordan Yearsley.

To my friends and family, thank for you filling my world with love, home-cooked meals, and care during the research, writing, and revision of this book. For those who housed me during my research trips (multiple times!), including Lauren Gardner, Jill Calhoun, Jess Strange, Eric Cabunoc, Andrew Kaplan, Dan Moody, Kate Roloson, Nicole Arrow, Katherine Crowley, and the loving "River Rat" Chicago community, thank you so much for opening your homes. To Liza Hale, Aliza Skolnik, and Katie Klein, my Cleveland family in Chicago, I am deeply thankful for our many meals, walks, and talks. For Katie, I am especially appreciative: you have witnessed many of the behind-the-scenes hours of this work and have been such an important source of support and happiness. To Laura Jo Hess, thank you for reminding me, always, that poetry exists.

Even though I have been away from Cleveland for many years, my family there has remained a constant source of encouragement. I'm lucky to be a part of such a big, loving circle of aunts, uncles, and cousins. Jackie and Robert, you are siblings and much more. Thank for you being supportive and loving friends. As we continue our lives, I am more and more grateful for our bond, as well as your wonderful partners Rob and Missy, and kids, Maddie, Emily, AJ, and Will. To my Kentucky family, Connie and Sammy Osborne, I have been touched by your enthusiasm, good humor, and support. Thank you for welcoming me (and this time-consuming project!) into your lives. To my partner in all things, Sammy Joe, your love and companionship can be best described as a sanctuary; you have helped foster a space of encouragement, creativity, and joy that has made writing a book possible. Thank you for being by my side for the highs and lows, and for taking out my extra commas. Arlo, sweet one, please know that your close company during the book's final phase gave the words a new meaning. To my parents, Brian and Pamela Gleisser, your unwavering support and excitement has been absolutely essential to the initiation and completion of this project. Thank you for being curious about art, people, and the world we live in, and for encouraging and nurturing my love of writing. I dedicate this book to you, and in memory of my grandparents, Ted and Idarose Luntz and Helga and Marcus Gleisser, whose incredible stories taught me from a young age that words, and their layered meanings, offer portals into the past and the future.

Notes

Introduction

1. Jean Toche, letter to Lil Picard, October 30, 1969, Lil Picard Papers, 1955–1972, Archives of American Art, Smithsonian Institution.
2. Jon Hendricks, interview by William Twersky, *WT_History Blog*, February 17, 2015, https://wthistory.wordpress.com/2015/04/17/transcript-of-my-interview-with-jon-hendricks/amp/.
3. Walter Laqueur, "The Origins of Guerrilla Doctrine," *Journal of Contemporary History* 10, no. 3 (1975): 341.
4. Roxanne Dunbar-Ortiz, *An Indigenous Peoples' History of the United States* (Boston: Beacon, 2014); Elizabeth Hinton, *America on Fire: The Untold Story of Police Violence and Black Rebellion since the 1960s* (New York: W. W. Norton, 2021).
5. Fidel Castro, *Fidel Castro's Tribute to Che Guevara* (New York: Merit, 1967), 1–14; Arif Dirlik, "The Third World," in *1968: The World Transformed* (Cambridge: Cambridge University Press, 1998), 301.
6. Kimberly Mair, *Guerrilla Aesthetics: Art, Memory, and the West German Urban Guerrilla* (Montreal: McGill-Queen's University Press, 2016); Odd Arne Westad, *The Global Cold War: Third World Interventions and the Making of Our Times* (Cambridge: Cambridge University Press, 2007), 193 ("guerrilla generation").
7. Robert Taber, *The War of the Flea: A Study of Guerrilla Warfare Theory and Practice* (New York: Lyle Stuart, 1965), 11.
8. Lil Picard, "Art," *East Village Other*, November 1969, 1. Jean Brown Papers, box 23, folder 9, Special Collections, Getty Research Institute, Los Angeles.
9. See, for example, Tom McDonough, ed., *Guy Debord and the Situationists International: Texts and Documents* (Cambridge, MA: MIT Press, 2002); Richard Kempton, *Provo: Amsterdam's Anarchist Revolt* (New York: Autonomedia, 2007); Luis Camnitzer, "The Tupamaros," in *Conceptualism in Latin American Art: Didactics of Liberation* (Austin: University of Texas Press, 2007), 45–47; Rika Hiro, "Between Absence and Presence: Exploring Video Earth's *What Is Photography?*," *Invisible Culture: An*

Electronic Journal for Visual Culture, no. 15 (2010), 79–101; Jeremy Varon, *Bringing the War Home: The Weather Underground, the Red Army Faction, and Revolutionary Violence in the Sixties and Seventies* (Berkeley: University of California Press, 2004); Mair, *Guerrilla Aesthetics*, 2016.

10. Hendricks and Twersky, *WT_History Blog*, 2015.
11. Jean Toche, conversation with author, June 2014.
12. Jon Hendricks, phone conversation with author, December 2, 2021.
13. Katherine McKittrick, *Demonic Grounds: Black Women and the Cartographies of Struggle* (Minneapolis: University of Minnesota Press, 2006); Simon Strick, *American Dorologies: Pain, Sentimentalism, Biopolitics* (New York: SUNY Press, 2014); José Esteban Muñoz, *Disidentifications: Queers of Color and the Performance of Politics* (Minneapolis: University of Minnesota Press, 1999); Alexander Weheliye, *Habeas Viscus: Racializing Assemblages, Biopolitics, and Black Feminist Theories of the Human* (Durham, NC: Duke University Press, 2014).
14. Sara Ahmed, *The Cultural Politics of Emotion* (New York: Routledge, 2004), 70–71.
15. Frank B. Wilderson III writes that race is a method of sustaining a "framework of recognition" that enacts colonialist humanist ideals of progress and civility. See Wilderson, *Red, White, and Black: Cinema and the Structure of U.S. Antagonism* (Durham, NC: Duke University Press, 2010), 9.
16. Chandan Reddy, *Freedom with Violence: Race, Sexuality, and the US State* (Durham, NC: Duke University Press, 2011); David Theo Goldberg, *The Racial State* (Oxford: Blackwell Publishers Ltd., 2002); Michael Omi and Howard Winant, *Racial Formation in the United States: From the 1960s to the 1980s* (New York: Routledge & Kegan Paul, 1986).
17. Ruth Wilson Gilmore, *Golden Gulag: Prisons, Surplus, Crisis, and Opposition in Globalizing California* (Berkeley: University of California Press, 2007), 28.
18. Various writers have used "guerrilla" to describe Asco's urban interventions, including C. Ondine Chavoya in his essay "Internal Exiles: The Interventionist Public and Performance Art of Asco," in *Space, Site, Intervention: Situating Installation Art*, ed. Erika Suderberg (Minneapolis: University of Minnesota Press, 2000), 189–208. Diarmuid Costello refers to Piper's *Catalysis* works as "early guerrilla performances" in the essay "Xenophobia, Stereotypes, and Empirical Acculturation: Neo-Kantianism in Adrian Piper's Performance-based Conceptual Art," in *Adrian Piper: A Reader* (New York: Museum of Modern Art, 2018), 172. Various exhibition catalogues and popular media stories refer to Pope.L as a "guerrilla" artist; see, for example, Oliver Basciano, "'I'm Not Jeff Koons!'—The Endurance Crawls, Weird Texts, and Guerrilla Brilliance of Pope.L," *Guardian*, July 18, 2021, https://www.theguardian.com/artanddesign/2021/jul/18/pope-l-jeff-koons-endurance-crawls-texts-guerrilla-brilliance-of-popel.
19. Hendricks and Twersky, *WT_History Blog*, 2015.
20. Kimberlé Crenshaw, "Demarginalizing the Intersection of Race and Sex: A Black

Feminist Critique of Antidiscrimination Doctrine, Feminist Theory and Antiracist Politics," *University of Chicago Legal Forum*, no. 1, article 8 (1989), 139–67; Sara Ahmed, "Declarations of Whiteness: The Non-Performativity of Anti-Racism," *Borderlands* (e-journal) 3, no. 2 (2004); Katherine McKittrick, *Dear Science and Other Stories* (Durham, NC: Duke University Press, 2021); bell hooks, *Teaching to Transgress: Education and the Practice of Freedom* (New York: Routledge, 1994), 71 ("white supremacist capitalist patriarchy"); Cathy Cohen, "Deviance as Resistance: A New Research Agenda for the Study of Black Politics," *Du Bois Review* 1, no. 1 (2004): 27–45.

21. Peggy Albers et al., "When Pictures Aren't Pretty: Deconstructing Punitive Literacy Practices," *Journal of Early Childhood Literacy* 14, no. 3 (September 2014): 291–318.
22. Michel Foucault, *Discipline and Punish: The Birth of the Prison*, trans. Alan Sheridan (New York: Vintage, 1977), 298.
23. Henrique Carvalho, Anastasia Chamberlen, and Rachel Lewis, "Punitiveness beyond Criminal Justice: Punishable and Punitive Subjects in an Era of Prevention, Anti-Migration, and Austerity," *British Journal of Criminology* 60, no. 2 (March 2020): 265–84, https://doi.org/10.1093/bjc/azz061.
24. Kathy O'Dell, *Contract with the Skin: Masochism, Performance Art, and the 1970s* (Minneapolis: University of Minnesota Press, 1998).
25. Since 2012, Piper prefers to be referred to as the "artist formerly known as African-American." Adrian Piper, "NEWS: September 2012," http://www.adrianpiper.com/news_sep_2012.shtml.
26. Micol Seigel draws from transnational perspectives and argues against the perceived neutrality of the comparative method. See Seigel, "Beyond Compare: Comparative Method after the Transnational Turn," *Radical History Review*, no. 91 (Winter 2005), 62–90.
27. See Claudia Calirman, *Brazilian Art under Dictatorship: Antonio Manuel, Artur Barrio, and Cildo Meireles* (Durham, NC: Duke University Press, 2012); Nelly Richards, "Margins and Institutions: Performances of the Chilean Avanzada," in *Corpus Delecti: Performance Art of the Americas*, ed. Coco Fusco (New York: Routledge, 2000), 214; Diana Taylor, *Disappearing Acts: Spectacles of Gender and Nationalism in Argentina's "Dirty War"* (Durham, NC: Duke University Press, 1997); Antawan Byrd, "Medu's Operative and Aesthetic Montage," in *The People Shall Govern! Medu Art Ensemble and the Anti-Apartheid Poster, 1979–1985* (New Haven, CT: Yale University Press, 2020), 26–33; Camnitzer, "Tupamaros," 45–47.
28. On the anticipation of threats of state violence and the police, see Seigel, *Violence Work*; Mark Neocleous, *The Fabrication of Social Order: A Critical Theory of Police Power* (Sterling, VA: Pluto Press, 2000).
29. See Randy Martin, *An Empire of Indifference: American War and the Financial Logic of Risk Management* (Durham, NC: Duke University Press, 2007); Richard Ericson and Kevin Haggerty, *Policing the Risk Society* (Toronto: University of Toronto Press, 1997); Eugene Rosa et al., *The Risk Society Revisited: Social Theory and Governance*

(Philadelphia: Temple University Press, 2014); Tom Baker and Jonathan Simon, *Embracing Risk: The Changing Culture of Insurance and Responsibility* (Chicago: University of Chicago Press, 2002); Anthony Giddens, "Risk and Responsibility," *Modern Law Review* 62, no. 1 (January 1999): 1–10.

30. Leigh Raiford, *Imprisoned in a Luminous Glare: Photography and the African American Freedom* (Chapel Hill: University of North Carolina Press, 2011), 150–52.

31. Christoph Kalter, "A Shared Space of Imagination, Communication, and Action: Perspectives on the History of the 'Third World,'" in *The Third World in the Global 1960s*, ed. Samantha Christiansen and Zachary A. Scarlett (New York: Berghahn Books, 2013), 24.

32. Umberto Eco, "Towards a Semiological Guerrilla Warfare," in *Faith in Fakes: Essays*, trans. William Weaver (London: Secker and Warburg, 1986), 143.

33. Germano Celant, "Notes on a Guerrilla War," *Flash Art*, no. 5 (1967).

34. McDonough, *Guy Debord*, 181–85.

35. Augusto Boal, *Theatre of the Oppressed*, trans. Charles A. McBride and Maria-Odilia Leal McBride (New York: Urizen Books, 1979); John Weisman, *Guerrilla Theater: Scenarios for Revolution* (Garden City, NY: Anchor Press, 1973); Martin Bradford, *The Theater Is in the Street: Politics and Performance in Sixties America* (Amherst: University of Massachusetts Press, 2004).

36. Julia Ault, *Alternative Art New York, 1965–1985* (New York: Social Text Collective, 2002), 6; Ben Sisario, "He's Got It Bad, or 'Baad,' for His Art," *New York Times*, January 20, 2010, http://www.nytimes.com/2010/01/24/theater/24vanpeebles.html.

37. Michael Shamberg, *Guerrilla Television* (New York: Holt, Rinehart and Winston, 1971), n.p.; Paul Ryan, "Cybernetic Guerrilla Warfare," *Radical Software*, no. 3 (Spring 1971), 1–2.

38. Warren Hinckle II, "Editorial Preface," *Scanlan's Monthly* 1, no. 8, "Suppressed Issue, Guerrilla War in the USA" (January 1971): 5.

39. Varon, *Bringing the War Home*, 9.

40. Rychetta Watkins, *Black Power, Yellow Power, and the Making of Revolutionary Identities* (Jackson: University Press of Mississippi, 2012), 55. Similarly, curator Jens Kastner's articulation of a 1960s "guerrilla-form" sees it as a template for imagination that emerged from the growing interrelation of social protest and artistic production in 1968. See Kastner, "Aspects of the Guerrilla Form: The Visual Arts and Social Movements around the Year 1968" in *68, Revolution I Love You: 1968 in Art, Politics and Philosophy* (Manchester: MIRIAD, 2008), 84–85. In addition, Watkin's research contributes to histories of radical activism that have corrected the initial narrative of the 1960s and 1970s, which tended to erase activists of color and centered white leftists. See Cynthia Young, *Soul Power: Culture, Radicalism, and the Making of a U.S. Third World Left* (Durham, NC: Duke University Press, 2006); Laura Pulido, *Black, Brown, Yellow and Left: Radical Activism in Los Angeles* (Berkeley: University of California Press, 2006).

41. Kodwo Eshun and Ros Gray, "The Militant Image: A Cine-Geography," *Third Text* 25, no. 1 (2011): 1–12.

42. The film was also screened at the Pentagon in 2003, as the Bush administration strategized for conflict in Iraq. Michael T. Kaufman, "The World: Film Studies; What Does the Pentagon See in 'Battle of Algiers'?" *New York Times*, September 7, 2003, 3.

43. "Mao and Che were worlds apart," historian Arif Dirlik observes, and yet what unites them "were First World images of the Third World and Third World notions that what worked against imperialism in one place would work equally well in another." Dirlik, "The Third World," in *1968: The World Transformed* (Cambridge: Cambridge University Press, 1998), 301.

44. Michel de Certeau, *The Practice of Everyday Life*, trans. Steven Rendall (Berkeley: University of California Press, 1984), 30–37.

45. María Lugones, "Tactical Strategies of the Streetwalker," in *Pilgrimages = Peregrinajes: Theorizing Coalition against Multiple Oppressions* (Lanham, MD: Rowman & Littlefield, 2003), 225.

46. Michael McClintock, *Instruments of Statecraft: U.S. Guerrilla Warfare, Counter-Insurgency, and Counter-Terrorism, 1940–1990* (New York: Pantheon, 1992), 48; 52; 136–74; Stuart Shrader, *Badges without Borders: How Global Counterinsurgency Transformed American Policing* (Oakland: University of California Press, 2019), 168–91.

47. For explications of the "punitive turn," see Deborah E. McDowell, Claudrena N. Harold, and Juan Battle, eds., *The Punitive Turn: New Approaches to Race and Incarceration* (Charlottesville: University of Virginia Press, 2013); Angela Davis, *Are Prisons Obsolete?* (New York: Seven Stories, 2003); Gilmore, *Golden Gulag*; David Garland, *Culture of Control: Crime and Social Order in Contemporary Society* (Chicago: University of Chicago Press, 2001); Naomi Murakawa, *The First Civil Right: How Liberals Built Prison America* (Oxford: Oxford University Press, 2014); Loic Wacquant, *Punishing the Poor: The Neoliberal Government of Social Insecurity* (Durham, NC: Duke University Press, 2009). For a canonical text that paved the way for thinking about crime as a story that becomes social phenomena, see Stuart Hall et al., *Policing the Crisis: Mugging, the State, and Law and Order* (London: Macmillan, 1978).

48. Marc Mauer, "The Endurance of Racial Disparity in the Criminal Justice System," in *Policing the Black Man: Arrest, Prosecution, and Imprisonment*, ed. Angela J. Davis (New York: Vintage, 2017), 34.

49. For a history of LEAA, see Murakawa, *First Civil Right*; Micol Seigel, *Violence Work: State Power and the Limits of Police* (Durham, NC: Duke University Press, 2018). On its funding, see Alex Vitale, *The End of Policing* (London: Verso, 2018), 50.

50. Camp, *Incarcerating the Crisis*, 3.

51. McDowell et al., *Punitive Turn*, 2–3.

52. Khalil Gibran Muhammad, "The Foundational Lawlessness of the Law Itself: Racial

Criminalization and the Punitive Roots of Punishment in America," *Daedalus* 151, no. 1, "Reimagining Justice: The Challenges of Violence and Punitive Excess" (Winter 2022): 107.

53. Muhammad, "Foundational Lawlessness," 107–20. He provides an excellent overview of the various punitive turns, synthesizing the research of Simon Balto, Donna Murch, Micol Seigel, Sarah Haley, Heather Ann Thompson, Naomi Murakawa, Dan Berger, Beth Richie, and Michelle Alexander, among others.
54. Muhammad, "Foundational Lawlessness," 116; Seigel, *Violence Work*, 3.
55. Urban Institute Report, "Criminal Justice Expenditures: Police, Corrections, and Courts," accessed October 23, 2022, https://www.urban.org/policy-centers/cross-center-initiatives/state-and-local-finance-initiative/state-and-local-backgrounders/criminal-justice-police-corrections-courts-expenditures#Question1Police.
56. Seigel, *Violence Work*, 3.
57. Jackie Wang, *Carceral Capitalism* (South Pasadena, CA: Semiotext(e), 2018); Rasul Mowatt, *The Geographies of Threat and the Production of Violence: The State and the City between Us* (New York: Routledge, 2021); Elizabeth Alexander, *The New Jim Crow: Mass Incarceration in the Age of Colorblindness* (New York: New Press, 2010).
58. See Robin D. G. Kelley's landmark text *Freedom Dreams: The Black Radical Imagination* (Boston: Beacon, 2002); Stefano Harney and Fred Moten, *The Undercommons: Fugitive Planning and Black Study* (Wivenhoe, England: Minor Compositions, 2013); McKittrick, *Dear Science*; Kevin Everod Quashie, *Black Aliveness; or, A Poetics of Being* (Durham, NC: Duke University Press, 2021); Fred Moten, *In the Break: The Aesthetics of the Black Radical Tradition* (Minneapolis: University of Minnesota Press, 2003); Uri McMillan, *Embodied Avatars: Genealogies of Black Feminist Art and Performance* (New York: New York University Press, 2015).
59. Stuart Schrader, *Badges without Borders: How Global Counterinsurgency Transformed American Policing* (Oakland: University of California Press, 2019), 176, citing FBI, "Racial Disturbances 1967," August 1967, Reports and Memos Related to Racial Riots 1967, box 5, PP Sherwin Markman, LBJL, 13a.
60. Max Felker-Kantor, *Policing Los Angeles: Race, Resistance, and the Rise of the LAPD* (Chapel Hill: University of North Carolina Press, 2018), 43, citing "Proceedings of the National Advisory Commission on Civil Disorders," November 2, 1967, 311, Urban Policy Research Institute Records, folder 15, box 38, Southern California Library, Los Angeles.
61. Allen Van Newkirk, "Detroit-Revolution in the Revolution," *Los Angeles Free Press*, August 4–10, 1967, 1, 14.
62. Van Newkirk, "Detroit-Revolution," 14–16.
63. Throughout this book, "brown" appears with the lowercase spelling, in keeping with current publications focusing on "brownness" in which the word is not capi-

talized. See, for example, José Esteban Muñoz, *The Sense of Brown* (Durham, NC: Duke University Press, 2020).

64. Charles W. McKinney Jr., "Riot," in *Keywords for African American Studies* (New York: New York University Press, 2018), 181.
65. Felker-Kantor, *Policing Los Angeles*, 49, citing Edward M. Davis, "America at the Crossroads," October 3, 1967, Police Department Records/82, notebook 1-A Speeches/Articles, box 2275, Los Angeles City Archives, Los Angeles.
66. Peter Paret and John Shy, *Guerrillas in the 1960s*, Princeton Studies in World Politics (Newark, NJ: Center for International Studies, 1962), 4.
67. Felker-Kantor, *Policing Los Angeles*, 43.
68. Schrader, *Badges without Borders*, 197.
69. Felker-Kantor, *Policing Los Angeles*, 53.
70. Edwin Willis, "Guerrilla Warfare Advocates in the United States," Report by Committee on Un-American Activities, House of Representatives, 90th Congress, 2nd Session, May 6, 1968, 21. For a history of Robert Williams and his influence on the formation of the Revolutionary Action Movement, see Kelley, *Freedom Dreams*, 69–93.
71. Ian Haney López, *Racism on Trial: The Chicano Fight for Justice* (Cambridge, MA: Belknap Press/Harvard University Press, 2003), 149.
72. Jordan T. Camp, *Incarcerating the Crisis: Freedom Struggles and the Rise of the Neoliberal State* (Oakland: University of California Press, 2016), 4.
73. Brian Jefferson, *Digitize and Punish: Racial Criminalization in the Digital Age* (Minneapolis: University of Minnesota Press, 2020), 134.
74. See Kara Keeling, *The Witch's Flight: The Cinematic, the Black Femme, and the Image of Common Sense* (Durham, NC: Duke University Press, 2007); Nikhil Pal Singh, "The Black Panthers and the Undeveloped Country of the Left," in *The Black Panther Party (Reconsidered)*, ed. Charles E Jones (Baltimore: Black Classic Press, 1998), 57–105; Raiford, *Imprisoned in a Luminous Glare*, 2011.
75. Keeling, *Witch's Flight*, 74.
76. Erica Edwards, *The Other Side of Terror: Black Women and the Culture of Empire* (New York: New York University Press, 2021), 49.
77. Simone Browne, *Dark Matter: On the Surveillance of Blackness* (Durham, NC: Duke University Press, 2015), 21.
78. Guerrilla Art Action Group, "Memo for the Staff and the Trustees of M.O.M.A.: Reference: The Three Demands of the Guerrilla Art Action Group of October 30, 1969," Jean Brown Papers, box 23, folder 9, GAAG, Getty Research Institute, Los Angeles.
79. Varon, *Bringing the War Home*, 90–91.
80. Varon, *Bringing the War Home*, 54.
81. Harry Gamboa Jr., phone conversation with author, March 3, 2018.

82. Inspiration for this emphasis on "doing" comes from Sylvia Wynter's discussion of a "deciphering turn." See Wynter, "Rethinking 'Aesthetics': Notes towards a Deciphering Practice," in *Ex-iles: Essays on Caribbean Cinema*, ed. Mbye Cham (Trenton, NJ: Africa World Press, 1992), 266–68.
83. Paul Schimmel, *Out of Actions: Between Performance and the Object, 1949–1979* (London: Thames & Hudson, 1998); Simon Armstrong, *Street Art* (London: Thames & Hudson, 2019); Nato Thompson, ed., *Interventionists: Users' Manual for the Creative Disruption of Everyday Life* (North Adams, MA: MASS MoCA, 2004); Claire Bishop, *Artificial Hells: Participatory Art and the Politics of Spectatorship* (New York: Verso, 2012); Shannon Jackson, *Social Works: Performing Art, Supporting Publics* (New York: Routledge, 2011); Frazer Ward, *No Innocent Bystanders: Performance Art and Audience* (Hanover, NH: Dartmouth College Press, 2012).
84. Saidiya Hartman, public talk, March 3, 2022, Buskirk-Chumley, Bloomington, IN. "Structural unlivability" is a central tenet explored within Afro-pessimism. See writings by Hartman, Hortense Spillers, Orlando Patterson, Jared Sexton, and Frank B. Wilderson in *Afro-Pessimism: An Introduction* (Minneapolis: Racked & Dispatched, 2017).
85. Nicole R. Fleetwood, *Marking Time: Art in the Age of Mass Incarceration* (Cambridge, MA: Harvard University Press, 2020), 2.
86. This framing is modeled on Brazilian sociologist Maria Edy Ferreira's work, as cited in Paulo Freire, *Pedagogy of the Oppressed* (1967; New York: Continuum, 1984), 83.
87. Ann Stoler, *Along the Archival Grain: Epistemic Anxieties and Colonial Common Sense* (Princeton, NJ: Princeton University Press, 2009); Seigel, *Violence Work*; Christina Sharp, *In the Wake: On Blackness and Being* (Durham, NC: Duke University Press, 2016); Gayle Rubin, "Thinking Sex: Notes for a Radical Theory of the Politics of Sexuality," in *Culture, Society, and Sexuality: A Reader*, ed. Richard Guy Parker and Peter Aggleton (London: UCL Press, 1999), 143–78. Alongside my development of the concept, "risk work" was used circa 2015 in sociological studies of health care to discuss the labor of assessing risk in the medical field. See Nicola K. Gale et al., "Towards a Sociology of Risk Work: A Narrative Review and Synthesis," *Sociology Compass* 10, no. 11 (November 2016): 1046–71.
88. Julia Bryan-Wilson, *Art Workers: Radical Practice in the Vietnam War Era* (Berkeley: University of California Press, 2009); Helen Molesworth, *Work Ethic* (University Park: Pennsylvania State University Press, 2003).
89. Audre Lorde, *Sister Outsider: Essays and Speeches* (Trumansburg, NY: Crossing Press, 1984); Trinh T. Minh-Ha, *Woman, Native, Other: Writing Postcoloniality and Feminism* (Bloomington: University of Indiana Press, 1989).
90. Joan Kee, *Models of Integrity: Art and Law in Post-Sixties America* (Oakland: University of California Press, 2019), 18.
91. François Pluchart, "Risk as the Practice of Thought," *Flash Art*, special issue, "Danger in Art" (1978): 40.
92. Jane Blocker, "Aestheticizing Risk in Wartime: the SLA to Iraq (2006)," in *The Aes-*

thetics of Risk, vol. 3 of SoCCAS [Southern California Consortium of Art Schools] Symposia (Distributed Art Publishers, 2008), 200.

93. Blocker, "Aestheticizing Risk," 191, 209, 217.
94. Robyn Wiegman, *Object Lessons* (Durham, NC: Duke University Press, 2012), 179.
95. George Lipsitz, *How Racism Takes Place* (Philadelphia: Temple University Press, 2011), 123.
96. Jessica Eaglin, "Technologically Distorted Conceptions of Punishment," *Washington University Law Review* 97 (2019): 483–543. I am also grateful to Micol Seigel for her astute observations that helped bring these connections forward.
97. Eaglin, "Technologically Distorted," 509.
98. Nikolas Rose, "At Risk of Madness," in Baker and Simon, *Embracing Risk*, 209–32. I am grateful to Michelle Smirnova for her insights on this topic.
99. Eaglin, "Technologically Distorted," 532.
100. Eaglin, "Technologically Distorted," 528.
101. Elizabeth Hinton, *From the War on Poverty to the War on Crime: The Making of Mass Incarceration in America* (Cambridge, MA: Harvard University Press, 2017).
102. Eduardo Bonilla-Silva's theorizing of "color-blind racism" offers a prescient study; he argues that this new ideology dates to the 1960s. See *Racism without Racists: Color-Blind Racism and the Persistence of Racial Inequality in America* (Lanham, MD: Rowman & Littlefield, 2014).
103. Jackie Wang's work on the racialized and gendered structures of innocence vis-à-vis policing has been crucial. See Wang, "Against Innocence: Race, Gender, and the Politics of Safety," in *Carceral Capitalism*, 260–95.
104. For examples of transtemporal analyses in art, see Huey Copeland, *Bound to Appear: Art, Slavery, and the Site of Blackness in Multicultural America* (Chicago: University of Chicago Press, 2013); Krista Thompson, "The Evidence of Things Not Photographed: Slavery and Historical Memory in the British West Indies," *Representations* 113, no. 1 (Winter 2011): 39–71; Cheryl Finley, *Committed to Memory: The Art of the Slave Ship Icon* (Princeton, NJ: Princeton University Press, 2018). For studies in art, law, and public policy see Rosalyn Deutsche, *Evictions: Art and Spatial Politics* (Cambridge, MA: MIT Press, 1996); Anthea Kraut, *Choreographing Copyright: Race, Gender, and Intellectual Property Rights in American Dance* (New York: Oxford University Press, 2016); Rebecca Zorach, ed., *Art against the Law* (Chicago: University of Chicago Press, 2015); Miwon Kwon, *One Place after Another: Site-Specific Art and Locational Identity* (Cambridge, MA: MIT Press, 2002); Hannah Feldman, *From a Nation Torn: Decolonizing Art and Representation in France, 1945–1962* (Durham, NC: Duke University Press, 2014).
105. Joshua Takano Chambers-Letson, *A Race So Different: Performance and Law in Asian America* (New York: New York University Press, 2013), 68.
106. Carman Moore, "Black Comedy: The USA v. Jean Toche," *Village Voice*, April 18, 1974. Jean Brown Papers, box 23, folder 10, Special Collections, Getty Research Institute, Los Angeles.

107. Hinton, *From the War on Poverty*, 155.
108. Ulrich Beck, "Foreword: Risk Society as Political Category," in Rosa et al., *Risk Society Revisited*, xxii–xxiii.
109. Herman Goldstein, "Toward Community-Oriented Policing: Potential, Basic Requirements, and Threshold Questions," *Crime & Delinquency* 33, no. 6 (1987): 6.
110. Paul Veyne, *Writing History: Essays on Epistemology*, trans. Mira Moore-Rinvolucri (Middletown, CT: Wesleyan University Press, 1984), 41.
111. Christina Hanhardt, *Safe Space: Gay Neighborhood History and the Politics of Violence* (Durham, NC: Duke University Press, 2013).

Chapter One

1. C. Ondine Chavoya, "Internal Exiles: The Interventionist Public and Performance Art of Asco," in *Space, Site, Intervention: Situating Installation Art*, ed. Erika Suderburg (Minneapolis: University of Minnesota Press, 2000), 197.
2. This chapter uses the designations "Chicano," "Chicana," and "Latino" to refer to the members of Asco—terms used by the artists themselves in the context of the 1970s and 1980s. I also use "Chicanx," an inclusive, nonbinary designation, to discuss individuals within a contemporary context.
3. Following C. Ondine Chavoya, I refer to Asco as a "collaborative artists' group" rather than an "art collective." See Chavoya, "Fleeting Inscriptions: Asco, Ephemera, and Intergroup Exchange in LA," *Living Collections Catalogue* (Walker Art Center), Spring/Summer 2020, https://walkerart.org/collections/publications/side-by-side/artists-groups-in-los-angeles-asco-and-los-four.
4. Marci R. McMahon, *Domestic Negotiations: Gender, Nation, and Self-Fashioning in US Mexican and Chicana Literature and Art* (Brunswick, NJ: Rutgers University Press, 2013), 138; Patssi Valdez, oral history interview with Jeffrey Rangel, May 26–June 2, 1999, Archives of American Art, Smithsonian Institution.
5. Sean Carillo, "'*¡Tenemos Asco!*' An Oral History of the Chicano Art Group," *Frieze*, no. 224, January 4, 2022, https://www.frieze.com/article/tenemos-asco-oral-history-chicano-art-group.
6. C. Ondine Chavoya and Rita Gonzalez, "Asco and the Politics of Revulsion," in *Asco: Elite of the Obscure, a Retrospective, 1972–1987*, ed. Chavoya and Gonzalez (Ostfildern, Germany: Hatje Cantz, 2011), 84.
7. Kellie Jones explains that the artists closed off the street momentarily by lighting flares in order to deter police from entering the area and arresting them. See Jones, *South of Pico: African American Arts in Los Angeles in the 1960s and 1970s* (Durham, NC: Duke University Press, 2017), 237.
8. Chavoya and Gonzalez, "Asco and the Politics of Revulsion," 84. See radio interview by Gabriel Gutierrez, *Morning Review with Gabriel Gutierrez*, KPFK, April 2, 2008.

9. C. Ondine Chavoya, "No-Movies: The Art of False Documents," in *Only Skin Deep: Changing Visions of the American Self*, ed. Coco Fusco and Brian Wallis (New York: International Center of Photography/Harry N. Abrams, 2003), 189, 199; Chon Noriega, "Your Art Disgusts Me: Early Asco 1971–75," *East of Borneo*, November 18, 2010, https://eastofborneo.org/articles/your-art-disgusts-me-early-asco-1971-75/ (originally published in *Afterall* 19 [Winter 2008]); Gronk, oral history interview with Jeffrey Rangel, January 20–23, 1997, Archives of American Art, Smithsonian Institution.
10. Philip Brookman and Amy Brookman, "Interview with ASCO," *CALIFAS: Chicano Art and Culture in California, Transcripts*, book 3, Collection Tloque Nahauque (University of California at Santa Barbara Davidson Library, 1983), 7–8.
11. John Giorno, "WPAX," artist statement in *Illegal America* (1982), n.p. See also "Investigation of Attempts to Subvert the United States Armed Services," report by House of Representatives Committee on Internal Security, May 1972, 7309–10.
12. Monica Castillo, "Overlooked No More: Ana Mendieta, a Cuban Artist Who Pushed Boundaries," *New York Times*, September 19, 2018, https://www.nytimes.com/2018/09/19/obituaries/ana-mendieta-overlooked.html.
13. Willoughby Sharp, "Elemental Gestures: Terry Fox," *Arts Magazine*, May 1970, 48–51.
14. Ursula Meyer, "The Eruption of Anti-Art," in *Idea Art: A Critical Anthology*, ed. Gregory Battcock (New York: Dutton, 1973), 125; Carman Moore, "Black Comedy: The USA v. Jean Toche," *Village Voice*, April 18, 1974. Jean Brown Papers, box 23, folder 10, Special Collections, Getty Research Institute, Los Angeles.
15. Moore, "Black Comedy."
16. Douglas Davis, "Death for Art's Sake," *Newsweek*, December 24, 1973, 68; Dorothy Sieberling, "The Art-Martyr," *New York Magazine*, May 24, 1976, 48.
17. Mans Wrange, "A Conversation with Chris Burden," in *Chris Burden* (Stockholm, Sweden: Magasin 3 Stockholm Konsthall, 1999), n.p.
18. Davis, "Death for Art's Sake," 68.
19. Davis, "Death for Art's Sake," 68; Richard Horvitz, "Chris Burden," *Artforum*, May 1976, n.p.
20. Peter Schjeldahl, "The Danger Artist," *New Yorker*, May 19, 2015, https://www.newyorker.com/culture/cultural-comment/danger-artist-chris-burden.
21. Both Asco and Burden have been called "guerrilla" artists or described as practicing "guerrilla-like" tactics. See, for example, Noriega, "Your Art Disgusts Me"; C. Ondine Chavoya, "Internal Exiles: The Interventionist Public and Performance Art of Asco," in *Space, Site, Intervention: Situating Installation Art*, ed. Erika Suderberg (Minneapolis: University of Minnesota Press, 2000), 189 ("guerrilla, or hit-and-run, tactics"); and Suzanne Lacy, discussing Burden in *Leaving Art: Writings on Performance, Politics, and Publics, 1974–2007* (Durham, NC: Duke University Press, 2010), 120.
22. Dana Friis-Hansen, "LA Hot and Cool: Temperaments and Traditions," in *LA, Hot and*

Cool, the Eighties, ed. Friis-Hansen et al. (Cambridge, MA: MIT List Visual Arts Center, 1988), 12.

23. Henri Lefebvre developed the idea of "the right to the city" in 1968. See Mark Purcell, "Possible Worlds: Henri Lefebvre and the Right to the City," *Journal of Urban Affairs* 36, no. 1 (2013): 141–54.
24. Kelly Lytle Hernandez reveals how the initial local jail in what is now modern Los Angeles was the foundational structure of US conquest. See Lytle Hernández, *City of Inmates: Conquest, Rebellion, and the Rise of Human Caging in Los Angeles, 1771–1965* (Chapel Hill: University of North Carolina Press, 2017).
25. Katherine McKittrick, *Demonic Grounds: Black Women and the Cartographies of Struggle* (Minneapolis: University of Minnesota Press, 2006), 4–5.
26. McKittrick, *Demonic Grounds*, xiii.
27. Valerie Cassel Oliver, "Putting the Body on the Line: Endurance in Black Performance," *Radical Presence: Black Performance in Contemporary Art* (Houston: Contemporary Arts Museum Houston, 2013), 14.
28. C. Ondine Chavoya, "Orphans of Modernism: The Performance of Asco," in *Corpus Delecti: Performance Art of the Americas*, ed. Coco Fusco (New York: Routledge, 2000), 253, 254.
29. Huey Copeland, "*Babel* Screened: On Race, Narcissism, and the Prediction of American Video Art," in *Black Is, Black Ain't* (Chicago: Renaissance Society/University of Chicago Press, 2013), 51.
30. George Lipsitz, "The Possessive Investment in Whiteness: Racialized Social Democracy and the 'White' Problem in American Studies," *American Quarterly* 47, no. 3 (1995): 359.
31. Chavoya, "Internal Exiles," 195.
32. "El Mexicano: Through the Eyes of the Gavachos; Profit Making: At the Expense of Our People," *La Raza* 1, no. 4 (1971): 23–24. Harry Gamboa Jr. Papers, box 8, folder 4, Special Collections, Stanford University.
33. Joseph R. Dominick, "Crime and Law Enforcement on Prime-Time Television," *Public Opinion Quarterly* 34, no. 2 (Summer 1973): 241–50.
34. Chon Noriega, "Stereotyping in Film in General and of the Hispanic in Particular," in *Latin Looks: Images of Latinas and Latinos in the U.S. Media*, ed. Clara E. Rodriguez (Boulder, CO: Westview Press, 1977), 35–39; Chon Noriega, *Shot in America: Television, the State, and the Rise of Chicano Cinema* (Minneapolis: Minnesota University Press, 2000), 35–50.
35. Harry Gamboa and Gronk, oral history interview with Jeffrey Rangel, April 1–16, 1999, Archives of American Art, Smithsonian Institution.
36. Harry Gamboa Jr., "City of Angels (1991)," in *Urban Exile: Collected Writings of Harry Gamboa Jr.*, ed. Chon Noriega (Minneapolis: University of Minnesota Press, 1998), 125.
37. David E. James, "No Movies: Projecting the Reel by Rejecting the Reel," in Chavoya

and Gonzalez, *Elite of the Obscure*, 182. James refers to *Decoy* as one of Asco's earliest No Movies.

38. C. Ondine Chavoya, "Pseudographic Cinema: Asco's No-Movies," *Performance Research: A Journal of the Performing Arts* 3, no. 1 (1998): 1–14.
39. Amelia Jones, "Traitor Prophets: Asco's Art as a Politics of the In-Between," in Chavoya and Gonzalez, *Elite of the Obscure*, 126.
40. Gronk, oral history interview, 1997.
41. Carillo, "*¡Tenemos Asco!*"
42. Laura Burnham, "Asco: Camus, Daffy Duck, and Devil Girls from East L.A.," *L.A. Style*, February 1987, 58.
43. Valdez, oral history interview with Jeffrey Rangel, 1999.
44. Edward Escobar, "The Dialectics of Repression: The Los Angeles Police Department and the Chicano Movement, 1968–1971," *Journal of American History* 79, no. 4 (March 1993): 1489.
45. George Sánchez, *Boyle Heights: How a Los Angeles Neighborhood Became the Future of American Democracy* (University of California Press, 2021), 9–10.
46. Sánchez, *Boyle Heights*, 9.
47. "South Central History" (2018), http://www.southcentralhistory.com/gang-history.php
48. "City, Navy Clamp Lid on Zoot-Suit Warfare," *Los Angeles Times*, June 9, 1943: n.p.
49. Willie Herrón, oral history interview with Jeffrey Rangel, February 5–March 17, 2000, Archives of American Art, Smithsonian Institution.
50. Escobar, "Dialectics of Repression," 1496. United States Commission on Civil Rights, California Advisory Committee, *Police-Community Relations in East Los Angeles, California: A Report of the California State Advisory to the United States Commission on Civil Rights* (Los Angeles), 1970, 19–20.
51. Chon Noriega, "No Introduction," in Gamboa, *Urban Exile*, 12.
52. Felker-Kantor, *Policing Los Angeles*, 67.
53. Frank Sifuentes, "Reflections on Law and Order in East Los Angeles," *Regeneración* 1, no. 8 (1970): 7. Harry Gamboa Jr. Papers, box 9, folder 10. Special Collections, Stanford University.
54. Sarah Ahmed, *Queer Phenomenology: Orientations, Objects, Others* (Durham, NC: Duke University Press, 2006), 140.
55. Ahmed, *Queer Phenomenology*, 142.
56. Michelle Alexander, *The New Jim Crow: Mass Incarceration in the Age of Colorblindness* (New York: New Press, 2011), 136.
57. Alexander, *New Jim Crow*, 136; citing Ryan Pintado-Vertner and Jeff Chang, "The War on Youth," *Colorlines* 2, no. 4 (Winter 1999–2000): 36.
58. US Congress, Senate Committee of the Judiciary, *Extent of Subversion in the "New Left": Testimony of Robert J. Thoms*, hearings before the Subcommittee to Investigate the Administration of the Internal Security Act and Other Internal Security

Laws, Part 1, January 20, 1970 (Washington, DC: US Government Printing Office, 1970), 22–24, and pullout section facing p. 38.

59. Sánchez, *Boyle Heights*, 186. See also Leticia Alvarado, *Abject Performances: Aesthetic Strategies in Latino Cultural Production* (Durham, NC: Duke University Press, 2018), 63.

60. Sánchez, *Boyle Heights*, 186; Committee on the Judiciary, 12.

61. Committee on the Judiciary, 12.

62. Gamboa, email correspondence with author, April 18, 2020.

63. Brian Jefferson, *Digitize and Punish: Racial Criminalization in the Digital Age* (Minneapolis: University of Minnesota Press, 2020), 62–64; Andrew Ferguson, "Policing Predictive Policing," *Washington University Law Review* 94, no. 5 (2017): 1132; David Correia and Tyler Wall, *Police: A Field Guide* (London: Verso, 2018), 185.

64. Jefferson, *Digitize and Punish*, 63–64.

65. Phillip Mitchell, "Optimal Selection of Police Patrol Beats," *Journal of Criminal Law and Criminology* 63, no. 4 (1973): 577.

66. Alvarado, *Abject Performances*, 80.

67. Jefferson, *Digitize and Punish*, 63.

68. Ruth Wilson Gilmore speaks of "organized abandonment" in *Golden Gulag: Prisons, Surplus, Crisis, and Opposition in Globalizing California* (Berkeley: University of California Press, 2007), 70–77.

69. Jefferson, *Digitize and Punish*, 53.

70. "Jerry Dreva Letters," May 17, 1974. Gronk Papers, box 1, folder 95, Chicano Research Center, University of California, Los Angeles.

71. Carlos Marighella, *Urban Guerrilla Minimanual* (1969; Vancouver, Canada: Pulp Press, 1974), 4. Political Pamphlets P2000354, Special Collections, Northwestern University.

72. Chavoya and Gonzalez, "Asco and the Politics of Revulsion," 84.

73. Chavoya, "Internal Exiles," 202.

74. Correia and Wall, *Police*, 185–87.

75. 18 U.S. Code § 2101.

76. Peter Babcox, Noam Chomsky, Judy Collins, Harvey Cox, Edgar Z. Friedenberg, et al., "The Committee to Defend the Conspiracy," *New York Review of Books*. June 19, 1969: n.p.

77. Felker-Kantor, *Policing Los Angeles*, 52.

78. Felker-Kantor, *Policing Los Angeles*, 52.

79. Felker-Kantor, *Policing Los Angeles*, 53.

80. Ian Haney López, *Racism on Trial: The Chicano Fight for Justice* (Cambridge, MA: Belknap Press/Harvard University Press, 2003), 149.

81. Deborah Cullen, "A Part and Apart: Contextualizing Asco," in Chavoya and Gonzalez, *Elite of the Obscure*, 217.

82. James, "No Movies," 182; this event is also referenced by Cullen, "A Part and Apart," 217.
83. Chavoya, "Internal Exiles," 203.
84. Escobar, "Dialectics of Repression," 1483.
85. Roberto Tejada, "Los Angeles Snapshots," in *Now Dig This! Art and Black Los Angeles, 1960–1980*, ed. Kellie Jones (Los Angeles: Hammer Museum, 2011), 72–73; Escobar, "Dialectics of Repression," 1499; "Police-Community Relations in East Los Angeles, California: A Report of the California State Advisory Committee to the United States Commission on Civil Rights," October 1970, 15.
86. Max Benavidez and Katie Vozoff, "The Wall: Image and Boundary, Chicano Art in the 1970s," in *Mexican Art of the 1970s: Images of Displacement* (Nashville, TN: Center for Latin American and Iberian Studies, Vanderbilt University, 1984), 48.
87. Harry Gamboa Jr., phone conversation with author, March 3, 2018.
88. *Los Angeles Times* 1971: 3, my emphasis. Peter Pitchess is the namesake of the "Pitchess Motion," a 1970s statute establishing a defendant's right to information about alleged officer misconduct or dishonesty. https://definitions.uslegal.com/p/pitchess-motion/.
89. Robert Goding-Williams, "Look, a Negro!," in *Reading Rodney King/Reading Urban Uprising*, ed. Goding-Williams (New York: Routledge, 1993), 169.
90. Carillo, "*¡Tenemos Asco!*"
91. Carillo, "*¡Tenemos Asco!*"
92. Chavoya, "Internal Exiles," 196.
93. *Mi Otro Yo—My Other Self*, 1982, documentary on Chicano art in Los Angeles recorded on videotape by Philip Brookman and Amy Brookman for *CALIFAS, Chicano Art and Culture in California*, audio recording. Foreign Languages and Area Collections, Harry Gamboa Jr. Papers, Special Collections, Stanford University.
94. James, "No Movies," 182.
95. Cullen, "A Part and Apart," 217.
96. Mike Davis, "Chinatown, Part Two? The 'Internationalization' of Downtown Los Angeles," *New Left Review*, no.164 (July/August 1987), 65.
97. "Chris Burden: Deadman." High Performance Archive, box 8, folder 9, Getty Research Institute, Los Angeles.
98. Frazer Ward, "Gray Zone: Watching Shoot," *October*, no. 95 (Winter 2001), 117–25.
99. Max Kozloff, "Pygmalion Reversed," *Artforum*, November 1975, 37; Christopher Knight, "Chris Burden and the Potential for Catastrophe," *Art Issues* 52 (March/April 1998): 18.
100. Chris Burden, public lecture at RISD, November 12, 1974. High Performance Archive, box 8, folder 8, Getty Research Institute, Los Angeles.
101. Chris Burden, interview with Jim Moisan, 1979. High Performance Archive, box 8, folder 8, Getty Research Institute, Los Angeles.

102. Peter Plagens, "He Got Shot—for His Art." *New York Times*, September 2, 1973, D1.
103. Burden, interview with Moisan, 1979.
104. Elizabeth Hinton, *From the War on Poverty to the War on Crime: The Making of Mass Incarceration in America* (Cambridge, MA: Harvard University Press, 2016), 219.
105. A. C. Germann, "Changing the Police—The Impossible Dream," *Journal of Criminal Law and Criminology* 62, no. 3 (1972): 420.
106. From John Baldessari et al., "L.A. Stories: A Roundtable," *Artforum*, October 2011, 247.
107. Mike Sonksen, "The History of South Central Los Angeles and Its Struggle with Gentrification," KCET, September 13, 2017, https://www.kcet.org/shows/city-rising/the-history-of-south-central-los-angeles-and-its-struggle-with-gentrification.
108. Felker-Kantor, *Policing Los Angeles*, 64–65.
109. Baldessari et al., "L.A. Stories," 243; S. Zaneta Kosiba-Vargas, "Harry Gamboa and ASCO: The Emergence and Development of a Chicano Art Group, 1971–1987" (PhD diss., University of Michigan, 1988), 207; Davis, "Chinatown, Part Two?," 77.
110. Plagens, "He Got Shot," D1.
111. Plagens would later explicitly dismiss Asco's work, writing of Gronk as a "succotash of Andy Warhol camp" whose work was funny and unserious, with no relevance for the avant-garde of Los Angeles. See Peter Plagens, letter to the editor, *Neworld* 5 (September/October 1980): 9.
112. Plagens, "He Got Shot," D1.
113. The law deemed criminal "any individual who reports, or causes any report to be made, to any city, county, or state department, district, agency, division, commission, or board, that an 'emergency' exists, knowing that the report is false." "False Report of an Emergency," California Penal Code 148.3, accessed April 2, 2020, https://www.shouselaw.com/false-report-emergency.html.
114. *Gossett v. Burnett*, 251 S.C. 548 (S.C. 1968). States have formulated the crime of creating a false emergency more recently (e.g., California Penal Code section 148.3, enacted 2002; Arizona Stat. 13-2907, enacted 1977), in response to doxing, swatting, and or other sorts of false 911 calls. I am grateful to Jarryd Page for his legal insights on this topic.
115. Penal code 148.3 (c).
116. Barbara Smith, "Burden Case Tried, Dismissed," *Artweek*, February 1973, 2.
117. Barbara Smith, "Art Piece Brings Arrest," *Artweek*, January 6, 1973, 4.
118. Smith, "Burden Case Tried," 2; Chris Burden interview, RISD, 1974.
119. Chris Burden interview, RISD, 1974.
120. Plagens, "He Got Shot," 87.
121. Burden, interview with Moisan, 1979.
122. Amelia Jones, "Lost Bodies: Early 1970s Los Angeles Performance Art in Art History," in *Live Art in LA: Performance Art in Southern California, 1970–1983*, ed. Peggy

Phelan (New York: Routledge, 2010), 126. This quote comes from Gronk in conversation with Amelia Jones, October 31, 2010.

123. Karen J. Pita Loor, "When Protest Is the Disaster: Constitutional Implications of State and Local Emergency Power," *Seattle University Law Review* 43, no. 1 (Fall 2019): 7.
124. Anthony Giddens, "Risk and Responsibility," *Modern Law Review* 62, no. 1 (January 1999): 3–4.
125. Gilmore, *Golden Gulag*, 11.
126. Randy Kennedy, "Chicano Pioneers," *New York Times*. August 25, 2011, https://www.nytimes.com/2011/08/28/arts/design/works-by-asco-at-the-los-angeles-museum.html.
127. Valdez refers to the 1975 performance as *Untitled*. Harry Gamboa Jr. documented it photographically and, as legal copyright holder, determines the photographs' title when they are reproduced. His title for the two images, *Pistol Whippersnapper movement 1* and *movement 2*, references a paper collage flyer he produced the following year, in 1976, which carries this title. For an extended discussion of *Pistol Whippersnapper* and its significance, see Faye Gleisser, "Asco, Chris Burden, and the Politics of the Misfire," *Journal of Visual Culture* 17, no. 3 (December 2018): 312–31.
128. Patssi Valdez, phone interview with author, May 28, 2014.
129. Burnham, "Asco," 408.
130. David A. Ross, "Chris Burden's Television," in *Chris Burden: A Twenty-Year Survey*, ed. Anne Ayres, Chris Burden, and Paul Schimmel (Newport Beach, CA: Newport Harbor Art Museum, 1988), n.p.
131. Burden's description for his performance is reprinted in Frazer Ward, *No Innocent Bystanders: Performance, Art, and Audience* (Hanover, NH: Dartmouth College Press, 2012), 102. In later interviews Burden has presented a different narrative of *TV Hijack*: "When, during the course of the interview, I was asked about some of my ideas, I enacted a hijack where I, with a knife, pretended to threaten the interviewer's life if the station stopped the live broadcast. *TV Hijack* was ultimately about who is in control over what's presented through the media." See Wrange, "Conversation with Chris Burden," 1999.
132. Ward, *No Innocent Bystanders*, 102.
133. Nick Stillman, "Do You Believe in Television? Chris Burden and TV," *East of Borneo*, October 10, 2010, https://eastofborneo.org/articles/do-you-believe-in-television-chris-burden-and-tv/.
134. For *Shoot*, see Gleisser, "Politics of the Misfire," 312–31.
135. United States Commission on Civil Rights, *Window Dressing on the Set: Women and Minorities in Television* (Washington, DC, August 1977), 50–51, 54.
136. Kosiba-Vargas, "Harry Gamboa and ASCO," 93.
137. Harry Gamboa Jr., "Silver Screenings the Barrio," *Equal Opportunity Forum* 6, no. 1 (1978): 7.

138. Valdez, oral history interview with Rangel, 1999.
139. Valdez, interview with author, 2014.
140. Valdez, oral history interview, 1999.
141. Anne Wagner, "Then and There: Anne Wagner on the Art of Chris Burden," *Artforum*, October 2011, 221.

Chapter Two

1. Adrian Piper, "IV. Concretized Ideas I've Been Working Around (January 1971)," in *Out of Order, Out of Sight*, vol. 1, *Selected Writings in Meta-Art, 1968–1992* (Cambridge, MA: MIT Press, 1996), 43.
2. Adrian Piper, "An Autobiographical Preface," which includes "Art as Catalysis (August 1970)," in *Out of Order, Out of Sight*, 1:32.
3. Adrian Piper, "Notes and Qualifications, September 1970," in *Talking to Myself: The Ongoing Autobiography of an Art Object* (Bruxelles: Hossmann Hamburg, MTL Bruxelles, 1974), 11. See also Adrian Piper, "II. Notes and Qualifications (September 1970)," in *Out of Order, Out of Sight*, 1:37.
4. See, for example, Diarmuid Costello, "Xenophobia, Stereotypes, and Empirical Acculturation: Neo-Kantianism in Adrian Piper's Performance-based Conceptual Art," in *Adrian Piper: A Reader* (New York: Museum of Modern Art, 2018), 172. Uri McMillan also ascribes a "guerrilla style" to Piper's Mythic Being, borrowing this formulation from José Esteban Muñoz's discussion of disidentification. See McMillan, *Embodied Avatars: Genealogies of Black Feminist Art and Performance* (New York: New York University Press, 2015), 139.
5. Adrian Piper, "My Calling (Cards) #1 and #2," in *Out of Order, Out of Sight*, 1:219.
6. Adrian Piper, "NEWS: September 2012." http://www.adrianpiper.com/news_sep_2012.shtml.
7. Lucy Lippard and Adrian Piper, "Catalysis: An Interview with Adrian Piper," *The Drama Review: TDR* 16, no. 1 (March 1972): 78.
8. Jean Toche, interview with author, June 5, 2014.
9. Toche, interview, 2014.
10. Jean Toche, statement written on behalf of the Ad Hoc Artists' Movement for Freedom, February 28, 1974. Jean Brown Papers, collection 890164, GAAG, box 23, folder 11, Getty Research Institute, Los Angeles.
11. Adrian Piper, "Passing for White, Passing for Black," *Transition* 58 (1992): 4–32. Reproduced in *Out of Order, Out of Sight*, 1:276.
12. Piper, "Preparatory Notes for *The Mythic Being* (1973–74)," in *Out of Order, Out of Sight*, 1:100–101.
13. Piper, "Preparatory Notes," 1:101.
14. Piper, "Preparatory Notes," 1:101–2.

15. Piper, "Preparatory Notes," 1:103–4; Tavia Nyong'o, *Afro-Fabulations: The Queer Drama of Black Life* (New York: New York University Press, 2019), 94 and, for a full discussion, chap. 3, "Brer Soul and the Mythic Being: Toward a Queer Logic of Dark Sense," 76–98.
16. Piper, "Preparatory Notes," 1:103.
17. Piper, "Preparatory Notes," 1:108–9.
18. Piper, "Art for the Art-World Surface Pattern," in *Out of Order, Out of Sight*, 1:164.
19. John Bowles, *Adrian Piper: Race, Gender, and Embodiment* (Durham, NC: Duke University Press, 2011), 138.
20. Carman Moore, "Black Comedy: The USA v. Jean Toche," *Village Voice*, April 18, 1974. Piper writes in March 1974, "The visual image of the Mythic Being appears publicly on a monthly basis in the Village Voice on the Gallery page." Adrian Piper, "Notes on the Mythic Being I–III," in *Out of Order, Out of Sight*, 1:117. Cherise Smith also writes about these images' appearance in the *Voice* between September 1973 and February 1975. See Smith, "Re-Member the Audience: Adrian Piper's Mythic Being Advertisements," *Art Journal* 66, no. 1 (Spring 2007): 47.
21. Hinton, *From the War on Poverty*, 128.
22. Hinton, *From the War on Poverty*, 128.
23. Anthropologist James C. Scott, in *Seeing Like a State: How Certain Schemes to Improve the Human Condition Have Failed* (New Haven, CT: Yale University Press, 1998), argues for the "indispensable role of practical knowledge, informal processes, and improvisation in the face of unpredictability" as a counter to the processes of simplification rendered by the state, whose pursuit of order and control gives way to "remarkably visual aesthetic terms" that "require a narrowing of vision" (6, 3, 11). Scott addresses the terms of order (forestry, grids, urbanization). I am interested instead in thinking about how the state summons its citizens to enact its envisioning of binaristic, simplified power relations through the forging of deputized looking.
24. Ren-yo Hwang, "Deviant Care for Deviant Futures: QTBIPoC Radical Relationalism as Mutual Aid against Carceral Care," *TSQ: Transgender Studies Quarterly* 6, no. 4 (2019): 561–64.
25. For insight into the longer histories of looking and surveillance, see Nicolas Mirzoeff, *The Right to Look: A Counterhistory of Visuality* (Durham, NC: Duke University Press, 2011); Nicole Fleetwood, *Troubling Vision: Performance, Visuality, and Blackness* (Chicago: University of Chicago Press, 2011); Simone Browne, *Dark Matter: On the Surveillance of Blackness* (Durham, NC: Duke University Press, 2015).
26. Jordan Berns, "Is There Something Suspicious about the Constitutionality of Loitering Laws?" *Ohio State Law Journal* 50, no. 3 (1989): 721.
27. David Theo Goldberg, *The Racial State* (Oxford: Blackwell, 2002), 104.
28. Peter W. Poulos, "Chicago's Ban on Gang Loitering: Making Sense of Vagueness and Overbreadth in Loitering Laws," *California Law Review* 83, no. 1 (January 1995): 399.
29. Anthony Romero, untitled public lecture, "Boundaries and Margins" series, Colby

College, Zoom, October 5, 2020. See also Tiffany Lethabo King, *The Black Shoals: Offshore Formations of Black and Native Studies* (Durham, NC: Duke University Press, 2019).

30. The documents came to the Getty by way of Jean Brown, a prominent collector of Fluxus and mail art, and a friend of Toche, who supported him during his trial in 1974.

31. See Jon Hendricks and Jean Toche, eds., *GAAG: The Guerrilla Art Action Group, 1969–1976: A Selection* (New York: Printed Matter, 1978). Following the anthology's format, as well as the artists' notations of their guerrilla art interventions, I refer to the work discussed here as "Open Letter to the Mayor of Boston."

32. When the Mythic Being series is featured in exhibitions and scholarship, the work is most often visually represented by images of *Cruising White Women*, *Getting Back*, and *Mythic Being: I Embody Everything You Most Hate and Fear*. In my research, I have yet to see *Loitering* appear as the focus of art-historical analysis.

33. Adrian Piper, email correspondence with author, November 21, 2019 (Café Pamplona); James Guttmann, zoom interview with author, December 31, 2021.

34. Poulos, "Chicago's Ban on Loitering Gangs," 385.

35. *The People's Law Dictionary*, ed. Gerald and Kathleen Hill, s.v. "loiter" (Fine Communication), https://dictionary.law.com/Default.aspx?typed=loiter&type=1.

36. Poulos, "Chicago's Ban on Loitering Gangs," 385.

37. Shirley Lung, "Criminalizing Work and Non-Work: The Disciplining of Immigrant and African American Workers," *University of Massachusetts Law Review* 14, no. 2, article 2 (2019): 324–25.

38. Michelle Alexander, *The New Jim Crow: Mass Incarceration in the Age of Colorblindness* (New York: New Press, 2011), 28–30.

39. Lung, "Criminalizing Work," 328–29; 323–24.

40. Lung, "Criminalizing Work," 323, 325.

41. Anna Pegler-Gordon, *In Sight of America: Photography and the Development of U.S. Immigration Policy* (Berkeley: University of California Press, 2009).

42. Treva Ellison, "The Strangeness of Progress and the Uncertainty of Blackness," in *No Tea, No Shade: New Writings in Black Queer Studies* (Durham, NC: Duke University Press, 2016), 326.

43. Ellison, "Strangeness of Progress," 324, 326.

44. Ellison, "Strangeness of Progress," 326.

45. Saidiya Hartman, *Wayward Lives, Beautiful Experiments: Intimate Histories of Social Upheaval* (New York: W. W. Norton, 2019), 243.

46. Hartman, *Wayward Lives*, 243.

47. Hartman, *Wayward Lives*, 224–25.

48. Piper, "Notes on the Mythic Being I–III," 1:124. Part II was written in January 1975 and first published in *Individuals: Post-Movement Art*, ed. Alan Sondheim (New York: E. P. Dutton), 1976.

49. Piper, "Notes on the Mythic Being," 1:123.

50. Piper, "Notes on the Mythic Being," 1:147.
51. Piper, "Notes on the Mythic Being," 1:138.
52. Adrian Piper, "The Mythic Being: Getting Back," in *Out of Order, Out of Sight*, 1:147. Written in 1980, but not published until 1996.
53. Bowles, *Adrian Piper*, 231.
54. Cherise Smith, *Enacting Others: Politics of Identity in Eleanor Antin, Nikki S. Lee, Adrian Piper, and Anna Deveare Smith* (Durham, NC: Duke University Press, 2011), 48.
55. Richard Powell, "Racial Imaginaries, from Charles White's Preacher to Jean-Peal Goude and Grace Jones' Nigger Arabesque," in *Back to Black: Art, Cinema, and the Racial Imaginary* (London: Whitechapel Art Gallery, 2005), 20.
56. Coco Fusco takes up this history and weaves together archival footage, simulated surveillance footage of many Davis "lookalikes," and trial transcripts from Angela Davis's case in her video piece *a/k/a Mrs. George Gilbert* (2004).
57. Adrian Piper, "Xenophobia and the Indexical Present II: Lecture (1992)," in *Out of Order, Out of Sight*, 1:263.
58. McMillan, *Embodied Avatars*, 137.
59. Piper, "Xenophobia," 1:263.
60. Alexander, *New Jim Crow*, 50.
61. Lauren Goluboff, *Vagrant Nation: Police Power, Constitutional Change, and the Making of the 1960s* (New York: Oxford University Press, 2016), 325.
62. Hinton, *From the War on Poverty*, 251, citing Reading Copies of Presidential Speeches and Statements, folder, "September 24, 1974, International Association of Chiefs of Police," box 1, Gerald Ford Presidential Library (GFPL); June 17, 1975, memorandum for Jim Connor from Dick Cheney, folder "Crime Message (2)," box 9, James E. Connor Files, GFPL.
63. *Coates v. City of Cincinnati*, 402 U.S. 611 (1971), https://supreme.justia.com/cases/federal/us/402/611/.
64. David Hudson Jr., "Coates v. City of Cincinnati," *The First Amendment Encyclopedia*, https://www.mtsu.edu/first-amendment/article/54/coates-v-city-of-cincinnati.
65. Petitioner's brief, *Papachristou v. City of Jacksonville*, 1971 WL 133167 (U.S.), 7 (U.S., 2004).
66. *Papachristou v. City of Jacksonville*, 405 U.S. 156 (1972), https://supreme.justia.com/cases/federal/us/405/156/.
67. Dorothy Roberts, "Race, Vagueness, and the Social Meaning of Order-Maintenance Policing," *Journal of Criminal Law and Criminology* 89, no. 3 (Spring 1999): 780.
68. "Loitering," N.Y. Pen Law 240.35 Section 240.35. Accessed August 5, 2014. http://codes.lp.findlaw.com/nycode/PEN/THREE/N/240/240.35.
69. Poulos, "Chicago's Ban on Loitering Gangs," 399.
70. Roberts, "Race, Vagueness," 784.
71. Roberts, "Race, Vagueness," 782–83.

72. Roberts, "Race, Vagueness," 783.
73. Berns, "Is There Something Suspicious," 735.
74. Geoffrey P. Alpert, John M. MacDonald, and Roger G. Dunham, "Police Suspicion and Discretionary Decision Making during Citizen Stops," *Criminology* 43, no. 2 (May 2005): 407–34.
75. The work of Tina Campt and Harvey Young on stillness and structural antiblack violence, as well as possibilities of refusal, has been invaluable. See Campt, *Listening to Images* (Durham, NC: Duke University Press, 2017); Young, *Embodying Black Experience: Stillness, Critical Memory, and the Black Body* (Ann Arbor: University of Michigan Press, 2010).
76. Huffa Frobes-Cross, "Action, Documentation, Documentary: The Early Photography of Allan Sekula, Martha Rosler, Fred Lonidier, and Phil Steinmetz," *World Records* 1 (2018), https://worldrecordsjournal.org/action-documentation-documentary/.
77. Guttmann, interview, 2021.
78. Guttmann, interview, 2021.
79. La Merr Jurelle Bruce, "Shore, Unsure: Loitering as a Way of Life," *GLQ: A Journal of Lesbian and Gay Studies* 25, no. 2 (April 2019): 352, citing *Merriam-Webster* and Dictionary.com.
80. Bruce, "Shore, Unsure," 353.
81. Adrian Piper, oral history interview with Josephine Withers, September 20, 1990, Archives of American Art, Smithsonian Institute.
82. Jean Toche, "Open Letter to: The Mayor of Boston, Boston, Mass. (October 21, 1974)." Jean Brown Papers, collection 890164, GAAG, box 23, folder 11, Getty Research Institute, Los Angeles.
83. Weather Underground Organization, *Osawatomie* 1, no. 3 (Spring 1975): 10.
84. John Kifner, "South Boston Crowd Attacks Black as Tensions Rise," *New York Times*, October 8, 1974, 1.
85. Louis Masur, *The Soiling of Old Glory: The Story of a Photograph That Shocked America* (New York: Bloomsbury, 2003), 1.
86. Kathleen Banks Nutter, "Militant Mothers: Boston, Busing, and the Bicentennial of 1976," *Historical Journal of Massachusetts*, Fall 2010, 52–75; Tahi L. Mottl, "The Analysis of Countermovements," *Social Problems* 27, no. 5, "Sociology of Political Knowledge Issue: Theoretical Inquiries, Critiques, and Explications" (June 1980): 620–35.
87. Bruce Gellerman, "'It Was like a War Zone': Busing in Boston," WBUR news, September 5, 2014, https://www.wbur.org/news/2014/09/05/boston-busing-anniversary.
88. Masur, *Soiling of Old Glory*, 48.
89. Masur, *Soiling of Old Glory*, 20.
90. Nikole Hannah-Jones, "It Was Never about Busing: Court-Ordered Desegregation Worked. But White Racism Made It Hard to Accept," *New York Times*, July 19, 2019,

https://www.nytimes.com/2019/07/12/opinion/sunday/it-was-never-about-busing.html.

91. Hannah-Jones, "It Was Never about Busing," 2019.
92. Paul Saba, "Monopoly Capitalists' Anti-Busing Movement Is an Attack on the Democratic Rights of the Black People and on the Unity of the Working Class," *Workers' Advocate*, December 15, 1975, https://www.marxists.org/history/erol/ncm-2/cousml-busing.htm.
93. Robert J. diGrazia, correspondence to Jean Toche, October 11, 1974. Jean Brown Papers, collection 890164, GAAG, box 23, folder 11, Getty Research Institute, Los Angeles.
94. Jean Toche, letter to FBI director Clarence Kelley, "Your withholding information in violation of the Freedom of Information Act. Appeal," November 17, 1975. Jean Brown Papers, collection 890164, GAAG, box 23, folder 12, Getty Research Institute, Los Angeles.
95. Robert J. diGrazia, correspondence to Jean Toche, October 11, 1974.
96. Jean Toche, "Open Letter to: The Mayor of Boston, Boston, Mass. (October 21, 1974)." Jean Brown Papers, collection 890164, GAAG, box 23, folder 11, Getty Research Institute, Los Angeles.
97. "Boston's Ordeal by Busing," *Newsweek*, October 21, 1974: 37.
98. Robert J. diGrazia, correspondence to Jean Toche, October 23, 1974, Jean Brown Papers, Collection 890164, GAAG, box 23, folder 11, Getty Research Center, Los Angeles, California.
99. Robert J. diGrazia, correspondence to Jean Toche, October 23, 1974.
100. Rory Judd Albert, "A Time for Reform: A Case Study of the Interaction between the Commissioner of the Boston Police Department and the Boston Police Patrolmen's Association: Technical Report," January 1975, 1–2, https://www.ncjrs.gov/pdffiles1/Digitization/25606NCJRS.pdf.
101. Albert, "Time for Reform," 5.
102. Albert, "Time for Reform," 2.
103. Stuart Schrader, "To Protect and Serve Themselves: Police in US Politics since the 1960s," *Public Culture* 31, no. 3 (2019): 609.
104. Albert, "Time for Reform," 17.
105. Albert, "Time for Reform," 17, citing a May 12, 1973, speech delivered by diGrazia to the Boston Social Welfare Seminar.
106. Albert, "Time for Reform," 48, 109.
107. Dana Chandler, phone interview with author, November 21, 2014.
108. Richard Ericson and Kevin Haggerty, *Policing the Risk Society* (Toronto: University of Toronto Press, 1997), 246.
109. Ericson and Haggerty, *Policing the Risk Society*, 246.
110. Ericson and Haggerty, *Policing the Risk Society*, 253–54.

111. Jarret S. Lovell, "Media Power and Information Control: A Study of Police Organizations and Media Relations" (PhD diss., Rutgers University, School of Criminal Justice, 2002), 2.
112. Lovell, "Media Power," 2.
113. Albert, "Time for Reform," 18.
114. Lovell, "Media Power," 16, 16–17.
115. I'm grateful to Jordana Cox for bringing forward this connection.
116. *United States v. Van Imschoot a/k/a Jean Toche*, 390 F. Supp. 994 (S.D.N.Y. 1974), https://casetext.com/case/united-states-v-van-imschoot.
117. Statement of Lucy R. Lippard, author and art critic, for Amnesty International affidavit, May 20, 1974. Jean Brown Papers, GAAG, box 23, folder 11, Getty Research Institute, Los Angeles.
118. J. Kozloff, A. Neel, Y. Rainer, et al., "On the Arrest of Jean Toche," *Artforum*, November 1974, 8.

Chapter Three

1. Darby English, "The Aesthetics of Dispossession: William Pope.L's Performance Interventions," in *How to See a Work of Art in Total Darkness* (Cambridge, MA: MIT Press, 2007), 255–311.
2. Lowry Stokes Sims, "Interview with Pope.L," in *William Pope.L: The Friendliest Black Artist in America©*, ed. Mark Bessire (Cambridge, MA: MIT Press, 2002), 62.
3. Neil V. McKittrick, 'The Homeless: Judicial Intervention on Behalf of a Politically Powerless Group," *Fordham Urban Law Journal* 16, no. 3 (1988): 427.
4. "Chronology," in *William Pope.L: The Friendliest Black Artist in America©*, 220.
5. Pope.L, audio file recording, my emphasis. *Pope.L: member, 1979–2001*, Museum of Modern Art, 2019, accessed February 2, 2020, https://www.youtube.com/watch?v=hJtmJUkc7h8.
6. Tehching Hsieh, email to author, October 20, 2021. Hsieh explains that the poster is based on the standard format of "wanted by USA" ads. Joan Kee has written that it is based on standard intake forms used to process foreign nationals. Kee, *Models of Integrity: Art and Law in Post-Sixties America* (Oakland: University of California Press, 2019), 132.
7. Kee, *Models of Integrity*, 132–39.
8. This telephone number was that of an active line. Tehching Hsieh, email correspondence with author, January 9, 2020.
9. Tehching Hsieh, correspondence with Jeannette Ingberman, January 28, 1982. Exit Art Papers, MSS 343, series I, box 283, folder 18, Fales Library, New York University.
10. Joan Kee, "Orders of Law in the *One Year Performances* of Tehching Hsieh," *American Art* 30, no. 1 (Spring 2016): 83.

11. Kee, *Models of Integrity*, 152; Larry Nathanson and Mike Pearl, "Gotta Have Art, Says Judge with a Heart," *New York Post*, June 22, 1982. Exit Art Papers, series II, subseries A, box 134, folder 5, Fales Library, New York University.
12. Jonathan Siskin, "Still Doing Time: On Tehching Hsieh," *New York: Viewpoint*. Exit Art Papers, series II, subseries A, box 134, folder 5, "Promotional materials," Fales Library, New York University.
13. Chris Thompson, "Afterbirth of a Nation: William Pope.L's Great White Way," *Women & Performance: A Journal of Feminist Theory* 14, no. 1 (2004): 67.
14. C. Carr, "In the Discomfort Zone," in Bessire, *William Pope.L*, 49.
15. Margaret Winslow, "Pope.L: The Body and Its Void," *Art Journal* (Winter 2020): 132–33; Carr, "Discomfort Zone," 50; Thompson, "Afterbirth of a Nation," 78.
16. Hilarie Sheets, "Pope.L's Group Crawl: Protest, Pathos, Provocation," *New York Times*, September 22, 2019, https://www.nytimes.com/2019/09/22/arts/design/popel-crawl-whitney-moma.html.
17. Frazer Ward, *No Innocent Bystanders: Performance Art and Audience* (Hanover, NH: Dartmouth College Press, 2012), 138.
18. Each of the yearlong performances carries a formal title, *One Year Performance*, followed by its dates. I utilize the works' more common, informal titles in this chapter.
19. Jill Johnston, "Tehching Hsieh: Art's Willing Captive," *Art in America*, September 2001, 143.
20. I'm grateful to historian Cara Caddoo for bringing out this incisive connection.
21. Kee, *Models of Integrity*, 134.
22. Jeanne Clare Feron, "Immigrants Court a New Life," May 7, 1978. *New York Times*. Section WC: 13.
23. Kee, *Models of Integrity*, 134.
24. Jeanette Ingberman, "Tehching Hsieh, One Year Performance 1981–1982" (1983), 1. Exit Art Papers, series I, box 2, folder 13, "Drafts/catalogue/final Outdoor Piece," Fales Library, New York University.
25. Kathy O'Dell, *Contract with the Skin: Masochism, Performance Art, and the 1970s* (Minneapolis: University of Minnesota Press, 1998).
26. Jeanette Ingberman, "Art and the Law in 20th Century America" (PhD diss., City University of New York, 1982), 18. Exit Art Papers, series I, box I, folder 4, Fales Library, New York University.
27. Gail Bederman, *Manliness and Civilization: A Cultural History of Gender and Race in the United States, 1880–1917* (University of Chicago Press, 1995), 221.
28. Richard Dyer, *White* (London: Routledge, 1997), 148.
29. Paul Achter, "'Military Chic' and the Rhetorical Production of the Uniformed Body," *Western Journal of Communication* 83, no. 3 (2019): 280.
30. Lara Shalson, *Performing Endurance: Art and Politics since 1960* (Cambridge: Cambridge University Press, 2018), 7, 12–13, 18.
31. Valerie Cassel Oliver, "Putting the Body on the Line: Endurance in Black Perfor-

mance," *Radical Presence: Black Performance in Contemporary Art* (Houston: Contemporary Arts Museum Houston, 2013), 14.

32. Ellen Wu, *Color of Success: Asian Americans and the Origins of the Model Minority* (Princeton, NJ: Princeton University Press, 2014), 252.
33. Kimberlé Crenshaw, "Demarginalizing the Intersection of Race and Sex: A Black Feminist Critique of Antidiscrimination Doctrine, Feminist Theory and Antiracist Politics," *University of Chicago Legal Forum*, no. 1, article 8 (1989), 139–67.
34. George Lipsitz, "Whiteness and War," in *Race, Identity, and Representation in Education*, 2nd ed., ed. Cameron McCarthy et al. (New York: Routledge, 2005), 98.
35. Lipsitz, "Whiteness and War," 96–97.
36. On Asian racialization and antiblackness, see Iyko Day, "Exclusion Acts," *Artforum*, online column, May 13, 2021, https://www.artforum.com/slant/iyko-day-on-asian-hate-through-the-prism-of-anti-blackness-85725.
37. Consider, for example, Richard Long's *A Line Made by Walking*, 1967; Vito Acconci's *Following Piece*, 1969; Yoko Ono's *Rape Piece*, 1969; Bas Jan Ader's *Fall 1* and *Fall 2*, 1970; Mierele Laderman Ukeles's *Hartford Wash*, 1973; Adrian Piper's *Mythic Being: Loitering*, 1974; Asco's *First Supper (After a Major Riot)*, 1974; Senga Nengudi's *Ceremony for Freeway Frets*, 1978; Papo Colo's *Superman 51*, 1978; Lorraine O'Grady's *Mlle Bourgeoise Noire*, 1980; David Hammons's *Bliz-aard Ball Sale*, 1983; and more.
38. In 1978, Pope.L explored the reception of "street people" in other *Meditation Square Pieces* like *Immolation Thunderbird*, a work he staged in front of Mary Boone art gallery in Soho.
39. Carr, "Discomfort Zone," 49; "chronology," *William Pope.L*, 220.
40. Martha Wilson, "William Pope.L" (interview), *BOMB*, no. 55 (Spring 1996), 51.
41. Wilson, "William Pope.L," 51.
42. Pope.L, public dialogue with Anthony Huberman, November 22, 2015, "IN. Practice Symposium," Renaissance Society, Chicago, Illinois.
43. Michael McMenamin, "From Dazzling to Dirty and Back Again: A Brief History of Times Square," Museum of the City of New York, July 14, 2015, blog, https://www.mcny.org/story/dazzling-dirty-and-back-again-brief-history-times-square
44. Katherine McKittrick, *Demonic Grounds: Black Women and the Cartographies of Struggle* (Minneapolis: University of Minnesota Press, 2006), 427.
45. Themis Chronopoulos, *Spatial Regulation in New York City: From Urban Renewal to Zero Tolerance* (New York: Routledge, 2011), 66.
46. Chronopoulos, *Spatial Regulation*, 70.
47. Fred Ferretti, "On Prostitution Row, Business Hums as Mayor Talks," *New York Times*, April 29, 1976, 42.
48. Nathaniel Sheppard Jr., "Beame and a Broadway Cast Call for Eradication of 'Porno Plague,'" *New York Times*, April 29, 1976, 42.
49. Chronopoulos, *Spatial Regulation*, 70.

50. Chronopoulos, *Spatial Regulation*, 70.
51. Chronopoulos, *Spatial Regulation*, 71.
52. McKittrick, *Demonic Grounds*, 397.
53. Anders Noren, "History of Homelessness in NYC," *Homelessness and Affordable Housing, NYC.* 2020. https://eportfolios.macaulay.cuny.edu/affordablehousingnyc/homelessness-in-nyc/
54. Rosalyn Deutsche, *Evictions: Art and Spatial Politics* (Cambridge, MA: MIT Press, 1996), 82.
55. Deutsche, *Evictions*, 73.
56. Deutsche, *Evictions*, 73.
57. Neil Smith, "Gentrification, the Frontier, and the Restructuring of Urban Space," in *Gentrification of the City*, ed. Neil Smith and Peter Williams (Boston: Allen and Unwin, 1986), 18–19.
58. McKittrick, *Demonic Grounds*, 425.
59. Fernando Natalici's photograph *Times Square* (1978) was displayed at gallery Lot 180 in 2014; http://www.lot180.com/#/times-square-1978-1/.
60. Bill Landis and Michelle Clifford, *Sleazoid Express* (Simon and Schuster, 2002); cited in https://briandanacamp.wordpress.com/2018/09/28/kung-fu-on-42nd-street/.
61. English, "Aesthetics of Dispossession," 265.
62. English, "Aesthetics of Dispossession," 261, 266.
63. English, "Aesthetics of Dispossession," 288.
64. André Lepecki, *Exhausting Dance: Performance and the Politics of Movement* (New York: Routledge, 2006), 97, 100.
65. Tiffany Barber, "William Pope.L's Budapest Crawl and Black Male Sports Bodies in Advertising in the 1990s," in *Out of Bounds: Racism and the Black Athlete* (Santa Barbara, CA: Praeger, 2014), 242–44.
66. Barber, "Budapest Crawl," 245, 241.
67. English, "Aesthetics of Dispossession," 288.
68. Jackie Wang, *Carceral Capitalism* (South Pasadena, CA: Semiotextl, 2018), 270–71.
69. Joel Trachtman, "Integrating Lawfare and Warfare," *Boston College International and Comparative Law Review* 39, no. 2 (2016): 272.
70. Ruth Wilson Gilmore in conversation with Chenjerai Kumanyika, "Ruth Wilson Gilmore Makes the Case for Abolition," *The Intercept* (podcast), June 10, 2020, https://theintercept.com/2020/06/10/ruth-wilson-gilmore-makes-the-case-for-abolition/.
71. Deutsche, *Evictions*, 279.
72. Rasul Mowatt, *The Geographies of Threat and the Production of Violence: The State and the City between Us* (New York: Routledge, 2021), 197.
73. McKittrick, "Homeless," 400.
74. Sheppard, "Beame and a Broadway Cast," 42.
75. McKittrick, "Homeless," 427.

76. David Church, *Grindhouse Nostalgia: Memory, Home Video, and Exploitation Film Fandom* (Edinburgh: Edinburgh University Press, 2015), 85, 96.
77. Brian Tochterman, *The Dying City: Postwar New York and the Ideology of Fear* (Chapel Hill: University of North Carolina Press, 2017), 178.
78. Samuel R. Delaney, *Times Square Red Times Square Blue* (1999; New York: New York University Press, 2019), 144.
79. Jack Halberstam, *In a Queer Time and Place: Transgender Bodies, Subcultural Lives* (New York: New York University Press, 2005), 13–14.
80. Wilson, "William Pope.L," 53.
81. "Pope.L: Crawl, ARTIST STORIES," produced by the Museum of Modern Art. Creative producers: Sara Bondinson and Kelly Cannon. 2019. Accessible on YouTube: https://www.youtube.com/watch?v=0N7OnQkch7s.
82. Tehching Hsieh, "Artist Biography," Sean Kelly Gallery, http://www.skny.com/artists/tehching-hsieh/bio/.
83. Jeanette Ingberman and Papo Colo, "Interview of Tehching Hsieh," *Artcom*, no. 18 (1982), 18. Exit Art Papers, series I, box 2, folder 14, Fales Library, New York University.
84. Frazer Ward, "Alien Duration: Tehching Hsieh, 1978–1999," *Art Journal* 65, no. 3 (2006): 11.
85. Ingberman and Colo, "Interview of Tehching Hsieh," 18.
86. Barry Kahn, "Sam Hsieh at Large in New York City," *Art in America*, Summer 1982, n.p.
87. Shalson, *Performing Endurance*, 131.
88. Simon Wu, "Get Out: Tehching Hsieh's Art of Survival in America," *Artforum*, June 8, 2022, https://www.artforum.com/slant/tehching-hsieh-s-art-of-survival-in-america-88707.
89. C. Carr, "The Fiery Furnace: Performance in the '80s, War in the '90s," *TDR* 49, no. 1 (Spring 2005): 20.
90. Chronopoulos, *Spatial Regulation*, 121.
91. Over a similar period, the citywide head count also fell by a third, from 31,600 in 1974 to 21,800 in 1982. *Police Department: City of New York, Annual Report 1984*, 7, https://www.ncjrs.gov/pdffiles1/Digitization/121490NCJRS.pdf.
92. Philip V. McHarris, "Disrupting Order: Race, Class, and the Roots of Policing," in *Violent Order: Essays on the Nature of Police*, ed. David Correia and Tyler Wall (Chicago: Haymarket Books, 2021), 34.
93. Wu, *Color of Success*, 198–99.
94. Wu, *Color of Success*, 182, 198.
95. James Kyung-Jin Lee, *Urban Triage: Race and the Fictions of Multiculturalism* (Minneapolis: University of Minnesota Press, 2004), 86. He cites "Success Story of One Minority Group in the U.S." *U.S. News & World Report*, December 26, 1966, 73–78, reprinted in *Roots: An Asian American Studies Reader*, ed. Amy Tachiki et al., 6–9 (Los Angeles: UCLA Asian American Studies Center, 1971).

96. Daryl Maeda, *Chains of Babylon: The Rise of Asian America* (Minneapolis: University of Minnesota Press, 2009), 1083.

97. Wu, *Color of Success*, 243.

98. Edward Morgan, *What Really Happened to the 1960s: How Mass Media Culture Failed American Democracy* (Lawrence: University Press of Kansas, 2010), 256.

99. Wu, *Color of Success*, 243. The idealized "law-abiding" stereotype of Japanese American and Chinese American citizens developed during the 1940s from different but complementary histories—Nissei and Issei recovery after internment during World War II, and the business savvy of Chinatowns—into what would become the assimilationist, nondelinquency discourse of the 1950s.

100. Kirby Farrell, "The Berserk Style in Post-Vietnam America," *Etnofoor* 13, no. 1 "Catastrophe" (2000): 15.

101. McKittrick, "Homeless," 427.

102. Ward, *No Innocent Bystanders*, 138.

103. I am grateful for Ellen Wu for drawing out this connection.

104. Jackie Wang, "Against Innocence: Race, Gender, and the Politics of Safety," in *Carceral Capitalism*, 260–95. See also *Afro-Pessimism: An Introduction* (Minneapolis: Racked & Dispatched, 2017), 11–12.

105. Tehching Hsieh, email correspondence with author. December 13, 2019.

106. Shalson, *Performing Endurance*, 133, my emphasis.

107. Kathleen Hughes, "Artist Explores Essence of the Daily Grind by Punching in Once an Hour for a Year," *Wall Street Journal*, April 24, 1981, n.p.

108. Nathanson and Pearl, "Gotta Have Art."

109. Kathleen Hughes, "Mr. Hsieh's Latest Performance: Keeping Warm Was the Easy Part," *Wall Street Journal*, July 11, 1982, 27.

110. Ingberman, "Art and the Law," 21.

111. Kee, *Models of Integrity*, 154.

112. *Afro-Pessimism*, 10; Kim TallBear, "Caretaking Relations, Not American Dreaming," *Kalfou* 6, no. 1 (2019): 24–41.

113. Richard Brilliant, "Reviewed Work," *Art Journal* 40, nos. 1–2 (1980): 431.

114. Bruce E. Mitchell, "Body Art: A Legal Policy Analysis (Jan. 1977)." In *Law, Ethics, and the Visual Arts: Cases and Materials*, ed. J. H. Merryman and A. E. Elsen (Philadelphia, PA: University of Pennsylvania Press, 1979), 3:173.

115. Mitchell, "Body Art," 3:173.

116. Mitchell, "Body Art," 3:171.

117. Mitchell, "Body Art," 3:173–74.

118. Mitchell, "Body Art," 3:174.

119. Mitchell, "Body Art," 3:175.

120. Ingberman and Colo, "Interview of Tehching Hsieh," 18.

121. *Illegal America* was the inaugural show for Exit Art, an alternative art space that Ingberman and Papo Colo later formalized at 548 Broadway in Soho.

122. Kate Linker, "Illegal America: Exhibition Review," *Artforum*, May 1982, n.p. Exit Art Papers, series I, box 1, folder 17, "Press clippings, 1981–2001," Fales Library, New York University.
123. Anna Pegler-Gordon, *In Sight of America: Photography and the Development of U.S. Immigration Policy* (Berkeley: University of California Press, 2009), 1–3.
124. On racial tensions in Chin's assault and trial, see Joshua Chambers-Letson, *A Race So Different: Performance and Law in Asian American* (New York: New York University Press, 2012), 89; Frank Wu, "Why Vincent Chin Matters," *New York Times*, June 22, 2012, http://www.nytimes.com/2012/06/23/opinion/why-vincent-chin-matters.html.
125. Lipsitz, "Whiteness and War," 80.
126. John Perreault, "Crimes of the Art," *Soho News*, March 2, 1982, 45; Exit Art Papers, series I, box I, folder 17, "Press clippings, 1982–2001," Fales Library, New York University.
127. Perreault, "Crimes of Art," 45.
128. Mitchell, "Body Art," 3:163.
129. Alexander, *New Jim Crow*, 136.
130. Allan Feldman, *Formations of Violence: The Narrative of the Body and Political Terror in Northern Ireland* (Chicago: University of Chicago Press, 1991), 109; cited in Ruth Wilson Gilmore, "Terror Austerity Race Gender Excess Theater," *Reading Rodney King/Reading Urban Uprising*, ed. Robert Gooding-Williams (New York: Routledge, 1993), 28.
131. McHarris, "Disrupting Order," 35.

Chapter Four

1. Josephine Withers, "Art Essay: The Guerrilla Girls," *Feminist Studies* 14, no. 2 (Summer 1988): 287.
2. Anna Chave, "The Guerrilla Girls' Reckoning," *Art Journal* 70, no. 2 (Summer 2011): 104; some minor discrepancies regarding the exact number exists in the discourse. See Ruben Cordova, "Taking It to the Street: The Guerrilla Girls' Struggle for Diversity," *Glasstire: Texas Visual Art*, November 28, 2021, https://glasstire.com/2021/11/28/taking-it-to-the-street-the-guerrilla-girls-struggle-for-diversity/.
3. Withers, "Art Essay," 285.
4. Chave, "Guerrilla Girls' Reckoning," 104.
5. Roberta Smith, "Waging Guerrilla Warfare against the Art World," *New York Times*, June 17, 1990, 1.
6. Chave, "Guerrilla Girls' Reckoning," 111.
7. Elizabeth Hess, "Guerrilla Girl Power: Why the Art World Needs a Conscience," in *But Is It Art? The Spirit of Art as Activism*, ed. Nina Felshin (Seattle: Bay Press, 1995), 327.

8. Julia de Burgos and Hannah Höch (Guerrilla Girls), oral history interview with Judith Olch Richards, Smithsonian American Art Archives, May 8, 2008.
9. Julia de Burgos, oral history interview, 2008.
10. "Gertrude Stein" et al., "Guerrilla Girls and Guerrilla Girls BroadBand: Inside Story," *Art Journal* 70, no. 2 (Summer 2011): 93.
11. Godzilla: Asian American Art Network, founded in 1990, may be another group with this origin story.
12. Howardena Pindell, interview with author, September 9, 2020. Pindell also discussed her hesitancy to publicize her role in PESTS in an interview with Uri McMillan. See McMillan, *Embodied Avatars: Genealogies of Black Feminist Art and Performance* (New York: New York University Press, 2015), 185.
13. Pindell, interview, 2020.
14. Howardena Pindell, letter to Martha Wilson, 1986. "Women of Color Research, 1986," Guerrilla Girls Records, box 6, folder 6, 2008.M.14, Getty Research Institute, Los Angeles.
15. Pindell, letter to Martha Wilson, 1986.
16. L. P., unpublished letter, 1987. Guerrilla Girls Records, box 30, folder 4, 2008.M.14, Getty Research Institute, Los Angeles.
17. PESTS, letter of solicitation, December 6, 1986. Guerrilla Girls Records, box 7, folder 1, 2008.M.14, Getty Research Institute, Los Angeles.
18. Chave, "Guerrilla Girls' Reckoning," 106. See also Trevor Stark, "Guerrilla Girls," in *This Will Have Been: Art, Love, and Politics in the 1980s* (New Haven, CT: Yale University Press, 2012), 181–83; McMillan, *Embodied Avatars*, 183.
19. Withers, "Art Essay," 289.
20. Sara Nogueira Silva and Chris Reed, "You Can't Always Get What You Want: Relative Anonymity in Cyberspace," *Scripted: A Journal of Law, Technology & Society* 12, no. 1 (2015): 37.
21. Jacquelyn Burkell, "Anonymity in Behavioral Research: Not Being Unnamed, But Being Unknown," *University of Ottawa Law and Technology Journal* (2006): 192.
22. Burkell, "Anonymity," 189.
23. Jasbir Puar, *Terrorist Assemblages: Homonationalism in Queer Times* (Durham, NC: Duke University Press, 2007), 124–25.
24. Hess, "Guerrilla Girl Power," 313.
25. See Cynthia Enloe, *Bananas, Beaches, and Babes: Making Feminist Sense of International Politics* (Berkeley: University of California Press, 1990); Alison Howell, "Forget 'Militarization': Race, Disability and the 'Martial Politics' of the Police and of the University," *International Feminist Journal of Politics* 20, no. 2 (2018): 117–36; Puar, *Terrorist Assemblages*; Josh Cerretti, *Abuses of the Erotic: Militarizing Sexuality in the Post–Cold War United States* (Lincoln: University of Nebraska Press, 2019).
26. Micol Siegel, *Violence Work: State Power and the Limits of Police* (Durham, NC: Duke University Press, 2018).

27. Dinah Prince, "Warfare in the World of Art," *Daily News*, October 16, 1985, 41.
28. For a history of guerrilla marketing, see Michael Serazio, *Your Ad Here: The Cool Sell of Guerrilla Marketing* (New York: New York University Press, 2013).
29. Guerrilla Girls, *Guerrilla Girls: The Art of Behaving Badly* (San Francisco: Chronicle Books, 2020), 9.
30. Cordova, "Taking It to the Street," 2021; Jane Bowles and Alma Thomas (Guerrilla Girls), oral history interview with Judith Olch Richards, Smithsonian American Art Archives, May 8, 2008.
31. Jane Bowles and Alma Thomas, oral history interview, 2008.
32. J. Phillip Thompson, "Broken Policing: The Origins of the 'Broken Windows' Policy," *New Labor Forum* 24, no. 2 (Spring 2015): 44
33. Lena Williams, "Spray Paint Sales Curbed in Graffiti War," *New York Times,* October 6, 1985, 56.
34. Mira Schor, "Girls Will Be Girls," *Artforum* 29, no. 1 (September 1990): 126.
35. Ellen Lubell, "Collage," *Village Voice*, December 10, 1985, 94.
36. Prince, "Warfare in the World of Art," 41.
37. Prince, "Warfare in the World of Art," 41.
38. Withers, "Art Essay," 286.
39. Paul Taylor, "Where the Girls Are," *Corporate Culture,* April 1987, 178.
40. Withers, "Art Essay," 286–87.
41. Frida Kahlo and Käthe Kollwitz, "Transgressive Techniques of the Guerrilla Girls," *Getty Research Journal*, no. 2 (2010), 203–8.
42. Stephen Salisbury, "Getting Militant about Women's Art," *Register* (Philadelphia), March 7, 1986, 3D.
43. Salisbury, "Getting Militant," 3D.
44. Lucy Lippard, "New Feminist Artists Show They Have a Mean Sense of Humor," *In These Times*, nos. 13–19 (November 1985), 20.
45. Walter Laqueur, "Interpretations of Terrorism: Fact, Fiction, and Political Science," *Journal of Contemporary History* 12, no. 1 (Jan. 1977): 1–42.
46. Puar, *Terrorist Assemblages*, xxiii.
47. Klare, "Interventionist Impulse," 63.
48. Suzi Gablik, "'We spell it like the Freedom Fighters': A Conversation with the Guerrilla Girls," *Art in America*, January 1994, 43.
49. Pippa Oldfield, "Calling the Shots: Women's Photographic Engagement with War in Hemispheric America, 1910–1990" (PhD diss., Durham University, 2016), 200–202, http://etheses.dur.ac.uk/11786/.
50. Peter Kornbluh, "Nicaragua: U.S. Proinsurgency Warfare against the Sandinistas," in *Low-Intensity Warfare*, 155.
51. Statement by Principal Deputy Press Secretary on the Achille Lauro Hijacking Incident, October 10, 1985, Ronald Reagan Presidential Library and Museum, https://

www.reaganlibrary.gov/archives/speech/statement-principal-deputy-press-secretary-speakes-achille-lauro-hijacking-incident.

52. L. P., correspondence with Guerrilla Girls, 1986. Guerrilla Girls Records, box 30, folder 4, 2008.M.14. Getty Research Institute, Los Angeles. Though undated, the letter was likely written in December 1986, as the author signs off, "I wish you all a Happy 1987."

53. William J. Choyke, "Experts: Determined Terrorism Unstoppable," *Philadelphia Inquirer*, March 7, 1986, 6B.

54. Sohail Daulatzai, *Black Star, Crescent Moon: The Muslim International and Black Freedom Beyond America* (Minneapolis: University of Minnesota Press, 2012), 89–90.

55. Puar, *Terrorist Assemblages*, 14–15.

56. Kathleen Belew, *Bring the War Home: The White Power Movement and Paramilitary America* (Cambridge, MA: Harvard University Press, 2018), 140–57.

57. Belew, *Bring the War Home*, 96.

58. Belew, *Bring the War Home*, 127.

59. Amanda Third, "Mediating the Female Terrorist: Patricia Hearst and the Containment of the Feminist Terrorist Threat in the United States in the 1970s," *Historical Social Research* 39, no. 3 (2014): 159.

60. Fattal, *Guerrilla Marketing*, 4.

61. Erina Duganne, "*The Nicaragua Media Project* and the Limits of Postmodernism," *Art Bulletin* 100, no. 1 (2018): 152.

62. Art Harris, "Sandinistas' Sister-in-Arms," *Washington Post*, October 4, 1984, n.p.

63. Harris, "Sandinistas' Sister-in-Arms," 1984.

64. Fattal, *Guerrilla Marketing*, 4.

65. L. P., correspondence, 1985. Guerrilla Girls Records, box 30, folder 2, 2008.M.14, Getty Research Institute, Los Angeles.

66. Guerrilla Girls, drafted recruitment letter, 1986. Guerrilla Girls Records, box 30, folder 3, 2008.M14, Getty Research Institute, Los Angeles.

67. Withers, "Art Essay," 285, 287.

68. "Alma Thomas" (Guerrilla Girl), oral history interview, 2008.

69. According to the group's chronology, the Guerrilla Girls' 1992 poster *Supreme Court Justice Supports Right to Privacy for Gays and Lesbians* is the first to address LGBTQ issues. See "The Guerrilla Girls' Complete Chronology," https://www.guerrillagirls.com/chronology-posters-books-stickers-actions.

70. Priscilla Wald. *Contagious: Cultures, Carriers, and the Outbreak Narrative* (Durham, NC: Duke University Press, 2008), 157.

71. Mary Ann Meyers, "AIDS: The Stranger in Our House," *Pennsylvania Gazette*, May 1988, 17.

72. Hess, "Guerrilla Girl Power," 324.

73. Edwards, *Other Side of Terror*, 60.
74. Pindell, interview, 2020.
75. PESTS newsletter, vol. 1, no. 3, "PESTS STRIP" (Fall/Winter 1987): 5.
76. In October 1986, the US Congress overturned President Reagan's veto of the Comprehensive Anti-Apartheid Act, passing it into law and imposing restrictions on economic transactions with South Africa. For an example of how anti-apartheid struggles were represented in contemporary art discourse see Allan Sekula, "The Body and the Archive," *October*, no. 39 (Winter 1986), 3–64.
77. PESTS newsletter, vol. 1, no. 3, "PESTS STRIP" (Fall/Winter 1987): 5.
78. Cordova, "Taking It to the Street," 2021.
79. Pindell, interview, 2020.
80. PESTS newsletter, vol. 1, no. 2, "PESTS STRIP," 1987. "P.E.S.T.S, 1986–89," Guerrilla Girls Records, box 7, folder 1, collection 2008.M.14, Getty Research Institute, Los Angeles.
81. PESTS newsletter, vol 1, no. 3, "PESTS STRIP" (Fall/Winter, 1987): 6.
82. McMillan, *Embodied Avatars*, 190, 194.
83. PESTS newsletter, vol 1, no. 3, "PESTS STRIP" (Fall/Winter, 1987): 4.
84. Kornbluh, "Nicaragua," 154.
85. Edwards, *Other Side of Terror*, 203; citing Toni Cade Bambara, "Community," box 3, Toni Cade Bambara Papers, Spelman College Archives, n.d.
86. Howardena Pindell, "Introduction," in *Autobiography: In Her Own Image* (New York: Gallery, 1988), 8.
87. PESTS newsletter, vol. 1, no. 3, "PESTS STRIP" (Fall/Winter, 1987): 7.
88. Withers, "Art Essay," 285; Hess, "Guerrilla Girl Power," 331.
89. Michael Selmi, "The Evolution of Employment Discrimination Law: Changed Doctrine for Changed Social Conditions," *GW Law Faculty Publications & Other Works*, no. 1110 (2014), 1.
90. Selmi, "Evolution," 4.
91. Selmi, "Evolution," 12.
92. Dean Spade, "Trans Laws and Politics on a Neoliberal Landscape," *Temple Political and Civil Rights Law Review* 18 (2009): 361.
93. Spade, "Trans Laws," 363.
94. Puar, *Terrorist Assemblages*, 27.
95. Hanhardt, *Safe Space*, 162.
96. Howardena Pindell, "Sticks and Stones (1988)," in *The Heart of the Question: The Writings and Paintings of Howardena Pindell* (New York: Midmarch Arts Press, 1997), 31.
97. Chave, "Guerrilla Girls' Reckoning," 104.
98. "Notes for Guerrilla Girls big meeting," Guerrilla Girls Records, box 30, folder 2, "1985," 2008.M.14, Getty Research Institute, Los Angeles.
99. Chave, "Guerrilla Girls' Reckoning," 110.

100. Nadja Sayej, "The Guerrilla Girls: 'We upend the art world's notion of what's good and what's right,'" *Guardian*, October 19, 2020, https://www.theguardian.com/artanddesign/2020/oct/19/the-guerrilla-girls-interview-art-world-rebels.

Epilogue

1. Zachary Small, "Artist Mounts Guerrilla Art Exhibition at Whitney Calling for Removal of Vice Chairman," *Hyperallergic*, December 11, 2018, https://hyperallergic.com/475476/artist-mounts-guerrilla-art-exhibition-at-whitney-calling-for-removal-of-vice-chairman/.
2. Tara Law, "The Story behind the Photo of a Family Running from Tear Gas at the U.S.-Mexico Border," *Time*, November 27, 2018. https://time.com/5464560/caravan-mexico-border-iconic-photo/.
3. Alex Greenberger, "To Remain Silent Is to Be Complicit: Whitney Staff Demand Action against Museum's Vice Chair of Board," *ARTnews*, November 30, 2018. https://www.artnews.com/art-news/news/remain-silent-complicit-whitney-staff-demand-action-museums-vice-chair-board-11437/.
4. Rafael Shimunov, interview with author, March 9, 2022.
5. Andrew W. Mellon Foundation, "Art Museum Staff Demographic Survey 2018," January 28, 2019, https://mellon.org/media/filer_public/b1/21/b1211ce7-5478-4a06-92df-3c88fa472446/sr-mellon-report-art-museum-staff-demographic-survey-01282019.pdf.
6. Jerald Pierce, "A Frye Art Museum Security Guard Takes Us on a Tour of His Favorite Piece," *Seattle Times*, August 18, 2022, https://www.seattletimes.com/entertainment/visual-arts/a-frye-art-museum-security-guard-takes-us-on-a-tour-of-his-favorite-pieces/; "Guarding the Art," Baltimore Museum of Art, March 27–July 10, 2022, https://artbma.org/exhibition/bma-security-officers-take-center-stage-as-guest-curators-of-a-new-exhibition-opening-in-march-2022/.
7. Sara Barnes, "Art Museum Security Guards Are Moonlighting as Curators to Arrange a Special Exhibition," *My Modern Met*, February 24, 2022, https://mymodernmet.com/baltimore-museum-of-art-guarding-the-art/.
8. Stefan Romer, "The *Inter-esse* When Pressing the Shutter-Release Button: For an Epistemology of Contentious and Committed Art Photography," in *The Militant Image Reader* (Graz: Camera Austria, 2015), 60.
9. Jean Toche, conversation with author, June 5, 2014.
10. Toche, conversation with author, 2014.
11. Toche, 2014.
12. Harry Gamboa Jr., phone conversation with author, March 3, 2018.
13. In September 2020, Pindell openly acknowledged in an interview that she began and organized PESTS. See Jillian Steinhauer, "At 77, Howardena Pindell Exorcises a

Chilling Memory from Childhood," *New York Times,* October 16, 2020, https://www.nytimes.com/2020/10/16/arts/design/howardena-pindell-shed-video.html.

14. Adrian Piper, *Escape to Berlin: A Travel Memoir* (Verlag: APRA Foundation Berlin, 2018).
15. Adrian Piper, "Personal Chronology," http://www.adrianpiper.com/personal_chrono.shtml.
16. Hawa Allen, "Fight or Flight: On Adrian Piper and the Escape to Freedom," *The Epiphanic,* July 9, 2018, https://epiphanyzine.com/features/2020/7/9/fight-or-flight-on-adrian-piper-and-the-escape-to-freedom.
17. Critical Art Ensemble, "Not So Quiet on the Western Front: A Report on Risk and Cultural Resistance within the Neoliberal Society of Fear," in *The Aesthetics of Risk,* vol. 3 of SoCCAS [Southern California Consortium of Art Schools] Symposia (Distributed Art Publishers, 2008), 360, 365.
18. Jordan T. Camp provides an excellent study of this oversight in *Incarcerating the Crisis: Freedom Struggles and the Rise of the Neoliberal State* (Oakland: University of California Press, 2016). For examples of texts that have pushed for the challenging of previous periodization and fragmentation, see Laia Barcells and Stathis Kalyvas, "International System and Technologies of Rebellion," *American Political Science Review* 104, no. 3 (2010): 415–29; Patrick Johnston and Seth Jones, "The Future of Insurgency," *Studies in Conflict and Terrorism* 36, no 1 (2013): 1–25; Edwards, *Other Side of Terror.*
19. Sarah Ahmed, *The Cultural Politics of Emotion* (New York: Routledge, 2004), 78.
20. Ahmed, *Cultural Politics of Emotion,* 79, emphasis in original.
21. "If You See Something Say Something Campaign," Campaign Partnership Guide, US Department of Homeland Security. https://www.dhs.gov/sites/default/files/publications/SeeSay-Overview508_1.pdf.
22. Stuart Schrader, "To Protect and Serve Themselves: Police in US Politics since the 1960s," *Public Culture* 31, no. 3 (2019): 602.
23. Andrew Ferguson, "Policing Predictive Policing," *Washington University Law Review* 94, no. 5 (2017): 1126.
24. Ferguson, "Policing Predictive Policing," 1113.
25. Ferguson, "Policing Predictive Policing," 1189.
26. Ellen Huet, "Server and Protect: Predictive Policing Firm PredPol Promises to Map Crime before It Happens," *Forbes,* February 11, 2015, https://www.forbes.com/sites/ellenhuet/2015/02/11/predpol-predictive-policing/?sh=5d6873164f9b.
27. Jackie Wang, *Carceral Capitalism* (South Pasadena, CA: semiotext(e), 2018), 41.
28. Brian Jefferson, *Digitize and Punish: Racial Criminalization in the Digital Age* (Minneapolis: University of Minnesota Press, 2020), 154–55.
29. Jefferson, *Digitize and Punish,* 156.
30. Jefferson, *Digitize and Punish,* 175.
31. Aaron Mak, "What Three Cities Are Spending on Police Compared with Everything

Else," June 19, 2020, https://slate.com/news-and-politics/2020/06/what-los-angeles-minneapolis-dallas-police-spend.html.

32. Mak, "What Three Cities Are Spending," 2020.
33. The Sentencing Project, "The Color of Justice: Racial and Ethnic Disparty in State Prisons," Accessed November 4, 2022, https://www.sentencingproject.org/app/uploads/2022/08/The-Color-of-Justice-Racial-and-Ethnic-Disparity-in-State-Prisons.pdf.
34. Million Dollar Hoods was founded in 2016 by Dr. Kelly Lytle Hernández and Dr. Danielle Dupuy in partnership with advocacy groups working to decarcerate California; https://milliondollarhoods.pre.ss.ucla.edu/.
35. Amina Cruz, phone conversation with author, February 23, 2022.
36. Cruz, phone conversation, 2022.
37. Lavie Raven interviewed by Rebecca Zorach, "Our Kids Don't Invent Guns," in *Art against the Law*, ed. Rebecca Zorach (Chicago: University of Chicago Press, 2015), 124.
38. Joy Harris, "New Anti-Riot Bills Threaten the Work of Social Practice Artists," *Hyperallergic*, August 19, 2021, https://hyperallergic.com/670742/new-anti-riot-bills-threaten-work-of-social-practice-artists/.
39. "A Judge Has Blocked the 'Anti-Riot' Law Passed in Florida after George Floyd Protests," National Public Radio/Associated Press, September 9, 2021, transcript at https://www.npr.org/2021/09/09/1035687247/florida-anti-riot-law-ron-desantis-george-floyd-black-lives-matter-protests.
40. Harris, "New Anti-Riot Bills."
41. Harris, "New Anti-Riot Bills."
42. Harris, "New Anti-Riot Bills."
43. Ren-yo Hwang, "Deviant Care for Deviant Futures: QTBIPoC Radical Relationalism as Mutual Aid against Carceral Care," *TSQ: Transgender Studies Quarterly* 6, no. 4 (2019): 567.
44. Sonic Insurgency Research Group, "About," Artist website, accessed March 2, 2022, https://www.s-i-r-g.net/about.
45. Josh Rios and Matt Joynt, "Notes on the Siren and Social Space," in *Spatial Justice 2.0: A Frame for Reclaiming Our Rights to Be, Thrive, Express, and Connect*, Design Studio for Social Intervention digital zine, p.13, accessed February 5, 2022, https://static1.squarespace.com/static/53c7166ee4b0e7db2be69480/t/5e629defadbcb60d977ec927/1583521265858/spatial_justice_zine_digital.pdf.
46. Rios and Joynt, "Notes on the Siren," 16. Rios and Joynt share that the Rumbler uses technology patented in the making of the Octavium, the first known subwoofer created in 1964 by Ramon Dones of El Cerrito, CA.
47. Rios and Joynt, "Notes on the Siren," 13, 14.

Bibliography

Achter, Paul. "'Military Chic' and the Rhetorical Production of the Uniformed Body." *Western Journal of Communication* 83, no. 3 (2019): 265–85.

Afro-Pessimism: An Introduction. Minneapolis: Racked & Dispatched, 2017. https://rackedanddispatched.noblogs.org/pdfs/

Ahmed, Sara. *The Cultural Politics of Emotion*. New York: Routledge, 2004.

——. *Queer Phenomenology: Orientations, Objects, Others*. Durham, NC: Duke University Press, 2006.

Albert, Rory Judd. "A Time for Reform: A Case Study of the Interaction between the Commissioner of the Boston Police Department and the Boston Police Patrolmen's Association: Technical Report." January 1975. Accessed July 20, 2020, https://www.ncjrs.gov/pdffiles1/Digitization/25606NCJRS.pdf

Alexander, Michelle. *The New Jim Crow: Mass Incarceration in the Age of Colorblindness*. New York: New Press, 2010.

Alpert, Geoffry P., John M. MacDonald, and Roger G. Dunham. "Police Suspicion and Discretionary Decision Making during Citizen Stops." *Criminology* 43, no. 2 (May 2005): 407–34.

Alvarado, Leticia. *Abject Performances: Aesthetic Strategies in Latino Cultural Production*. Durham, NC: Duke University Press, 2018.

Andrew W. Mellon Foundation. "Art Museum Staff Demographic Survey 2018." January 28, 2019. https://mellon.org/media/filer_public/b1/21/b1211ce7-5478-4a06-92df-3c88fa472446/sr-mellon-report-art-museum-staff-demographic-survey-01282019.pdf

Armstrong, Simon. *Street Art*. London: Thames & Hudson, 2019.

Ault, Julia. *Alternative Art New York, 1965–1985*. New York: Social Text Collective, 2002.

Ayres, Anne, Chris Burden, and Paul Schimmel, eds. *Chris Burden: A Twenty-Year Survey*. Newport Beach, CA: Newport Harbor Art Museum, 1988.

Baker, Tom, and Jonathan Simon. *Embracing Risk: The Changing Culture of Insurance and Responsibility*. Chicago: University of Chicago Press, 2002.

Baldessari, John, Thomas Crow, Harry Gamboa Jr., Liz Larner, Andrew Perchuk, Ali Subotnick, Maurice Tuchman, and Helene Winer; Richard Meyer and Michelle Kuo, moderators. "L.A. Stories: A Roundtable." *Artforum*, October 2011, 240–49.

Barber, Tiffany. "William Pope.L's Budapest Crawl and Black Male Sports Bodies in Advertising in the 1990s." In *Out of Bounds: Racism and the Black Athlete*, 231–54. Santa Barbara, CA: Praeger, 2014.

Barnes, Sara. "Art Museum Security Guards Are Moonlighting as Curators to Arrange a Special Exhibition." *My Modern Met*, February 24, 2022. https://mymodernmet.com/baltimore-museum-of-art-guarding-the-art

Beck, Ulrich. "Foreword: Risk Society as Political Category." In *The Risk Society Revisited: Social Theory and Governance*, ed. Eugene Rosa et al., xiii–xxiii. Philadelphia: Temple University Press, 2014.

Bederman, Gail. *Manliness and Civilization: A Cultural History of Gender and Race in the United States, 1880–1917*. Chicago: University of Chicago Press, 1995.

Belew, Kathleen. *Bring the War Home: The White Power Movement and Paramilitary America*. Cambridge, MA: Harvard University Press, 2018.

Benavidez, Max, and Kate Vozoff. "The Wall: Image and Boundary, Chicano Art in the 1970s." In *Mexican Art of the 1970s: Images of Displacement*, 48–55. Nashville, TN: Center for Latin American and Iberian Studies, Vanderbilt University, 1984.

Berns, Jordan. "Is There Something Suspicious about the Constitutionality of Loitering Laws?" *Ohio State Law Journal* 50, no. 3 (1989): 717–36.

Bessire, Mark, ed. *William Pope.L: The Friendliest Black Artist in America©*. Cambridge, MA: MIT Press, 2002.

Bewley, Jon, and Jonty Tarbuck. *Chris Burden*. Newcastle: Locus+, 2007.

Bishop, Claire. *Artificial Hells: Participatory Art and the Politics of Spectatorship*. New York: Verso, 2012.

Blocker, Jane. "Aestheticizing Risk in Wartime: The SLA to Iraq (2006)." In *The Aesthetics of Risk*. Vol. 3 of SoCCAS [Southern California Consortium of Art Schools] Symposia, 191–223. Distributed Art Publishers, 2008.

Boal, Augusto. *Theatre of the Oppressed*. Trans. Charles A. McBride and Maria-Odilia Leal McBride. New York: Urizen Books, 1979.

Bonilla-Silva, Eduardo. *Racism without Racists: Color-Blind Racism and the Persistence of Racial Inequality in America*. Lanham, MD: Rowman & Littlefield, 2014.

Bowles, John. *Adrian Piper: Race, Gender, and Embodiment*. Durham, NC: Duke University Press, 2011.

Bradford, Martin. *The Theater Is in the Street: Politics and Performance in Sixties America*. Amherst: University of Massachusetts Press, 2004.

Brookman, Philip, and Amy Brookman. "Interview with ASCO." *CALIFAS: Chicano Art and

Culture in California, Transcripts, book 3. Collection Tloque Nahauque. University of California at Santa Barbara Davidson Library, 1983.

Browne, Simone. *Dark Matter: On the Surveillance of Blackness*. Durham, NC: Duke University Press, 2015.

Bruce, La Merr Jurelle. "Shore, Unsure: Loitering as a Way of Life." *GLQ: A Journal of Lesbian and Gay Studies* 25, no. 2 (April 2019): 352–61.

Bryan-Wilson, Julia. *Art Workers: Radical Practice in the Vietnam War Era*. Berkeley: University of California Press, 2009.

Burkell, Jacquelyn. "Anonymity in Behavioural Research: Not Being Unnamed, but Being Unknown." *University of Ottawa Law and Technology Journal* (2006): 191–203.

Burnham, Laura. "Asco: Camus, Daffy Duck, and Devil Girls from East L.A." *L.A. Style*, February 1987.

Byrd, Antawan. "Medu's Operative and Aesthetic Montage." In *The People Shall Govern! Medu Art Ensemble and the Anti-Apartheid Poster, 1979–1985*, 26–33. New Haven, CT: Yale University Press, 2020.

Calirman, Claudia. *Brazilian Art under Dictatorship: Antonio Manuel, Artur Barrio, and Cildo Meireles*. Durham, NC: Duke University Press, 2012.

Camnitzer, Luis. *Conceptualism in Latin American Art: Didactics of Liberation*. Austin: University of Texas Press, 2007.

Camp, Jordan T. *Incarcerating the Crisis: Freedom Struggles and the Rise of the Neoliberal State*. Oakland: University of California Press, 2016.

Campt, Tina. *Listening to Images*. Durham, NC: Duke University Press, 2017.

Carillo, Sean. "'*¡Tenemos Asco!*' An Oral History of the Chicano Art Group." *Frieze*, no. 224. January 4, 2022. https://www.frieze.com/article/tenemos-asco-oral-history-chicano-art-group

Carr, C. "The Fiery Furnace: Performance in the '80s, War in the '90s." *TDR* 49, no. 1 (Spring 2005): 19–28.

———. "In the Discomfort Zone." In *William Pope.L: The Friendliest Black Artist in America©*, ed. Mark Bessire, 48–53. Cambridge, MA: MIT Press, 2002.

Carvalho, Henrique, Anastasia Chamberlen, and Rachel Lewis. "Punitiveness beyond Criminal Justice: Punishable and Punitive Subjects in an Era of Prevention, Anti-Migration, and Austerity." *British Journal of Criminology* 60, no. 2 (March 2020): 265–84. https://doi.org/10.1093/bjc/azz061

Cassel Oliver, Valerie. "Putting the Body on the Line: Endurance in Black Performance." In *Radical Presence: Black Performance in Contemporary Art*, 14–19. Houston: Contemporary Arts Museum Houston, 2013.

Castillo, Monica. "Overlooked No More: Ana Mendieta, a Cuban Artist Who Pushed Boundaries." *New York Times*, September 19, 2018. https://www.nytimes.com/2018/09/19/obituaries/ana-mendieta-overlooked.html

Castro, Fidel. *Fidel Castro's Tribute to Che Guevara*. New York: Merit, 1967.

Cerretti, Josh. *Abuses of the Erotic: Militarizing Sexuality in the Post–Cold War United States.* Lincoln: University of Nebraska Press, 2019.

Certeau, Michel de. *The Practice of Everyday Life.* Trans. Steven Rendall. Berkeley: University of California Press, 1984.

Chambers-Letson, Joshua Takano. *A Race So Different: Performance and Law in Asian America.* New York: New York University Press, 2013.

Chave, Anna. "The Guerrilla Girls' Reckoning." *Art Journal* 70, no. 2 (Summer 2011): 103–11.

Chavoya, C. Ondine. "Fleeting Inscriptions: Asco, Ephemera, and Intergroup Exchange in LA." *Living Collections Catalogue* (Walker Art Center), Spring/Summer 2020. https://walkerart.org/collections/publications/side-by-side/artists-groups-in-los-angeles-asco-and-los-four

———. "Internal Exiles: The Interventionist Public and Performance Art of Asco." In *Space, Site, Intervention: Situating Installation Art,* ed. Erika Suderberg, 189–208. Minneapolis: University of Minnesota Press, 2000.

———. "No-Movies: The Art of False Documents." In *Only Skin Deep: Changing Visions of the American Self,* ed. Coco Fusco and Brian Wallis, 199–203. New York: International Center of Photography/Harry N. Abrams, 2003.

———. "Orphans of Modernism: The Performance of Asco." In *Corpus Delecti: Performance Art of the Americas,* ed. Coco Fusco. New York: Routledge, 2000.

———. "Pseudographic Cinema: Asco's No-Movies." *Performance Research: A Journal of the Performing Arts* 3, no. 1 (1998): 1–14.

Chavoya, C. Ondine, and Rita Gonzalez, eds. *Asco: Elite of the Obscure, a Retrospective, 1972–1987.* Ostfildern, Germany: Hatje Cantz, 2011.

Choyke, William J. "Experts: Determined Terrorism Unstoppable." *Register* (Philadelphia), March 7, 1986, 6B.

Chronopoulos, Themis. *Spatial Regulation in New York City: From Urban Renewal to Zero Tolerance.* New York: Routledge, 2011.

Church, David. *Grindhouse Nostalgia: Memory, Home Video, and Exploitation Film Fandom.* Edinburgh: Edinburgh University Press, 2015.

Cohen, Cathy. "Deviance as Resistance: A New Research Agenda for the Study of Black Politics." *Du Bois Review* 1, no. 1 (2004): 27–45.

Copeland, Huey. "*Babel* Screened: On Race, Narcissism, and the Predication of American Video Art." In *Black Is, Black Ain't,* 44–55. Chicago: Renaissance Society/University of Chicago Press, 2013.

———. *Bound to Appear: Art, Slavery, and the Site of Blackness in Multicultural America.* Chicago: University of Chicago Press, 2013.

Cordova, Ruben. "Taking It to the Street: The Guerrilla Girls' Struggle for Diversity." *Glasstire: Texas Visual Art,* November 28, 2021. https://glasstire.com/2021/11/28/taking-it-to-the-street-the-guerrilla-girls-struggle-for-diversity/

Costello, Diarmuid. "Xenophobia, Stereotypes, and Empirical Acculturation: Neo-

Kantianism in Adrian Piper's Performance-based Conceptual Art." In *Adrian Piper: A Reader*, 166–215. New York: Museum of Modern Art, 2018.

Crenshaw, Kimberlé. "Demarginalizing the Intersection of Race and Sex: A Black Feminist Critique of Antidiscrimination Doctrine, Feminist Theory and Antiracist Politics." *University of Chicago Legal Forum*, no. 1 (1989), 139–67.

Critical Art Ensemble. "Not So Quiet on the Western Front: A Report on Risk and Cultural Resistance within the Neoliberal Society of Fear." In *The Aesthetics of Risk*. Vol. 3 of SoCCAS [Southern California Consortium of Art Schools] Symposia, 357–75. Distributed Art Publishers, 2008.

Daulatzai, Sohail. *Black Star, Crescent Moon: The Muslim International and Black Freedom beyond America*. Minneapolis: University of Minnesota Press, 2012.

Davis, Angela. *Are Prisons Obsolete?* New York: Seven Stories, 2003.

Davis, Douglas. "Death for Art's Sake." *Newsweek*, December 24, 1973, 68.

Davis, Mike. "Chinatown, Part Two? The 'Internationalization' of Downtown Los Angeles." *New Left Review*, no.164 (July/August 1987), 65–86.

Day, Iyko. "Exclusion Acts." *Artforum*, online column, May 13, 2021. Accessed January 2022, https://www.artforum.com/slant/iyko-day-on-asian-hate-through-the-prism-of-anti-blackness-85725

Delaney, Samuel R. *Times Square Red Times Square Blue*. 1999; New York: New York University Press, 2019.

Deutsche, Rosalyn. *Evictions: Art and Spatial Politics*. Cambridge, MA: MIT Press, 1996.

Dirlik, Arif. "The Third World." In *1968: The World Transformed*, 295–318. Cambridge: Cambridge University Press, 1998.

Dominick, Joseph R. "Crime and Law Enforcement on Prime-Time Television." *Public Opinion Quarterly* 34, no. 2 (Summer 1973): 241–50.

Duganne, Erina. "*The Nicaragua Media Project* and the Limits of Postmodernism." *Art Bulletin* 100, no. 1 (March 2018): 146–68.

Dunbar-Ortiz, Roxanne. *An Indigenous Peoples' History of the United States*. Boston: Beacon, 2014.

Dyer, Richard. *White*. London: Routledge, 1997.

Eaglin, Jessica. "Technologically Distorted Conceptions of Punishment." *Washington University Law Review* 97 (2019): 483–543.

Eco, Umberto. *Faith in Fakes: Essays*. Trans. William Weaver. London: Secker and Warburg, 1986.

Edwards, Erica. *The Other Side of Terror: Black Women and the Culture of US Empire*. New York: New York University Press, 2021.

Ellis, Treva. "The Strangeness of Progress and the Uncertainty of Blackness." In *No Tea, No Shade: New Writings on Black Queer Studies*. Durham, NC: Duke University Press, 2016.

English, Darby. *How to See a Work of Art in Total Darkness*. Cambridge, MA: MIT Press, 2007.

Enloe, Cynthia. *Bananas, Beaches, and Babes: Making Feminist Sense of International Politics.* Berkeley: University of California Press, 1990.

——. *Maneuvers: The International Politics of Militarizing Women's Lives.* Berkeley: University of California Press, 2000.

Ericson, Richard, and Kevin Haggerty. *Policing the Risk Society.* Toronto: University of Toronto Press, 1997.

Escobar, Edward. "The Dialectics of Repression: The Los Angeles Police Department and the Chicano Movement, 1968–1971." *Journal of American History* 79, no. 4 (March 1993): 1483–1514.

Eshun, Kodwo, and Ros Gray. "The Militant Image: A Cine-Geography." *Third Text* 25, no. 1 (2011): 1–12.

Farrell, Kirby. "The Berserk Style in Post-Vietnam America." *Etnofoor* 13, no. 1, "Catastrophe" (2000): 7–31.

Fattal, Alexander L. *Guerrilla Marketing: Counterinsurgency and Capitalism in Colombia.* Chicago: University of Chicago Press, 2018.

Feldman, Allan. *Formations of Violence: The Narrative of the Body and Political Terror in Northern Ireland.* Chicago: University of Chicago Press, 1991.

Feldman, Hannah. *From a Nation Torn: Decolonizing Art and Represenation in France, 1945–1962.* Durham, NC: Duke University Press, 2014.

Felker-Kantor, Max. *Policing Los Angeles: Race, Resistance, and the Rise of the LAPD.* Chapel Hill: University of North Carolina Press, 2018.

Ferguson, Andrew. "Policing Predictive Policing." *Washington University Law Review* 94, no. 5 (2017): 1109–89.

Ferretti, Fred. "On Prostitution Row, Business Hums as Mayor Talks." *New York Times,* April 29, 1976, 42.

Finley, Cheryl. *Committed to Memory: The Art of the Slave Ship Icon.* Princeton, NJ: Princeton University Press, 2018.

Fleetwood, Nicole. *Troubling Vision: Performance, Visuality, and Blackness.* Chicago: University of Chicago Press, 2011.

——. *Marking Time: Art in the Age of Mass Incarceration.* Cambridge, MA: Harvard University Press, 2020.

Foucault, Michel. *Discipline and Punish: The Birth of the Prison.* Trans. Alan Sheridan. New York: Vintage, 1977.

Freire, Paulo. *Pedagogy of the Oppressed.* 1967; New York: Continuum, 1984.

Friis-Hansen, Dana, et al., eds. *LA, Hot and Cool, the Eighties.* Cambridge, MA: MIT List Visual Arts Center, 1988.

Frobes-Cross, Huffa. "Action, Documentation, Documentary: The Early Photography of Allan Sekula, Martha Rosler, Fred Lonidier, and Phil Steinmetz." *World Records* 1 (2018). https://worldrecordsjournal.org/action-documentation-documentary/

Gablik, Suzi. "'We spell it like the Freedom Fighters': A Conversation with the Guerrilla Girls." *Art in America,* January 1994, 43–47.

Gale, Nicola K., et al. "Towards a Sociology of Risk Work: A Narrative Review and Synthesis." *Sociology Compass* 10, no. 11 (November 2016): 1046–71.

Gamboa, Harry, Jr. "Silver Screenings the Barrio," *Equal Opportunity Forum* 6, no. 1 (1978): 7.

———. *Urban Exile: Collected Writings of Harry Gamboa Jr.* Ed. Chon Noriega. Minneapolis: University of Minnesota Press, 1998.

Garland, David. *Culture of Control: Crime and Social Order in Contemporary Society*. Chicago: University of Chicago Press, 2001.

Gellerman, Bruce. "'It Was like a War Zone': Busing in Boston." WBUR News, September 5, 2014. Accessed December 2018, https://www.wbur.org/news/2014/09/05/boston-busing-anniversary

Germann, A. C. "Changing the Police—The Impossible Dream." *Journal of Criminal Law and Criminology* 62, no. 3 (1972): 416–21.

Giddens, Anthony. "Risk and Responsibility." *Modern Law Review* 62, no. 1 (January 1999): 1–10.

Gilmore, Ruth Wilson. *Golden Gulag: Prisons, Surplus, Crisis, and Opposition in Globalizing California*. Berkeley: University of California Press, 2007.

Gilmore, Ruth Wilson, and Chenjerai Kumanyika. "Ruth Wilson Gilmore Makes the Case for Abolition." *The Intercept* (podcast). June 10, 2020. https://theintercept.com/2020/06/10/ruth-wilson-gilmore-makes-the-case-for-abolition/

Gilroy, Paul. *The Black Atlantic: Modernity and Double Consciousness*. Cambridge, MA: Harvard University Press, 1993.

Gleisser, Faye. "Asco, Chris Burden, and the Politics of the Misfire." *Journal of Visual Culture* 17, no. 3 (December 2018): 312–31.

Goding-Williams, Robert, ed. *Reading Rodney King/Reading Urban Uprising*. New York: Routledge, 1993.

Goldberg, David Theo. *The Racial State*. Oxford: Blackwell, 2002.

Goldstein, Herman. "Toward Community-Oriented Policing: Potential, Basic Requirements, and Threshold Questions." *Crime & Delinquency* 33, no. 6 (1987): 6–30.

Goluboff, Lauren. *Vagrant Nation: Police Power, Constitutional Change, and the Making of the 1960s*. New York: Oxford University Press, 2016.

Greenberger, Alex. "To Remain Silent Is to Be Complicit: Whitney Staff Demand Action against Museum's Vice Chair of Board." *ARTnews*, November 30, 2018. https://www.artnews.com/art-news/news/remain-silent-complicit-whitney-staff-demand-action-museums-vice-chair-board-11437/

Guerrilla Girls. *Guerrilla Girls: The Art of Behaving Badly*. San Francisco: Chronicle Books, 2020.

Halberstam, Jack. *In a Queer Time and Place: Transgender Bodies, Subcultural Lives*. New York: New York University Press, 2005.

Hall, Stuart, et al. *Policing the Crisis: Mugging, the State, and Law and Order*. London: Macmillan, 1978.

Hanhardt, Christina. *Safe Space: Gay Neighborhood History and the Politics of Violence*. Durham, NC: Duke University Press, 2013.

Hannah-Jones, Nikole. "It Was Never about Busing: Court-Ordered Desegregation Worked. But White Racism Made It Hard to Accept." *New York Times,* July 19, 2019. https://www.nytimes.com/2019/07/12/opinion/sunday/it-was-never-about-busing.html

Harney, Stefano, and Fred Moten. *The Undercommons: Fugitive Planning and Black Study*. Wivenhoe, England: Minor Compositions, 2013.

Harris, Art. "Sandinistas' Sister-in-Arms." *Washington Post*, October 4, 1984, n.p.

Harris, Joy. "New Anti-Riot Bills Threaten the Work of Social Practice Artists." *Hyperallergic*, August 19, 2021. https://hyperallergic.com/670742/new-anti-riot-bills-threaten-work-of-social-practice-artists/

Hartman, Saidiya. *Wayward Lives, Beautiful Experiments: Intimate Histories of Social Upheaval*. New York: W. W. Norton, 2019.

Heathfield, Adrian, and Tehching Hsieh. *Out of Now: The Lifeworks of Tehching Hsieh*. Cambridge, MA: MIT Press, 2009.

Hendricks, Jon, and Jean Toche, eds. *GAAG: The Guerrilla Art Action Group, 1969–1976: A Selection*. New York: Printed Matter, 1978.

Hess, Elizabeth. "Guerrilla Girl Power: Why the Art World Needs a Conscience." In *But Is It Art? The Spirit of Art as Activism*, ed. Nina Felshin, 312–27. Seattle: Bay Press, 1995.

Hinckle, Warren, II. "Editorial Preface." *Scanlan's Monthly: Suppressed Issue, Guerrilla War in the USA* 1, no. 8 (January 1971): 2–5.

Hinton, Elizabeth. *America on Fire: The Untold Story of Police Violence and Black Rebellion since the 1960s*. New York: W. W. Norton, 2021.

——. *From the War on Poverty to the War on Crime: The Making of Mass Incarceration in America*. Cambridge, MA: Harvard University Press, 2016.

Hiro, Rika. "Between Absence and Presence: Exploring Video Earth's *What Is Photography?*" *Invisible Culture: An Electronic Journal for Visual Culture*, no. 15 (2010), 79–101.

hooks, bell. *Teaching to Transgress: Education and the Practice of Freedom*. New York: Routledge, 1994.

Horvitz, Richard. "Chris Burden." *Artforum*, May 1976, 24–31.

Howell, Alison. "Forget 'Militarization': Race, Disability and the 'Martial Politics' of the Police and of the University." *International Feminist Journal of Politics* 20, no. 2 (2018): 117–36.

Huet, Ellen. "Server and Protect: Predictive Policing Firm PredPol Promises to Map Crime before It Happens." *Forbes*, February 11, 2015. Accessed April 1, 2022, https://www.forbes.com/sites/ellenhuet/2015/02/11/predpol-predictive-policing/?sh=5d6873164f9b

Hughes, Kathleen. "Artist Explores Essence of the Daily Grind by Punching in Once an Hour for a Year." *Wall Street Journal*, April 24, 1981.

———. "Mr. Hsieh's Latest Performance: Keeping Warm Was the Easy Part." *Wall Street Journal*, July 11, 1982, 27.

Hwang, Ren-yo. "Deviant Care for Deviant Futures: QTBIPoC Radical Relationalism as Mutual Aid against Carceral Care." *TSQ: Transgender Studies Quarterly* 6, no. 4 (2019): 559–78.

Ingberman, Jeanette. "Art and the Law in 20th Century America." PhD diss., City University of New York, 1982. Exit Art Papers, series I, box I, folder 4, Fales Library, New York University.

Ingberman, Jeanette, and Papo Colo. "Interview of Tehching Hsieh." *Artcom*, no. 18 (1982), 18.

Jackson, Shannon. *Social Works: Performing Art, Supporting Publics*. New York: Routledge, 2011.

James, David E. "No Movies: Projecting the Reel by Rejecting the Reel." In *Asco: Elite of the Obscure, a Retrospective, 1972–1987*, ed. C. Ondine Chavoya and Rita Gonzalez, 179–91. Ostfildern, Germany: Hatje Cantz, 2011.

Jefferson, Brian. *Digitize and Punish: Racial Criminalization in the Digital Age*. Minneapolis: University of Minnesota Press, 2020.

Johnston, Jill. "Tehching Hsieh: Art's Willing Captive." *Art in America*, September 2001, 140–43.

Jones, Amelia. "Lost Bodies: Early 1970s Los Angeles Performance Art in Art History." In *Live Art in LA: Performance Art in Southern California, 1970–1983*, ed. Peggy Phelan, 115–84. New York: Routledge, 2010.

———. "Traitor Prophets: Asco's Art as a Politics of the In-Between." In *Asco: Elite of the Obscure, a Retrospective, 1972–1987*, ed. C. Ondine Chavoya and Rita Gonzalez, 102–10. Ostfildern, Germany: Hatje Cantz, 2011.

Jones, Kellie. *South of Pico: African American Arts in Los Angeles in the 1960s and 1970s*. Durham, NC: Duke University Press, 2017.

Kahlo, Frida, and Käthe Kollwitz. "Transgressive Techniques of the Guerrilla Girls." *Getty Research Journal*, no. 2 (2010), 203–8.

Kahn, Barry. "Sam Hsieh at Large in New York City." *Art in America*, Summer 1982, n.p.

Kalter, Christoph. "A Shared Space of Imagination, Communication, and Action: Perspectives on the History of the 'Third World.'" In *The Third World in the Global 1960s*, ed. Samantha Christiansen and Zachary A. Scarlett. New York: Berghahn Books, 2013.

Kee, Joan. *Models of Integrity: Art and Law in Post-Sixties America*. Oakland: University of California Press, 2019.

———. "Orders of Law in the *One Year Performances* of Tehching Hsieh." *American Art* 30, no. 1 (Spring 2016): 73–91.

Keeling, Kara. *The Witch's Flight: The Cinematic, the Black Femme, and the Image of Common Sense*. Durham, NC: Duke University Press, 2007.

Kelley, Robin D. G. *Freedom Dreams: The Black Radical Imagination*. Boston: Beacon, 2002.

Kempton, Richard. *Provo: Amsterdam's Anarchist Revolt.* New York: Autonomedia, 2007.

Kifner, John. "South Boston Crowd Attacks Black as Tensions Rise." *New York Times,* October 8, 1974, 1. Accessed July 20, 2020, https://www.nytimes.com/1974/10/08/archives/south-boston-crowd-attacks-black-as-tensions-rise-south-boston.html

Klare, Michael, and Peter Kornbluh, eds. *Low-Intensity Warfare: Counterinsurgency, Proinsurgency, and Antiterrorism in the Eighties.* New York: Pantheon, 1988.

Knight, Christopher. "Chris Burden and the Potential for Catastrophe." *Art Issues* 52 (March/April 1998).

Kosiba-Vargas, Zaneta. "Harry Gamboa and Asco: The Emergence and Development of a Chicano Art Group, 1971–1987." PhD diss., University of Michigan, 1988.

Kozloff, Max. "Pygmalion Reversed." *Artforum,* November 1975, 30–37.

Kraut, Anthea. *Choreographing Copyright: Race, Gender, and Intellectual Property Rights in American Dance.* New York: Oxford University Press, 2016.

Kwon, Miwon. *One Place after Another: Site-Specific Art and Locational Identity.* Cambridge, MA: MIT Press, 2002.

Kyung-Jin Lee, James. *Urban Triage: Race and the Fictions of Multiculturalism.* Minneapolis: University of Minnesota Press, 2004.

Lacy, Suzanne. *Leaving Art: Writings on Performance, Politics, and Publics, 1974–2007.* Durham, NC: Duke University Press, 2010.

Lacy, Suzanne, and Leslie Labowitz. "Feminist Media Strategies for Political Performance." In *The Feminism and Visual Culture Reader,* ed. Amelia Jones, 302–13. London: Routledge, 2003.

Laqueur, Walter. "Interpretations of Terrorism: Fact, Fiction, and Political Science." *Journal of Contemporary History* 12, no. 1 (Jan. 1977): 1–42.

———. "The Origins of Guerrilla Doctrine." *Journal of Contemporary History* 10, no. 3 (1975): 341–82.

Lepecki, André. *Exhausting Dance: Performance and the Politics of Movement.* New York: Routledge, 2006.

Lippard, Lucy. "New Feminist Artists Show They Have a Mean Sense of Humor." *In These Times,* nos. 13–19 (November 1985), 20.

Lippard, Lucy, and Adrian Piper. "Catalysis: An Interview with Adrian Piper." *The Drama Review: TDR* 16, no. 1 (March 1972): 76–78.

Lipsitz, George. *How Racism Takes Place.* Philadelphia: Temple University Press, 2011.

———. "The Possessive Investment in Whiteness: Racialized Social Democracy and the 'White' Problem in American Studies." *American Quarterly* 47, no. 3 (1995): 369–87.

———. "Whiteness and War." In *Race, Identity, and Representation in Education,* 2nd ed., ed. Cameron McCarthy et al., 78–110. New York: Routledge, 2005.

Loor, Karen J. Pita. "When Protest Is the Disaster: Constitutional Implications of State and Local Emergency Power." *Seattle University Law Review* 43, no. 1 (Fall 2019): 1–70.

López, Ian Haney. *Racism on Trial: The Chicano Fight for Justice.* Cambridge, MA: Belknap Press/Harvard University Press, 2003.

Lorde, Audre. *Sister Outsider: Essays and Speeches.* Trumansburg, NY: Crossing Press, 1984.

Lovell, Jarret S. "Media Power and Information Control: A Study of Police Organizations and Media Relations." PhD diss., Rutgers University, School of Criminal Justice, 2002.

Lugones, María. *Pilgrimages = Peregrinajes: Theorizing Coalition against Multiple Oppressions.* Lanham, MD: Rowman & Littlefield, 2003.

Lung, Shirley. "Criminalizing Work and Non-Work: The Disciplining of Immigrant and African American Workers." *University of Massachusetts Law Review* 14, no. 2, article 2 (2019): 290–348.

Lytle Hernández, Kelly. *City of Inmates: Conquest, Rebellion, and the Rise of Human Caging in Los Angles, 1771–1965.* Chapel Hill: University of North Carolina Press, 2017.

Maeda, Daryl. *Chains of Babylon: The Rise of Asian America.* Minneapolis: University of Minnesota Press, 2009.

Mair, Kimberly. *Guerrilla Aesthetics: Art, Memory, and the West German Urban Guerrilla.* Montreal: McGill–Queen's University Press, 2016.

Marighella, Carlos. *Urban Guerrilla Minimanual.* 1969; Vancouver: Pulp Press, 1974.

Martin, Randy. *An Empire of Indifference: American War and the Financial Logic of Risk Management.* Durham, NC: Duke University Press, 2007.

Masur, Louis. *The Soiling of Old Glory: The Story of a Photograph That Shocked America.* New York: Bloomsbury, 2003.

Maurer, Marc. "The Endurance of Racial Disparity in the Criminal Jusitce System." In *Policing the Black Man: Arrest, Prosecution, and Imprisonment*, ed. Angela J. Davis. New York: Vintage, 2017.

McClintock, Michael. *Instruments of Statecraft: U.S. Guerrilla Warfare, Counter-Insurgency, and Counter-Terrorism, 1940–1990.* New York: Pantheon, 1992.

McDonough, Tom, ed. *Guy Debord and the Situationists International: Texts and Documents.* Cambridge, MA: MIT Press, 2002.

McDowell, Deborah, Claudrena N. Harold, and Juan Battle, eds. *The Punitive Turn: New Approaches to Race and Incarceration.* Charlottesville: University of Virginia Press, 2013.

McHarris, Philip V. "Disrupting Order: Race, Class, and the Roots of Policing." *Violent Order: Essays on the Nature of Police*, ed. David Correia and Tyler Wall, 32–48. Chicago: Haymarket Books, 2021.

McKinney, Charles W., Jr. "Riot." In *Keywords for African American Studies*, 179–83. New York: New York University Press, 2018.

McKittrick, Katherine. *Dear Science.* Durham, NC: Duke University Press, 2021.

———. *Demonic Grounds: Black Women and the Cartographies of Struggle.* Minneapolis: University of Minnesota Press, 2006.

McKittrick, Neil V. "The Homeless: Judicial Intervention on Behalf of a Politically Powerless Group." *Fordham Urban Law Journal* 16, no. 3. (1988): 389–440.

McMahon, Marci R. *Domestic Negotiations: Gender, Nation, and Self-Fashioning in US Mexican and Chicana Literature and Art*. Brunswick, NJ: Rutgers University Press, 2013.

McMillan, Uri. *Embodied Avatars: Genealogies of Black Feminist Art and Performance*. New York: New York University Press, 2015.

Minh-Ha, Trinh T. *Woman, Native, Other: Writing Postcoloniality and Feminism*. Bloomington: University of Indiana Press, 1989.

Mitchell, Bruce E. "Body Art: A Legal Policy Analysis (Jan. 1977)." In *Law, Ethics, and the Visual Arts: Cases and Materials*, ed. J. H. Merryman and A. E. Elsen, vol. 1. Philadelphia: University of Pennsylvania Press, 1979.

Mitchell, Phillip. "Optimal Selection of Police Patrol Beats." *Journal of Criminal Law and Criminology* 63, no. 4 (1973): 577–84.

Meyer, Ursula. "The Eruption of Anti-Art." In *Idea Art: A Critical Anthology*, ed. Gregory Battcock. New York: Dutton, 1973.

Mirzoeff, Nicolas. *The Right to Look: A Counterhistory of Visuality*. Durham, NC: Duke University Press, 2011.

Molesworth, Helen. *Work Ethic*. University Park: Pennsylvania State University Press, 2003.

Moore, Carman. "Black Comedy: The USA v. Jean Toche." *Village Voice*, April 18, 1974.

Morgan, Edward. *What Really Happened to the 1960s: How Mass Media Culture Failed American Democracy*. Lawrence: University Press of Kansas, 2010.

Moten, Fred. *In the Break: The Aesthetics of the Black Radical Tradition*. Minneapolis: University of Minnesota Press, 2003.

Mottl, Tahi L. "The Analysis of Countermovements." *Social Problems* 27, no. 5, "Sociology of Political Knowledge Issue: Theoretical Inquiries, Critiques, and Explications" (June 1980): 620–35.

Mowatt, Rasul. *The Geographies of Threat and the Production of Violence: The State and the City between Us*. New York: Routledge, 2021.

Muhammad, Khalil Gibran. "The Foundational Lawlessness of the Law Itself: Racial Criminalization and the Punitive Roots of Punishment in America." *Daedalus* 151, no. 1, "Reimagining Justice: The Challenges of Violence and Punitive Excess" (Winter 2022): 107–20.

Muñoz, José Esteban. *Disidentifications: Queers of Color and the Performance of Politics*. Minneapolis: University of Minnesota Press, 1999.

Murakawa, Naomi. *The First Civil Right: How Liberals Built Prison America*. Oxford: Oxford University Press, 2014.

Nathanson, Larry, and Mike Pearl. "Gotta Have Art, Says Judge with a Heart." *New York Post*, June 22, 1982.

Neocleous, Mark. *The Fabrication of Social Order: A Critical Theory of Police Power*. Sterling, VA: Pluto Press, 2000.

Nogueira Silva, Sara, and Chris Reed. "You Can't Always Get What You Want: Relative

Anonymity in Cyberspace." *Scripted: A Journal of Law, Technology & Society* 12, no. 1 (June 2015): 37–50.

Noriega, Chon. "No Introduction." In *Urban Exile: Collected Writings of Harry Gamboa Jr.*, ed. Chon Noriega, 1–22. Minneapolis: University of Minnesota, 1998.

——. *Shot in America: Television, the State, and the Rise of Chicano Cinema*. Minneapolis: Minnesota University Press, 2000.

——. "Stereotyping in Film in General and of the Hispanic in Particular." In *Latin Looks: Images of Latinas and Latinos in the U.S. Media*, ed. Clara E. Rodriguez, 35–39. Boulder, CO: Westview Press, 1977.

——. "Your Art Disgusts Me: Early Asco, 1971–75." *East of Borneo*, December 18, 2010. Accessed April 15, 2015. http://www.eastofborneo.org/articles/your-art-disgusts-me-early-asco-1971-75

Nutter, Kathleen Banks. "Militant Mothers: Boston, Busing, and the Bicentennial of 1976." *Historical Journal of Massachusetts*, Fall 2010, 52–75.

Nyong'o, Tavia. *Afro-Fabulations: The Queer Drama of Black Life*. New York: New York University Press, 2019.

O'Dell, Kathy. *Contract with the Skin: Masochism, Performance Art, and the 1970s*. Minneapolis: University of Minnesota Press, 1998.

Omi, Michael, and Howard Winant. *Racial Formation in the United States: From the 1960s to the 1980s*. New York: Routledge, 1986.

Oldfield, Pippa. "Calling the Shots: Women's Photographic Engagement with War in Hemispheric America, 1910–1990." PhD diss., Durham University, 2016. http://etheses.dur.ac.uk/11786/

Paret, Peter, and John Shy. *Guerrillas in the 1960s*. Princeton Studies in World Politics. Newark, NJ: Center for International Studies, 1962.

Pegler-Gordon, Anna. *In Sight of America: Photography and the Development of U.S. Immigration Policy*. Berkeley: University of California Press, 2009.

Perreault, John. "Crimes of the Art." *Soho News*, March 2, 1982.

Pierce, Jerald. "A Frye Art Museum Security Guard Takes Us on a Tour of His Favorite Piece." *Seattle Times*, August 18, 2022. https://www.seattletimes.com/entertainment/visual-arts/a-frye-art-museum-security-guard-takes-us-on-a-tour-of-his-favorite-pieces/

Pindell, Howardena. *Autobiography: In Her Own Image*. New York: Gallery, 1988.

——. *The Heart of the Question: The Writings and Paintings of Howardena Pindell*. New York: Midmarch Arts Press, 1997.

Picard, Lil. "Art." *East Village Other*, November 1969, 1.

Piper, Adrian. *Escape to Berlin: A Travel Memoir*. Verlag: APRA Foundation Berlin, 2018.

——. "NEWS: September 2012." http://www.adrianpiper.com/news_sep_2012.shtml

——. *Out of Order, Out of Sight: Selected Writings in Meta-Art, 1968–1992*. Cambridge, MA: MIT Press, 1996.

Plagens, Peter. "He Got Shot—for His Art." *New York Times,* September 2, 1973, D1, 87.

Pluchart, François. "Risk as the Practice of Thought." *Flash Art*, special issue, "Danger in Art," 1978.

Poulos, Peter W. "Chicago's Ban on Gang Loitering: Making Sense of Vagueness and Overbreadth in Loitering Laws." *California Law Review* 83, no. 1 (January 1995): 379–417.

Prince, Dinah. "Warfare in the World of Art." *Daily News*, October 16, 1985, 41.

Puar, Jasbir. *Terrorist Assemblages: Homonationalism in Queer Times*. Durham, NC: Duke University Press, 2007.

Pulido, Laura. *Black, Brown, Yellow and Left: Radical Activism in Los Angeles*. Berkeley: University of California Press, 2006.

Quashie, Kevin Everod. *Black Aliveness; or, A Poetics of Being*. Durham, NC: Duke University Press, 2021.

Raiford, Leigh. *Imprisoned in a Luminous Glare: Photography and the African American Freedom*. Chapel Hill: University of North Carolina Press, 2011.

Reddy, Chandan. *Freedom with Violence: Race, Sexuality, and the US State*. Durham, NC: Duke University Press, 2011.

Richards, Nelly. "Margins and Institutions: Performances of the Chilean Avanzada." In *Corpus Delecti: Performance Art of the Americas*, ed. Coco Fusco. New York: Routledge, 2000.

Roberts, Dorothy. "Race, Vagueness, and the Social Meaning of Order-Maintenance Policing." *Journal of Criminal Law and Criminology* 89, no. 3 (Spring 1999): 775–836.

Romer, Stefan. "The *Inter-esse* When Pressing the Shutter-Release Button: For an Epistemology of Contentious and Committed Art Photography." In *The Militant Image Reader*. Graz: Camera Austria, 2015.

Rosa, Eugene, et al. *The Risk Society Revisited: Social Theory and Governance*. Philadelphia: Temple University Press, 2014.

Rubin, Gayle. "Thinking Sex: Notes for a Radical Theory of the Politics of Sexuality." In *Culture, Society, and Sexuality: A Reader*, ed. Richard Guy Parker and Peter Aggleton, 143–78. London: UCL Press, 1999.

Ryan, Paul. "Cybernetic Guerrilla Warfare." *Radical Software*, no. 3 (Spring 1971), 1–2.

Saba, Paul. "Monopoly Capitalists' `Busing Movement Is an Attack on the Democratic Rights of the Black People and on the Unity of the Working Class." *Workers' Advocate*, December 15, 1975. https://www.marxists.org/history/erol/ncm-2/cousml-busing.htm

Salisbury, Stephan. "Getting Militant about Women's Art." *Philadelphia Inquirer*, March 7, 1986, 3D.

Sánchez, George. *Boyle Heights: How a Los Angeles Neighborhood Became the Future of American Democracy*. Oakland: University of California Press, 2021.

Schor, Mira. "Girls Will Be Girls." *Artforum* 29, no. 1 (September 1990): 26.

Schimmel, Paul. *Out of Actions: Between Performance and the Object, 1949–1979*. London: Thames & Hudson, 1998.

Schjeldahl, Peter. "The Danger Artist." *New Yorker,* May 19, 2015. https://www.newyorker.com/culture/cultural-comment/danger-artist-chris-burden

Schrader, Stuart. *Badges without Borders: How Global Counterinsurgency Transformed American Policing.* Oakland: University of California Press, 2019.

——. "To Protect and Serve Themselves: Police in US Politics since the 1960s." *Public Culture* 31, no. 3 (2019): 601–23.

Scott, James C. *Seeing Like a State: How Certain Schemes to Improve the Human Condition Have Failed.* New Haven, CT: Yale Universtiy Press, 1998.

Seigel, Micol. "Beyond Compare: Comparative Method after the Transnational Turn." *Radical History Review*, no. 91 (Winter 2005), 62–90.

——. *Violence Work: State Power and the Limits of Police.* Durham, NC: Duke University Press, 2018.

Selmi, Michael. "The Evolution of Employment Discrimination Law: Changed Doctrine for Changed Social Conditions." *GW Law Faculty Publications & Other Works*, no. 1110 (2014).

Serazio, Michael. *Your Ad Here: The Cool Sell of Guerrilla Marketing.* New York: New York University Press, 2013.

Shalson, Lara. *Performing Endurance: Art and Politics since 1960.* Cambridge: Cambridge University Press, 2018.

Shamberg, Michael. *Guerrilla Television.* New York: Holt, Rinehart, and Winston, 1971.

Sharp, Christina. *In the Wake: On Blackness and Being.* Durham, NC: Duke University Press, 2016.

Sharp, Willoughby. "Elemental Gestures: Terry Fox." *Arts Magazine*, May 1970, 48–51.

Sheets, Hilarie. "Pope.L's Group Crawl: Protest, Pathos, Provocation." *New York Times,* September 22, 2019. https://www.nytimes.com/2019/09/22/arts/design/popel-crawl-whitney-moma.html

Sheppard, Nathaniel, Jr. "Beame and a Broadway Cast Call for Eradication of 'Porno Plague.'" *New York Times,* April 29, 1976, 42.

Sieberling, Dorothy. "The Art-Martyr," *New York Magazine,* May 24, 1976, 48.

Sifuentes, Frank. "Reflections on Law and Order in East Los Angeles." *Regeneración* 1, no. 8 (1970): 7.

Singh, Nikhil Pal. "The Black Panthers and the Undeveloped Country of the Left." In *The Black Panther Party (Reconsidered)*, ed. Charles E. Jones, 57–105. Baltimore: Black Classic Press, 1998.

Sisario, Ben. "He's Got It Bad, or 'Baad,' for His Art." *New York Times.* January 20, 2010. http://www.nytimes.com/2010/01/24/theater/24vanpeebles.html

Small, Zachary. "Artist Mounts Guerrilla Art Exhibition at Whitney Calling for Removal of Vice Chairman." *Hyperallergic*, December 11, 2018. https://hyperallergic.com/475476/artist-mounts-guerrilla-art-exhibition-at-whitney-calling-for-removal-of-vice-chairman/

Smith, Barbara. "Art Piece Brings Arrest," *Artweek*, January 6, 1973, 4.

——. "Burden Case Tried, Dismissed," *Artweek*, February 1973, 2.

Smith, Cherise. *Enacting Others: Politics of Identity in Eleanor Antin, Nikki S. Lee, Adrian Piper, and Anna Deveare Smith*. Durham, NC: Duke University Press, 2011.

——. "Re-Member the Audience: Adrian Piper's Mythic Being Advertisements." *Art Journal* 66, no. 1 (Spring 2007): 46–58.

Smith, Neil. "Gentrification, the Frontier, and the Restructuring of Urban Space." In *Gentrification of the City*, ed. Neil Smith and Peter Williams. Boston: Allen and Unwin, 1986.

Smith, Roberta. "Waging Guerrilla Warfare against the Art World." *New York Times,* June 17, 1990, 1.

Sonksen, Mike. "The History of South Central Los Angeles and Its Struggle with Gentrification." KCET, September 13, 2017. https://www.kcet.org/shows/city-rising/the-history-of-south-central-los-angeles-and-its-struggle-with-gentrification

Spade, Dean. "Trans Laws and Politics on a Neoliberal Landscape." *Temple Political and Civil Rights Law Review* 18 (2009): 353–73.

Stark, Trevor. "Guerrilla Girls." In *This Will Have Been: Art, Love, and Politics in the 1980s*, 181–83. New Haven, CT: Yale University Press, 2012.

Stoler, Laura Ann. *Along the Archival Grain: Epistemic Anxieties and Colonial Common Sense*. Princeton, NJ: Princeton University Press, 2009.

Steinhauer, Jillian. "At 77, Howardena Pindell Exorcises a Chilling Memory from Childhood." *New York Times,* October 16, 2020. https://www.nytimes.com/2020/10/16/arts/design/howardena-pindell-shed-video.html

Strick, Simon. *American Dorologies: Pain, Sentimentalism, Biopolitics*. New York: SUNY Press, 2014.

Taber, Robert. *The War of the Flea: A Study of Guerrilla Warfare Theory and Practice*. New York: Lyle Stuart, 1965.

TallBear, Kim. "Caretaking Relations, Not American Dreaming." *Kalfou* 6, no. 1 (2019): 24–41.

Taylor, Diana. *Disappearing Acts: Spectacles of Gender and Nationalism in Argentina's "Dirty War."* Durham, NC: Duke University Press, 1997.

Taylor, Paul. "Where the Girls Are." *Corporate Culture*, April 1987, 178.

Tejada, Roberto. "Los Angeles Snapshots." In *Now Dig This! Art and Black Los Angeles, 1960–1980*, ed. Kellie Jones, 69–83. Los Angeles: Hammer Museum, 2011.

Third, Amanda. "Mediating the Female Terrorist: Patricia Hearst and the Containment of the Feminist Terrorist Threat in the United States in the 1970s." *Historical Social Research* 39, no. 3 (2014): 150–75.

Thompson, Chris. "Afterbirth of a Nation: William Pope.L's Great White Way." *Women & Performance: A Journal of Feminist Theory* 14, no. 1 (2004): 63–90.

Thompson, Krista. "The Evidence of Things Not Photographed: Slavery and Historical Memory in the British West Indies." *Representations* 113, no. 1 (Winter 2011): 39–71.

Thompson, J. Phillip. "Broken Policing: The Origins of the 'Broken Windows' Policy." *New Labor Forum* 24, no. 2 (Spring 2015): 42–47.

Thompson, Nato, ed. *Interventionists: Users' Manual for the Creative Disruption of Everyday Life*. North Adams, MA: MASS MoCA, 2004.

Tochterman, Brian. *The Dying City: Postwar New York and the Ideology of Fear*. Chapel Hill: University of North Carolina Press, 2017.

Trachtman, Joel. "Integrating Lawfare and Warfare." *Boston College International and Comparative Law Review* 39, no. 2 (2016): 267–82.

Van Newkirk, Allen. "Detroit-Revolution in the Revolution." *Los Angeles Free Press*, August 4–10, 1967, 1, 14.

Varon, Jeremy. *Bringing the War Home: The Weather Underground, the Red Army Faction, and Revolutionary Violence in the Sixties and Seventies*. Berkeley: University of California Press, 2004.

Veyne, Paul. *Writing History: Essays on Epistemology*. Trans. Mira Moore-Rinvolucri. Middletown, CT: Wesleyan University Press, 1984.

Vitale, Alex. *The End of Policing*. London: Verso, 2018.

Wacquant, Loïc. *Punishing the Poor: The Neoliberal Government of Social Insecurity*. Durham, NC: Duke University Press, 2009.

Wagner, Anne. "Then and There: Anne Wagner on the Art of Chris Burden." *Artforum*, October 2011, https://www.artforum.com/print/201108/then-and-there-the-art-of-chris-burden-29040.

Wald, Priscilla. *Contagious: Cultures, Carriers, and the Outbreak Narrative*. Durham, NC: Duke University Press, 2008.

Wang, Jackie. *Carceral Capitalism*. South Pasadena, CA: Semiotext(e), 2018.

Ward, Frazer. "Alien Duration: Tehching Hsieh, 1978–1999." *Art Journal* 65, no. 3 (2006): 6–19.

——. "Gray Zone: Watching Shoot." *October*, no. 95 (Winter 2001), 117–25.

——. *No Innocent Bystanders: Performance Art and Audience*. Hanover, NH: Dartmouth College Press, 2012.

Watkins, Rychetta. *Black Power, Yellow Power, and the Making of Revolutionary Identities*. Jackson: University Press of Mississippi, 2012.

Weheliye, Alexander. *Habeas Viscus: Racializing Assemblages, Biopolitics, and Black Feminist Theories of the Human*. Durham, NC: Duke University Press, 2014.

Weisman, John. *Guerrilla Theater: Scenarios for Revolution*. Garden City, NY: Anchor Press, 1973.

Westad, Odd Arne. *The Global Cold War: Third World Interventions and the Making of Our Times*. Cambridge: Cambridge University Press, 2007.

Wiegman, Robyn. *Object Lessons*. Durham, NC: Duke University Press, 2012.

Wilderson, Frank B., III. *Red, White, and Black: Cinema and the Structure of U.S. Antagonism*. Durham, NC: Duke University Press, 2010.

Williams, Lena. "Spray Paint Sales Curbed in Graffiti War." *New York Times*, October 6, 1985, 56.

Willis, Edwin. "Guerrilla Warfare Advocates in the United States." Report by Committee on Un-American Activities. House of Representatives 90th Congress 2nd Session. May 6, 1968.

Wilson, Martha. "William Pope.L" (interview). *BOMB*, no. 55 (Spring 1996), 50–55.

Winslow, Margaret. "Pope.L: The Body and Its Void." *Art Journal*, Winter 2020, 132–34.

Withers, Josephine. "Art Essay: The Guerrilla Girls." *Feminist Studies* 14, no. 2 (Summer 1988): 284–300.

Wrange, Mans. *Chris Burden*. Stockholm, Sweden: Magasin 3 Stockholm Konsthall, 1999.

Wu, Ellen. *Color of Success: Asian Americans and the Origins of the Model Minority*. Princeton, NJ: Princeton University Press, 2014.

Wu, Frank. "Why Vincent Chin Matters." *New York Times*, June 22, 2012. http://www.nytimes.com/2012/06/23/opinion/why-vincent-chin-matters.html

Wu, Simon. "Get Out: Tehching Hsieh's Art of Survival in America." *Artforum*, June 8, 2022. https://www.artforum.com/slant/tehching-hsieh-s-art-of-survival-in-america-88707

Wynter, Sylvia. "Rethinking 'Aesthetics': Notes towards a Deciphering Practice." In *Ex-iles: Essays on Caribbean Cinema*, ed. Mbye Cham, 238–79. Trenton, NJ: Africa World Press, 1992.

Young, Cynthia. *Soul Power: Culture, Radicalism, and the Making of a U.S. Third World Left*. Durham, NC: Duke University Press, 2006.

Young, Harvey. *Embodying Black Experience: Stillness, Critical Memory, and the Black Body*. Ann Arbor: University of Michigan Press, 2010.

Zorach, Rebecca, ed. *Art against the Law*. Chicago: University of Chicago Press, 2015.

Index

abolitionism, 5–6, 31, 63, 76, 126–27, 194
Abramović, Marina, 116
Acconci, Vito, 24, 116, 143
Achter, Paul, 117
ACLU (American Civil Liberties Union), 43
aftercrimes, 40, 47–49, 60
agitprop, 21, 31, 155, 157
Ahmed, Sara, 5, 44, 55, 188
AI-5 ban, 10
AIDS, 155, 168
AIDS Coalition to Unleash Power (ACT-UP), 155
Akasegawa, Gempei, 143
Alexander, Michelle, 44, 81, 85
Algeria, 3–4, 13. See also *Battle of Algiers, The*
Allen, Hawa, 187
Amnesty International, 105
Anaheim, 45–46
anonymity, 155; and Guerrilla Girls, 148, 150, 179–80; of Guerrilla Girls versus PESTS, 31, 155; and PESTS, 169, 179; social politics of, 156–57, 168–69; and Hsieh, 115
Ant Farm, 12
antiblackness, 6, 22–23, 68, 93, 120, 169, 179, 185; and Hsieh, 30, 139, 141; and place-making, 81; and policing, 85, 91, 186; and Pope.L, 30, 109; and racial capitalism, 141; and Reagan Administration, 19; and surveillance, 19; and vagrancy, 82, 141
anticolonial movements, 4, 6, 19, 85
antiloitering laws, 82, 88, 91; origins of, 80; and Piper, 77, 85; and Pope.L, 109, 119, 137; and public space, 77, 109; and queer spaces, 15; and Toche, 77; unconstitutionality of, 85, 87; and white supremacy, 81. *See also* Jim Crow laws; policing
Anti-Riot Act (1968), 15, 30, 48, 59, 76; and Burden, 59–60
antivagrancy laws, 81–83, 85–86, 91, 109, 124, 137
antiwar (activism), 11, 15, 49, 51, 71–72, 89–90, 106, 134
apartheid, 10, 43, 169, 174, 236n76
Arbery, Ahmaud, 31
Argentina, 4, 10
Arnoldi, Chuck, 54
arrests, 1–2, 5, 7, 10, 26–28, 29, 55, 75, 86, 147, 159, 188; of Asco, 34, 43, 61, 66; by Boston police, 100; of Burden, 35–36, 40, 53–54, 58, 59, 61; and busing, 101;

arrests (*continued*)
in Chicago, 192; at Chicano Moratorium demonstration, 49; of Cruz, 192–93; of Hsieh, 111–12, 137, 139, 141, 144; and *Illegal America*, 145; and loitering, 80; of Lonidier, 89–90; in Milwaukee, 128; in New York City, 122; versus non-arrests, 146, 183; of Pope.L, 109, 130; of Toche, 72, 74, 95, 103, 105, 186. *See also* Black Codes; Davis, Angela; Papachristou, Margaret

art discourse, 39, 112, 147; and "guerrilla," 9, 182, 184; and police, 22–23, 38, 56; and risk, 27, 141; and whiteness, 30, 40, 67

Artforum, 105, 139, 144, 187

Artists Labor Force, 172

art law, 27, 30–31, 40, 114, 120, 141–43, 146

Art v War, 31, 182–84

Art Workers Coalition (AWC), 1, 5, 24, 74

Asco, 25, 37–43, 51–52, 59–68, 89, 188, 204n18; and Burden, 28, 33, 35, 37–39, 62, 72, 190; disbandment of, 187; and East Los Angeles, 9, 30, 33, 49, 55–56; and *First Supper (After a Major Riot)*, 48–49, 61; and guerrilla tactics, 6–7, 28, 37, 40; meaning in Spanish, 34; and *Pistol Whippersnapper*, 63–64, 219n127; and police/policing, 21, 30, 46, 49, 55, 72, 187, 190; and punitive literacy, 51, 55; and *Spray Paint LACMA*, 61, 146, 192. *See also* No Movies

Asian Americans, 12, 27, 124, 144–45, 151; and anti-Asianness, 30, 81, 141, 144; as "model minority," 135–36, 139

Astorga, Nora, 166

Auerbach, David, 73, 79–80, 88

Baldessari, John, 56, 58

Bambara, Toni Cade, 174

Banks, Valerie, 93

Barber, Tiffany, 126

Battle of Algiers, The, 13, 167, 207n42. *See also* Algeria

Beame, Abraham, 103, 122, 128

Beck, Ulrich, 28, 188

Bederman, Gail, 117

Belew, Kathleen, 166

Belgium, 1, 71

Berlin, 114, 187

Beuys, Joseph, 24

Beydler, Gary, 65

Black Codes, 81, 91. *See also* antivagrancy laws

Black Emergency Cultural Coalition, 2

Black Lives Matter, 31, 193

Black Panthers/Black Panther Party for Self-Defense, 2, 18–20, 34, 84, 161; and FBI, 18, 84; founding of, 11, 135; and police, 4, 11, 18–19, 48

Black studies, 8, 10, 25, 38–39, 91, 120, 127, 168

Blocker, Jane, 25

body art, 21, 53, 141–42. *See also* performance art

Bolivia, 3

Boston, 9, 28, 92, 95, 99–103, 105; and integration of schools, 93–94; and Toche, 9, 30, 77–78, 92, 96–97, 103, 105. *See also* busing; diGrazia, Robert J.

Boston Police Department, 9, 92, 94–96, 98–99, 100–103. *See also* diGrazia, Robert J.

Bowles, John, 84

Brazil, 4, 10, 46, 150

Bread and Puppet Theater, 12

"broken windows" policy, 159, 168

Browne, Simone, 19

Bruce, La Merr Jurelle, 91

Bryan-Wilson, Julia, 24

Burden, Chris, 6, 24, 40, 56, 67, 119, 143–44, 197; arrest and trial of, 54–55, 59–62,

140; and Asco, 28, 30, 33, 35, 37–40, 62–63, 72, 190; *Coals to Newcastle*, 144; *Deadman*, 35, 39, 52–54, 58, 61–63, 68; *Interiorization*, 35–36, 58, 63; and legal precedent, 27, 40, 146; and Los Angeles, 9, 28, 30, 35, 38–39, 52, 59; *Shoot*, 35–37, 116; *TV Hijack*, 9, 63, 65–66, 68
Burkell, Jacquelyn, 155
Bush, George W., 188
busing, 93–94; and white antibusing protest, 9, 96, 102
Butler, Jim, 61

California, 11, 19, 35, 90, 189, 192; Army National Guard, 56; art world in, 56; Black Conference Committee, 45; border with Mexico, 144; and Burden, 59, 65; Council of Criminal Justice, 45; and diGrazia, 100; Penal Code, 59; and Reagan, 136. *See also* Anaheim; Los Angeles; Oakland; Sacramento; San Francisco; Santa Ana; Santa Cruz; Watts (California)
Camp, Jordan T., 18
carceral state/system/society, 27, 81, 143, 147, 156, 185–86; and art-world theater, 184; "carceral aesthetics," 22, 23; "carceral apparatus," 190, 194; "carceral archipelago," 8; "carceral care," 76; "carceral geography," 82, 194; "carceral humanism," 194; crisis of, 18; and debt, 15; formalism of, 194; harm of, 135; history of, 15; politics of, 134; studies of, 8, 10; and welfare, 25. *See also* prison studies
Carmichael, Stokely. *See* Ture, Kwame
Cassel Oliver, Valerie, 39, 119
Castelli, Leo, 140, 149, 152, 180
Castro, Fidel, 3
Catalysis (Piper), 69–70, 72, 91, 204n18. *See also* Piper, Adrian
Celant, Germano, 12
censorship, 10, 65, 67, 152, 171, 179
Certeau, Michel de, 13
Chambers-Letson, Joshua, 27
Chandler, Dana, 100, 197
Chauvin, Derek, 193
Chave, Anna, 150
Chavoya, C. Ondine, 39, 41, 47, 204n18
Cheney, Dick, 85
Chicago, 11, 116, 192, 194, 199–200
Chicano Brown Berets, 11, 45, 48, 51
Chicanos, 49–52, 65, 123; and Asco, 9, 33–34, 38, 46, 61, 65, 67; Brown Berets, 11, 48; and Los Angeles, 30, 34, 40, 42–44, 50, 52, 62; and *The Magnificent Seven*, 41; and National Chicano Moratorium Committee, 49–51
Chin, Vincent, 144
China, 18; and immigration to US, 81, 109, 139, 144; and Mao Zedong (Tse-tung), 4, 20
Chinese Americans, 119, 135, 144. *See also* Hsieh, Tehching
Chinese Red Guard Party, 11
Chronopoulos, Themis, 122
Church, David, 129
CIA (Central Intelligence Agency), 17, 163
citation, 114, 139, 141, 146–47. *See also* arrests; policing
Civil Rights Acts, 48, 177
Cleaver, Eldridge, 44
Coals to Newcastle (Burden), 144. *See also* Burden, Chris
Coates, Dennis, 86
COINTELPRO, 18–19
Cold War, 16, 18, 188
Colo, Papo, 131, 142; and Exit Art, 231n121
Colombia, 166, 191
communism, 3–4, 18, 163, 166, 168
conceptualism, 24, 34–35, 39, 141
conceptual photography, 33, 89, 187

Copeland, Huey, 27, 39, 197
counterinsurgency, 6, 13, 17, 56, 156, 163, 188–89
Crenshaw, Kimberlé, 119
criminality, 18, 27, 30, 41, 46, 56, 59, 61, 65, 81, 90, 194; and art, 116, 140, 146; of Hsieh, 139; and Pope.L and Hsieh, 120; racialized, 30, 61, 136; and "racial state," 76–77; "status criminality," 82; and stereotypes, 40
criminal law, 14, 26, 46, 116
criminology, 189
critical disability theory, 5, 181
critical ethnic studies, 6
critical race theory, 5
Crow, Thomas, 58
Cruz, Amina, 31, 191–93, 197
Cuba, 3, 17–18, 106, 166, 174

Daulatzai, Sohail, 165
Davis, Angela, 44, 84
Davis, Edward, 17, 50. *See also* LAPD (Los Angeles Police Department)
Davis, Mike, 58
Deadman (Burden), 35, 39, 53–54, 61–62, 68, 142; and arrest and trial of Burden, 27, 36; and Los Angeles, 52, 58; scholarly readings of, 66. *See also* Burden, Chris
Debayle, Anastasio Somoza, 163
Debray, Regis, 4
Decolonize This Place, 183
Decoy Gang War Victim (Asco), 33–35, 39, 41, 46–47, 49, 61, 68, 187. *See also* Asco; No Movies
Deitch, Jeffrey, 74
Delaney, Samuel, 129
deputized discernment, 30, 75, 77, 80, 82, 91, 103, 106–7; definition of, 75–76; and Piper and *Loitering*, 92, 107; and press conferences, 102; and Toche, 94, 103, 106
DeSantis, Ron, 193
Detroit, 16–18, 94, 173; and murder of Chin, 144
Deutsche, Rosalyn, 123, 211n104
dictatorship, 10, 163, 166
Diggers, 12
diGrazia, Robert J., 77–78, 92, 94–96, 98–101, 103, 105–6. *See also* Boston Police Department
Dillon, C. Douglas, 72, 103, 105–6
direct action, 21, 71
displacement, 11, 17, 52, 56, 65, 123, 147
Douglas, Emory, 12
Dreva, Jerry, 46
Dunlap, Bruce, 35
Dyer, Richard, 117

Eaglin, Jessica, 26, 198
Eco, Umberto, 12
Edwards, Erica, 19, 168, 174
Egypt, 164, 183
Ellison, Treva, 81–82
Elsen, Albert, 141
El Teatro Campesino, 12
endurance, 30–31, 39, 108, 114–20, 136, 142, 156; and bodybuilding, 117–18; and discourses of urban renewal, 120, 123; and fitness culture, 118; and Hsieh, 30–31, 108, 112, 116, 119–20, 131, 140, 142, 147; and Pope.L, 30–31, 108, 112, 114–15, 119–20, 126, 131; as problematic term, 116
endurance art, 112, 114, 116, 131
England, 80
English, Darby, 125–26
Enloe, Cynthia, 156
Erdmann, Martin, 140
Eregbu, Alexandria, 23

Ericson, Richard, 101
Eshun, Kodwo, 13
exile, 10, 115, 187

false emergency (crime), 35, 53, 55, 59, 61, 140, 218n114
Fanon, Frantz, 4
FBI, 16, 18, 35, 44, 48, 84, 106, 165; director Clarence Kelley, 100; and PESTS, 174; and Toche, 72, 95, 103, 105. *See also* Hoover, J. Edgar
Fekner, John, 155
Feldman, Allan, 147
Feldman, Ronald, 152
Felker-Kantor, Max, 43, 56
Ferguson, Andrew, 189
Fergusson, Claire, 111
Finley, Cheryl, 27
First Supper (After a Major Riot) (Asco), 48–49, 51–52, 61, 68. *See also* Asco
Flash Art, 12, 24, 116
Fleetwood, Nicole, 22–23
Floyd, George, 31, 193
Fluxus, 24, 222n30
Ford, Gerald, 85
Foucault, Michel, 8
Fox, Terry, 35
France, 4
Franklin Furnace, 116, 134
Friis-Hansen, Dana, 37
Frobes-Cross, Huffa, 90
Frye, Marquette, 56. *See also* Watts (California)
fugitive, 16, 25; Black women's cartographies, 38; Angela Davis as, 84; fugitivity, 91; world-making, 82

Gamboa, Harry, Jr., 40, 43–47, 67, 197; and Asco, 21, 33, 49, 52, 55, 63, 187; on *Decoy Gang War Victim*, 34–35; and FBI, 84; and National Chicano Moratorium, 51; *Pistol Whippersnapper*, 64; *Spray Paint LACMA*, 41; and Valdez, 63, 68
gang violence, 9, 32–34. See also *Decoy Gang War Victim* (Asco)
Garrity, Arthur, 93
Gates, Daryl, 48, 100
genocide, 3, 11, 15, 25
geography, 5, 14, 39; and Banks, 93; carceral, 82; "geographic relevancy," 38–39; and interfaces, 63; of Los Angeles, 38, 56; and policing, 45; racial, 52; and risk categories, 26. *See also* Ellison, Treva; Jordan Jefferson, Brian; McKittrick, Katherine; Mowatt, Rasul; Smith, Neil; Wilson Gilmore, Ruth
Germany, 4, 12
Getty Research Institute, 78, 104, 150, 152, 155, 164, 171, 176
Gibran Muhammad, Khalil, 14
Giddens, Anthony, 62
Gidra, 12
Gillette, Frank, 18
Giorno, John, 34
Glenn, Allison, 23, 199
Goldberg, David Theo, 77
Goldstein, Herman, 28
Gowles, Charles, 152
Gran Fury, 155
Gray, Ros, 13
Green, Wilder, 2
Gronk. *See* Nicandro, Glugio "Gronk"
Guerrilla Art Action Group (GAAG), 2, 4–5, 7, 71, 78, 97–98, 143
Guerrilla Girls, 6–7, 149–52, 156–69, 171–72, 180, 197; creation of, 9, 31, 148; and PESTS, 28, 31, 148, 155–57, 173, 177–80
guerrilla tactics, 4, 7, 27–30, 84, 139, 179, 182, 185; and anticolonial struggles,

guerrilla tactics (*continued*)
11; and art law, 31; and Asco, 37–38, 72; and Burden, 37–38, 72; and endurance, 112; and Guerrilla Art Action Group (GAAG), 4, 71; and Guerrilla Girls, 7, 155–56; and *Guerrilla Television*, 12; and guerrilla warfare, 3; "hit and run," 68, 72; and *Illegal America*, 143; juridical interpretations of, 40; and marketing, 39, 157, 234n28; and PESTS, 7, 155–56; and policing, 6, 9–10, 14–17, 189; and Pope.L, 146; and Reagan Administration, 31, 163; and risk, 6, 21, 27, 38, 181; as transnational, 10; and US counterinsurgency, 6; and white artists, 22
guerrilla theater, 70–71
guerrilla warfare, 2–4, 12–13, 18, 29, 93, 145, 188; and FBI, 84; and Guerrilla Girls, 173; and Reagan administration, 31, 174; and urban policing, 16, 93
Guevara, Ernesto "Che," 3, 19–20, 151
Guttmann, Jim, 78–79, 88, 90

Haacke, Hans, 89
Haggerty, Kevin, 101
Halberstam, Jack, 129
Hanhardt, Christina, 32
Hannah-Jones, Nikole, 94
Hartman, Saidiya, 22, 82
Harvard University, 9, 30, 73, 79–80, 82, 90, 92. *See also* Mythic Being; Piper, Adrian
Havana, 3–4, 16. *See also* Cuba
Hearst, Patricia (Patty), 63, 65, 84
Hendricks, Jon, 98, 104, 184, 197; and Guerrilla Art Action Group (GAAG), 2, 5, 7, 71; and "Malevich action," 1–2, 7, 20; and Toche, 1–2, 4–5, 7, 20–21, 71–72, 103–5, 184
Herrón III, Willie, 33–34, 41, 43, 49, 187
Hinckle, Warren, 12
Hinton, Elizabeth, 75
Hoffman, Abbie, 34
Hollywood, 12, 41, 67. *See also* Los Angeles
Holzer, Jenny, 155
homelessness, 109, 123, 126; and anti-homeless laws, 15; and "homeless person" 125, 127, 141. *See also* unhoused
Hoover, J. Edgar, 18, 48. *See also* FBI
Horvitz, Robert, 36–37
House Committee on Un-American Activities, 18
Hoving, Thomas, 106
Howell, Alison, 156
Hsieh, Tehching, 6–7, 25, 132, 134, 136–47, 197; arrest of, 111–12, 139; and endurance, 30, 112, 116, 118–20, 131, 140, 142, 147; and *Illegal America*, 116, 137, 139, 143; and immigration, 109–11; and *Outdoor Piece*, 9, 111–13, 115–16, 120, 131–35, 137; and Pope.L, 28, 30, 108, 112, 115–16, 118–20, 130, 136–37, 147; and Taiwan, 9, 30, 109, 131; *Time Clock Piece*, 115; trial of, 139–41, 146; *Wanted by U.S. Immigration Service*, 9, 109–12, 115–16, 120, 137–39, 144–45
Hughes, Kathleen, 140
Hwang, Ren-yo, 76, 194

Illegal America (exhibition), 30, 114, 137, 139, 142–43, 145–46
Indigenous peoples, 3, 11, 15, 22, 25, 91, 127, 166
Ingberman, Jeanette, 116, 131, 139–40, 142–44; and Exit Art, 231n121
installation art, 24, 140
Interiorization (Burden), 35–36
intersectional/ity, 8, 119, 156, 179
Israel, 59, 164
Italy, 4, 116, 164

Janis, Sidney, 152
Japan, 4, 81, 114, 143–44, 150; and immigration to US, 81, 144
Japanese Americans, 136
Jean-Louis, Andre Yvon, 92–93, 96, 99–100
Jim Crow laws, 16, 81, 91, 96. *See also* Black Codes; white supremacy
Johnson, Lyndon B., 6, 14, 18, 86
Jones, Amelia, 41, 218n122
Jordan Jefferson, Brian, 45, 190
Joynt, Matt, 194. *See also* Sonic Insurgency Research Group
Judson Church, 1
Juvenile Justice and Delinquency Prevention Act, 85. *See also* Omnibus Crime Control and Safe Streets Act

Kahn, Barry, 131, 139
Kalter, Christoph, 11
Kanders, Warren B., 182–83
Kansas City, 35–36, 58, 61, 63, 100. *See also* Burden, Chris; *Interiorization* (Burden)
Kee, Joan, 24, 111, 116, 141
Keeling, Kara, 19
Kelley, Clarence, 100
Kelling, George, 159
Kennedy, Peter, 73–74
Kerner Commission, 16, 75. *See also* National Advisory Commission on Civil Disorders
Klinghoffer, Leon, 164
Knight, Christopher, 53
Koch, Edward, 103, 122–24, 128, 136
Korda, Alberto, 2–3
Kornbluh, Peter, 163, 174
Kozloff, Max, 53
Kyung-Hoon, Kim, 182

LaForge, Ellen, 124
LA, Hot and Cool, the Eighties, 37
LAPD (Los Angeles Police Department), 16–17, 43, 45, 48–51, 55–56, 191; and Public Disorder Investigation Division (PDID), 48. *See also* Davis, Edward; Reddin, Thomas; Watts (California)
Latin America, 3, 11, 16, 151, 163, 165. *See also* Argentina; Brazil; Chicanos; Cuba; Mexican Americans; Mexico
law enforcement. *See* policing
Law Enforcement Assistance Act (LEAA), 14, 17
lawfare, 127–28, 130–31, 135, 137, 143, 145–46, 188
lawlessness, 129
Lepecki, André, 126
Levinson, Jay, 157
Lindsay, John, 103, 122
Linker, Kate, 144–45
Lippard, Lucy, 70, 105, 162
Lipsitz, George, 25, 39, 120
Livingston, Jane, 60
Living Theater, 12
Lloyd, Tom, 5
Lonidier, Fred, 89–90, 197
Lorde, Audre, 24
Los Angeles, 30, 33, 40; and Asco, 38, 49, 61, 72; and Burden, 35, 38, 59, 61, 72; East Los Angeles, 7, 20, 28, 30, 32–34, 38, 42–44, 49–50; and Gamboa, 44–45; Getty Research Institute in, 78; as home of predictive policing, 29, 189, 191; police, 16–17, 20, 28, 42–45, 48, 72, 100; and punitive literacy, 38, 44, 189, 191; and Riko Mizuno Gallery, 52, 60. *See also* LAPD (Los Angeles Police Department)
Los Angeles County, 11, 43, 45–46, 191
Los Angeles County Museum (LACMA), 40, 60, 62. *See also* Livingston, Jane; *Spray Paint LACMA*
Lovell, Jarret, 101

low-intensity warfare/conflict, 6, 13, 31, 163
Lugones, María, 13
Lung, Shirley, 81
Lutjeans, Phyllis, 36, 63, 65

Magnificent Seven, The, 41
Malevich, Kazimir, 1–2, 4
"Malevich action," 4, 7, 20, 184. *See also* Guerrilla Art Action Group (GAAG); Hendricks, Jon; Toche, Jean
Manning, Peter, 102
Marighella, Carlos, 4, 46
Marsh, Ken, 18
Massachusetts, 30, 73, 88. *See also* Boston; Boston Police Department
mass media, 12, 48; and AIDS, 168; and art, 34; and Astorga, 166; and Black Panther Party for Self-Defense, 18; and Black September, 59; and gentrification, 123; and Guerrilla Girls, 159–60, 168, 173; and guerrillas, 163; guerrilla television, 18, 37; hijacking/hoax, 7, 9, 21; and immigration; and No Movie, 41; and police work, 101; and policing, 52, 135; print, 13; and racialized criminality, 30, 46, 61; and Reagan, 174; television (TV), 38, 65, 67, 101; and *TV Hijack*, 65–66, 219n131, 116; and violence, 36, 51, 135; and white men, 66; and "Zoot Suit Warfare," 43. *See also* social media
McBrien, Rose, 140
McKinney, Charles W., Jr., 17
McKittrick, Katherine, 38
McMillan, Uri, 85, 173, 220n4, 233n12
McPartland, Scott, 124–25
Melton, Eugene Eddie, 86
Mendieta, Ana, 35
Mendieta, Raquelín, 35
Merryman, John, 141
Metropolitan Museum of Art, 71–72, 103, 105, 150
Mexican Americans, 33–34, 43, 51, 56, 65–66
Mexico, 4, 66, 144, 182–83, 191; and migration to US, 42, 191
Meyer, Ursula, 35
Meza, Maria, 182–83
Milwaukee, 128, 137
Minh-ha, Trinh T., 24
Minimalism, 24, 53
Minneapolis, 11, 193. *See also* Floyd, George; Native American Indian Movement
Mitchell, Bruce E., 141–43, 146
Mitchell, Phillip S., 45–46, 58
Mizuno, Riko, 52, 60, 66
Molesworth, Helen, 24
Moore, Carman, 35
Mowatt, Rasul, 127, 198
Mulford, Don, 19
multicultural/ism, 24, 152, 178
Munich Olympics (1972), 59
Museum of Modern Art (MoMA), 71–72, 103, 115, 148, 151, 180; and "carceral aesthetics," 22; and "Malevich action," 1–2, 4, 20; and MoMA PS.1, 22
Mythic Being, 9, 72–74, 83, 85, 220n4; *The Mythic Being*, 77–79, 146. *See also* Piper, Adrian

Natalici, Fernando, 124
National Advisory Commission on Civil Disorders, 16. *See also* Kerner Commission
National Chicano Moratorium Committee, 49–51, 89–90
National Crime Information Center (NCIC), 18

Native American Indian Movement, 11
Native Americans, 11, 15, 22, 25, 51, 91, 127, 183
Netherlands, 4
Newark, 16–17, 121
Newton, Huey, 11
New York City, 1, 30, 59, 112, 122–24, 126, 128–29; and Art v War, 182; Center for Constitutional Rights in, 197; Chinatown, 28, 31, 116, 134–37; East Village, 4, 148, 158; and Eco, 12; and Guerrilla Girls, 9, 152, 158–59, 167; immigration officials, 111, 116; Metropolitan Museum of Art (Met), 71–72, 105–6, 150; Metropolitan Transit Authority, 188; and PESTS, 9, 152, 173; and Piper, 69, 72, 74, 91; and policing, 27, 103, 119, 135, 159, 189; and Pope.L, 9, 27, 114, 119; Soho, 28, 115, 134, 148, 158–59, 171–72; Times Square, 9, 31, 109, 122–30, 134–37, 146; and Toche, 71–72, 74, 103, 187; Tribeca, 111, 116, 134–35; and Young Lords, 11. *See also* Metropolitan Museum of Art; *Times Square Crawl* (Pope.L); Whitney Museum of American Art
New York State, 87, 139
New York Times, 51, 56, 94, 136; and Burden, 36, 54, 58, 61, 66
Nicandro, Glugio "Gronk," 33–35, 41, 46, 49, 62–63, 65, 187
Nicaragua, 163, 166, 174
Nitz, Michael, 144–45
Nixon, Richard, 15, 100
No Movies, 41–43, 58, 60. *See also* Asco
Noriega, Chon, 41, 43, 200
Nyong'o, Tavia, 73

Oakland, 11
Omnibus Crime Control and Safe Streets Act, 14, 75, 85. *See also* Juvenile Justice and Delinquency Prevention Act
Oppenheim, Dennis, 24, 143
Organization of Latin American Solidarity, 16
Outdoor Piece, 9, 112, 115–16, 120, 131–35, 137, 143. *See also* Hsieh, Tehching

Paint (dot) Red Repetitions (Hsieh), 131. *See also* Hsieh, Tehching
Palestine, 4, 59, 164, 183
Papachristou, Margaret, 86
Papachristou v. City of Jacksonville, 86–87, 90
Parada, Esther, 174
Paris, 4, 12
Patriot Act, 188
Patterson, Orlando, 22
Peoples' Video Theatre, 18
performance art, 24, 39, 116, 119, 140–42; and Burden, 59, 62; and guerrilla, 32, 185
performance studies, 8, 10, 27, 73, 155, 173
Perreault, John, 145
PESTS, 6–7, 25, 152, 161, 169, 171–80; establishment of, 9, 31, 151; and Guerrilla Girls, 28, 148, 151, 155–57, 169; and Pindell, 151, 187
Phoenix, 128
photography, 33, 51, 89, 174, 187. *See also* conceptual photography
Picard, Lil, 1, 4–5
Picasso, Pablo, 72
Pindell, Howardena, 151–52, 169, 172–73, 175, 178–79, 187, 197
Pinder, Kym, 23
Piper, Adrian, 25, 82, 84, 99, 107, 146, 187–88, 197; and Art Workers Coalition (AWC), 24; *Calling (Card) #1* and *#2*,

Piper, Adrian (*continued*)
69, 85; and Cambridge, 9, 30, 77, 79–80, 82, 90, 92, 146; *Catalysis*, 70, 91; and guerrilla, 6–7, 70–71; and Mythic Being, 9, 73–74, 77–80, 83, 85, 107; *The Mythic Being*, 85, 88–92, 103; and New York City, 72–73, 88, 91; and Toche, 28, 30, 69, 71–72, 74, 77, 106–7
Pistol Whippersnapper (Gamboa), 63–64. *See also* Asco; Gamboa, Harry, Jr.
Pita Loor, Karen, 62
Pitchess, Peter, 49, 51
Plagens, Peter, 54, 58–59, 61–62
Pluchart, François, 24, 116
policing, 6–9, 41, 48, 58–60, 66, 190; and Anti-Riot Act of 1968, 59; and Asco, 21, 30, 34, 38–39, 42, 49, 55, 58; and Black Panther Party for Self-Defense, 11; and "broken windows" paradigm, 159, 168; and Burden, 30, 35, 39, 54, 58, 61; and crime maps, 124, 189–90; in East Los Angeles, 20, 28–29, 34, 42–45, 50, 52, 56; and loitering, 15, 30, 82, 86–88, 99–100, 103, 106–7, 129; in Los Angeles, 16–17, 45–46, 48–50, 100, 189, 191; Los Angeles as home of computerized predictive algorithms, 29, 38, 189, 191; in New York City, 109, 114, 121–25, 128, 135, 158–59, 184, 189; overpolicing, 11, 46; and predictive methods, 15, 38, 40, 45–46, 49, 55, 72, 189–91; and racialized punitive relations, 11, 15–16, 38, 59, 112, 190; reform of, 28–30, 76–77, 87, 94–95, 99, 100, 103; underpolicing, 23, 194; in Watts, 17, 43, 56, 100; in West Los Angeles, 28, 30, 35, 43–44, 55, 58; as white, 4, 11, 16, 19, 54, 56, 90, 99, 109; and white gangs, 43; and white supremacy, 82. *See also* Boston Police Department; diGrazia, Robert J.; false emergency (crime); LAPD (Los Angeles Police Department); predictive policing; PredPol; Reddin, Thomas
Pontecorvo, Gillo, 13. See also *Battle of Algiers, The*
Pope.L, 6–7, 25, 118–30, 135, 139, 142, 197; and crawling as symbolic act, 125–26; and endurance, 30, 114, 116, 118–20; *Great White Way*, 114; and Hsieh, 28, 108, 109, 115–16, 118–20, 137, 139, 142, 147; and loitering, 137; and New York City, 9, 30, 108, 109, 112, 114, 121–24, 128; and New York City statues, 27, 119; non-arrest of, 146; and police, 9, 27, 30, 109, 115, 121–23, 129–30; and tactical crawling, 130, 146; *Times Square Crawl*, 108, 110, 112, 114, 120–22, 124, 129–30, 136; *Tompkins Square Crawl*, 114
Powell, Richard, 84
predictive policing, 15, 31, 40, 49, 189–90; in Los Angeles, 29, 38, 45, 55, 72, 191. *See also* LAPD (Los Angeles Police Department); policing; PredPol
PredPol, 189–90; and metadata, 190
Prince, Dinah, 159, 161
prison, 8, 145, 164; budgets, 14; and conditions of imprisonment, 23, 24, 59, 76; construction, 15; history of, 81; and Sentencing Project, 191. *See also* arrests; Black Codes
prison studies, 8, 18. *See also* carceral state/system/society; prison
Puar, Jasbir, 155–56, 162, 165, 178
public safety, 19, 25, 59, 89, 122, 128–29, 147, 162; ordinances, 51. *See also* policing
Puerto Rican Young Lords, 2, 11, 34, 161
Puerto Rico, 11, 183
Puleo, Risa, 23
punitive literacy, 1, 7, 27, 30, 67, 120, 147, 189; and Asco, 38, 40, 67; and Burden,

52–53; and Cruz, 191–93; definitions of, 8; and "guerrilla," 19; and Guerrilla Girls, 159, 168; and Hsieh, 127, 131, 141; and *Illegal America*, 143; and Los Angeles, 38, 191; periodization of, 29, 112; and Piper, 107; and police departments, 99; and Pope.L, 129; and Shimunov, 182–83, 185; and Sonic Insurgency Research Group (SIRG), 194; and "stop and frisk," 44; and terrorism, 188; and white artists, 7–9, 22–25, 38–40, 56, 58
punitive turn, 14–15, 188–89, 208n53

queer and trans studies, 76, 194
queer intimacy, 87
queer sociality, 129

racial capitalism, 81, 141, 182
racism, 6, 26, 67, 86, 92, 120; and antiblackness, 22, 82, 85, 186; and Asco, 41–42; and Boston Police Department, 94; and capitalism, 81; color-blind, 26, 80; environmental, 58, 191; and gender, 147; and Guerrilla Girls, 148, 150–52, 167–68, 177; and PESTS, 152, 169, 171–72, 174, 177, 179; and Piper, 69, 85; and policing, 22–23, 44, 169, 186; and Toche, 71, 94. *See also* antiblackness; Black Codes; Jim Crow laws; slavery; white supremacy
Radical Presence (exhibition), 39. *See also* Cassel Oliver, Valerie
Raiford, Leigh, 11
Ratner, Michael, 186
Raven, Lavie, 192
Reagan, Ronald, 6, 15, 19, 31, 136, 166, 174; and AIDS, 168; and Guerrilla Girls, 156, 159, 162, 164; and Latin America, 163; and low-intensity conflict, 6, 31, 163; Reagan Doctrine, 163; and terrorism, 164; "War on Drugs," 168
Red Army Faction, 12
Reddin, Thomas, 16–17
Regeneración, 34
resistance, 13, 21, 23, 29, 32, 179, 185, 194; and endurance, 116; feminist, 157; and Pope.L, 126; and punitiveness, 10, 28; to state violence and regulation, 6, 18
Revolutionary Action Movement, 18
Rhode Island School of Design, 53
Rios, Josh, 194. *See also* Sonic Insurgency Research Group
risk management, 6, 14–15, 17, 38, 95, 120, 127, 181
risk work, 1, 22, 25, 27, 29, 62, 68, 181; and anonymity, 155; and art history, 67; and Asco, 61; and Burden, 63, 66; as a framework, 23, 186; and graffiti, 185, 192; and Guerrilla Girls, 157, 162, 180; and Hsieh, 131, 137, 140, 143; in Los Angeles, 40, 56; and PESTS, 157, 174; and policing, 23, 31, 185; and Pope.L, 131, 146; and punitive literacy, 31, 67, 193; and security state, 186; and state violence, 40; and white supremacy, 32
Roberts, Dorothy, 87–88
Robinson, Cedric, 81
Rodia, Sabato, 56
Rodin, Auguste, 117
Romero, Anthony, 77, 194. *See also* Sonic Insurgency Research Group
Rosler, Martha, 88
Ryan, Paul, 12

Sacramento, 19
Safariland, 183
Salazar, Rubén, 49–50
Salisbury, Stephan, 161
Samuels, Larry, 190
Sánchez, George, 43
San Diego, 89–90
Sandoval, Humberto, 49

San Francisco, 11, 35
San Francisco Mime Troupe, 12
Santa Ana, 35, 45–46, 66
Santa Cruz, 189
Saxbe, William, 94
Schjeldahl, Peter, 36
Schor, Mira, 159
Schrader, Stuart, 189
Schwarzenegger, Arnold, 117–18
Seale, Bobby, 11, 18
Section 8 funds, 123
segregation, 16–17, 56, 59
Seigel, Micol, 15, 23, 198, 205n26
Sekula, Allan, 89
sentencing, 14, 26, 139–40. *See also* carceral state/system/society; lawfare; policing; prison
settler colonialism, 3, 77
Sexton, Jared, 22
sexuality, 6, 87–88, 156
Shafrazi, Tony, 27, 72, 103, 142
Shalson, Lara, 118, 132
Shamberg, Michael, 12
Sharp, Christina, 23
Shaw, Elizabeth, 2
Sheehan, Maura, 158
Shimunov, Rafael, 182–85, 197. *See also* Art v War
Shoot (Burden), 35–37, 66, 116. *See also* Burden, Chris
Sifuentes, Frank, 44
Sims, Lowery Stokes, 108
Situationists, 12
slavery, 3, 11, 16, 27, 91, 126, 174
smart phones, 190
Smith, Barbara, 60–61, 65
Smith, Cherise, 84
Smith, Neil, 123
Smithsonian American Art Museum, 150, 200
social media, 150, 183–84
social practice, 21, 193–94
sociology, 8, 14, 24, 28, 62
Sonic Insurgency Research Group, 31, 77, 194
South Africa, 10, 169, 236n76
Soviet Union, 3
Spain, 3, 114
Speakes, Larry M., 164
Spillers, Hortense, 22
Spray Paint LACMA (Asco), 41, 49, 61, 68, 146, 192
Standing Rock Dakota Access Pipeline, 183
Stanford, Max, 18
Steinbaum, Bernice, 152
Stewart, Potter, 86
Stoler, Ann, 23
street theater, 12
Supreme Court (US), 44, 85–86, 136, 235n69; and *Coates v. City of Cincinnati*, 86; and *Terry v. Ohio*, 44, 76
surveillance studies, 19
surveillance technology, 14–15, 28, 184. *See also* predictive policing
SWAT teams, 29, 38, 48
Symbionese Liberation Army, 65

Taber, Robert, 4
Tactical Police Force, 93, 101
Taiwan, 9, 30, 109, 131
Taylor, Breonna, 23, 31
Taylor, Paul, 160–61
tear gas, 48–49, 182–83
Third, Amanda, 166
Thompson, Krista, 27, 197
Times Square Crawl (Pope.L), 9, 120–21, 125–30, 136, 146; as "endurance art," 112, 114; photographs of, 108, 124; and police, 109, 114, 122–24, 127–30. *See also* New York City; Pope.L
Toche, Jean, 74, 103–5, 142, 186–88, 197;

arrest of, 72; and Art Workers Coalition (AWC), 24, 74; and Boston, 9, 30, 77, 92, 94–101, 103; and Burden, 27, 146; and FBI, 105–6; and Guerrilla Art Action Group (GAAG), 2, 4–7; and Hendricks, 1–2, 4, 7, 20–21, 72, 104, 184; and "Malevich action," 1–2, 4, 20, 184; and Piper, 27, 69–74, 77, 106–7

Tompkins Square Crawl (Pope.L), 114. *See also* Pope.L

trans studies, 76, 181, 194

Trinh, Cindy, 183, 197

Trump, Donald, 183

Tupamaros, 10

Ture, Kwame, 16

TV Hijack (Burden), 9, 36, 63, 65–66, 68, 219n131. *See also* Burden, Chris

unhoused, 30, 119, 136. *See also* homelessness

United States, 5, 9, 60, 156, 169, 181–82, 186, 191; armed services, 35; art museums in, 184; attorney general, 9, 92, 94; border with Mexico, 182–83; census, 172; Chinese Exclusion Act (1882), 81, 144; Civil War, 81, 91; Commission on Civil Rights, 66; Congress, 11, 14, 26, 28, 48, 82, 163; Constitution, 19, 27, 86–87; courts in, 93; and Cuba, 174; genocide of Indigenous people, 25; and Guerrilla Girls, 150, 164; and guerrilla tactics in art, 6–7, 22, 112; and guerrilla warfare, 3–4, 12, 18; and Hsieh, 30, 131, 139, 144; jails, 191; "model minority" myth in, 139; National Guard, 16, 56; Naturalization Act (1870), 81; Natural Origins Act (1924), 81; Page Act (1875), 81, 144; and Piper, 85, 187–88; and policing, 6, 16–17, 22–23, 28, 84, 94, 99, 127; punitive turn in, 14–15; and Rally for Nuclear Disarmament, 134; and Reagan Doctrine, 163, 166; Reconstruction, 81; Senate, 45, 103; and slavery, 16, 19, 25; State Department, 163; and terrorism, 164–65; and Toche, 71, 105; and Vietnam War, 49, 166. *See also* Patriot Act; Supreme Court (US)

urbanization, 16–17, 32, 42, 52, 119, 155; and urban renewal, 15, 30, 52, 61, 109, 122, 123, 129–30, 134, 188

Urban Subjects (collective), 185

Uruguay, 4, 10, 124

vagrancy, 75, 81–83, 85–86, 91, 109, 141. *See also* antivagrancy laws

Valdez, Patssi, 33–34, 41–42, 49, 63, 65, 67–68, 187, 197

Van Peebles, Melvin, 12

Van Raay, Janice (Jan), 1–2, 5

Varon, Jeremy, 12, 20

Vautier, Ben, 24

Veyne, Paul, 29

Viennese Action, 143

Vietnam, 2–4, 35, 93, 117, 120, 163, 165–66; and Asco, 38; and Burden, 36; Chicanos in, 49; guerrilla fighters in, 11, 17, 165; North Vietnamese fighters in, 4; refugees from, 116; and Viet Cong tactics, 17

Village Voice, 35, 74, 159

Volunteer Lawyers for the Arts, 140

Wang, Jackie, 126, 190

Wanted by U.S. Immigration Service (Hsieh), 9, 109–11, 115–16, 120, 137–39, 143–45. *See also* Hsieh, Tehching

Ward, Frazer, 53, 115, 200

"War on Crime," 6, 14–15, 86

"War on Drugs," 15, 168

"War on Terror," 31, 88, 168–69, 188

Watkins, Rychetta, 12

Watts (California), 16–18, 43, 46, 100. *See also* Los Angeles
Watts Towers, 56
Weather Underground, 12, 20, 92
Wentzy, James, 134
whiteness, 6, 22–25, 38–39, 81, 127, 146–47, 151–52, 168; and Burden, 40, 66–68; logics of, 93; making of, 19, 90; and masculinity, 117, 119, 142; and PESTS, 175, 178; and policing, 93, 191, 194; and schools, 93; and surveillance, 19, 90; and vagrancy, 82
white supremacy, 8, 17, 32, 81–82, 96, 165, 179, 186; and white gangs, 43. *See also* Black Codes; Jim Crow laws; segregation
Whitney Museum of American Art, 114–15, 117–18, 148, 182–84; Biennial, 148
Wiegman, Robyn, 25
Wilderson, Frank B., 22, 204n15
Williams, Regina, 93
Williams, Robert, 18
Willis, Edwin, 18
Wilson, James Q., 159
Wilson, Martha, 151, 171
Wilson Gilmore, Ruth, 6, 63, 81, 127
Wise, Howard, 5
Withers, Josephine, 167
World War II, 24, 81
Wu, Ellen, 136, 198
Wu, Simon, 134

xenophobia, 17, 41, 147, 150, 179

Young Lords. *See* Puerto Rican Young Lords